UNDERSTANDING AND USING

English Grammar

FOURTH EDITION

TEACHER'S GUIDE

Martha Hall
Betty S. Azar

PEARSON
Longman

UNDERSTANDING AND USING

English Grammar

FOURTH EDITION

TEACHER'S GUIDE

UNDERSTANDING AND USING

English Grammar

FOURTH EDITION

TEACHER'S GUIDE

RESOURCE DISC

PEARSON
Longman

Martha Hall
Betty S. Azar

Understanding and Using English Grammar, Fourth Edition
Teacher's Guide

Pearson Education, 10 Bank Street, White Plains, NY 10606

Staff credits: The people who made up the **Understanding and
Using English Grammar, Fourth Edition, Teacher's Guide** team,
representing editorial, production, design, and manufacturing,
are Dave Dickey, Christine Edmonds, Ann France,
Amy McCormick, Robert Ruvo, and Ruth Voetmann.

Text composition: S4Carlisle Publishing Services
Text font: Helvetica

ISBN 10: 0-13-205211-3
ISBN 13: 978-0-13-205211-5

Printed in the United States of America
8 9 10—V011—14 13

Contents

Preface

This *Teachers' Guide* is intended as a practical aid to teachers. You can turn to it for notes on the content of a unit and how to approach the exercises, for suggestions for classroom activities, and for answers to the exercises in the text.

General teaching information can be found in the introduction. It includes:

- the rationale and general aims of *Understanding and Using English Grammar*
- classroom techniques for presenting charts and using exercises
- suggestions on using the *Workbook* in connection with the student book
- supplementary resource texts
- comments on differences between American and British English
- a key to the pronunciation symbols used in this *Guide*

The rest of the *Guide* contains detailed notes and instructions for teaching every chapter. Each chapter contains three main parts: the chapter summary, the background notes on charts and exercises (found in the gray shaded boxes), and the bulleted step-by-step instructions for the charts and most of the exercises.

- The Chapter Summary explains the objective and approach of the chapter. It also explains any terminology critical to the chapter.
- The gray background notes boxes contain additional explanations of the grammar point, common problem areas, and points to emphasize. These notes are intended to help the instructor plan the lessons before class.
- The bulleted step-by-step instructions contain detailed plans for conducting the lesson in class.

The back of the *Guide* contains the answer key for the student book and an index.

Acknowledgments

The author would like to thank Joe and Megan Kelliher for their kindness and cajoling during the writing of this book. In addition, she is grateful for the supportive and creative atmosphere fostered at The New England School of English, her ESL "home" for more than ten years.

Introduction

General aims of *Understanding and Using English Grammar*

Understanding and Using English Grammar is a high-intermediate to advanced level ESL/EFL developmental skills text. In the experience of many classroom teachers, language learners like to spend at least some time on grammar with a teacher to help them. The process of looking at and practicing grammar becomes a springboard for expanding the learners' abilities in speaking, writing, listening, and reading.

Most students find it helpful to have special time set aside in their English curriculum to focus on grammar. Students generally have many questions about English grammar and appreciate the opportunity to work with a text and teacher to make sense out of the sometimes confusing array of forms and usages in this strange language. These understandings provide the basis for advances in usage ability as students experiment, both in speaking and writing, with ways to communicate their ideas in a new language.

Teaching grammar does not mean lecturing on grammatical patterns and terminology. It does not mean bestowing knowledge and being an arbiter of correctness. Teaching grammar is the art of helping students make sense, little by little, of a huge, puzzling construct, and engaging them in various activities that enhance usage abilities in all skill areas and promote easy, confident communication.

The text depends upon a partnership with a teacher; it is the teacher who animates and directs the students' language learning experiences. In practical terms, the aim of the text is to support you, the teacher, by providing a wealth and variety of material for you to adapt to your individual teaching situation. Using grammar as a base to promote overall English usage ability, teacher and text can engage students in interesting discourse, challenge their minds and skills, and intrigue them with the power of language as well as the need for accuracy to create understanding among people.

Suggestions for the Classroom

PRESENTING THE GRAMMAR CHARTS

Each chart contains a concise visual presentation of the structures to be learned. The majority of the charts are preceded by a quick Warm-up exercise designed to help students discover the grammar before the presentation of the chart (see the Exercise Types section for a more detailed discussion of the Warm-up exercises). Presentation techniques often depend upon the content of the chart, the level of the class, and students' learning styles. Not all students react to the charts in the same way. Some students need the security of thoroughly understanding a chart before trying to use the structure. Others like to experiment more freely with using new structures; they refer to the charts only incidentally, if at all.

Given these different learning strategies, you should vary your presentation techniques and not expect students to "learn" or memorize the charts. The charts are just a starting point for class activities and a point of reference. Some charts may require particular methods of presentation, but generally any of the following techniques are viable.

Technique #1:   Present the examples in the chart, perhaps highlighting them on the board. Add your own examples, relating them to your students' experience as much as possible. For example, when presenting simple present tense, talk about what students do every day: come to school, study English, etc. Elicit other examples of the target structure from your students. Then proceed to the exercises.

Technique #2:   Elicit target structures from students before they look at the chart in the textbook. Ask leading questions that are designed so the answers will include the target structure. (For example, with present progressive, ask: "What are you doing right now?") You may want to write students' answers on the board and relate them to selected examples in the chart. Then proceed to the exercises.

Technique #3:   Instead of beginning with a chart, begin with the first exercise after the chart, and as you work through it with students, present the information in the chart or refer to examples in the chart.

Technique #4:   Assign a chart for homework; students bring questions to class. (You may even want to include an accompanying exercise.) With advanced students, you might not need to deal with every chart and exercise thoroughly in class. With intermediate students, it is generally advisable to clarify charts and do most of the exercises in a section.

Technique #5:   Some charts have a preview exercise or pretest. Begin with these, and use them as a guide to decide what areas to focus on. When working through the chart, you can refer to the examples in these exercises.

With all of the above, the explanations on the right side of the chart are most effective when recast by the teacher, not read word for word. Keep the discussion focus on the examples. Students by and large learn from examples and lots of practice, not from explanations. In the charts, the explanations focus attention on what students should be noticing in the examples and the exercises.

ADDITIONAL SUGGESTIONS FOR USING THE CHARTS

The Here-and-Now Classroom Context

For every chart, try to relate the target structure to an immediate classroom or "real-life" context. Make up or elicit examples that use the students' names, activities, and interests. For example, when introducing possessive adjectives, use yourself and your students to present all the sentences in the chart. Then have students refer to the chart. The here-and-now classroom context is, of course, one of the grammar teacher's best aids.

Demonstration Techniques

Demonstration can be very helpful to explain the meaning of structures. You and your students can act out situations that demonstrate the target structure. For example, the present progressive can easily be demonstrated (e.g., "I *am writing* on the board right now"). Of course, not all grammar lends itself to this technique.

Using the Board

In discussing the target structure of a chart, use the classroom board whenever possible. Not all students have adequate listening skills for "teacher talk," and not all students can visualize and understand the various relationships within, between, and among structures. Draw boxes, circles, and arrows to illustrate connections between the elements of a structure.

Oral Exercises with Chart Presentations

Oral exercises usually follow a chart, but sometimes they precede it so that you can elicit student-generated examples of the target structure as a springboard to the discussion of the grammar. If you prefer to introduce a particular structure to your students orally, you can always use an oral exercise prior to the presentation of a chart and its written exercises, no matter what the given order in the text.

The Role of Terminology

Students need to understand the terminology, but you shouldn't require or expect detailed definitions of terms, either in class discussion or on tests. Terminology is just a tool, a useful label for the moment, so that you and your students can talk to each other about English grammar.

BALANCING TEACHER AND STUDENT TALK

The goal of all language learning is to understand and communicate. The teacher's main task is to direct and facilitate that process. The learner is an active participant, not merely a passive receiver of rules to be memorized. Therefore, many of the exercises in the text are designed to promote interaction between learners as a bridge to real communication.

The teacher has a crucial leadership role, with "teacher talk" a valuable and necessary part of a grammar classroom. Sometimes you will need to spend time clarifying the information in a chart, leading an exercise, answering questions about exercise items, or explaining an assignment. These periods of "teacher talk" should, however, be balanced by longer periods of productive learning activity when the students are doing most of the talking. It is important for the teacher to know when to step back and let students lead. Interactive group and pairwork play an important role in the language classroom.

EXERCISE TYPES

Warm-up Exercises

Newly created for the 4th edition, the Warm-up exercises precede all of the grammar charts that introduce new material. They serve a dual purpose. First, they have been carefully crafted to help students discover the target grammar as they progress through each Warm-up exercise. Second, they are an informal diagnostic tool for you, the teacher, to assess how familiar the class is with the target structure. While the Warm-ups are intended to be completed quickly, you may wish to write students' responses on the board to provide visual reinforcement as you work through the exercise.

Preview Exercises

The purpose of these exercises is to let students discover what they do and do not know about the target structure in order to engage them in a chart. Essentially, preview exercises illustrate a possible teaching technique: assess students first as a springboard for presenting the grammar in a chart.

In truth, almost any exercise can be used as a preview. You do not need to follow the order of material in the text. Adapt the material to your own needs and techniques.

First Exercise after a Chart

In most cases, this exercise includes an example of each item shown in the chart. Students can do the exercise together as a class, and the teacher can refer to chart examples where necessary. More advanced classes can complete it as homework. The teacher can use this exercise as a guide to see how well students understand the basics of the target structure(s).

General Techniques for Fill-in (written) Exercises

The fill-in or written exercises in the text require some sort of completion, transformation, discussion of meaning, listening, or a combination of such activities. They range from those that are tightly controlled and manipulative to those that encourage free responses and require creative, independent language use. Following are some general techniques for the written exercises:

Technique A: A student can be asked to read an item aloud. You can say whether the student's answer is correct or not, or you can open up discussion by asking the rest of the class if the answer is correct. For example:

> TEACHER: Juan, would you please read number 3?
> STUDENT: Ali *speaks* Arabic.
> TEACHER (to the class): Do the rest of you agree with Juan's answer?

The slow-moving pace of this method is beneficial for discussion not only of grammar items, but also of vocabulary and content. Students have time to digest information and ask questions. You have the opportunity to judge how well they understand the grammar.

However, this time-consuming technique doesn't always, or even usually, need to be used, especially with more advanced classes.

Technique B: You read the first part of the item and pause for students to call out the answer in unison. For example:

> TEXT entry: "Ali *(speak)* _____ Arabic."
> TEACHER (with the students looking at their texts): Ali . . . .
> STUDENTS (in unison): speaks (with possibly a few incorrect responses scattered about)
> TEACHER: speaks Arabic. *Speaks.* Do you have any questions?

This technique saves a lot of time in class, but is also slow-paced enough to allow for questions and discussion of grammar, vocabulary, and content. It is essential that students have prepared the exercise by writing in their books, so it must be assigned ahead of time as homework.

Technique C: Students complete the exercise for homework, and you go over the answers with them. Students can take turns giving the answers, or you can supply them. Depending on the importance and length of the sentence, you may want to include the entire sentence, or just the answer. Answers can be given one at a time while you take questions, or you can supply the answers to the whole exercise before opening it up for questions. When a student gives an answer, the other students can ask him/her questions if they disagree.

Technique D: Divide the class into groups (or pairs) and have each group prepare one set of answers that they all agree is correct prior to class discussion. The leader of each group can present its answers.

Another option is to have the groups (or pairs) hand in their set of answers for correction and possibly a grade.

It's also possible to turn these exercises into games wherein the group with the best set of answers gets some sort of reward (perhaps applause from the rest of the class).

One option for correction of group work is to circle or mark the errors on the one paper the group turns in, make photocopies of that paper for each member of the group, and then hand back the papers for students to correct individually. At that point, you can assign a grade if desired.

Of course, you can always mix Techniques A, B, C, and D — with students reading some aloud, with you prompting unison response for some, with you simply giving the answers for others, or with students collaborating on the answers for others. Much depends on the level of the class, their familiarity and skill with the grammar at hand, their oral-aural skills in general, and the flexibility or limitations of class time.

Technique E: When an exercise item has a dialogue between two speakers, A and B, ask one student to be A and another B, and have them read the entry aloud. Then, occasionally say to A and B: "Without looking at your text, what did you just say to each other?" (If necessary, let them glance briefly at their texts before they repeat what they've just said in the exercise item.) Students may be pleasantly surprised by their own fluency.

Technique F: Some exercises ask students to change the form but not the substance (e.g., to change the active to the passive, a clause to a phrase, and question to a noun clause, etc.), or to combine two sentences or ideas into one sentence that contains a particular structure (e.g., an adjective clause, a parallel structure, a gerund phrase, etc.). Generally, these exercises are intended for class discussion of the form and meaning of a structure. The initial stages of such exercises are a good opportunity to use the board to draw circles and / or arrows to illustrate the characteristics and relationships of a structure. Students can read their answers aloud to initiate class discussion, and you can write on the board as problems arise. Or students can write their sentences on the board themselves. Another option is to have them work in small groups to agree upon their answers prior to class discussion.

Open–ended Exercises

The term "open–ended" refers to those exercises in which students use their own words to complete or respond to sentences, either orally or in writing.

Technique A: Exercises where students must supply their own words to complete a sentence should usually be assigned for out-of-class preparation. Then, in class students can read their sentences aloud and the class can discuss the correctness and appropriateness of the completions. Perhaps you can suggest possible ways of rephrasing to make a sentence more idiomatic. Students who don't read their sentences aloud can revise their own completions based on what is being discussed in class. At the end of the exercise discussion, you can tell students to hand in their sentences for you to look at or simply ask if anybody has questions about the exercise and not have them submit anything to you.

Technique B: If you wish to use a completion exercise in class without having previously assigned it, you can turn the exercise into a brainstorming session in which students try out several completions to see if they work. As another possibility, you may wish to divide the class into small groups and have each group come up with completions that they all agree are correct and appropriate. Then use only those completions for class discussion or as written work to be handed in.

Technique C: Some completion exercises are done on another piece of paper because not enough space has been left in the textbook. It is often beneficial to use the following progression: (1) assign the exercise for out-of-class preparation; (2) discuss it in class the next day, having students make corrections on their own papers based on what they are learning from discussing other students' completions; (3) then ask students to submit their papers to you, either as a requirement or on a volunteer basis.

Paragraph Practice

Some writing exercises are designed to produce short, informal paragraphs. Generally, the topics concern aspects of the students' lives to encourage free and relatively effortless communication as they practice their writing skills. While a course in English rhetoric is beyond the scope of this text, many of the basic elements are included and may be developed and emphasized according to your students' needs.

For best results, whenever you give a writing assignment, let your students know what you expect: "This is what I suggest as content. This is how you might organize it. This is how long I expect it to be." If at all possible, give your students composition models, perhaps taken from good compositions written by previous classes, perhaps written by you, perhaps composed as a group activity by the class as a whole (e.g., you write on the board what students tell you to write, and then you and your students revise it together).

In general, writing exercises should be done outside of class. All of us need time to consider and revise when we write. And if we get a little help here and there, that's not unusual. The topics in the exercises are structured so that plagiarism should not be a problem. Use in-class writing if you want to evaluate your students' unaided, spontaneous writing skills. Tell them that these writing exercises are simply for practice and that — even though they should always try to do their best — mistakes that occur should be viewed simply as tools for learning.

Encourage students to use a basic dictionary whenever they write. Point out that you yourself never write seriously without a dictionary at hand. Discuss the use of margins, indentation of paragraphs, and other aspects of the format of a well-written paper.

Error-Analysis Exercises

For the most part, the sentences in this type of exercise have been adapted from actual student writing and contain typical errors. Error-analysis exercises focus on the target structures of a chapter but may also contain miscellaneous errors that are common in student writing at this level (e.g., final -s on plural nouns or capitalization of proper nouns). The purpose of including them is to sharpen the students' self-monitoring skills.

Error-analysis exercises are challenging, fun, and a good way to summarize the grammar in a unit. If you wish, tell students they are either newspaper editors or English teachers; their task is to locate all the mistakes and then write corrections. Point out that even native speakers have to scrutinize, correct, and revise their own writing. This is a natural part of the writing process.

The recommended technique is to assign an error-analysis exercise for in-class discussion the next day. Students benefit most from having the opportunity to find the errors themselves prior to class discussion. These exercises can, of course, be handled in other ways: seatwork, written homework, group work, or pairwork.

Let's Talk Exercises

The fourth edition of *Understanding and Using English Grammar* has even more exercises explicitly set up for interactive work than the last edition had. In these exercises, students can work in pairs, in groups, or as a class. Interactive exercises may take more class time than they would if teacher-led, but it is time well spent, for there are many advantages to student-student practice.

When students are working in pairs or groups, their opportunities to use what they are learning are many times greater than in a teacher-centered activity. Obviously, students working in groups or pairs are often much more active and involved than in teacher-led exercises.

Pairwork and group work also expand student opportunities to practice many communication skills at the same time in that they are practicing target structures. In peer interaction in the classroom, students have to agree, disagree, continue a conversation, make suggestions, promote cooperation, make requests, and be sensitive to each other's needs and personalities — the kinds of exchanges that are characteristic of any group communication, whether in the classroom or elsewhere.

Students will often help and explain things to each other during pairwork, in which case both students benefit greatly. Ideally, students in interactive activities are "partners in exploration." Together they go into new areas and discover things about English usage, supporting each other as they proceed.

Pairwork and group work help to produce a comfortable learning environment. In teacher-centered activities, students may sometimes feel shy and inhibited or may experience stress. They may feel that they have to respond quickly and accurately and that *what* they say is not as important as *how* they say it — even though you strive to convince them to the contrary. When you set up groups or pairs that are noncompetitive and cooperative, students usually tend to help, encourage, and even joke with one another. This encourages them to experiment with the language and to speak more often.

- Pairwork Exercises: Tell the student whose book is open (usually Partner A) that she / he is the teacher and needs to listen carefully to his / her partner's responses. Vary the ways in which students are paired up, including having them choose their own partners, counting off, or drawing names / numbers from a hat. Walk around the room and answer questions as needed.

- Small Group Exercises: The role of group leader can be rotated for long exercises, or one student can lead the entire exercise if it is short. The group can answer individually or chorally, depending on the type of exercise. Vary the ways in which you divide the class into groups and choose leaders. If possible, groups of 3-5 students work best.

- Class Activity (teacher-led) Exercises:

  a. You, the teacher, conduct the oral exercise. (You can always choose to lead an oral exercise, even when the directions specifically call for pairwork; exercise directions calling for group or pairwork work are suggestions, not ironclad instructions.)

  b. You don't have to read the items aloud as though reading a script word for word. Modify or add items spontaneously as they occur to you. Change the items in any way you can to make them more relevant to your students. (For example, if you know that some students plan to watch the World Cup soccer match on TV soon, include a sentence about that.) Omit irrelevant items.

  c. Sometimes an item will start a spontaneous discussion of, for example, local restaurants or current movies or certain experiences your students have had. These spur-of-the-moment dialogues are very beneficial to your class. Being able to create and encourage such interactions is one of the chief advantages of a teacher leading an oral exercise.

Discussion of Meaning Exercises

Some exercises consist primarily of you and your students discussing the meaning of given sentences. Most of these exercises ask students to compare the meaning of two or more sentences (e.g., *You should take an English course* vs. *You must take an English course).* One of the main purposes of discussion-of-meaning exercises is to provide an opportunity for summary comparison of the structures in a particular unit.

Basically, the technique in these exercises is for you to pose questions about the given sentences, and then let students explain what a structure means to them (which allows you to find out what they do and do not understand). You can summarize the salient points as necessary. Students have their own inventive, creative way of explaining differences in meaning. They shouldn't be expected to sound like grammar teachers. Often, all you need to do is listen carefully and patiently to a student's explanation, and then clarify and reinforce it by rephrasing it somewhat.

Listening Exercises

Depending on your students' listening proficiency, some of the exercises may prove to be easy and some more challenging. You will need to gauge how many times to replay a particular item. In general, unless the exercise consists of single sentences, you will want to play the dialogue or passage in its entirety to give your students some context. Then you can replay the audio to have your students complete the task.

It is very important that grammar students be exposed to listening practice early on. Native speech can be daunting to new learners; many say that all they hear is a blur of words. Students need to understand that what they see in writing is not exactly what they should expect to hear in normal, rapidly spoken English. If students can't hear a structure, there is little chance it will be reinforced through interactions with other speakers. The sooner your students practice grammar from a listening perspective, the more confidence they will develop and the better equipped they will be to interact in English.

The two audio CDs can be found at the back of *Understanding and Using English Grammar*. There are 97 listening exercises in the text, all marked with a headphone icon. They reinforce the grammar being taught — some focusing on form, some on meaning, most on both.

You will find an audio tracking list at the back of the student book to help you locate a particular exercise on the CD. The listening scripts for all the exercises are also in the back of the student book, beginning on page 451.

Pronunciation Exercises

A few exercises focus on pronunciation of grammatical features, such as endings of nouns or verbs and contracted or reduced forms.

Some phonetic symbols are used in these exercises to point out sounds which should not be pronounced identically; for example, /s/, /Pz/, and /z/ represent the three predictable pronunciations of the grammatical suffix which is spelled -s or -es. It is not necessary for students to learn the complete phonetic alphabet; they should merely associate each symbol in an exercise with a sound that is different from all others. The purpose is to help students become more aware of these final sounds in the English they hear to encourage proficiency in their own speaking and writing.

In the exercises on spoken contractions, the primary emphasis should be on students' hearing and becoming familiar with spoken forms rather than on their accurate pronunciation of these forms. The most important part of most of these exercises is for students to listen to the oral production and become familiar with the reduced forms. Initially, it can sound strange for students to try to pronounce reduced forms; because of their lack of experience with English, they may be even less understandable when they try to produce these forms.

Language learners know that their pronunciation is not like that of native speakers; therefore, some of them are embarrassed or shy about speaking. In a pronunciation exercise, they may be more comfortable if you ask groups or the whole class to say a sentence in unison. After that, individuals may volunteer to speak the same sentence. Students' production does not need to be perfect, just understandable. You can encourage students to be less inhibited by having them teach you how to pronounce words in their languages (unless, of course, you're a native speaker of the students' language in a monolingual class). It's fun — and instructive — for the students to teach the teacher.

Expansions and Games

Expansions and games are important parts of the grammar classroom. The study of grammar is (and should be) fun and engaging. Some exercises in the text are designated as Games. In this *Teacher's Guide*, other exercises have Expansions that follow the step-by-step instruction. Both of these activity types are meant to promote independent, active use of target structures.

The atmosphere for the activities should be relaxed, and not necessarily competitive. The goal is clearly related to the chapter's content, and the reward is the students' satisfaction in using English to achieve that goal. (For additional games and activities, see *Fun with Grammar: Communicative Activities for the Azar Grammar Series,* by Suzanne W. Woodward.)

MONITORING ERRORS

In Written Work

When marking papers, focus mainly on the target grammar structure. Praise correct usage of the structure. Depending on the level of your class, you may want to simply mark but not correct errors in the target structure, and correct all other errors yourself. However, if development of writing skills is one the principal goals in your class, you will probably want the students to correct most of their errors themselves. Regardless of how you mark errors, tell your students that these writing exercises are simply for practice and that – even though they should always try to do their best — mistakes that occur should be viewed simply as tools for learning.

You may notice that some errors in usage seem to be the result of the students' study of the most recent grammar structure. For example, after teaching perfect tenses you may notice students using past perfect more than they had previously, but not always using it correctly. This is natural and does not seem to be of any lasting harm. View the students as experimenting with new tools. Praise them for reaching out toward what is new usage for them, even as you correct their errors. Grammar usage takes time to gel. Don't expect sudden mastery, and make sure your students don't expect that either. Encourage risk-taking and experimentation; students should never be afraid of making mistakes. In language acquisition, a mistake is nothing more than a learning opportunity.

In Oral Work

Students should be encouraged to monitor each other to some extent in interactive work, especially when monitoring activities are specifically assigned. (You should remind them to give some *positive* as well as corrective comments to each other.) You shouldn't worry about "losing control" of students' language production; not every mistake needs to be corrected. Mistakes are a natural part of learning a new language. As students gain experience and familiarity with a structure, their mistakes will begin to diminish.

Similarly, students shouldn't worry that they will learn one another's mistakes. Being exposed to imperfect English in an interactive classroom is not going to impede their progress in the slightest. In today's world, with so many people using English as a second language, students will likely be exposed to all levels of English proficiency in people they meet — from airline reservation agents to new neighbors from a different country to a co-worker whose native language is not English. Encountering imperfect English is not going to diminish their own English language abilities, either now in the classroom or later in different English-speaking situations.

Make yourself available to answer questions about correct answers during group work and pairwork. If you wish, you can take some time at the end of an exercise to call attention to mistakes that you heard as you monitored the groups. Another possible way of correcting errors is to have students use the answer key in the back of the book to look up their own answers when they need to. If your edition of the student book comes without the answer key, you can make student copies of the answers from the separate *Answer Key* booklet.

OPTIONAL VOCABULARY

Students benefit from your drawing attention to optional vocabulary for many reasons. English is a vocabulary-rich language, and students actively want to expand both their passive and active vocabulary in English. By asking students to discuss words, even words you can safely assume they recognize, you are asking students to use language to describe language and to speak in a completely spontaneous way (they don't know which words you will ask them about). Also, asking students to define words that they may actually know or may be familiar with allows students a change of pace from focusing on grammar, which may be particularly challenging at any given time. This gives students a chance to show off what they do know and take a quick mini-break from what may occasionally feel like a "heavy" focus on grammar.

One way to review vocabulary, particularly vocabulary that you assume students are familiar with, is to ask them to give you the closest synonym for a word. For example, if you ask students about the word *optimistic,* as a class you can discuss whether *positive, hopeful,* or *happy* is the closest synonym. This is, of course, somewhat subjective, but it is a discussion that will likely engage students. Similarly, for a more advanced group, you can ask them for the closest antonym of a given word, and thus for *optimistic* students could judge among, *sad, negative,* and *pessimistic,* for example. However you choose to review optional vocabulary, most students will greatly appreciate and profit from your doing so.

HOMEWORK

The textbook assumes that students will have the opportunity to prepare most of the written exercises by writing in their books prior to class discussion. Students should be assigned this homework as a matter of course.

Whether you have students write their answers on paper for you to collect is up to you. This generally depends upon such variables as class size, class level, available class time, your available paper-correcting time, not to mention your preferences in teaching techniques. Most of the exercises in the text can be handled through class discussion without the students needing to hand in written homework. Most of the written homework that is suggested in the text and in the chapter notes in this *Teacher's Guide* consists of activities that will produce original, independent writing.

POWERPOINTS

An additional resource included with this *Teacher's Guide*, the ten PowerPoint lessons are designed for use in the classroom as "beyond-the-book" activities based on real-world readings. These lessons would serve ideally as a whole-class review prior to a test. Or you may want to break them up in shorter chunks and use them as short reviews after completing a section of charts. Depending on the level of your class, you may want to make copies of the readings for students to study as homework before the lesson. The PowerPoints are also available for download at *AzarGrammar.com*.

Additional Resources

USING THE *WORKBOOK*

The *Workbook* contains self-study exercises for independent study, with a perforated answer key located at the end of the book. If you prefer that students not have the answers to the exercises, ask them to hand in the answer key at the beginning of the term (to be returned at the end of the term). Some teachers may prefer to use the *Workbook* for in-class teaching rather than independent study.

The *Workbook* mirrors the *Student Book*. Exercises are called "exercises" in the *Student Book* and "practices" in the *Workbook* to minimize confusion when you make assignments. Each practice in the *Workbook* has a content title and refers students to appropriate charts in the *Student Book* and in the *Workbook* itself.

Workbook practices can be assigned by you or, depending upon the level of maturity or sense of purpose of the class, simply left for students to use as they wish. They may be assigned to the entire class or only to those students who need further practice with a particular structure. They may be used as reinforcement after you have covered a chart and exercises in class or as introductory material prior to discussing a chart in class.

In addition, students can use the *Workbook* to acquaint themselves with the grammar of any units not covered in class. Earnest students can use the *Workbook* to teach themselves.

TEST BANK

The *Test Bank for Understanding and Using English Grammar* is a comprehensive bank of quizzes and tests that are keyed to charts or chapters in the student book. Each chapter contains a variety of short quizzes which can be used as quick informal comprehension checks or as formal quizzes to be handed in and graded. Each chapter also contains two comprehensive tests. Both the quizzes and the tests can be reproduced as is, or items can be excerpted for tests that you prepare yourself.

AZAR INTERACTIVE

Students learn in many ways and benefit from being exposed to grammar in a variety of contexts. This computer-based program is keyed to the text and provides all-new exercises, readings, listening and speaking activities, and comprehensive tests. You can use this program concurrently with the text or as an independent study tool. You can assign the whole chapter to the entire class, or you can customize the exercises to particular students. For example, for those students who are proficient in written work, but need practice with oral production, you can assign the speaking, listening, and pronunciation exercises. Another way to assign exercises would be based on the target structure. If you notice that a student is struggling with a particular grammar point or section, you can assign the corresponding exercises for further out of class study. In addition, the chapter tests can be used as effective reviews prior to an in-class test.

Fun with Grammar

Fun with Grammar: Communicative Activities for the Azar Grammar Series, is a teacher resource text by Suzanne W. Woodward with communicative activities correlated to the Azar-Hagen Grammar Series. It is available as a text or as a download on *AzarGrammar.com.*

AzarGrammar.com

Another resource is *AzarGrammar.com.* This website is designed as a tool for teachers. It includes a variety of additional activities keyed to each chapter of the student book including additional exercise worksheets, vocabulary worksheets, and song-based activities tied to specific grammar points. This website is also a place to ask questions you might have about grammar (sometimes our students ask real stumpers), as well as also being a place to communicate with the authors about the text and to offer teaching/exercise suggestions.

Notes on American vs. British English

Students are often curious about differences between American and British English. They should know that the differences are minor. Any students who have studied British English (BrE) should have no trouble adapting to American English (AmE), and vice versa.

Teachers need to be careful not to inadvertently mark differences between AmE and BrE as errors; rather, they should simply point out to students that a difference in usage exists.

Differences in Grammar

Differences in article and preposition usage in certain common expressions follow. These differences are not noted in the text; they are given here for the teacher's information.

AmE	BrE
be in **the** hospital	be in Ø hospital
be at **the** university (be in college)	be at Ø university
go to **a** university (go to college)	go to Ø university
go to Ø class/be in Ø class	go to **a** class/be in **a** class
in **the** future	in Ø future (OR in **the** future)
did it **the next** day	did it Ø next day (OR **the** next day)
haven't done something **for/in** weeks	haven't done something **for** weeks
ten minutes **past/after** six o'clock	ten minutes **past** six o'clock
five minutes **to/of/till** seven o'clock	five minutes **to** seven o'clock

Differences in Spelling

Variant spellings can be noted but should not be marked as incorrect in student writing. Spelling differences in some common words follow.

AmE	BrE
jewelry, traveler, woolen	jewellry, traveller, woollen
skillful, fulfill, installment	skilful, fulfil, instalment
color, honor, labor, odor	colour, honour, labour, odour
-ize (realize, apologize)	-ise/ize (realise/realize, apologise/apologize)
analyze	analyse
defense, offense, license	defence, offence, licence (n.)
theater, center, liter	theatre, centre, litre
check	cheque (bank note)
curb	kerb
forever	for ever/forever
focused	focused/focussed
fueled	fuelled/fueled
practice (n. and v.)	practise (v.); practice (n. only)
program	programme
specialty	speciality
story	storey (of a building)
tire	tyre

DIFFERENCES IN VOCABULARY

Differences in vocabulary usage between AmE and BrE usually do not significantly interfere with communication, but some misunderstandings may develop. For example, a BrE speaker is referring to underpants or panties when using the word "pants," whereas an AmE speaker is referring to slacks or trousers. Students should know that when American and British speakers read each other's literature, they encounter very few differences in vocabulary usage. Similarly, in the United States Southerners and New Englanders use different vocabulary, but not so much as to interfere with communication. Some differences between AmE and BrE follow.

AmE	BrE
attorney, lawyer	barrister, solicitor
bathrobe	dressing gown
can (of beans)	tin (of beans)
cookie, cracker	biscuit
corn	maize
diaper	nappy
driver's license	driving licence
drug store	chemist's
elevator	lift
eraser	rubber
flashlight	torch
jail	gaol
gas, gasoline	petrol
hood of a car	bonnet of a car
living room	sitting room, drawing room
math	maths (e.g., a maths teacher)
raise in salary	rise in salary
rest room	public toilet, WC (water closet)
schedule	timetable
sidewalk	pavement, footpath
sink	basin
soccer	football
stove	cooker
truck	lorry, van
trunk (of a car)	boot (of a car)
be on vacation	be on holiday

Key to Pronunciation Symbols

THE PHONETIC ALPHABET (SYMBOLS FOR AMERICAN ENGLISH)

Consonants

Phonetic symbols for most consonants use the same letters as in conventional English spelling: /b, d, f, g, h, k, l, m, n, o, p, r, s, t, v, w, y, z/.*

Spelling consonants that are <u>not</u> used phonetically in English: c, q, x.

A few additional symbols are needed for other consonant sounds.
/ θ / (Greek theta) = voiceless *th* as in **th**in, **th**ank
/ δ / (Greek delta) = voiced *th* as in **th**en, **th**ose
/ ŋ / = *ng* as in si**ng**, thi**nk** (but not in da**n**ger)
/ š / = *sh* as in **sh**irt, mi**ss**ion, na**ti**on
/ ž / = *s* or *z* in a few words like plea**s**ure, a**z**ure
/ č / = *ch* or *tch* as in wa**tch**, **ch**urch
/ ĵ / = *j* or *dge* as in **j**ump, le**dge**

*Slanted lines indicate phonetic symbols.

<u>Vowels</u>

The five vowels in the spelling alphabet are inadequate to represent the 12-15 vowel sounds of American speech. Therefore, new symbols and new sound associations for familiar letters must be adopted.

Front	**Central**	**Back** (lips rounded)
/i/ or /iy/ as in *beat*		/u/, /u:/, or /uw/ as in *boot*
/I/ as in *bit*		/ʊ/ as in *book*
/e/ or /ey/ as in *bait*		/o/ or /ow/ as in *boat*
		/ɔ/ as in *bought*
/ɛ/ as in *bet*	/ə/as in *but*	
/æ/ as in *bat*	/a/ as in *bother*	

Glides: /ai/ or /ay/ as in *bite*
/ɔi/ or /Oy/ as in *boy*
/æ/ or /aw/ as in a*bout*

British English has a somewhat different set of vowel sounds and symbols. You might want to consult a standard pronunciation text or BrE dictionary for that system.

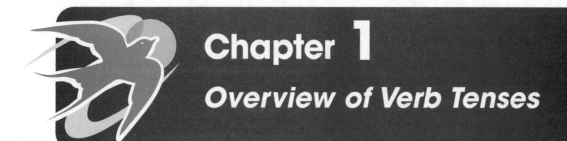

Chapter 1
Overview of Verb Tenses

CHAPTER SUMMARY

OBJECTIVE: To provide a general overview of all twelve verb tenses. The intention is for students to understand that some logical relationships exist among the verb tenses. This chapter will serve as a review for many students and will strengthen students' ability to recognize and use the verb tenses.

APPROACH: Students at this level are probably somewhat familiar with all of the verb tenses (with the possible exceptions of the future perfect and future perfect progressive, two little-used tenses). In presenting the initial charts in this chapter, you can help the students understand the overall patterns in the English tense system (for example, that all progressive tenses indicate that an activity is / was / will be in progress or that all perfect tenses indicate that one activity occurs before another activity or time.) Then as you proceed through the chapter, you can refer to Chart 1-5 to put each tense within the framework of English verb tenses. For example, you can relate the use of the past progressive (*I was sitting in class at this time yesterday*) to present progressive (*I am sitting in class right now*).

TERMINOLOGY: Simple tenses are formed without an auxiliary or helping verb, and the tense is indicated in the ending of the verb.

"Progressive" is also called "continuous," and always contains an *-ing* participle in addition to a helping verb. This form is used to indicate verbs that are in progress.

Perfect verbs include a form of the verb *have* and indicate that one action is completed in relation to another one.

You may want to review the terms "main clause" and "time clause" with students, in preparation for this chapter.

❑ **EXERCISE 1.** Let's talk: interviews and introductions. Page 1
Time: 15–20 minutes

This exercise assumes that students know how to ask and answer basic questions in English. (You may wish to give a short review of question word order if the need arises during class discussion, but primarily this first exercise is not intended to focus on any grammar in particular. You may, however, wish to refer the students to the Appendix if problems such as word order arise). This exercise also assumes that the students don't know each other. If all the students are already acquainted, they could pretend to be famous persons being interviewed by television reporters and make up entirely different questions.

- First, write your name in sentence form. For example:

  My name is Martha.

- Then ask students what question they would need to ask in order to get this information from you, prompting the following response, which you should also write on the board:

  What is your name?

- As a class, in pairs, or groups, have students create a correct question for each topic.

- Write students' questions on the board and discuss whether they ask for the desired information. For example:

  If a student suggests *How you say your name?* to obtain the information for item 2, help students correct the question in terms of grammar and vocabulary to *How do you spell your name?*

- Now ask students to interview one another, and review as a class. Circulate and jot down common mistakes for later review.

  Optional Vocabulary
  origin
  current residence
  field

❑ **EXERCISE 2.** Let's talk: preview of verb tenses. Page 1
Time: 10–15 minutes

This exercise can be used to introduce almost all the essential information contained in Charts 1-1 through Chart 1-5 by discussing each item in detail and drawing the diagrams of various tenses from Chart 1-5 on the board. Or this exercise can simply be used as a quick review of the tenses prior to individual presentation of Charts 1-1 through 1-5.

- Introduce the exercise by writing the following sentence (or any other sentence that will lead students to *What are you doing right now?*) on the board.

  I am teaching grammar class.

- Write **what** + form of **do** on the board and ask students to form a related question.

  What are you doing right now?
  I am teaching grammar class.

- Then draw the time line of that verb tense and write another practice sentence on the board if needed.
- Work through the other verb tenses in this manner.
- Divide students into pairs and instruct them to help one another decide which tense is needed.
- See the Teaching Suggestions in the front of this book for a variety of ways to teach this type of exercise.

CHART 1-1. The Simple Tenses. Page 2
Time: 10 minutes

The purpose of this chart is to help students understand the relationships in form and meaning among the three simple tenses. Not all possible uses of each tense are included in this chart. This chart and the subsequent charts in this chapter are meant as an overview. A more detailed discussion of the individual tenses occurs in subsequent chapters.

- Draw the basic diagram from the book, with arrows indicating now, past, and future.
- Read the name of the first tense (simple present) and draw the illustrating tense time line next to it.
- Write two example sentences illustrating form and meaning of the tense on the board beneath the time line, and highlight the verb.
- Use the example sentences given or generate your own. If you generate your own, be sure to use regular verbs to clearly show the verb form. For example:

  Marta practices yoga every day.

  Chi-Wei walks to class every morning.

- Follow the same procedure with the other two simple tenses. Write the name of the tense, draw the appropriate time line, and write two sample sentences to illustrate the form of each tense.
- Explain that time words and phrases such as *every day* used in chart example (b), *yesterday* used in (c), *last night* used in (d), *tomorrow* used in (e), and *tonight* used in (f) are important indicators of which tense to use.

❏ EXERCISE 4. Let's listen and talk. Page 2
Time: 10–15 minutes

- Play the audio through once without stopping. Then replay the audio one item at a time, giving students time to write their answers.
- Review the audio answers as a class.
- Give students a few minutes to decide whether each item is true for them.
- Have pairs or small groups share their answers.
- Then ask specific questions to engage students and learn a bit more about them. For example:

  You said you didn't cook your own dinner last night, Maria. Did you go out to eat?

  Expansion: Write the following professions on stick-on name tags, index cards, or pieces of scrap paper. Tape one on the back of each student so that no student can see which professional role he or she is wearing.

accountant	construction worker
farmer	salesperson
doctor	administrative assistant
lawyer	computer programmer
bus or train driver	delivery person
physicist	teacher
professional athlete	plumber

Explain that the purpose of this game is to use the present tense to create sentences that will help each person guess the profession on their tag or card. Give students a few minutes to get up and look at each other's name tags and jobs without telling each other what his / her jobs are. Have students sit down again, and model one profession with a student. For example, if the student's tag says "accountant," you could create sentences such as these:

This person uses math daily.

This person likes numbers.

This person balances the checkbooks for companies.

CHART 1-2. The Progressive Tenses. Page 3
Time: 10–15 minutes

As their name indicates, progressive tenses show actions in progress at a given point in time. These tenses are also referred to as "continuous."

In present progressive, this time is either right now or occasionally, these days, or these times. For example:

Gas prices are rising.

In past progressive tense, the time is in the past and the action in progress is often "interrupted" by a simple past tense verb.

Future progressive is used to describe an action that will be in progress and is often interrupted by a simple future verb.

It is critical that students understand whether the action **is, was,** or **will be** in progress. A second action (often indicated by a simple past or simple future action) may interrupt the verb in progress and can serve as a time reference.

- Write the name of the first progressive tense (present progressive) from the chart and draw its tense time line on the board.
- Write two sample sentences on the board to illustrate the time line. You can copy the exact sentences from the chart or make up examples of your own.
- Follow the above procedure when presenting the other progressive tenses, taking time to highlight the *be* auxiliary verb and the *-ing* participle.
- Emphasize the usefulness of the secondary verb (used in the time clause) in each sample sentence by explaining the following:

  In (b) Tom was sleeping when I arrived.

  "When I arrived" is in the past tense and interrupted the action in the main clause, which was already in progress in the past.

  In (c) Tom will be sleeping when we arrive.

  "When we arrive" indicates future, and this action will interrupt the prediction that Tom will be sleeping.

❏ EXERCISE 6. Let's listen and talk. Page 3
Time: 10 minutes

• Write the following cues on the board as a reference for students as they listen:

now = is / are + -ing

past = was / were + -ing

future = will be + -ing

• When asking students to supply additional information, write their answers on the board with correct verb forms for further reinforcement. For example:

At midnight last night, Marco wasn't sleeping.

You ask: *What were you doing, Marco?*

Write the student reply on the board: *I was finishing my homework at midnight last night.*

CHART 1-3. The Perfect Tenses. Page 4
Time: 10–15 minutes

Students may need more explanation of this chart than for the preceding two charts. With all perfect tenses, an action has either been completed at an indefinite time in the past (present perfect), had been completed before a more recent event in the past (past perfect), or will have been completed by a particular time in the future (future perfect).

It is important to emphasize the idea of completion with each perfect tense. It may also be helpful for students to know that many Americans don't use the past perfect when speaking and that future perfect is also not very common. Future perfect is unique — in order to understand its meaning and use, students must view the future from the perspective of a particular future action already having been completed.

As you generate sentences, make sure to use regular verbs in order to keep the focus on the general uses of the perfect tenses. Irregular tenses will be dealt with in more detail in later chapters.

• Present each tense in turn. Write the name of the tense, draw and label the appropriate time line for each tense, and write the example sentences beneath each one.

• After you highlight each perfect tense, take time to ask students which action (in the case of past perfect and future perfect) happened or will have happened first.

❏ EXERCISE 8. Let's listen and talk. Page 4
Time: 10–15 minutes

• Let students know that this exercise has two parts; first they are going to listen and fill in the blanks, then they are going to circle *yes* or *no*.

• Play the audio through once without stopping. Then play it again, pausing after each item to give students time to write.

• In pairs, have students compare their answers.

• Then play the audio again to check answers. Replay as necessary whenever questions arise.

• Give students a few minutes to decide which questions are true for them. Then put students in small groups to discuss their answers.

• After they have had time to discuss their answers, ask specific questions to reinforce the grammar, such as:

You: *I heard Max say that before he went to bed last night, he hadn't finished all of his homework. Max, what had you finished before you went to bed last night?*

Max: *I had finished an email to my girlfriend in Germany.*

You: *Okay, so before Max went to bed last night, he had finished an email to his girlfriend.*

Which action happened first?

❏ EXERCISE 9. Warm-up. Page 5
Time: 10–15 minutes

This exercise can be teacher-led or done as pairwork. Regardless, taking the time to review student answers and ask individual students the warm-up questions will help ensure that enough time is allotted for each tense.

CHART 1-4. The Perfect Progressive Tenses. Page 5
Time: 15–20 minutes

The perfect progressive tense expresses an action that has already been in progress when interrupted by another action (either in past or future). Unlike the perfect tenses just explored, the focus here is on progress and continuation rather than completion. However, like past perfect and future perfect tenses, these progressive perfect tenses are used to show one action in relation to another.

• Explain that the perfect progressive tenses show actions that have not yet been completed, in relation to another point in time (or event).

• Present each section of the chart, writing the name of the tense, drawing the time line and writing sample sentences beneath each one.

• Draw each progressive time line with an arrow indicating continuation.

• Highlight the targeted form *have / has + been + -ing* for each example sentence.

CHART 1-5. Summary Chart of Verb Tenses.
Pages 6–7
Time: 15–20 minutes

This two-page chart is an overview of the verb tenses. If you have not already made a wall chart or transparency of the verb tense chart, you may want to create one as a handy reference for Chapters 2-4. Students are likely to be less comfortable with the tenses presented in the second half of this chart. Be prepared to take more time with these sections.

By the end of this section of Chapter 1, students should feel prepared to explore the perfect tenses at length in upcoming chapters. As with the first part of Chart 1-5, reinforce comprehension by having students assist you in drawing the simple time lines and writing example sentences on the left-hand side of the board before contrasting these with the progressive forms on the right-hand side.

- Draw each simple tense time line and corresponding sentence on the left side of the board.
- On the right side of the board, do the same with the progressive tenses and sentences.
- Highlight the relationships both vertically (present, past, future) and horizontally by contrasting the various tenses.

❑ EXERCISE 11. Looking at grammar.
Pages 6–7
Time: 10–15 minutes

- Have students complete the first part of Exercise 11 as instructed.
- Then have students compare their answers, using the chart as a guide.

Expansion: Write the names of all the verb tenses on the board and number them. Draw all twelve diagrams and letter them. Then ask students to match the tense names with the correct diagram.

❑ EXERCISE 12. Let's talk. Page 8
Time: 10 minutes

The purpose of this exercise is to consolidate the information the students have received to this point. This exercise is essentially only additional examples of tense usage. It also seeks to promote the learning of the names of the tenses, which is helpful for student-teacher communication during units on verb tense usage.

Expansion: If you are doing this as a class, draw the Chart 1-5 time lines on the board and ask students to identify which diagram applies to which example. If students are working in pairs or small groups, have them draw the time lines that represent each tense.

❑ EXERCISE 15. Warm-up: listening. Page 9
Time: 10–15 minutes

This activity is a good chance to assess students' grasp of spelling rules.

- Play the example part of the audio, and then answer any questions.
- Play the audio through once without stopping.
- Then play it again, pausing after each item.
- Have students compare answers with a partner.
- Assign a student to each item, and have them write their answer on the board.
- As a class, correct spelling as needed.

CHART 1-6. Spelling of -ing and -ed Forms.
Page 10
Time: 15–25 minutes

Briefly discuss the spelling rules illustrated by each group of examples so that students become familiar with the content of the chart and can refer to it later.

Refer back to this chart as you work through Exercises 16 and 17.

Another option is to work through this chart as you review the answers to the Warm-up (Exercise 15).

- Present each category as listed on the left by first writing the numbered description on the board. For example:

    1. Verbs That End in a Consonant and -e

- Write one of the base forms given in the book next to the category on the board. For example:

    hope

- Ask students if they know the -ing and the -ed form, and ask for the spelling. If no one knows the answer, explain how to make the transformation and write it on the board.
- Present the two spelling exceptions below the chart, reminding students that particularly with spelling rules, certain exceptions always exist.

❑ EXERCISE 16. Looking at spelling. Page 10
Time: 10–15 minutes

Even if students don't know the meaning of some of the words in these exercises, they should be able to spell the forms correctly. After the students have written the correct forms, supply vocabulary definitions for the class as necessary.

- Complete one part at a time, giving students a few minutes to write their answers.
- Then have students check their work by comparing answers with a partner.

• As a class, review the correct answers by asking various students to write their answers on the board.

Expansion: Have students come up with sentences to go with each of the verbs now written on the board.

❑ **EXERCISE 17.** Looking at spelling. Page 11
Time: 10–15 minutes

Optional Vocabulary

ruin	boil
pat	tape
earn	

❑ **EXERCISE 19.** Let's talk and write. Page 12
Time: 5–10 minutes

This exercise works well as a homework assignment because it gives students a chance to produce the tenses on their own. In addition, it gives them an opportunity to practice English outside of class.

• Prepare students for each of the activities by discussing what types of questions they will need to ask in order to successfully write about a classmate, a native speaker, or a particular place.
• Have students brainstorm what tenses they will need to use for each of the writing activities before choosing one.

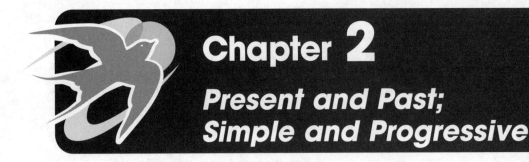

Chapter 2
Present and Past; Simple and Progressive

CHAPTER SUMMARY

OBJECTIVE: To explore four high-frequency verb tenses, reviewing and reinforcing the students' ability to use them, and to introduce some finer points of tense usage.

APPROACH: The text presents and compares the simple present and present progressive, including their use with non-progressive verbs, and then moves on to the simple past and past progressive. The simple past section includes pronunciation of -ed endings and special practice with irregular verbs.

TERMINOLOGY: "Progressive" is also called "continuous" in some texts. A clause is a structure containing a subject and a verb. A clause may be either independent (also called a main clause) or dependent (subordinate clause).

Optional Chapter Introduction Activity
(can be done before or after Exercise 1)
Time: 10–20 minutes

• Ask two students what they do first when they wake up in the morning. Write their answers on the board.

  Yao gets dressed, brushes his teeth, and then eats breakfast.

  Maria drinks a cup of coffee as soon as she gets up.

• Ask two other students what they are doing right now, and write their answers on the board.

  Paulo is listening to the teacher.

  Mieko is writing in her notebook.

• Underline the tenses and ask students to explain the differences (the first set of sentences is about regularly scheduled actions or habits; the second set of sentences shows what is happening right now).

• Ask two other students what they did last weekend, and write their answers on the board.

• Ask two other students what they were doing at 7:30 P.M. last night. Write their answers on the board.

• Underline the tenses in the four new sentences, and ask students to explain the differences.

• Ask students which set of sentences describes actions completed in the past.

• Elicit that the second set of sentences shows what was happening (ongoing) at a specific time in the past.

❑ **EXERCISE 1.** What do I already know?
Page 13
Time: 10–20 minutes

> This exercise can be used as a pretest, pairwork, or a whole-class activity. The purpose is for students to discover which grammar points they need to pay special attention to in this chapter.
>
> The text assumes that students do not know all the grammar covered in this exercise. If your students can do this exercise without any difficulty or questions, they may not need to study this chapter.
>
> While this exercise previews the grammar found in Chapter 2, it also includes grammar not found in the chapter. The chapter assumes the students are already familiar with non-target grammar, such as word order in questions, parallel structures, and the use of final -s / -es. You may wish to take some time in class to review these points. (questions and negatives in the Appendix; parallel structure in Chapter 16, and final -s / -es in Chapter 6)

• Introduce the exercise and its purpose — for students to discover areas of the language that they need to study.

• Give students time to do the exercise individually.

• As a class, discuss correct answers. If time permits, have students write their answers on the board.

Optional Vocabulary
consist
gases
political situation

❑ **EXERCISE 2.** Warm-up. Page 13
Time: 5–10 minutes

Part I
• After students complete Part 1, ask the class, *Who reads a newspaper every day?* Ask a student who did not raise a hand to make a sentence that is true for him / her. For example:

  I don't read a newspaper every day. OR *I read my email every day.*

- Ask the class, *Who is sitting next to someone from Asia?* Ask one of the students who did not raise his / her hand to make a true sentence. For example:

  I am not sitting next to someone from Asia.
  OR
  I am sitting next to someone from Spain.

Part II
- Ask students what a general truth is and what a daily habit is. Ask students what habit or daily practice is most important to them and write them on the board.
- Discuss student responses, especially unique or funny ones.

Optional Vocabulary
revolve
general truth
daily habit

CHARTS 2-1 and 2-2. Simple Present.
Present Progressive. Page 14
Time: 10–15 minutes

> Now that students have covered preliminary materials on the English tense system, the text focuses on each tense in more detail.
>
> Throughout the rest of the chapters on verb tenses, the exercises contain questions, negatives, contractions, and mid-sentence adverbs. These topics are assumed to be primarily review at this level, but most students still need to work with them. You may wish to refer students to the Appendix during your class instruction.

- Make a large chart on the board with the headings *General Truth* in the left column, *Habit* in the middle column, and *In Progress* in the right column.
- Ask different students to read the example sentences from Charts 2-1 and 2-2.
- Ask the class if the sentence is a habit, a truth, or if it's in progress. Write the item letter — (a), (b), etc. — in the correct column. Work through all the example sentences.

Expansion: Help students create their own sentences for each category, using their own lives as content. Ask the class which heading each new sentence should go under, and write the sentence on the board. When each heading has two or three sentences, underline the verbs and have students discuss the differences among them.

❏ EXERCISE 3. Let's talk. Page 14
Time: 15–25 minutes

Part I
- Divide students into pairs or small groups. Then model the activity with one group.
- Circulate and help each group with their discussion.

Part II
- Review the meaning of *generalizations,* another word for *general truth,* as well as the vocabulary in both the topics and verbs lists.
- Model the exercise with a student or group before assigning the task to the whole class.

❏ EXERCISE 5. Listening. Page 15
Time: 5–10 minutes
- Remind students that more than one completion may be correct.
- Ask students to close their books, and play the audio through once.
- Have students open their books, and give them a moment to look over the time phrases.
- Play the audio again, stopping after each item.
- Optional: After going through all the items, have students compare their answers with a partner.
- Elicit the correct answers from the class, either orally or on the board. Then listen a final time for confirmation.

Expansion: Before playing the audio the second time, go through the time phrases and have students suggest which tenses go with each time phrase. For example, they should be able to predict that *right now* calls for present progressive tense.

❏ EXERCISE 6. Let's talk: class activity.
Page 15
Time: 10–20 minutes

Expansion: Bring in cards with harder-to-guess actions written on them, such as *blow a bubble, floss your teeth, surf,* etc. Also bring in some blank cards for students to write their own hard-to-guess ideas.

CHART 2-3. Non-Progressive Verbs. Page 16
Time: 15–25 minutes

> The key point here is the difference between "states" and "activities." The intention of this chart and its terminology is simply to inform the students that certain common verbs are usually <u>not</u> used in the progressive.
>
> In the list of non-progressive verbs, even the verbs without asterisks can occasionally be used in the progressive. The text, however, only concentrates on the usual, most frequent use of these verbs.
>
> The list of non-progressive verbs is by no means complete. For the most part, it stresses only those verbs used in the exercises. Depending on the level of your class and the amount of time you have, you may want to mention these additional non-progressive verbs used to describe states: *astonish, concern, equal, impress, involve, lack, measure, regret, satisfy.*

- Write the term "non-progressive" on the board, and then write two or three sample sentences, using verbs from the chart.
- Illustrate the impossibility of progressive with these non-progressive verbs by adding a sample incorrect progressive sentence for each. For example:

  CORRECT: *Paulina belongs to the tennis team.*

  INCORRECT: *Paulina ~~is belonging to~~ the tennis team.*

- Move to the section of the chart showing verbs that can be either progressive or non-progressive.
- Write two sample sentences for a few more verbs included in this chart, and discuss the difference in meaning. For example:

  Coffee smells good. vs. *Mei-Lin is smelling her coffee.*

❏ EXERCISE 11. Let's write. Page 19
Time: 20–30 minutes

- To introduce this assignment, have the class brainstorm ideas for a sample composition that might begin with *I am sitting in my English class . . .* as a way of explaining what you want.
- Compose a paragraph on the board using several student sentences. Write the sentences exactly as they are spoken.
- Then revise the writing with the help of the class, and focus the students' attention on verb tenses and time words.

  Expansion: Ask students to imagine they are somewhere else. Have them describe either orally or in writing what they are doing. The rest of the class has to guess what the locale is. For example:

  I am sitting on an uncomfortable chair. People are rushing by me pulling or carrying their suitcases. Others are looking at their watches and pacing. Where am I? (Airport/Train Station etc.)

CHARTS 2-4 and 2-5. Regular and Irregular Verbs. Irregular Verb List. Pages 20–21
Time: 15–25 minutes

The lists and groups in these charts serve as a handy reference tool for students. Many of them will already be familiar with the categories of irregular verbs presented here.

You may want to spend three to five minutes a day quizzing the class on irregular verb forms as ongoing review throughout several weeks of the term. This can be done orally and / or using the board. Give students a verb, and ask them to say all three principal parts of the verb. Correct their pronunciation and / or spelling.

- Write the three common verb forms (*Simple, Simple Past, Past Participle*) on the board.
- Elicit some time words commonly associated with each, e.g., *every day, yesterday,* and *since last year.* Write them on the board under the verb form.
- Ask a student to choose a regular verb.

- Use that verb to create three sentences on the board; one in simple present, one in simple past, and one in present perfect. For example:

  I watch a movie every Friday night. I watched a movie last night. I have watched that movie three times this month.

- Using the same verb, write a present perfect progressive sentence on the board. Point out the present participle. Remind students of the use of present participles in forming progressive tenses.

❏ EXERCISES 12–19: Pages 22–25

Exercises 12–19 review irregular verb forms in the simple past tense. The exercises can be done over several class periods. They also work well for the last five minutes of class. They can then be repeated at a later time, after a few days or weeks, for review, or as test items.

The Listening exercises (Exercises 12,14,16) provide practice hearing, distinguishing, and then spelling the verb forms. To reinforce spelling, it is helpful to have students write their answers on the board when reviewing these exercises.

The Let's talk exercises (Exercises 13,15,17) should go at a fast pace, almost like a game. The directions call for pairwork, but you may want to lead the exercises yourself, in which case responses can be individual or the whole class together. Students should be encouraged to respond as quickly as possible rather than taking time to formulate their answers first.

Additional ideas for teaching these exercises can be found in the Teaching Suggestions at the beginning of this book.

❏ EXERCISE 12. Listening. Page 22
Time: 10–15 minutes

- Ask students to look over the sentences in situation 1. Tell them they need to change each simple present verb they hear into the correct simple past form.
- Play the audio, stopping after each item. Play the audio again straight through.
- Ask individual students to write their answers on the board. Discuss and correct as necessary.
- Give students time to preview the next situation, and then follow the same steps.

❏ EXERCISE 15. Let's talk: pairwork. Page 24
Time: 10–15 minutes

  Expansion: Ask students to create their own questions about what they did the previous weekend.

❏ EXERCISE 16. Listening. Page 24
Time: 5–10 minutes

Optional Vocabulary
temperature
fever

Expansion: Connect the grammar to your students' lives by encouraging mini-discussions. For example, when going through Exercise 16 with students, find out what home remedies (as in item 11) are popular in their countries for problems such as colds, fevers, toothaches, headaches, etc.

❏ EXERCISE 18. Listening. Page 25
Time: 10 minutes

Expansion: For more intensive listening practice, make this a dictation exercise. After finishing the exercise, choose three or four sentences and play the audio for them again. Have students write the entire sentences. Review as a class by asking individual students to write their sentences on the board, and correct as a class.

❏ EXERCISE 19. Listening. Page 25
Time: 10–15 minutes

Part I
• Play the story once. Then play the statements and have students circle their answers. Review answers as a class and replay story if needed.

Part II
• Play the story again. Have students complete the cloze exercise with the verbs they hear. Replay if needed.
• Have individual students (in turn) read the completed story aloud and get help from peers when a correction is needed.

Optional Vocabulary

peacefully	intruder
thief	sneaking around
sliding door	sirens
managed to (do something)	crack
operator	

❏ EXERCISE 20. Warm-up: listening. Page 26
Time: 5–10 minutes

This warm-up gives students the chance to hear the correct pronunciation of simple past endings.

Be prepared to exaggerate the sounds of the endings even more than the audio does in order to ensure students can hear and recognize the difference.

• Write the three endings (/t/, /d/, /əd/) on the board. Demonstrate the sound of each ending. As you answer questions and review answers, point to the correct ending to help those students who have trouble hearing the different sounds.

• Play the examples and then elicit the answers. Demonstrate the pronunciation of each word while pointing to the correct ending.
• Play the audio for items 1–9, and review the answers as a class.

CHART 2-6. Regular Verbs: Pronunciation of -ed Endings. Page 27
Time: 10–15 minutes

Failure to include pronunciation suffixes such as -ed and -s is common among learners of English. Since these sounds are unstressed, students often don't hear them. If students don't hear the suffixes, then they tend not to use them in their own production, whether written or oral. Concentrating on the spoken forms of the -ed suffix may help students correct ingrained usage problems with this form in their own production. Students are not expected to stop and figure out the correct pronunciation while speaking, but the awareness of the three differing forms may help them hear these suffixes more readily and internalize them more easily.

• Demonstrate (and as needed, exaggerate) the difference between a voiceless and a voiced consonant by having students put their hands to their throats. Then have students repeat after you:

    vowel   foul

• Students should feel their voice box vibrate when they say the "v" sound but not when they make the "f" sound.
• Point out that in both *vowel* and *foul,* students' teeth and lips are in exactly the same position.
• Give your students the following examples and ask them to again put their hands on their voice boxes to feel the differences:

    dip—tip   zip—sip   bill—pill

• Explain that the final consonant of the base form (whether voiceless or voiced) changes the -ed ending from /t/ to /d/.
• Write the following examples on the board and have students repeat the correct pronunciation after you.

    stamp — stamped (/t/ ending because the "p" sound in stamp is voiceless)

    stab — stabbed (/d/ ending because the "b" sound in stab is voiced)

❏ EXERCISES 21 and 22. Listening. Listening and pronunciation. Page 27
Time: 5–10 minutes each exercise

Be sure to write the three endings (/t/, /d/, /əd/) on the board. As you review each correct answer, point to the correct ending to help those students who have trouble hearing the different sounds. You might want to number the three endings as well so they can be referenced more easily.

- Play the audio through once without stopping.
- Play it again and stop the audio after each verb.
- Ask students which ending they hear. Play it more than once if necessary. Go through items as slowly as necessary for students to hear the endings.
- Ask individual students to read their answers aloud.

Optional Vocabulary (Exercise 22)

blinked	mopped
yawned	vacuumed
stretched	dusted

Expansion: (Exercise 22) Expand students' vocabulary for everyday gestures (e.g., blink, yawn, stretch) by teaching others, such as *wink, sigh, nod, shake your head, roll your eyes, shudder, shiver,* and *shrug.*

❏ **EXERCISE 23.** Let's talk: small groups.
Page 28
Time: 10–15 minutes

- Model the exercise with a group.
- While groups are working, write the grid from the book on the board.
- Assign one group to each column and have them write their answers on the board.
- Discuss and correct the grid as a class. You may need to pronounce some verbs for the class.

CHARTS 2-7 and 2-8. Simple Past. Past Progressive. Page 29
Time: 10–20 minutes

At this point you may wish to explain that a clause is a structure that has a subject and a verb, and make the distinction between a main or independent clause and a dependent clause. (Students will concentrate on complex sentences in later chapters.) This text assumes that students are quite familiar with sentences containing basic adverb clauses of time using *when, while, before,* and *after.* A more detailed discussion of adverb clauses appears in Chapter 17. At this point, keep the focus on verb tenses, with minimal attention to complex structures.

Note in (g) and (h): In sentences with *when,* the progressive usually occurs in the main clause. In sentences with *while,* the progressive usually occurs in the *while*-clause.

- Ask specific students about their actions the previous evening.

    Galina, what were you doing at 8:07 last night?
    What were you doing at 8:07 last night, Luis?

- Write students' responses on the board as correct sentences.

    At 8:07 P.M., Galina was taking a shower and preparing to meet her friends.
    At 8:07 P.M., Luis was emailing his wife in Madrid.

- Explain that a specific point in time can also be described by an event that took place then. If we imagine the phone rang at 8:07 P.M., we can make a time clause using this information:

    When the phone rang, . . .

- Write the following (or other sentences created from student information) on the board:

    When the phone rang, Galina was taking a shower.
    When the phone rang, Luis was emailing his wife in Madrid.

- Explain that *while* can also be used to make a time clause.
- Write the following (or other sentences created from student information) on the board:

    The phone rang while Galina was taking a shower.
    The phone rang while Luis was emailing his wife in Madrid.

- Have various students read sample sentences from charts 2-7 and 2-8 aloud.
- Emphasize and elaborate on targeted grammar by rephrasing questions. For example:

    What was Luis already doing (or in the middle of doing) when the phone rang?

Expansion: Play the game "Alibi" with your students. The point of the game is that a crime has been committed (e.g., *My grammar book was stolen last night!*) and students have to construct alibis, or explanations for where they were when the crime took place.

Prepare index cards with events in simple verb form and corresponding times listed. Using this information, students provide an alibi for where they were and what they were doing at a particular time by making sentences from the actions and times listed on their cards. For example:

    7:30   walk to grocery store
    8:00   meet friend for coffee
    9:00   go to movie theater

You can either make up a "crime" (*Help! My grammar book was stolen last night!*) or simply ask students to explain what they were doing at a particular time to get the ball rolling. For example:

    You: *A crime was committed last night at 7:30. What were you doing? OR I called you at 7:30 last night. What were you doing?*

    Marcella, using the information on your card, tell me what you were doing at that time.

    Marcella: *I was walking to the grocery store.*

❏ **EXERCISE 28.** Let's talk: pairwork. Page 31
Time: 10–15 minutes

Optional Vocabulary

overseas	run a red light
slip	pay attention to
park illegally	

❏ EXERCISE 29. Grammar and listening.
Page 32
Time: 10–15 minutes

Optional Vocabulary
United Nations
multilingual

Expansion: Discuss your students' first day of class with them. Ask students questions such as:

Were you nervous when you got to class?

Did you recognize any other students?

What did you bring with you on the first day?

Students should be able to answer using past progressive and simple past appropriately. This activity can also be used as preparation for Exercise 32.

❏ EXERCISE 30. Let's talk. Page 32
Time: 10–30 minutes

A pantomime is performed silently. Ideas are communicated by gestures and movements, not by words. Be sure to give students sufficient time to think about how they will perform their pantomime.

This pantomime exercise should generate spontaneous use of the target structures — past verbs. Be sure to focus attention on the correct use of the verb tenses because, in the excitement of the activity, students may tend to slip into present or uninflected forms. The grammar focus should be on consistent use of past verbs. You may wish to let other errors go by uncorrected.

- Model the activity by demonstrating a pantomime yourself or asking a volunteer to do so.
- Then ask the class to describe what happened using past verbs.
- Give students sufficient time to perform and the audience time to produce the correct targeted structures.
- ALTERNATIVE: Divide the class into small groups and follow the above steps. Each group can appoint a leader to watch the time limit and monitor the use of past verbs.

Expansion: Before class, write the additional pantomime activities listed below on index cards. Give these to students to use in addition to the actions in the book.

putting on makeup and checking one's appearance in the mirror

making a fruit salad or smoothie (peeling a banana is a distinctly recognizable action)

making a toast or speech

preparing and flipping pancakes

listening to music while walking down a crowded street

getting ready for bed, brushing and flossing teeth, etc.

trying to wake up when the alarm rings

making a bed

emptying the dryer, folding and/or ironing clothes

putting in or taking out contact lenses

checking your messages on a cell phone or answering machine

❏ EXERCISE 31. Let's write. Page 32
Time: 10–20 minutes

This can be done as a timed writing exercise in class immediately following a pantomime or as a homework assignment.

- Elicit time words from the class and write them on the board. Some examples are: *first, next, then, after.*

Expansion: Write one description paragraph as a whole-class activity, with you writing on the board as students suggest sentences. Then revise the paragraph with the help of the class, and focus attention on chronological organization and use of time words as connective devices.

❏ EXERCISE 32. Let's write. Page 32
Time: 10–20 minutes

This exercise pulls all of the grammar in Chapter 2 together and works well as a homework assignment.

When you mark students' papers, focus mainly on the use of verb tenses. Other errors should be given less attention. Add an enthusiastic note of praise or encouragement for good work.

- Spend a few moments discussing students' first experiences to help them recall details that will enhance interest. For example:

What did you notice when you were on your way from the airport / train / ship?

Who was the first person you met?

How did you feel? Did you feel nervous or excited or tired?

- Remind students to use time words to clearly illustrate when events occurred: *first, next, then, after that, before, when, while,* etc. If comparing to present-day feelings, discuss time words for the present time.

CHART 2-9. Using Progressive Verbs with *Always.* Page 33
Time: 10–15 minutes

The structure in this chart may not be especially significant in a student's overall language usage ability, but it's fun and can be used to point out that a grammatical form can convey a speaker's emotional attitude. The chart and the following exercises are also good places for students to practice conveying emotion in speech through sentence stress and intonation.

- Ask students to describe the annoying habits of people in their lives.
- Use their information to create sentences on the board. Emphasize the "annoying" factor by inserting *always* between auxiliary and progressive participle.

- Have students read through Chart 2-9 aloud, and encourage them to add drama and emotion to the sentences.

□ **EXERCISE 34.** Let's talk. Page 33
Time: 10–15 minutes

Optional Vocabulary
mess up   crack one's knuckles
brag

Expansion: Elicit real-life annoying habits ("pet peeves") from the class. Pet peeves are behaviors that annoy one person especially, even more so than do other irritating behaviors. For example, someone who is always on time may find other people being five or ten minutes late particularly annoying or consider lateness a pet peeve. Put a few "annoyed" sentences on the board such as:

He is always talking on the phone.

She is forever chewing gum.

I am constantly doing laundry.

Then ask students to create sentences based on their own pet peeves.

□ **EXERCISE 35.** In your own words. Page 33
Time: 10–15 minutes

Optional Vocabulary
stand someone
hassle (problem)

Expansion: Discuss cross-cultural differences related to this topic. Possible questions:

How late do you have to be to be thought "late," and what are the social consequences?

Is it okay to ask someone how old she is or how much money he makes?

Is it considered rude to eat fast food in public?

What do Americans always do that the rest of the world finds annoying?

Direct students to use *always* and progressive forms when describing their own culture's pet peeves.

CHART 2-10. Using Expressions of Place with Progressive Verbs. Page 34
Time: 10–15 minutes

The point of this chart is that the prepositional phrases of place can have two positions: (1) the neutral position at the end of the clause or (2) the focus position, which emphasizes the expression of place between *be* and the main verb.

In answer to *what*-questions, the neutral position is used because the emphasis is then on the activity. In answer to *where*-questions, the focus position is used.

- Explain to students that one way to alter emphasis or meaning of a sentence is by changing word order.
- Use student-generated information to create sentences and write them on the board. For example:

Li-Tzu was in the library studying. vs.
Li-Tzu was studying in the library.

- Like the samples above, your sentences should illustrate the different emphasis created by placing the expression of place between the auxiliary and the *-ing* verb.

Chapter 3

Perfect and Perfect Progressive Tenses

CHAPTER SUMMARY

OBJECTIVE: To explore the perfect and perfect progressive tenses, which have complex references to time and duration of activities or situations.

APPROACH: The text promotes familiarity with past and present participles, necessary for students to use perfect and perfect progressive tenses correctly. The text illustrates time expressions used with *since* and *for*, examines *has / have* contractions common in spoken English, and compares present perfect tense with simple past. The present perfect progressive section includes work on identifying when the progressive form is called for. Finally, the remainder of the chapter discusses past perfect tense and combines its use with simple past tense to distinguish two past times within one sentence.

TERMINOLOGY: A "past participle" is the third principal part of a verb (e.g., *go-went-**gone**-going*). The past participle is used with an auxiliary in the perfect tenses and in the passive voice. It can also function as an adjective.

❏ EXERCISE 1. Let's talk: pairwork. Page 36
Time: 10–15 minutes

This exercise gives students the chance to recall and produce past participles in context. Though students will probably make mistakes, they will gain confidence using irregular verb past participles.

• Remind students that they will be using the irregular verb forms that they studied in the previous chapter.
• Remind students that a question with *your* as in item 10 requires an answer with *my*.
• As a follow-up activity, ask students to spell some of the past participles in the exercise, either orally or on the board. Be sure to include *hidden*, *stolen*, and *forgotten* since these are particularly troublesome.

❏ EXERCISE 2. Let's listen and talk. Page 37
Time: 15–20 minutes

You may need to explain that *ever* in a present perfect question means "at least once in your lifetime." It is not used in the answer to a question. You may also want to explain that an acceptable alternative to *No, I haven't* is *No, I never have.*

• Play the audio at least twice, giving students time to write their answers.
• Assign a student to each item and have them write their answers on the board.
• Replay the audio and check the answers on the board as a class.
• Give students a few minutes to answer each question. Then have pairs tell about themselves.

Expansion: Use the completed version of this exercise as content for an information exchange done in rotating pairs. Instruct students to arrange themselves in two lines facing one another. (If you have odd numbers, you will need to provide instructions and model with the extra student.) Partners ask the questions from Exercise 2 and exchange answers until you instruct them to switch. When you do, the last student in one of the lines moves to the first position of the same line, and everyone in this line "rotates" one space to the left, giving everyone in both lines a new partner. After students have had three or four partners, have them return to their seats. Ask each student to provide one statement about a class member, based on what was learned from this exchange. Write students' answers on the board, correcting as you do so. For example:

You: *Who can tell me something about Lucia?*
Carlo: *She has never lost her wallet.*
Eu-Jin: *She has never slept in a tent.*

❏ EXERCISE 3. Warm-up. Page 37
Time: 5 minutes

• Give students a few minutes to complete the sentences.
• Ask questions that will lead students to why simple past tense is required in items 1 and 4. For example:

You: *When did you take your first English class, Kenichi?*

Kenichi: *I took my first English class in 2006.*

You: *Okay, why do we need simple past "took" here?*

Kenichi: *The time 2006 is over, and the action was completed in the past.*

CHART 3-1. Present Perfect. Page 38
Time: 15–20 minutes

The use of the present perfect illustrated in examples (a)–(e) carries the same meaning as the present perfect progressive: it expresses the <u>duration</u> of an activity that began in the past and continues into the present. The present perfect is used to express the duration of a "state," but the present perfect progressive is used to express the duration of an "activity." Note that the verbs in (a)–(e) are non-progressive. (See Chart 2-3.)

Special attention may need to be paid to (h), where *have* is an auxiliary verb and *had* is the main verb.

• Ask students questions about when they moved to their current residence, and confirm that they still live there now. For example:

> You: *Chie, when did you move here?*
>
> Chie: *I moved here in 2000.*
>
> You: *And you still live here today, in ____, right?*
>
> Chie: *Yes.*

• Draw and write:

Chie has lived here since 2000 / for ____ years.

• Explain that present perfect tense (formed with **has / have** + *past participle*) is used for an action that started in the past and continues in the present.
• Using the time line technique, present the other two sections of the chart: present perfect for unspecified time and present perfect for a repeated event.
• Double-check that students have understood by asking them to explain how present perfect differs from simple past, and put their responses on the board.

❏ EXERCISE 4. Looking at grammar.
Page 39
Time: 5–10 minutes

Remind students that *since* and *for* are used with present perfect tense to show an action begun in the past and continuing in the present.

Frequent problems occur with *since*. *Since* may be followed by (1) a specific day or date (*1998, Friday, last January, etc.*) or (2) a clause with a past tense verb (*since I was twelve years old, since he came to this city, etc.*). Be sure to point out that it is incorrect to use durational phrases such as *since two years* or *since a long time*. In those cases, *for* is used.

It is advisable to discourage the use of time phrases with *ago* following *since* (e.g., *since three days ago*). Such phrases are sometimes used very informally by native speakers, for instance in a short answer, but are likely to be misused by the learners at this point.

❏ EXERCISE 8. Let's talk. Page 41
Time: 5–10 minutes

Expansion: Instruct students to come up with four or five present perfect questions of their own to ask their partner(s). For example: *How many times have you been in love? How many times have you been outside your country?*

Have students use their own questions as well as those in the text to gain information about one another. Each student can then present a sentence about one other person to the class.

❏ EXERCISE 9. Let's write and talk. Page 41
Time: 10–20 minutes

This exercise provides an effective way for students to use the target grammar creatively. For homework the previous day, have students prepare four truths and two lies about themselves in order to participate in this activity.

❏ EXERCISE 10. Warm-up: Listening.
Page 41
Time: 10 minutes

• Ask students to close their books and number 1–6 on a piece of paper.
• Explain that they'll be listening for the words *have* and *has* in the sentences but that the words have been shortened, or reduced.
• Play the audio through once, pausing after each item, so students can write which word they think was used, *have* or *has*.
• Have students open their books, then play the audio again straight through.
• Discuss as a class how *have* and *has* are pronounced.

CHART 3-2. *Have* and *Has* in Spoken
English. Page 42
Time: 10–15 minutes

> Here, reduced speech describes the sound of helping verbs (*has / have*) contracted with the preceding nouns and / or question words. Students should know that they will hear reduced speech frequently in everyday conversation with native speakers. The students' focus should be kept on recognizing and understanding reduced speech rather than producing it.

• Copy the example sentences from the left-hand side of the chart onto the board.
• Write the three pronunciation symbols on the board and number them:
    1. / v /   2. / əv /   3. / z /
• Point to the appropriate symbols whenever modeling a sound in order to help students hear the differences.
• Exaggerate your pronunciation of the reduced speech in each one.
• Explain that these contractions are rarely used in writing, and then only in informal writing.

❏ EXERCISE 11. Listening. Page 42
Time: 10–15 minutes

• Play the example on the audio.
• If the symbols are still on the board from your chart explanation, point to the appropriate symbol as you read the example. If not, write them on the board and point to them when appropriate.
• Play the audio once without stopping.
• Then play the audio again, stopping after each item. You may need to play the audio more than once.
• Have individual students write their answers on the board, and discuss as a class.

❏ EXERCISE 12. Warm-up. Page 43
Time: 5 minutes

• Have two students take the roles of the boy and girl and have them read the dialogue aloud.
• Ask students to explain the time frame in both cases.

CHART 3-3. Present Perfect vs. Simple Past.
Page 43
Time: 10–20 minutes

> Students are often confused about the differences between the simple past and present perfect. Specifically, once they are introduced to present perfect, they either tend to overuse it or not use it all. This chart clarifies the differences in meaning and usage between the two tenses.

• Ask students for an example sentence in the simple past. For example:

    You: *Layla, what did you do last night?*
    Layla: *I finished my project at 9:00 last night.*
    You: *Okay, so Layla finished her project at 9:00 last night.*

• Draw and write:

    9:00 P.M. last night   *now*
    |————————|———————————X———————————|
    Layla finished her project at 9:00 P.M. last night.

• Now ask a leading question resulting in the present perfect tense. For example:

    You: *Has anyone visited Paris?*
    Roberto: *Yes.*
    You: *Okay, so we know Roberto visited Paris, but we don't know when. To express this, we can use the present perfect tense, which is formed from has / have + past participle.*

• Draw and write:

    some time before now   *now*
    |————————|———————————?———————————|
    Roberto has visited Paris.

• Repeat that while we know Roberto has visited Paris in the past, we don't know (and are not concerned with) when he did so.
• Draw on the board time lines from Chart 3-3 for example sentences (a)–(d).
• Write two columns on the board as follows:

    <u>Present Perfect</u>   *vs.*   <u>Simple Past</u>
    unknown time in past   *specific time in past*
    still in progress   *completed in past*

• Keep the columns on the board as students work through Exercises 13 and 14.

❏ EXERCISE 13. Looking at grammar.
Page 44
Time: 10 minutes

Optional Vocabulary
arid   pass away
late-breaking news   wiser

❏ EXERCISE 14. Let's talk: find someone
who . . . . Page 45
Time: 5–10 minutes

• Give students a few minutes to read through items 1–6 and answer any vocabulary questions.
• Model the example with the help of two students.
• Model follow-up questions for your students.

    What did you . . . ?
    Why did you . . . ?
    When did you . . . ?
    Where did you . . . ?

Expansion: This "find someone who" exercise can be expanded to give students an opportunity to practice making small talk while using the target grammar. If possible, turn the activity into a "party" by playing background music at a low volume. Doing so can help students feel less self-conscious when speaking. Instruct students to meet, greet, and gather as much information about one another as they can. You can signal that students should move on to a new conversation partner by stopping the music and restarting it, instructing them to change. You can circulate and take notes or, if your full participation is needed to keep the activity moving, become one of the party guests yourself. To wrap up the activity, have students return to their seats, and ask each student to tell one interesting fact about another student.

CHART 3-4. Present Perfect Progressive.
Page 46
Time: 10–20 minutes

In examples (e)–(h), it can be challenging for students to understand when to use present perfect and when they must use present perfect progressive. In many cases, both are acceptable. Because of this, you should anticipate that students will need extra examples and discussion to feel confident distinguishing which form of the present perfect to use.

• First, write the example sentence for present progressive tense as follows:

   I am teaching grammar class right now.

• Then draw the diagram from the chart on the board, and write the following sentence:

   I have been teaching grammar class since _____.
   (Add whatever time is true for you that day.)

• Explain that both tenses deal with actions in progress, but the present progressive simply states that an action is in progress *at the moment of speaking,* while the present perfect progressive gives the *duration up to now of an action in progress.*

• Explain that present perfect progressive tense is used to emphasize the duration of an activity over time, and ask questions that bring out good examples, such as:

   How long have you been studying English?
   How long have you been playing tennis?
   How long have you been practicing kung fu?
   How long have you been wearing contact lenses?

• Write students' answers on the board.

   Mie has been studying English for six years.
   Alexandre has been playing tennis since he was seven.
   Juan has been practicing kung fu for ten months.
   Malka has been wearing contact lenses since she turned sixteen.

• Explain that the tense is often used with the following time expressions: *for, since, all day, all week, all morning.*

❑ EXERCISE 17. Let's write. Page 47
Time: 10–20 minutes

This exercise works very well as homework; you can assign one, two, or all three time frames.

Expansion: Divide the class into three groups and assign each group a tense time frame. Group 1 will use present perfect progressive, Group 2 will use simple past, and Group 3 will use present perfect to write their descriptions. Ask students to use as many of the verbs provided beneath the picture as possible in their descriptions. Have them also come up with other verbs which can be used to talk about the picture. After 10 or 15 minutes, have the groups take turns reading their own descriptions aloud while the other two groups assess the accuracy of the grammar used.

❑ EXERCISE 18. Listening. Page 48
Time: 5–10 minutes

• Explain to students that they will be listening for parts of a real conversation and, therefore, not every blank will be completed with target grammar.
• Play the audio through once without stopping. Then play it again, stopping after each sentence.
• In pairs, have students compare their answers.
• Play the audio again so that the pairs of students can check their answers.

❑ EXERCISE 19. Looking at grammar.
Page 48
Time: 10–15 minutes

This exercise presents those cases in which both present perfect and present perfect progressive are acceptable. Let your students know that in some cases, the difference is so subtle that native speakers can't even articulate why they have chosen one tense and not the other.

• Explain that present perfect progressive emphasizes *duration of time,* while present perfect shows an emphasis on *completion.* For example:

   I have been reading <u>War and Peace</u> for two weeks.
   vs.
   I have read 200 pages of <u>War and Peace</u>.

• Tell your students that another subtle distinction is that present perfect progressive is more often used for *recent activity,* and present perfect is more often used for *an indefinite time in a more distant past.* For example:

   I have been traveling in Asia.
   vs.
   I have traveled in Asia.

• Explain that the first sentence suggests the time frame is recent, and the second suggests that the travel happened at some unknown time before now.

❏ EXERCISE 21. Let's write. Page 49
Time: 15–20 minutes

This is a summary review activity for the present perfect, present perfect progressive, and simple past.

Before assigning either topic, prepare students in class by writing some student-generated sentences on the board, and discuss which would make the best topic or introductory sentence. Students can then continue in class or at home. Or consider scheduling extra time for brainstorming a composition as a class, prior discussion of topics often leads to better compositions.

When assigning the task, be sure to clearly explain the expected length and grammar focus of the assignment.

- For topic 1, if the students seem shy about speaking frankly of their experiences in your class, ask some leading questions such as:

    What was your first impression of this building? This room?

    What do you remember about your classmates on the first day? Your teacher?

    Who did you talk to?

    Did you think the class was going to be too easy? Too hard?

- Then move into questions with the present perfect.

    How long have you been attending this class?

    What topics of English grammar have we studied? Have been easy for you? Have been hard for you?

    What are some fun things we've done in this class since that first day?

- For topic 2, ask questions to get students thinking about their final days at home.

    What did you do the last day before you left?

    What kinds of things did you pack before coming here?

    Did you have a good-bye party with your family or friends before you left?

    Did you sleep well the night before you traveled, or were you too anxious? What were you nervous about before you traveled here?

- Next, move into questions with present perfect.

    How have you been spending your time since you came here?

    In addition to English, what have you been learning about?

    How have you been enjoying the weather, food, and culture of your new setting?

    Have you been communicating with your friends and family at home? Have you been telephoning or using email?

CHART 3-5. Past Perfect. Page 50
Time: 10–20 minutes

The most important concept for students to grasp is that <u>two</u> events in the past are necessary to use past perfect. The <u>earlier</u> event uses the past perfect tense.

Sometimes students have the incorrect notion that past perfect shows that events took place a long, long time ago. Be ready to clarify this misunderstanding by emphasizing that in using the past perfect, <u>when</u> an event occurred in the past is important only in relation to another time in the past.

The expression *by the time* usually needs some explanation. It conveys the idea that one event was, or will be, completed before another event. It usually signals that either the past perfect (simple or progressive) or the future perfect (simple or progressive) needs to be used in the main clause. In fact, this phrase is used to signal only those tenses in the exercises in the text — even though it is possible to use other tenses when a "state" rather than an "event" is being expressed. For example: *The doctor came at six. By that time, it **was** too late* (state). *The patient **was** dead* (state) OR ***had died*** (event).

In some cases, such as (d) and (f), simple past can be used in place of past perfect in informal English. In other words, it is often, but by no means always, possible to use the simple past in place of the past perfect. The past perfect is relatively formal, and students will tend to encounter this tense more in written English than in spoken English.

Reviewing the chart's notes on the use of past perfect tense with *before* and *after* (c)–(f), reported speech (g) and (h), and use in written text (i) will help students know where and in what contexts to anticipate the tense's use.

- Using student-generated information, draw a time line that shows two past events. For example:

    Juan left at 4:00 P.M. Pedro called him at 6 P.M.

- Write an example illustrating the two tenses combined in one sentence. For example:

    four hours ago   two hours ago   now

    Juan had already left when Pedro called him.

- Work through the first examples (a)–(f), illustrating the combination of simple past and past perfect tenses on the board with time lines.

- Depending on your class, assess whether to present and discuss examples (g)–(j) formally. You may choose to skip these points for now to give your students a chance for immediate controlled practice.

❑ EXERCISE 23. Looking at grammar.
Page 51
Time: 10–20 minutes

> The most challenging aspect of this exercise is for students to accurately identify which action happened first. Students need to think about the situation as it is described in order to do this logically, and you may need to ask leading questions to help them do so consistently.

Optional Vocabulary

roam	emigrate
become extinct	relocate
embarrassment	settle

❑ EXERCISE 25. Warm-up: listening. Page 52
Time: 5 minutes

- As students have worked with reduced speech earlier, ask a student to explain what reduced speech is.
- Ask students to predict how *had* will sound when reduced.

CHART 3-6. *Had* in Spoken English. Page 53
Time: 5–10 minutes

> The goal here is to help students understand the situations in which *had* is reduced. When *had* is used as a main verb, it cannot be reduced. When had is part of the past perfect, it is usually reduced. As in earlier pronunciation exercises which focused on reduction, the aim here is not for students to produce the target structure but rather to train their ears to better hear the structure in everyday English.

- Ask your students questions in order to elicit two sentences in which *had* is an auxiliary. For example:

  Had anyone already studied present perfect tense before we studied it in this chapter?

  Had anyone already visited the United States before she came to this class?
- Write students' responses.

  Francine had already studied present perfect tense.

  Xie had already visited Boston.
- Then ask questions which elicit *had* as the main verb.

  Did anyone have a problem when they first arrived here?

  Did any of you have a concern during your first week of classes?
- Write students' responses.

  Mieko had a problem.

  Jasmine had a concern.
- Give students a few moments to study the two sets of sentences, and then ask them what the difference is between the two sets. If students are struggling with this, you can prompt them by underlining the simple past and past perfect verb forms in the sentences.

- Next, using normal, relaxed spoken English, read all four sentences aloud. Ask students if they heard any differences, and encourage them to try to explain the differences.
- In the first two sentences on the board, cross out the word *had* and write the phonetic sounds below.
- To show students that they can't reduce *had* to /d/ in the sentences about Mieko and Jasmine, have students try to do so. They will say some form of *Mieko'd a problem,* which fails as a sentence because the main verb isn't clear.

❑ EXERCISE 27. Listening. Page 53
Time: 5–10 minutes.

> Point out to students that the reduced sound for *had* and *would* is the same. Explain that they can tell which auxiliary is being used by looking at the verb form that follows /d/. If it's the past participle, the /d/ = *had*. If it's the simple form of the verb, then /d/ = *would*.

CHART 3-7. Past Perfect Progressive. Page 55
Time: 10–15 minutes

> The past perfect progressive is only possible when more than one past event is being discussed. The past perfect progressive is used to indicate that the earlier action had been in progress and was interrupted by the more recent simple past action.
>
> This tense is used infrequently. It is more common in formal written English, with the possible exception of its use in reported speech.

- Draw time lines and write examples on the board to illustrate an ongoing past perfect action interrupted by a more recent simple past action. For example:

  3:00 P.M.   5:00 P.M.   now

  —x x x x x x x x x———————————|

  It is now 7:30 P.M.

  Mara had been waiting for two hours when Lara's flight arrived at 5:00 P.M.
- Ask students what actions occurred in the sentence. Then ask them which action occurred first.
- After students have given the correct answer, explain that the past perfect progressive is only possible when more than one past event is being discussed.

❑ EXERCISES 32–37. Pages 57–59

> Exercises 32–37 provide comprehensive review of the tenses presented in Chapters 1–3. You may want to ask students to recall all of the tenses they remember and write these on the board before beginning these exercises.

18   Chapter 3

❏ EXERCISE 33. Listening. Page 58
Time: 5 minutes

- Before playing the audio, write the names of tenses as column headings on the board and ask students to predict time words that go with various tenses. For example:

Simple Past	Present Perfect	Past Perfect
ago, last week	since, for, ever, never	already

❏ EXERCISE 35. Let's talk. Page 59
Time: 10–15 minutes

In order to keep momentum up, give students a time limit. Because the next exercise is a variation on this theme, it is a good idea to conduct this "chain story" creation as a class, thus preparing students for the next exercise.

❏ EXERCISE 37. Let's write. Page 59
Time: 15–30 minutes

You may notice that some errors in verb tense usage seem to be the result of the students' study of verb tenses. For example, you may notice students trying to use past perfect more than they previously had but not always using it correctly. Don't despair. It is natural and does not seem to be of any lasting harm. View the students as experimenting with new tools. Praise them for reaching out to what is new usage for them, even as you correct their errors. Their study of verb tenses is providing a foundation for growth as they gain experience and familiarity with English. Grammar usage takes time to gel. Don't expect sudden mastery — and make sure that your students don't expect that either.

- Tell your students that they should plan on writing about 300 to 400 words (or six to ten sentences) once they have refined the topic.
- Have students get into small groups to discuss the topic and share ideas.
- Explain to students that the questions are only intended to guide their ideas. They should not simply answer every question in order. To facilitate this, ask students leading questions about the topics, themselves, worldwide events that took place the year of their birth, or simply ask them about their family structure, where they lived, etc.
- Discuss the meaning of the phrase *state of the world* with your students by asking them about the state of the world today
- Offer your own history and have students help you write the start of your story or theirs on the board.
- Have students complete the writing out of class.

Expansion: Because this exercise requires using many verb tenses, you can create your own error-analysis exercise by copying some of the incorrect sentences your students produce. Make sure that every student in the class has one of their errors represented. You can also include miscellaneous, non-target errors if you know that the class can easily correct these as well. Edit the student writing somewhat: don't include errors that would get you into a whole new discussion of unfamiliar grammar. For example:

Student writing: *I enjoied to grow myself up in Mexico City. I had had a happy child time there, My parents taked good care of there children.*

Used as an error-analysis exercise item:

I enjoied growing up in Mexico City. I had had a happy childhood there. My parents taked good care of there children.

Chapter **4**
Future Time

CHAPTER SUMMARY

OBJECTIVE: To explore and learn the most common ways to express future time. This chapter emphasizes *will* and *be going to* future forms, present tense future, and briefly introduces the less common future perfect tenses.

APPROACH: This text defines the simple future as a verb form that expresses an event or situation that will, to the best of the speaker's knowledge, occur in future time. Using modals and periphrastic (i.e., phrasal) modals to express future time is covered in Chapters 9 and 10.

TERMINOLOGY: For ease of classroom communication, the text refers to both the *will* + *simple form* and *be going to* + *simple form* as the simple future tense.

❏ EXERCISE 1. What do I already know?
Page 60
Time: 5–10 minutes

This exercise is a quick way to tap into students' existing knowledge of present and future tenses. Depending on the level of your class, you may want to spend more time reviewing the time words and contexts of each item.

- Give students a few minutes to circle their answers.
- Have students read the sentences and their choices aloud.
- Ask students to explain which words in each sentence helped them make their choices.

❏ EXERCISE 2. Warm-up. Page 60
Time: 5–10 minutes
- Since this complex task occurs at the beginning of the chapter, put students in pairs to complete the task.
- While pairs are working, choose a few students to write the items on the board.
- As a class, discuss and correct the sentences on the board.

CHART 4-1. Simple Future: *Will* and *Be Going To.* Page 61
Time: 15–25 minutes

This chart introduces the two basic forms for expressing the future. It does not show their difference in function or meaning. (See Chart 4-2.)

It is useful to spend some time on the pronunciation of the reduced forms (*'ll* and *gonna*). Model the reduced forms for students, but don't rush them to use them in their speech. Remind students that good enunciation is important for new language learners and that normal contracted speaking will occur naturally as they gain experience with the language. Be sure to point out that *'ll* is used both in speech and in very informal writing but that *gonna* is never used in writing.

- Ask students their plans for the following day or weekend. For example:

  Alessandra, what will you do this weekend?
  Chien, what are you going to do this weekend?

- Using students' information, write sentences demonstrating that both *will* and *be going to* can be used for simple future. For example:

  Alessandra will visit her cousin this weekend.
  Chien is going to play softball this weekend.

- Go over the chart with the class, and ask students to read the example sentences (a)–(l) aloud.

❏ EXERCISES 3-7. Pages 61 and 62

Exercises 3–7 give students the opportunity to practice the two simple future forms in listening and speaking contexts. The exercises build in complexity, ending with students creating sentences using the future tenses. The focus here is not on the differences in meaning but rather on the correct forms of the tenses.

❏ EXERCISE 3. Listening. Page 61
Time: 5 minutes
- Read the example sentences aloud, exaggerating the pronunciation of the contractions.
- Then play the examples on the audio so students can hear different people pronouncing *will* or *'ll*.

- Play the audio through once without stopping. Then go back and play each item at least twice.
- Review answers as a class, replaying any items as needed.

❏ **EXERCISE 4.** Pronunciation. Page 62
Time: 5–10 minutes

> The contraction of *will* is natural in conversation; this exercise gives students practice in hearing these forms and trying to produce them themselves.

❏ **EXERCISE 7.** Let's talk: small groups.
Page 62
Time: 10–15 minutes

> This speaking exercise gives students a chance to practice using the *be going to* form of the simple future freely and creatively.

- Explain that the goal of the exercise is to produce future forms in statements and questions. Then explain that students will reach the goal by imagining themselves and their classmates in specific jobs in the future.
- See the Teaching Suggestions in the front of this book for a discussion of how to lead Let's Talk exercises effectively.

Expansion: To turn this activity into a game, have students keep their future occupation to themselves. Instruct them not to reveal the name of their profession. They should only discuss the specific duties or expectations of their future jobs, leaving others to guess what the profession is. For example: Student A has been given the future occupation of politician.

Student A says:

I am going to meet many people and shake lots of hands every day.
I am going to make many speeches.
I am going to travel a lot.
I am going to change the world.
I am going to read newspaper articles about myself.

Other students guess what Student A's future role is:

Are you going to be an actor?
Are you going to be a famous athlete?
Are you going to be a politician?

CHART 4-2. *Will* vs. *Be Going To.* Page 63
Time: 10–20 minutes

> Students often want to know the difference between *will* and *be going to*. This chart compares three different meanings for *will* and *be going to*: prediction, prior plan, and willingness.

- Put the three headings from the chart (*Prediction, Prior Plan, Willingness*) on the board.
- Using student-generated information, write one *will* sentence and one *be going to* sentence under the heading *Prediction*. If students' responses don't quite work, make your own predictions about topics that interest your class.
- Highlight the verb forms so that students easily see that *will* and *be going to* have the same meaning and can both be used to make predictions. For example:

  Prediction
  Brazil <u>will win</u> the next World Cup.
  Germany <u>is going to win</u> the next World Cup.

- Next, ask a couple of students what they are going to do this coming weekend, and write their responses on the board using *be going to* under the heading *Prior Plan*.
- Highlight the *be going to* verb form in each sample sentence and explain that for plans made before the moment of speaking, *be going to* is used. For example:

  Prior Plan
  Makiko <u>is going to</u> visit her friend in New York.
  Juan <u>is going to</u> make dinner for his family.

- Then elicit examples of willingness from students by deliberately dropping a pen or book near a student's feet.
- Ask the student if he/she will pick the object up for you. Because of the cue that you have given the student (*Will you get that for me?*), he/she may automatically say *I will*.
- Even if the student says nothing or incorrectly says *I'm going to pick that up,* you can use this brief demonstration to teach the correct form.
- Explain that the student didn't know and <u>couldn't know</u> that you were going to drop something and then ask him/her to pick it up. So there was no prior plan to do so.
- Explain that the <u>only</u> correct future form for a decision made at the moment of speaking is the *will* future.
- Give students the example of a telephone ringing or a knock on the door. Because we don't know in advance when such actions will happen, we <u>can't</u> make prior plans to respond to them.
- Write the examples you have discussed under the heading *Willingness* and highlight the verb forms.
- Remind students that the *will* future is frequently spoken and written as a contraction, particularly with the pronoun *I*. For example:

  Willingness
  (The phone rings.)
  I <u>will answer</u> it / <u>I'll answer</u> it.
  (Someone knocks on the door.)
  I <u>will get</u> it / <u>I'll get</u> it.

- Explain that the negative form of the *will* future is used to express refusal or, in the case of an inanimate object or machine, inability to function.
- Write some examples of this particular usage on the board. For example:

  Beatriz's uncle is afraid of flying and <u>won't travel</u> by plane.

*I don't know what is wrong with it, but my computer
<u>won't turn on</u>.*

- Go over Chart 4-2 with students, asking students to read the sample sentences (a)–(f) aloud.
- Draw students' attention to Situation 1 and Situation 2 below Chart 4-2.
- Have one student read A and one B in Situation 1 and two different students read A and B in Situation 2.
- Ask a few students to tell you what they will do three or four weekends from now. As some won't yet have any plans, encourage them to use either *will* or *be going to* forms.

❏ **EXERCISES 9 and 10.** Page 64

Exercises 9 and 10 require students to think critically about the meaning and context of each sentence in order to know what form of future they need to use. If you feel that students are struggling with Exercise 9, complete it as a class, discussing the reason for choosing each correct form. Write key phrases that show either willingness or evidence of future plans on the board. If Exercise 9 seems to come easily to your group, you may want to have them complete Exercise 10 (and give them even more intensive practice), before reviewing both exercises.

❏ **EXERCISE 9.** Looking at grammar.
Page 64
Time: 10 minutes

- Because students need to understand the context in these sentences in order to successfully complete the exercise, take time to review any vocabulary questions.
- See the Teaching Suggestions in the front of the book for suggestions on incorporating optional vocabulary in the lesson.

Optional Vocabulary

front-row seats	grab
creative	engaged
patient	accustomed
elementary	

❏ **EXERCISE 13.** Warm-up. Page 66
Time: 5 minutes

The directions ask students to explain what they notice about the verbs in blue. Students should notice that these verbs are all in present tense, and when preceded by a time word or phrase such as *after, as soon as,* and *when,* the time expressed is future and not present.

- Students may automatically complete these sentences using a main clause in a future tense. If they don't, correct their tense, but also respond to the content of

their completions. For example:

Juan, are you really going to go home and go to sleep after you leave this class? But it's still morning!
I am shocked that not one student in this class is going to open his grammar book as soon as he goes home tonight.

CHART 4-3. Expressing the Future in Time Clauses. Page 67
Time: 15–20 minutes

The focus of this chart is on verb usage in complex sentences containing dependent (subordinate) adverb clauses, called "time clauses" here. The structure of sentences with these clauses is discussed more thoroughly in Chapter 17.

Learners naturally feel that it is "logical" to use future tense in the time clause as well as in the main clause. Point out that this is not "traditional" English usage. There are certain patterns and systems within a language, but a language should not be expected to be logical.

The meaning of *until* is sometimes difficult for learners to grasp, as in (e). It means that a situation will exist, then change.

- Using some of the time words included in the chart, elicit from the class two sentences combining time clauses (first) and main clauses in future tense. Write the sentences on the board. For example:

   As soon as Marco gets up tomorrow, he will call his mother.
   After Flavia leaves school on Friday, she will go to the airport.

- Now come up with two sentences in which the time clause comes after the main clause.

   Pei-weng will take the TOEFL test after she returns to Taiwan.
   Lars will leave for the mountains when his father arrives.

- Explain that when the time clause precedes the main clause, a comma separates the two.
- Tell students that no comma is needed when the time clause follows the main clause.
- Underline the present tense structure of the time clause in one color, and highlight the future tense structure of the main clause in a different color. Highlight commas as necessary.
- Go over Chart 4-3 with students, asking them to read sentences (a)–(h) aloud.

❏ **EXERCISE 14.** Looking at grammar.
Page 67
Time: 5–10 minutes

- Tell students that by drawing brackets around the time clause, they are distinguishing the time clause from the main clause.

Optional Vocabulary

sweep	elections	harbor
front porch	tide	

❑ EXERCISE 15. Looking at grammar.
Page 67
Time: 5–10 minutes

Optional Vocabulary

nap	B.A. (bachelor's degree)
junior in college	M.A. (master's degree)
graduate degrees	Ph.D. (doctorate degree)

❑ EXERCISE 16. Let's talk: interview.
Page 68
Time: 10–15 minutes

- Put students into groups of three.
- Instruct students to first make questions from the cues in each example individually, and then to ask the other students in their group their questions.
- As a class, have students give you the questions they formed for each of the five examples and put these on the board. For example:

  1. *What are you going to do after you wake up tomorrow?*

- Ask students to report on their partners' responses, and write some (or all) of these responses on the board. For example:

  You: *Ming, what is Javier going to do after he wakes up tomorrow?*

  Ming: *After Javier wakes up tomorrow, he is going to finish his grammar homework.*

- Continue until you have received a few answers for each of the five questions and written two or three responses for each on the board.
- Analyze any mistakes by writing the sentences on the board and calling on the class for help with correction.

CHART 4-4. Using the Present Progressive and the Simple Present to Express Future Time.
Page 69
Time: 10–15 minutes

> The present progressive, when used to express future time, must relate to a planned event or definite intention.
>
> The simple present, when used to express future time, is limited to scheduled events.
>
> These tenses are frequently used to express future time, especially in conversational English. The difficulty for students is to learn the limitations on using these tenses to mean future time.

- Ask students if they have any plans for the coming weekend or holiday.
- Co-create present progressive sentences on the board using the present progressive for planned future events. For example:

  Jun is having dinner with his girlfriend tomorrow night.

  Maria is traveling to Miami on Friday.

- Have three students read example sentences (a)–(c) aloud in turn.
- Introduce the use of simple present for future regularly scheduled events by asking students when the next class is.
- Write their responses on the board using simple present tense, and remind them that you can do so because your class is a regularly scheduled event.

  Our class meets at 9:00 two days from now.

- Have three students read sentences (d)–(f) aloud and refer to the notes on the right-hand side of the chart as needed.

❑ EXERCISE 19. Looking at grammar.
Page 70
Time: 5–10 minutes

Expansion: Prepare index cards for each student, with his / her name written on it. These cards will later be given out, one per student (no student should receive his own name). Students will use the present progressive form of the future to describe another classmate's planned activities.

Tell students they need to 1) talk to every student in class and 2) find out at least three details about their classmates' plans for the coming weekend. Have students stand up, walk around the room, and ask each other what they are doing this coming weekend. After 10–15 minutes of gathering information, they should all sit down again. You will now distribute the name cards to each student, making sure that each class member receives another class member's name.

Now explain to the class that they have to look at the name of the person on the card and recall what his/her upcoming plans are. They will then use the present progressive to pretend to be that person. The other class members will have to guess who the speaker is pretending to be. For example, Vilson from Brazil might say:

This weekend my parents are arriving from Taiwan, and they are taking me shopping in Chinatown so I can have some Chinese food in my apartment. I am showing my parents all around Portland on Saturday. Although they have traveled all over Asia, they have never been to the United States before, and they want to see an American city.

On Sunday, we are driving to the mountains because my mother has always wanted to see the leaves change colors.

Who am I?

Classmates:

Hsu-wei. You're Hsu-wei . . . because she told us that her parents were arriving from Taiwan this weekend! Yeah . . . and Hsu-wei also said that they were driving to the mountains because her mom has always wanted to see the leaves change colors. And she also said she was going shopping for Chinese food in Chinatown with her parents.

❏ EXERCISE 20. Let's write. Page 71
Time: 10–25 minutes

> This is an imaginative writing exercise. Beginning this exercise in class with the ideas below helps students grasp the idea of expanding on the basic topic of travel plans.
>
> You may want to teach the idiomatic phrase "money is no object," meaning students should pretend they have enough money and time to go absolutely wherever they want and to do whatever they want.
>
> Use a map if possible. If you have time, photocopy mini-maps of the world. You may also want to print a copy of an itinerary from the internet.

- Explain what an itinerary is: a plan for a trip that shows the places to be visited, the route, the arrival and departure dates, hotels, and transportation.
- Break students into small groups to brainstorm their first destination.
- Remind students that the more specific their plans are and the more detailed their itinerary is, the more interesting the end result will be.
- Have them think about where they will depart from, what means and class of travel they will take, and what time of day they will arrive at their first destination.
- Write specific questions on the board to help students brainstorm and help them to think of as many details for their upcoming itinerary as possible. For example:

  Where are you leaving from?

  How are you traveling? Are you going first-class in a plane or sailing via luxury cruise ship? Are you driving across the continent of Africa in your Land Rover or being chauffeured from Heathrow airport to Buckingham Palace in a Rolls Royce?

  Who is accompanying you?

  What time are you arriving at your first destination?

  How long are you staying there?

  What kind of accommodations are you staying in, etc.

- Tell students that once they have written a few initial sentences, the rest can be completed for homework.

CHART 4-5. Future Progressive. Page 71
Time: 10–15 minutes

> Future progressive is most commonly used in response to questions about what will already be in progress at one specific future time. When planning a meeting or conference that has many sequenced steps or events, future progressive comes in very handy. (For example: *At 9:35, the seminar will be wrapping up.*)
>
> This tense is also used informally to talk about what is predicted to be happening at an unspecified time in the future. For example, *I'll be calling you soon* or *You'll be speaking English in no time.* This use occurs primarily in spoken English and shows a warmth and familiarity among the speakers and listeners.

- Draw this time line on the board, and using student-generated information, illustrate future progressive tense.

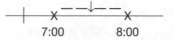

  Tomorrow, Giles is leaving his apartment at 7:00 A.M.

  At 8:00 A.M., he will arrive at school.

  At 7:30 A.M., Giles will be driving to school.

- Explain that the general form is *will* + progressive (*be* + *-ing* form) of the verb.
- If using the *be going to* form of the future, the future progressive form is *be going to* + *be* + *-ing.*

  Tomorrow, Giles is leaving his apartment at 7:00 A.M.

  He is going to arrive at school at 8:00 A.M.

  At 7:30 A.M., Giles is going to be driving to school.

- Have students read sentences (a)–(d) from the chart aloud, taking turns.

❏ EXERCISES 22 and 23. Looking at grammar. Page 72
Time: 5–10 minutes per exercise

> Since both Exercise 22 and 23 are short, you may want to do the first two items of each as a class, and then assign the rest as homework.
>
> Remind students that the references to specific times in the future will help them know which tense to use.

CHART 4-6. Future Perfect and Future Perfect Progressive. Page 73
Time: 10–20 minutes

> The future perfect and future perfect progressive are the two <u>least</u> used tenses in English. The tenses are primarily found in academic literature more than everyday prose or speech, so you don't need to spend a great deal of time on them.

- Draw the time line and use student-generated information to illustrate future perfect.

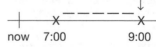

  Marco will finish his doctorate in June of 2016.

  I will see Marco in July of 2016.

  By the time I see Marco, he will have finished his doctorate.

- Using another student's information, draw a time line and illustrate the use of the future perfect progressive.

  Irene will start studying at 7:00 P.M.

  At 9:00 P.M., her roommate will return to the apartment.

Irene will have been studying for two hours by the time her roommate gets home.

- Explain that future perfect progressive is used to show the duration of an event that will be in progress before another event takes place.
- Select different students to read aloud the examples (a)–(c) from the left-hand side of Chart 4-6.

❏ **EXERCISE 25.** Looking at grammar.
Page 73
Time: 10–15 minutes

This exercise includes past, present, and future perfect, and progressive tenses. The text tries to help students understand the future perfect and future perfect progressive by comparing them to other tenses with which the students are more familiar.

❏ **EXERCISE 26.** Let's talk or write. Page 74
Time: 10–15 minutes

Expansion: With a more advanced class, you can do this exercise with books closed, with you reading the cue from the text about Bill's activities yesterday and asking the questions about tomorrow. Because students haven't prepared for this exercise, they will need to justify their choices spontaneously, gaining speaking practice this way. You can separate students into groups or teams or simply encourage them to shout out responses and corrections.

❏ **EXERCISE 27.** Let's talk or write. Page 75
Time: 10–25 minutes

This exercise is ideal for a final homework exercise reviewing future tenses. It can be started in class and completed as homework, or you can take an entire class to work on it. This can be continued at home and collected as a final written assignment.

- Give students time to read through all the topics. Answer any vocabulary or content questions they may have.
- Briefly read through each of the topics, and ask a few provocative questions for each topic to prompt students' brainstorming. For example:

  Types of transportation: Will we have personal space ships? Air cars?
  Energy sources: Will we be using the tides? Hydrogen?

- Put students in small groups, and have them choose their top three topics and brainstorm ideas for them.
- Stop the exercise with 10 minutes to spare in order to give students time to begin writing their ideas.
- Remind students when writing paragraphs that sometimes they need to mix past, present, and future tenses. For example:

  In the past, people used horses for transportation. Today we use cars and airplanes, but in the future, everyone will fly their own private rocket ship.

- See the Teaching Suggestions in the front of this book for further discussion on working with writing exercises.

Chapter 5
Review of Verb Tenses

CHAPTER SUMMARY

OBJECTIVE: To review the verb tenses taught in detail in Chapters 1–4.

APPROACH: Chapter 5 provides practice with all the verb tenses previously presented. As a result, this is the only chapter in the book which does not contain any charts.

When students have to pick the appropriate tense(s) according to context and meaning, it is important that they have opportunities to discuss their choices and explore misunderstandings. One of your many roles is to help students become sensitive monitors and effective editors of their own English use.

Now that the foundation for verb tense usage has been laid, the students need both guided and free practice and, most important, lots of out-of-class language experiences as the complex process of language acquisition proceeds. You may wish to tell your students that they shouldn't expect to become instant experts in verb-tense usage after studying these first five chapters, but that you expect their development to be excellent and their ultimate goal easily reachable. Sometimes students equate second language learning with other academic pursuits. They may feel that once they study a chapter in mathematics or chemistry, they are masters of the information it contains — and expect the same results in a language class. You may wish to discuss with your students the many ways in which the study of a language is different from other courses of study.

❏ **EXERCISE 1.** What do I already know?
Page 76
Time: 10–15 minutes

This exercise can be done individually, in small groups, or as a whole class. It can also be used as a quick pretest to assess students' strengths and weaknesses.

❏ **EXERCISE 3.** Let's talk. Page 78
Time: 10–15 minutes

Short answers are natural in conversations. However, in this exercise students are practicing verb tenses, so they should answer in complete sentences.

If this exercise is teacher-led, approach each item conversationally; add extra words, expand upon topics, rephrase questions, and put the questions in relevant contexts. These questions are in the text merely to suggest ideas as you engage the students in an oral review of verb tenses.

In items where there are several related questions, ask a question and wait for the response, then follow that answer with the next question to the same student. Don't stop for corrections or explanations until the item (the conversation) is completed.

If the exercise is used for pairwork or group work, the students can simply monitor each other and check with you as necessary.

❏ **EXERCISE 4.** Listening. Page 78
Time: 10 minutes

Be sure students have their books closed when you play the audio for Part I. This will help them concentrate on listening for the meaning.

❏ **EXERCISE 5.** Let's talk and write. Page 79
Time: 5–10 minutes to relate story; 20 minutes to write

Assign this task as homework the day before. Ask students to think about the sequence of events and the tenses required to tell their story successfully.

This is not a dictation exercise, so Student A should listen to Student B's complete story and then report it in a written paragraph. Student A can take notes but should not try to write everything down word for word.

• After putting students in pairs, announce a time limit (perhaps 5 minutes) so that the stories are not too long.
• Tell students that they should both tell their stories first. Then they can both write at the same time.

Expansion: This assignment can be turned into a group discussion and writing project. It may help students if you ask them to begin their story with an opener such as *I have never been so embarrassed / confused / scared / annoyed as the time I. . . .*

In groups of three or four, students share their anecdotes in class and decide which one would work best as a written narrative to share with the entire group. Together, the members of the small group work on writing the story using the first person singular narrator ("I") and adding in detailed and descriptive language to engage the reader or listener. You may discuss whether the account should be 100 percent accurate or whether embellishments are welcome.

Collect the group-written narratives and redistribute them so that each group has another group's story. One member of each group reads the story aloud, and the whole class has to guess which class member is the real narrator.

❏ EXERCISE 6. Looking at grammar.
Page 79
Time: 10–15 minutes

This exercise is intended as a model for the writing assignment that follows in Exercise 7.

Optional Vocabulary
botanical gardens	balloon race
barely	time to breathe

❏ EXERCISE 7. Let's write. Page 80
Time: 10–20 minutes

It may help to co-write a letter together as a class on the board first. You can either use yourself as subject, and have students help you put your own activities into the proper tenses and sequence, or you can choose to author the letter as one class member.

You may wish to require students to use each of the twelve tenses at least once. This may result in forced sentences, but students usually find it challenging and fun. If you choose to do this, refer them to Chart 1-5 so they can review which verb forms they need to use.

- Put students into small groups to brainstorm what they want to say.
- Help them define their topic by writing some specific questions on the board and having students answer these questions first. For example:

  What have you been doing recently?

  What do you do every day?

  What have you done since the last time you contacted the person you are writing to?

  What are you planning to do this weekend?

  What are you going to achieve or complete this coming month?

- Tell students to respond to the questions and then elaborate on them in order to write a letter.

❏ EXERCISE 9. Looking at grammar.
Page 80
Time: 15–20 minutes

This exercise is ideal for students to work through alone. Remind students to pay attention to the context and look for any time cues they can find. In addition, there are a number of vocabulary items for you to review with students.

- After students have completed the exercise, ask various students to read a few sentences at a time aloud so that the whole class hears the passage as a cohesive text.
- Discuss any sentences that have produced varying responses.
- Ask general comprehension questions about the passage as a whole. For example:

  What is the main topic of the passage?

  What are some of the mythical explanations for earthquakes discussed in the text?

  What countries do these mythical explanations come from?

  According to scientists, what do catfish do before an earthquake happens?

  What animals appear to be sensitive and able to predict earthquakes?

  How could these animals help humans?

- Ask students if their culture(s) has / have similar mythical explanations for natural phenomena, and use this as a discussion springboard.

Optional Vocabulary
ancient	wave	predict
estimates	strike	instruments
trembles	brick	sufficiently
catfish	concrete	

❏ EXERCISE 10. Let's talk: pairwork.
Page 82
Time: 20–25 minutes

Decide on famous people for students to role-play beforehand. Be prepared with a list of enough famous living people that you can assign one to each pair.

- Before beginning the activity, discuss what a "nosy" reporter is. As a class, generate a list of nosy questions a reporter might ask.
- If there is time, have students read their articles aloud. Invite classmates to correct grammar and usage. After they read their articles, students can reveal the identity of the famous person interviewed.

❏ **EXERCISE 11.** Let's talk: small groups.
Page 82
Time: 10–15 minutes

> This exercise gives students a chance to use the target grammar to talk about the class and its members. Encourage students to be somewhat dramatic and humorous in describing the class, its members, and activities to date.

- Bring in a few copies of news releases to distribute to students beforehand.
- Ask students what a news release contains, and, using the samples you have brought in, explain that news releases contain easily understandable information.
- Tell students that the news release shouldn't be longer than a few paragraphs and that students should use the specific bulleted points listed in the text to guide their discussion and writing.

Expansion: Use the most descriptive sentences created by the small groups in order to co-create one news release for the whole class on the board. You may want to copy this down and make photocopies to distribute to everyone in the class.

❏ **EXERCISE 12.** Let's talk and write.
Page 82
Time: 5–10 minutes, over multiple days

> This activity is designed to be spread out over a period of days with only a few students giving speeches each day. Students who are not speaking should take notes in order to practice listening skills. They can also note (1) questions to ask for additional information and (2) problems with verb tenses or pronunciation. These notes can be used for discussion after each speech.

> As a preparation for this exercise, you may wish to bring a newspaper article to class and have the class work together to make a two- or three-minute summary so that the students understand exactly what you expect.

❏ **EXERCISE 13.** Check your knowledge.
Page 82
Time: 10–15 minutes

- If you decide to use the expansion below, don't let students look through Exercise 13 in advance.

Expansion: Put students into two teams for this error-correction exercise. You will need a watch with a second hand in order to give each team a suitable amount of time (45 seconds). Teams keep their books closed. Write the incorrect sentence on the board and assign it to one team. As a group, the team whose turn it is has to identify the problem and correct it completely within 45 seconds or whatever amount of time you allot. If the team successfully does both, it gets two points. If the team identifies the problem but does not provide a corrected version, the team earns only one point. The correction phase then goes to the other team, which now has the opportunity to gain an extra point by providing a grammatical correction. The team with the most points at the end of the competition wins.

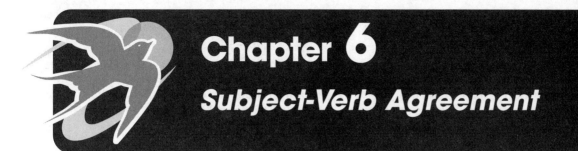

Chapter 6
Subject-Verb Agreement

CHAPTER SUMMARY

OBJECTIVE: To review and master correct usage of final -*s* / -*es* and subject-verb agreement.

APPROACH: Correct use of final -*s* / -*es* is a common problem among English language learners. Even though students may "know" the grammar for using the final -*s* / -*es* suffix, they are still not consistent in using it correctly in their own production, both oral and written. To help with self-monitoring and the development of correct patterns of production, this chapter focuses on final -*s* / -*es* and singular-plural distinctions, beginning with a review of some rules for spelling and pronouncing the final -*s* / -*es* suffix. The main sections deal with the problem of number: quantities and various aspects of singular-plural agreement between subject and verb.

TERMINOLOGY: The term "expression of quantity" is used for any quantifier (e.g., *some of, a lot of, several of, two of*), determiner (e.g., *no, each, every, some, any*), or predeterminer (e.g., *all, both*) that expresses amount or size.

❑ **EXERCISE 1.** What do I already know?
Page 84
Time: 5–10 minutes

This exercise can be used as a short pretest or preview of the chapter. You may wish to tell students that you know this exercise is "too easy" but that for the average learner, problems with singular-plural persist through many years of English study and use; thus, this review of basics.

- Give students a few minutes to add -*s* or -*es,* then discuss. Possible points of discussion:

    grammatical explanations for final -s / -es

    pronunciation of -s / -es: /s/, /z/, and /əz/

    variations in spelling: -s vs. -es; -ys vs. -ies

    basic grammar terminology: noun, verb, adjective, singular, plural

    the basic structure of the simple sentence: subjects and verbs and complements

- Since it is assumed students are familiar with most of the points above, they should be able to provide much of the information with only occasional prompting from you.

- Be sure to write the correct answers on the board so that everyone can focus on which words do or do not have a final -*s* / -*es.*

CHART 6-1. Final -*s* / -*es:* Use, Pronunciation, and Spelling. Page 85
Time: 10–20 minutes

Most students are probably well aware of the elementary grammar in this chart but still sporadically or even frequently omit final -*s* / -*es.* This chart seeks to reinforce student awareness of -*s* / -*es* by a review of rules and an emphasis on oral production.

Encourage correct production of final -*s* / -*es* by exaggerating your own correct pronunciation. Remind students that mistakes with this basic point may make their accent sound more "foreign" than it would otherwise sound. Most adult learners speak an accented English, but most also want to minimize their accents. By becoming vigilant about the correct pronunciation of final -*s* / -*es* and self-correcting as much as possible, students can minimize their own accents.

- Write the three phonetic symbols /s/, /z/, and /əz/ on the board. Model the sounds for the students. As you work through the chart and following exercises, point to the appropriate symbol when discussing a particular pronunciation to help those students who may not be able to hear the differences yet.

- Present each ending and its particular pronunciation systematically, using your students' lives as a context for sentences. For example:

    Pavlo likes books and movies.

- Highlight or underline the -*s* endings:

    *Pavlo likes book*s*, and movie*s*.*

- Point out that the final -*s* is pronounced differently after different nouns. For example, After *book* (a voiceless ending sound, /k/), the -*s* is pronounced like /s/. After *movie* (a voiced ending sound, /i/[ee]), the -*s* is pronounced like /z/.

- Have students repeat each sound after you.

❏ **EXERCISE 3.** Listening and pronunciation.
Page 85
Time: 5 minutes

- Pointing to the three phonetic symbols /s/, /z/, and /əz/ on the board, model the target sounds again. Tell students they will be listening for these sounds.
- Play the audio through once with no pauses and have students write their answers. Explain that while they may not be 100 percent certain the first time they listen, they should still write down an answer.
- Play the audio through again, pausing after each item.
- Have pairs compare their answers by pronouncing the words aloud.
- Check for correct answers by having individual students read each item aloud. Point to the correct symbol (/s/, /z/, or /əz/) on the board, and correct pronunciation as necessary.

Expansion for Exercises 3–5: Divide the class into two teams. Flip a coin to decide which team will begin the game. Spell a word aloud or write it on the board. The first person in the first team's line must then pronounce the plural of the word correctly. If he/she does, then the team gets a point, and the next word goes to the second team. If the first student does not pronounce the word correctly, then the first person in the second team's line can try. Continue until every student on each team has had a turn.

❏ **EXERCISE 6.** Let's talk: pairwork. Page 86
Time: 5–10 minutes

Expansion: Have students come up with two or three additional sentences of their own. Encourage students to think of unusual occupations or examples of human or animal behavior that can follow the model.

CHART 6-2. Basic Subject-Verb Agreement.
Page 87
Time: 10–15 minutes

The grammatical term "third person" refers to this pattern:

Singular: ***I*** = the person who is speaking, the "first person"

you = the person who is being spoken to, the "second person"

he/she/it or **a singular or noncount noun** = the person or thing that is being discussed, the third person.

Plural: ***we*** = the speaker and included persons, the "first person plural" form

you = all persons who are being spoken to or included in the audience, the "second person plural" form

they or **a plural noun** = people or things that are being discussed, the "third person plural" form

- Using your students as topics, write a simple present sentence on the board. For example:

  Lin studies English.

- Point out that the subject *Lin* is singular and therefore the verb, *studies,* is also singular.
- Draw an arrow from the singular subject to the verb it determines, and highlight the verb's third person singular -*s* ending.

  Lin studie͜s English.

- Diagramming is particularly helpful when presenting subjects followed by prepositional phrases, adjective clauses, or gerunds. Exaggerate this point by writing a very long sentence that starts with a subject followed by a prepositional phrase (or adjective clause) that contains both plural and singular nouns. For example:

  The article from the Internet about the lives of scientists in the eighteenth century and their wives and children seems a bit boring.

- Write a few complex sentences on the board, such as:

  The book Seok is reading amuses her.
  Learning new vocabulary words challenges students.

- Have students come to the board and diagram the sentences.
- Give students the opportunity to read aloud the sample sentences (a)–(k), on the left-hand side of the chart.

❏ **EXERCISE 8.** Looking at grammar.
Page 87
Time: 5–10 minutes

Students must be able to identify the grammatical subject, then select the correct form of the verb. The grammatical subject may not be the logical subject. Subjects with *every* and *each* (e.g., *every man, woman, and child*) may seem to be plural because the expression can logically be seen to refer to many people, but the grammatical concept of *every* and *each* is singular. Naturally, this is a difficult point for learners.

Optional Vocabulary

lettuce	cabbage
subjects	rich in (vitamin C)
astound	protected
syllabus	overpriced

❏ **EXERCISE 9.** Listening. Page 88
Time: 5–10 minutes

Optional Vocabulary

calculations	expectations
thesaurus	sign language
routine	

CHART 6-3. Subject-Verb Agreement: Using Expressions of Quantity. Page 89
Time: 10–15 minutes

> Make sure students understand that with *some, most, all,* and *fractional* (*two-thirds, one-half,* etc.) expressions of quantity, they need to find the noun that follows the expression to know whether a singular or plural verb is needed. In contrast, the expressions *one, each,* and *every* always require singular verbs no matter what follows them.

- Ask one student to read item (a) and another to read item (b) aloud.
- Ask the class how and why examples (a) and (b) are different. Point out how that affects the verb.
- Continue to work through the pairs of example sentences (c)–(h) with different students reading them aloud. Stress the certainty and consistency of these examples.
- To further illustrate this point, write contrasting examples from students' lives, such as the ones below, and have students explain the differences in meaning:

Singular Verb	Plural Verb
Some of the movie was too violent for Lina.	*Some of the movies today are too violent for Lina.*
A lot of Jin-Young's notebook is full of grammar notes.	*A lot of the students' notebooks are full of grammar notes.*
One-half of Marta's birthday cake is gone.	*One-half of Marta's birthday presents are gone.*
Most of Abdullah's weekend is busy.	*Most of Abdullah's weekends are busy.*

- Emphasize that the expression of quantity preceding the noun (e.g., *some of, two-thirds of, a lot of,* etc.) does <u>not</u> determine the verb in (a)–(h). It is the noun that determines the verb, not the quantifier.
- Continue asking students to read aloud the rest of the chart.
- Provide clarification (by referring to notes on the left side of the chart) and write more example sentences on the board as needed.

❑ EXERCISE 11. Looking at grammar.
Page 89
Time: 10–20 minutes

Optional Vocabulary

rotten	enclosures	materials
required	approximately	calcium
roam	chief	excused

❑ EXERCISE 12. Looking at grammar.
Page 90
Time: 5–10 minutes

Expansion: Point out the sentence ending above each column, which ends with an adjective. Ask students for additional adjectives that can be used to complete the sentences. Write the three or four most sophisticated or interesting options on the board. Have students rotate into new groups so they can have new partners and continue the completions with new adjectives.

❑ EXERCISE 13. Warm-up. Page 90
Time: 5–10 minutes

- Have students complete and then read their responses aloud.
- Discuss any interesting and/or unusual completions, particularly if doing so leads to more spontaneous use of *there is / there are.*

CHART 6-4. Subject-Verb Agreement: Using *There + Be.* Page 91
Time: 5–10 minutes

> Like much of this chapter, this chart will serve as review for most students.
>
> The structure *there + be + noun* conveys the idea that something exists and has a very different meaning from *They are there,* in which *there* represents a particular place. Be sure students understand the word *there* has no meaning in and of itself. The structure itself (*there + be + noun*) conveys the meaning that something exists.
>
> Stress that the verb agrees with the noun following *be; there* is neither singular nor plural.

❑ EXERCISE 16. Let's talk. Page 92
Time: 5–10 minutes

Expansion: Before class, write a number of unusual places on index cards. These may include the following:

a laboratory	*a hospital or a clinic*
a beach	*a mechanic's workshop*
a beauty salon	*a pet store*
a barber shop	*a water park / an amusement park*
a doctor's / dentist's office	
a factory	*a gym*
a restaurant	*a swimming pool*
a bar	*an airport or a train station*
an Internet café	*a grocery store*
an embassy / a state department office	*an open-air market*

Give students cards and ask them to create *There is / There are* sentences as clues. These clues are then presented to the class orally, and the rest of the class must guess the location based on them.

❏ EXERCISE 17. Let's talk and write.
Page 92
Time: 5–10 minutes

- Give students time to complete their answers and write their four true sentences about their current city or town.
- Put students in pairs or small groups and have them first discuss their yes / no items.
- Instruct students to be ready to defend their opinion by linking it to the four sentences they wrote about their current city or town.

Expansion: Have students write sentences about their hometown or city or another favorite location. Students can then argue that places are better or worse than the city / town they are all in now, based on what they have produced.

ALTERNATIVE: For a simplified version, assign half the class the role of arguing the superior quality of life in a rural setting and the other half defending the superior quality of life in an urban setting. Once students have prepared appropriate *There is / There are* statements, you can mediate a whole-class debate.

❏ EXERCISE 18. Warm-up. Page 92
Time: 5–10 minutes

> The exercise may be difficult for some students, so you may want to present it concurrently with the chart and its rules on irregularities.

- Explain that all of the sentences are correct.
- See if students can articulate how / why certain nouns ending in -s are actually single entities or concepts by asking leading questions such as:

  What do you know about the United Nations? (Although it's comprised of many nations, it is one organization, so it's singular.)

  When we say seven kilometers, are we counting each one, or do we mean the distance as a total?

- Let students know that in some cases they need to simply learn that certain words (for example, *news*) are always singular, though this may not make sense to them.

CHART 6-5. Subject-Verb Agreement: Some
Irregularities. Page 93
Time: 10–20 minutes

> Let students know that as these are irregularities, they are not predictable, and the best approach is to learn these exceptions by rote. One way to present these irregularities (which are not in keeping with what students have learned about subject-verb agreement) is to diagram and highlight example sentences showing that the subject and verb don't agree.

- Write a few irregular sentences on the board. For example:

  Today's news were interesting. vs. Today's news was interesting.

- Highlight the plural final *-s* in the subject and then draw a line through the expected plural verb.

  Today's news ~~were~~ interesting. vs. Today's news was interesting.

- Then connect the plural subjects to their singular verbs. Be sure to emphasize that though this is not expected, the irregularity is correct.

  Today's news ~~were~~ interesting. vs. Today's news <u>was</u> interesting.

❏ EXERCISE 19. Looking at grammar.
Page 94
Time: 10–15 minutes

Optional Vocabulary

established	rabies
respected	infectious
seek	fatal
statistics	susceptibility
branch	venom
riot	instances

❏ EXERCISE 20. Game. Page 94
Time: 10–15 minutes

Expansion: Each team has the opportunity to provide the correct answer to each of the nine statements given in turn, based on the team's general knowledge. In addition, extra points are gained by each team's coming up with accurate sentences about the other two choices presented in parentheses for items 2, 3, 4, 8, and 9. Not every team may be able to come up with additional sentences, but it can be engaging for students to show their knowledge of non-linguistic fields and to produce sentences on the spot. This expansion requires the teacher to know enough or prepare enough facts about all choices for each item so that she / he can judge whether the additional sentences are correct. Have students work in teams, and keep score on the board. For example:

  1. (*The Scots, The Irish, The English*) <u>are</u> famous for educational institutions like Oxford and Cambridge.

Examples of possible additional sentences offered by a team:

The Scots are famous for inventing golf.

The Scots are well known for their traditional universities, such as St. Andrews and Edinburgh.

The Scots are famous for their production of woolen goods.

The Irish are famous for their writers, such as Yeats and Wilde.

The Irish are well known for their exaggerated story telling, which is called "blarney."

❏ EXERCISE 21. Let's talk. Page 95
Time: 10–15 minutes

Some of these discussion questions will be more productive than others. Because people find it easy to talk about themselves and their preferences, items 1 and 6 may work well with little elaboration. However, you may need to model what is meant by item 2 and / or ask leading questions of students yourself in order to engage them in items 3 and 4.

For example, items 3 and 4 may be rephrased as follows:

What do books and school supplies cost here / in Japan / in your country?

How far do most people commute to work or school here / in Brazil / in your country?

Correct students immediately when you hear them make mistakes with third person -*s* and / or subject-verb agreement irregularities.

❏ EXERCISES 22 and 23. Looking at grammar. Pages 95 and 96
Time: 5–10 minutes each

These can be done as fast drills; you say the cue, and the students respond with *is* or *are*. Or students could work in pairs / small groups. In addition to oral practice, you could ask the students to write out complete sentences.

❏ EXERCISE 24. Let's talk. Page 96
Time: 10–15 minutes

These statements can be a great springboard for on-the-spot discussions, but you may need to rephrase some of them to fully engage students.

- Give students time to work independently.
- Put students in pairs or small groups to discuss their opinions. Emphasize that they need to add at least three sentences explaining the reasons for their opinions.

Optional Vocabulary
immunizations
lack
customs

❏ EXERCISE 27. Check your knowledge. Page 98
Time: 10–20 minutes

- As you review the exercise with students, have them read the correct answers aloud in turn and explain how they arrived at their answers. For example:

  What is the subject?
  Does this subject agree with the verb?

- Then explain answers to the class.

Optional Vocabulary
satellites   profound
orbiting   deteriorate
long-range   out-of-the-way

❏ EXERCISE 28. Let's talk. Page 99
Time: 10–20 minutes

- Assign students groups that will best take advantage of their strengths and weaknesses. Allow students to exchange ideas freely without one student dominating the discussion.
- While the groups are summarizing their points to present to the whole class, circulate among the groups and discuss the enormous benefit of participating in challenging social situations, such as speeches and the necessity of students' taking risks and making mistakes, all of which are essential for language acquisition.

Expansion: Instead of, or in addition to, their oral summary, have groups write short paragraphs stating their conclusions and paying special attention to subject-verb agreement.

❏ EXERCISE 29. Let's talk and write. Page 99
Time: 10–15 minutes

Expansion: Because many folktales and fairy tales have similar concepts and constructs, but with some variations on a theme or motif, discuss the basic plots of common fairy tales as a class first. Write some key elements on the board. For example, for "The Ugly Duckling":

ugly duckling
rejected by others
transformation
becomes beautiful swan

The above may be enough information to prompt others to share related fairy tales or legends.

Chapter 7
Nouns

CHAPTER SUMMARY

OBJECTIVE: To review and gain control of such important features of English grammar as the singular / plural and count / noncount distinctions, possessive forms, articles, and some expressions of quantity.

APPROACH: The text presents regular and irregular plural nouns, possessive nouns, using nouns as modifiers and count / noncount distinctions. There are then separate sections on article usage and expressions of quantity, with exercises devoted to particular expressions and the challenges they pose.

TERMINOLOGY: Some grammar books and dictionaries refer to "noncount" nouns as "mass" or "uncountable" nouns. The term "expression of quantity" is used for any quantifier (e.g., *some of, a lot of, two of*), determiner (e.g., *no, each, every, some, any*) or predeterminer (e.g., *all, both*) that expresses amount or size.

❑ **EXERCISE 1.** What do I already know?
Page 100
Time: 5–10 minutes

> Students will know some of the plural nouns and will benefit from trying to spell them. Be sure to model the correct pronunciation of plurals.

Expansion: A traditional classroom game is a spelling bee. Students all stand. The teacher says a word to one student; that student repeats the word and then must spell it correctly letter by letter from memory. If the spelling is incorrect, the student sits down. The next student who is standing must then spell the same word. If the spelling is correct, he / she remains standing and the teacher says a new word to the next student. The game continues in this way until only one student, the "champion speller," remains standing.

In the case of a spelling bee with plural endings, the teacher can say the word, and the student spells it adding the appropriate ending. Some possible words: *custom, disease, skyscraper, appearance, hospital, career, calendar, label, mask, ladder, mirror, ghost, ticket, passenger, occasion; wish, ash, leash, boss, kiss, mess, choice; itch, pitch, patch, ditch; hoax, wax, hex, fox; fairy, balcony, diary, berry, penalty, mystery, enemy, holiday, category;* and any of the words in Chart 7-1. For additional words, consult a list of frequently misspelled

words, but avoid words with variant American / British spellings (e.g., *color / colour, airplane / aeroplane, program / programme, judgment / judgement*).

❑ **EXERCISE 2.** Warm-up. Page 100
Time: 5 minutes

- Give students time to complete the items on their own, and then ask individual students to write their answers on the board.
- Correct spelling together as necessary.

CHART 7-1. Regular and Irregular Plural Nouns. Page 101
Time: 10–20 minutes

> This chart is an introduction and a reference, not something to be memorized precisely. Encourage students to consult their dictionaries when in doubt about the plural form of a noun — just as native speakers have to do. Sometimes native speakers (including, you might tell your students, the author of this text) need to look up, for example, the spelling of the plural form of words that end in *-o*.
>
> In (f): You can point out that the final *-o* is followed by *-s* and not *-es* when the noun is a shortened form (e.g., *auto-automobile, memo-memorandum*) and when the *-o* is preceded by another vowel (e.g., *studio, video*). Again, encourage students to consult their dictionaries when in doubt.
>
> The list in the chart is not inclusive. Others that could be mentioned, especially if your students grasp these noun patterns readily, include: in (g): *buffaloes / buffalos, haloes / halos;* in (i): *waifs, oafs, serfs, sheriffs, tariffs;* in (j): *one moose — two moose; one reindeer — two reindeer;* in (l): *vita — vitae.*
>
> Many of the foreign plurals in examples (k)–(m) are used primarily in academic English; the text seeks only to make learners aware that some nouns in English have these odd plural forms. Students will learn and remember only those that are useful to them.
>
> If students ask why some nouns are irregular, you might explain that throughout its history, the English language has had close contact with other European languages. It has been influenced by German, Danish, Latin, Greek, and especially French; a few forms from those languages occur in some English words today.

- Explain that the chart includes more words than students are likely to use or remember, but that by including many examples, students will recognize patterns and make smart guesses when faced with new nouns.
- Begin by presenting the most common patterns: (a), (b), and (c). Write three headings on the board:

    (a) Final -s (b) Final -es (c) change to -ies

    most nouns ending in -sh,-ch,-s,-z,-x ending in -y
- Now ask students questions to elicit examples of the common patterns presented in (a)–(c). You will need to tailor your questions to elicit useful examples. For example:

    Ugur, how much luggage did you bring with you when you came to the United States?

    I brought three suitcases.
- Once you have the example sentence, ask the class which heading it belongs under, and write it below the appropriate one.
- Next, present an example sentence or two for each remaining section of the chart by writing headings on the board and the examples underneath.
- With most of these patterns, you can continue to elicit example sentences from students and write them under headings on the board, as described above.
- Because some students will know some irregular plurals and some -oes and -ves endings, you may want to present these categories first.
- For the less familiar patterns and foreign words, it may work best to write a heading and provide a sample yourself — without trying to elicit it from students.
- Remind students that they should turn to the chart for reference as much as needed.
- Remind students that the point of exercises following the chart is not memorization but recognition of the categories given.

❏ EXERCISE 3. Game. Page 102
Time: 10–20 minutes

- Model the directions first by writing a category on the board and asking students to refer back to the list to find nouns that fit it.
- Break students into groups of three to five members and explain that if another team member asks for an explanation of the choice, the team has to provide one.

Expansion: If your students like the game and want to continue, use these extra (and more challenging) categories:

  Things found in the living room
  (*videos, lamps, radios, photos, mementos, shelves*)
  Things found in the kitchen
  (*potatoes, tomatoes, loaves, knives, fish, shrimp*)
  Points of view or academic positions
  (*beliefs, hypotheses, theses*)

Roles in musical performances
(*heroes, solos, sopranos*)
Things used to decorate the human body
(*tattoos, scarves*)
People/things found in an office
(*men, women, memos, chiefs [as in CEO], data, media, shelves*)

❏ EXERCISE 5. Looking at grammar.
Page 103
Time: 10–15 minutes

- Give students a 5–7 minute time limit to complete as much as possible independently.
- Assign a student to each item and have them write their answers on the board.
- Ask different students to read each item aloud, and then discuss as a class if the spelling is correct.
- Correct pronunciation changes carefully, to heighten students' awareness of the spelling changes (e.g., you can exaggerate the correct pronunciation of *women*.)

Optional Vocabulary

process	steep
load	cliff
cart	phenomenon

❏ EXERCISE 6. Looking at grammar.
Page 104
Time: 10–15 minutes

Because subject-verb agreement is a focus here and students are used to error-correction practice where they correct each error, you may need to repeatedly remind them of the directions to change only nouns (not verbs).

If your students find the content too difficult, you stop after paragraph 3. Not every exercise needs to be done in its entirety by every student. You could make this optional or extra-credit homework, too.

- Have students make corrections independently or in groups.
- Remind students that they should focus on the verb when deciding whether the noun needs to be corrected.
- Review as a class.

Optional Vocabulary

bacterium	virus
organism	particle
consist of	reproduce
cell	infect
tuberculosis	treat
pneumonia	

CHART 7-2. Possessive Nouns. Page 105
Time: 10–15 minutes

> Another way to explain the possessive form is to say that a noun always adds 's in writing, e.g., *boy's, men's.* However, in the case of a noun that already ends in *-s,* we take away the second *-s* and leave the apostrophe.
>
> *boy* + *'s* = *boy's*   (singular, possessive)
>
> *men* + *'s* = *men's*   (irregular plural, possessive)
>
> *boys* + *'s* = *boys's*   (plural, possessive) you take away the *-s: boys'*

- Write the word "apostrophe" and an apostrophe (') on the board. Ask students what structures need apostrophes, prompting them to say *contractions.*
- Tell students that possessive forms (which show belonging or ownership) also use apostrophes.
- Write two headings on the board, *Singular Possessive* and *Plural Possessive.*
- Using a student's name, write a possessive sentence under the appropriate heading, and explain that possessive forms add 's. For example:

  Jana's cell phone is in her backpack.

- Change the student's actual name to *the student,* and write the new sentence under the *Singular Possessive* heading. For example:

  The student's cell phone is in her backpack.

- With the help of students, change *student's, cell phone,* and *backpack* to plurals.
- Remind students that rather than doubling the *-s,* the apostrophe comes after the final *-s* in a regular plural possessive.
- Elicit from students any other words that need to be changed to plural forms, and write the new sentence on the board under the *Plural Possessive* heading. For example:

  The students' cell phones are in their backpacks.

- Now change the word *students'* to *men's* and *women's,* and explain that when the plural is irregular and doesn't end in *-s,* the apostrophe 's comes after the final letter.
- Write a new heading under *Plural Possessive* — *Irregular Plural Possessive* — and put the newest sentence under this heading. For example:

  The men's and women's cell phones are in their backpacks.

❏ **EXERCISE 8.** Looking at grammar.
Page 105
Time: 10–15 minutes

- Assign one of the nine completions to the first nine students who finish, and ask them to write the complete sentences on the board.
- Students who did not write the original sentences on the board should be asked to make any necessary corrections.
- Review as a class.

❏ **EXERCISES 9 and 10.** Looking at grammar. Pages 105–106
Time: 10–20 minutes each

> Both of these exercises are error corrections. You may want to break the students into groups to work through the exercises, assign only the first few of each exercise, or assign both exercises as homework.
>
> Please see the Teaching Suggestions in the front of this book for effective use of error-correction exercises.

Optional Vocabulary: Exercise 9

aboard	diplomat
space shuttle	invariably
housing problem	numerous

Optional Vocabulary: Exercise 10

petroleum	mythological
storage	encounter
evaluate	destruction
trustworthiness	

❏ **EXERCISE 11.** Warm-up. Page 106
Time: 5 minutes

> **Expansion:** As students complete the warm-up, write the following words on the board in columns as below. Have students come to the board to draw lines matching nouns that act as adjectives in common combinations. This expansion activity will help students realize that they already know many of these phrases, before they see Chart 7-3.
>
> (Correct matches: *school bus, library card, television program, hardware store, hair salon, fruit salad.*)

school	card
library	bus
television	store
hardware	program
hair	salad
fruit	salon

CHART 7-3. Using Nouns as Adjectives.
Page 107
Time: 10–15 minutes

> Some grammar books use the term "noun adjunct" for a noun that modifies another noun. Some grammar books refer to noun-noun combinations as one type of "compound noun."

- Write the following headings on the board:

  Noun as Adjective　　*Noun*

- Explain that nouns can describe other nouns and that when nouns are used in this way, their form is singular.
- Look around the room with students to see what adjective noun-noun combinations present themselves, and write these on the board with each part under the appropriate heading.

Noun as Adjective	*Noun*
class	project
grammar	book

- Write the incorrect example from Chart 7-3, *vegetables soup,* on the board. Remind students that plural forms are not generally used as modifiers. Cross out *vegetables* and replace with *vegetable.*
- Ask a student how old he / she is and create a hyphenated adjective — number (+ *year-old*) from this information. Write a sentence describing the student and his age on the board. For example:

  Lorenzo is a twenty-seven-year-old Italian lawyer.

- Emphasize in the above example that *-year* is not plural.

❏ EXERCISE 12. Looking at grammar.
Page 107
Time: 10 minutes

> Note: In general, a hyphen is used when two (or more) words used as a modifer to a noun have one meaning when the appear together: *a man-eating tiger* (it's not *a man tiger* or *an eating tiger;* it's *a man-eating tiger* — two words which together give one meaning, as though they were one word). (Other examples are: *salt-and-pepper hair, a part-time job, a matter-of-fact attitude, a two-hour movie.*

- Have students first complete this exercise independently and then read their answers aloud.
- When you read or listen to students' answers, pay special attention to two common problems: 1) the modifying noun must be in singular form, and 2) the article a/an is required for singular count nouns.
- Point out the use of hyphens (-) in adjective phrases containing numbers. It is useful to have students write their answers on the board, as some of them may be unfamiliar with the use of the hyphen.

CHART 7-4. Count and Noncount Nouns.
Page 109
Time: 10 minutes

> Some noncount nouns, like *furniture,* are also called "mass nouns" in other grammar books.
>
> The count/noncount distinction is one of the most difficult points for students to control.

Some common mistakes that students make are the following:

Incorrect	Correct Count Form	Correct Noncount Form
many homeworks	*many assignments*	*a lot of homework*
some slangs	*some slang expressions*	*some slang*
many vocabularies	*many vocabulary words/items*	*a large vocabulary*

- Present the chart by writing examples (a) and (b) on the board.
- Reiterate that *chairs* can be counted by numbers and that noncount nouns or categories, such as *furniture,* cannot be preceded by actual numbers but rather by expressions of quantity.
- Tell your students that this count / noncount distinction is not always easy to predict or recognize but that they have already encountered it many times.
- Ask your students how much homework they had the previous night. If the answers they generate are correct, put them on the board as you hear them. If the answers need correction, remind students that *homework* can't be counted but that *assignments* can. For example:

  Bengt had a lot of homework last night, but Per only had a little homework.

  Bengt had five assignments, but Per only had two assignments.

- Remind students that count nouns are preceded by *a / an* in the singular and take final *-s / -es* in the plural.
- Write student-generated examples of this point on the board and underline the articles and final *-s / -es.* For example:

  Luisa received a letter and an email yesterday.

  Luisa received two messages from home yesterday.

- Explain that noncount nouns are preceded by expressions of quantity but not by *a / an* or *one.*
- Explain that noncount nouns have no plural form and so, do not take a final *-s / -es.*
- Write an example of a sentence using a noncount noun on the board, and draw attention to the lack of indefinite article and final *-s / -es.* For example:

  Luisa received some _ mail_ yesterday.

❏ EXERCISE 16. Looking at grammar.
Page 109
Time: 10 minutes

> The purpose of this exercise is to help students understand the two charts that follow (7-5 and 7-6). You can use this exercise as a means of discussing the ideas presented in Chart 7-5.

- In item 1, point out that a noncount noun refers to a "whole" that is made up of different parts. Explain that *furniture* is the "whole" and *chairs, tables, desks* are the different parts. You may also want to use the term "category" to explain this concept.
- In items 4 and 5, compare noncount and count usages of the same word, *iron;* the meaning of each use is different.

Optional Vocabulary

scenery	rusty
press	wrinkled

Expansion: Give each student two cards (or the students can use their own paper). On one, write a large letter "C" and on the other write "NC." As you and your students read each sentence aloud, pause after each noun while the students hold up the card that identifies the noun in question as count or noncount. In this way, you can quickly see if students are incorrectly identifying any nouns, and the students can have a little fun with this grammar point.

CHARTS 7-5 and 7-6. Noncount Nouns. Some Common Noncount Nouns. Page 110
Time: 20–25 minutes

The concept of a noncount noun is covered in Chart 7-5, followed by a list of common noncount examples in Chart 7-6.

If it helps your students to understand, use the term "mass" to explain the idea of "a whole" or "a category."

As pointed out in examples (e) and (f) of Chart 7-5, some nouns can be used as either count or noncount. Some of the nouns in Chart 7-6 also have count uses. A noun is count or noncount depending on how it is used and the speaker's intended meaning. No noun is inherently count or noncount. The words listed in Chart 7-6 are usually or always used as noncount nouns, but you may wish to discuss some of those with dual uses: *glass* (a material) vs. *a glass* (a container for drinking); *tea* (a drink) vs. *teas* (kinds of tea); *pepper* (a spice) vs. *a pepper* (a vegetable); *bridge* (a card game) vs. *a bridge* (a way or structure across a river); *time* (an abstract concept) vs. *times* (occurrences).

- Present the different kinds of noncount nouns in Chart 7-5, (a)–(d), by writing an example sentence of each on the board.
- Next to each example sentence write a term that will help students understand the category: (a) *whole category;* (b) *liquids, solids, gases, or mass of particles;* (c) *abstractions;* (d) *phenomena of nature).*
- Explain that units of measure are used to quantify liquids or masses of particles, and refer students to the asterisked list below the chart.
- Explain that many nouns have both count and noncount uses, and write the examples in (e) and (f) on the board.

- Tell students that they are not expected to memorize all the nouns in Chart 7-6 but that the chart provides a handy reference, which categorizes common noncount nouns according to the distinctions in Chart 7-5.
- Look through Chart 7-6 with your students and discuss any questions that may arise.

❏ EXERCISE 17. Looking at grammar.
Page 111
Time: 10–15 minutes

- Give students time to do this exercise on their own, and remind them not to make any changes in the unitalicized words.
- Have students read their corrected sentences aloud taking turns. Ask students to exaggerate their pronunciation so that final *-s / -es* can be heard.
- You may want to begin this exercise in class and assign the remainder as homework.

Optional Vocabulary

harmful	reduce	grain
substance	reward	

❏ EXERCISE 19. Looking at grammar.
Page 112
Time: 10–15 minutes

- Give students time to complete the exercise on their own.
- Ask various students to put their answers on the board, and the class as a whole will correct these.
- Tell students to raise their C and NC cards (from the previous Expansion) after certain nouns, e.g., *change* (NC) and *coins* (C) in item 1.

Optional Vocabulary

sea level	satisfied
precipitation	metropolitan

❏ EXERCISE 20. Warm-up. Page 113
Time: 5–10 minutes

- The illustrations in this warm-up help students articulate correct article usage they see, so give them sufficient time to think through the pictures.
- Improvise additional questions to help students discuss the use of definite and indefinite articles. For example:

Dialogue 1
Are Tom and Anna talking about the same cat?

Dialogue 2
Has Anna met the cat Tom is talking about?

Dialogue 3
Do Tom and Anna think an independent nature is a quality of most cats or just a few?

CHART 7-7. Basic Article Usage. Page 114
Time: 10–20 minutes

Articles are very difficult for students to understand and use correctly. Many languages do not have articles. Languages that do have articles use them differently from English. Articles are, in many teachers' experiences, difficult to teach. There are many nuances, complex patterns of use, and idiomatic variations. Students who are frustrated trying to understand and use articles should be reminded that articles are just a small component of English. Proficiency in using articles improves with experience; it cannot be obtained overnight by learning "rules."

The exercises that follow the chart point out some contrasts in usage that should help students understand the differences among *a/an, the,* and the absence of any article (symbolized by Ø).

Some students may need a reminder about using *an* instead of *a.* English speakers prefer not to pronounce another vowel sound after the article "a." Therefore, they put "n" between the two vowel sounds.
For example:
a + apple → an apple;
a + old man → an old man;
a + umbrella → an umbrella
(But note that *a university* has no "n" because the "u" has a "y" or consonant sound.)
a + other → another (Tradition causes this to be written as one word.)

- Present Part I: Using *A / An or Ø*: Generic Nouns by explaining that an indefinite article or no article is used to talk about the noun very generally when describing or defining the noun.
- Write the example sentences from the chart on the board under the heading *Generic Nouns.* You may want to include a noun preceded by *an.*

    A banana is yellow.
    An egg is oval.
    Bananas are yellow.
    Fruit is good for you.

- Make sure that students understand that when they see such descriptive sentences that no real bananas, eggs, or fruit are being discussed but that the noun represents all the real bananas, eggs, and fruit.
- Present Part II: Using *A / An or Some*: Indefinite Nouns by writing the sentences from the chart or some examples of your own on the board under the heading *Indefinite Nouns.*

    I ate a banana. I ate an apple.
    I ate some bananas. I ate some apples.
    I ate some fruit.

- Explain that this time, the indefinite article does refer to a real, concrete noun but that it is one or some of many real things.
- Present Part III: Using *The:* Definite Nouns

- Write the sentences from the chart on the board.

    Thank you for the banana.
    Thank you for the bananas.
    Thank you for the fruit.

- Explain that a noun is definite (and needs a definite article) when both speaker and listener are referring to the same real object or specific thing.

❑ EXERCISE 24. Game. Page 117
Time: 15–20 minutes

One way to play the game is to eliminate each player who can't remember the whole list beginning with "A." The game continues until there is only one player who can recite the whole list or until everyone left can recite the whole list from A to Z. For the classroom, however, it is better to make the game noncompetitive. The purpose is for students to have fun while they are practicing a grammar point.

- Divide the class into groups of six to ten and explain the game.
- Explain that each group can try to do the whole alphabet; set a time limit (15–20 minutes) and let the groups get as far in the alphabet as they can. To shorten the game, you could assign only half the alphabet to each group.
- Tell students to try to play without taking a lot of notes, but it would be all right if they needed to jot down a few notes to jog their memory when it's their turn to speak. It would also be all right for the students to help each other remember the list and remind each other about the use of *a / an* and *some.*
- Accept all strange or funny answers as long as they conform to the correct article usage and begin with the appropriate letter of the alphabet.
- Remind students to focus on the correct use of *a / an* and *some.* Allow students to begin their items with an adjective; *a bald monkey,* for example, could be used for the letter "B" (but not the letter "M").

CHART 7-8. General Guidelines for Article
Usage. Page 118
Time: 10–15 minutes

This chart gives students needed guidelines for using articles, and in particular, helps students understand when the definite article *the* is required. Keep students' focus on the need to use a definite article when both speaker and listener are discussing the same specific thing.

- With your class, create sample sentences that refer to objects in the classroom that all students can see and refer to.

- Explain that when everyone in the discussion knows what is being discussed, the definite article is required. For example:

    The clock says 10:25.

    The door is closed.

    The board is covered with vocabulary and grammar notes.

    The student next to Su-Jin looks tired.

- Present guideline (a) by referring to the sentences above as well as the examples in the chart.

- Now ask students to describe something or someone they saw the previous day. Use their information to write a first sentence, introducing an object with an indefinite article and then referring to this object with the definite article, *the.* For example:

    Yesterday Juana and Milo saw <u>some</u> students performing a play outside. <u>The</u> students were dressed in brightly colored clothes.

- Explain that the definite article is used for the second mention of an indefinite noun because at that point, the speaker can be sure the listener does know what is being referred to.

- Ask students to tell you their favorite foods or animals. Write their sentences on the board, and emphasize that you are omitting an article altogether because they are making generalizations about count nouns.

- Emphasize that no article is needed by including the definite article and then crossing it out. For example:

    Belzan loves to eat ~~the~~ pears.

    Miki is a big fan of ~~the~~ pandas.

- Show students that a singular count noun always needs either an article, *this* or *that,* or a possessive pronoun by writing sample sentences on the board using students' information. For example:

    Mikail has a notebook.

    Mikail has that notebook.

    Mikail has his notebook.

❏ EXERCISE 26. Looking at grammar.
Page 118
Time: 10–15 minutes

- Because this exercise is a series of dialogues, students can work in pairs, or two students can read one dialogue to the whole class. If working in pairs, have students switch roles for each item.

- Explain to the class that what is in the speaker's mind determines which article to use. If the speaker believes the listener knows which thing or person the speaker is referring to, the speaker will use *the.* If not, the speaker will use *a/an, some,* or Ø.

Optional Vocabulary
leak
swerved
pothole

❏ EXERCISE 28. Grammar and speaking.
Page 120
Time: 10–15 minutes

> Because this exercise asks students to discuss and share their opinions on a variety of matters, students may prefer to complete this exercise in small groups or pairs. Encourage students to give personal examples when explaining whether they agree or disagree with the statements. You may want to assign this as homework the night before to give students ample time to think through the topics and formulate opinions.

- Give students time to complete the sentences and then agree or disagree with them on their own.

- Then divide students up into pairs or small groups, and have them work through the exercise, explaining whether they agree or disagree with each statement and giving examples from their own experiences.

- Have students share their opinions with the class as a whole, or pick one or two questions to discuss as a class.

❏ EXERCISE 30. Listening. Page 121
Time: 10 minutes

- Ask students to close their books and listen to the audio once focusing on the main ideas and content.

- Have students open their texts, listen again, and fill in the blanks with *a, an,* or *the.*

- After you review the completions with students, ask them questions about the content of the talk. For example:

    Where did and how did the term "computer bug" originate?

    What machine was Thomas Edison working on when he first coined the term "bug"?

Optional Vocabulary
phonograph
attributed

❏ EXERCISE 31. Warm-up. Page 121
Time: 5–10 minutes

> This warm-up will help students realize what they already know and will help them recognize what sounds wrong to them.

- Give your students a few minutes to eliminate expressions of quantity that can't be used with the given noun phrases, and then review the correct answers.

- Discuss the term "expressions of quantity" and point out differences in their usage with count and noncount nouns.

CHART 7-9. Expressions of Quantity Used with Count and Noncount Nouns. Page 122
Time: 10–15 minutes

> A *lot of* and *lots of* have the same meaning. Both are somewhat informal, with *lots* being the more informal.

- Ask students to give you a few random count nouns. Unusual nouns will be more fun for students. For example:

    artichoke, hiccup, dog collar

- Using one of these nouns, write an example for each expression of quantity in sections (a) and (b) of the chart on the board under the heading *Count Only*. Repeat that all of the expressions in (a) and (b) can only be used with count nouns.
- Now ask your class for a few unusual noncount nouns. For example:

    compassion, protein, arrogance

- Using one of these noncount nouns, write example phrases using the expressions from (c) under the heading *Noncount Only*.
- Now, using the count and noncount nouns chosen for the above boardwork, write the expressions of quantity from (d) in front of both nouns. Label this list *Count and Noncount*.

❏ **EXERCISE 34.** Looking at grammar.
Page 124
Time: 10–15 minutes

- Explain to students that they cannot change any words in the original sentences in italics, but they will need to change the nouns to their correct forms.
- Emphasize count / noncount distinctions with expressions of quantity as you go through the exercise, and ask students to explain these to you as they review their answers.

❏ **EXERCISE 35.** Let's talk: interview.
Page 125
Time: 10–15 minutes

Expansion: Before class, prepare index cards with additional sentence starters for students to use when interviewing classmates, such as:

I can't respect people who want to have a lot of. . .
People in (name of country) don't have enough. . .
My parents always wanted me to gain a lot of. . .
I have very few . . . , but I have a lot of. . .
The leaders of modern nations need to have a great deal of. . .
Doctors should have a lot of. . .
I am disappointed when my friends don't have any. . .

After students have had a chance to interview one another, discuss what was learned in terms of what was most predictable and what was most surprising. Alternatively, students can give another student's

response while the remainder of the class has to guess who said what. For example:

Student A: *This person said she is disappointed when her friends don't have any patience with students trying to learn a new language. Who said this?*

Student B: *I think it was Marazita because she explained that her friends' lack of patience with foreigners really frustrated her the other day when we were chatting about our own countries.*

CHART 7-10. Using *A Few* and *Few; A Little* and *Little*. Page 126
Time: 10–15 minutes

> This is difficult grammar for most learners, and it can be difficult to explain. The chart compares the meanings by saying *a few* and *a little* give a positive idea and indicate that something exists or is present. The chart then explains that *few* and *little* give a negative idea and indicate that something is "largely absent." You may need to explain the term *largely* (meaning "for the most part"), as some learners may not be familiar with it.
>
> Sometimes students think there must be a difference in quantity between *a few* and *few*. They ask How many is "a few" and how many is "few"? They think that *few friends* is less than *a few friends*. But, the real difference can rest in the speaker's attitude: *a few* reflects a positive opinion of the quantity, and *few* reflects a negative or diminishing opinion, even if the quantity is the same in both cases.
>
> For example, Sam and Sara are new students in college. In two weeks, Sam has made three friends and Sara has made three friends. Sam's mother is very pleased. She says *Sam's getting along fine. He's made a few friends and likes his teachers.* Sara's mother, however, thinks Sara should have made lots of friends by now and worries that she is not adjusting to her new college. She says *Sara doesn't like her classes and has few friends. I'm worried about her.* In each case, the number of friends is the same, but the speaker's attitude is different.
>
> The following chart may be helpful for students:
>
> | _Count_ | _Noncount_ |
> | --- | --- |
> | *few = not many* | *little = not much* |
> | *a few = some* | *a little = some* |

- With your students, create sentences that show that *a few* and *a little* give a positive idea. For example:

    Junko has made a few new friends this month.
    Guillaume has a little time to spend with his girlfriend this weekend.

- Explain that when you remove the indefinite article in each sentence above, you don't change the quantity. However, doing so changes the speaker's / writer's attitude about the quantity.

- Rewrite the sentences above without the article *a* and add explanatory notes in parentheses. For example:

  Junko has made few new friends this month. (She does not have many new friends.)

  Guillaume has little time to spend with his girlfriend this weekend. (He doesn't have much time to spend with his girlfriend.)

- Repeat that using the expression of quantity without the indefinite article gives a negative idea that the quantity (whatever it actually may be) is not sufficient.
- Remind students that even if this concept seems a bit confusing, they will get used to the distinction when they hear it. They should refer to Chart 7-10 for support as needed.

❑ **EXERCISE 37.** Looking at grammar.
Page 126
Time: 5–10 minutes

This exercise approaches the grammar by using parallel meanings. Discuss the meaning of each sentence in terms of what is "largely present" or "largely absent."

- Tell students that they have to understand the speaker's attitude (positive or negative) when replacing the italicized words with *a few, very few, a little,* or *very little.*

Optional Vocabulary

dreary	prevent
programs	hinges
squeaks	

❑ **EXERCISE 40.** Let's talk. Page 128
Time: 10–20 minutes

- Put students into pairs or small groups.
- Tell students that in addition to deciding whether Dan and Eva have *too much / many, too few / little,* or *just the right amount / number,* they should be prepared to justify their decisions to the class. For example:

  They have too few tea bags to last a week. If they both have tea in the morning, they will run out after just one day.

CHART 7-11. Singular Expressions of Quantity: *One, Each, Every.* Page 129
Time: 10 minutes

You might want to refer to Chart 6-2 Basic Subject-Verb Agreement, which identified *each* and *every* as singular in number.

Each, every, and *one* are common sources of errors. For that reason, they receive special emphasis here.

Be sure to note the concept of "specificity": a noun is made specific by fronting it with *the,* a possessive, or a demonstrative adjective. One can say *one of the students, one of my students,* or *one of those students,* but one cannot say *one of students.*

- Using student-generated examples or those from the chart, write example sentences on the board using *one, each* and *every* as seen in (a), (b) and (c).
- Then write the heading + *Singular Count Nouns* above the student examples and underline the singular count nouns in each sentence.
- Ask students to create sentences using *one of, each of,* and *every one of* and write them on the board. Write the heading + *Specific Plural Count Nouns* above them and underline the plural nouns.

CHART 7-12. Using *Of* in Expressions of Quantity. Page 131
Time: 10–15 minutes

As described in the background notes for Chart 7-11, students need to understand the concept of specificity and be able to distinguish nonspecific (*book, desk, cookie*) nouns from specific versions of the same (*the book, my desk, that cookie*) nouns.

Emphasize that some expressions of quantity *always* include *of,* whether they are followed by a nonspecific or a specific noun.

- With your students, generate examples of *one* and *many* + nonspecific nouns and write them on the board.

  Expressions of Quantity — No "Of" with Nonspecific Nouns
  Manuel purchased one ticket.
  Jae-Lien saw many movies.

- Then come up with examples of expressions that include *of* when used with specific nouns and put these on the board.

  "Of" Used with Specific Nouns
  One of those bags belongs to Valentina.
  Many of Ahmed's books are translations from Arabic.

- Finally, write on the board some examples from the chart that always include *of.* This section of the board should be titled:

  Expressions That Always Include "Of"
  The majority of the students in this school speak several languages in addition to English.
  Most of Kazuhiro's friends also enjoy playing pool.
  Hardly any of Juanita's days here have been wasted.

❏ EXERCISE 45. Looking at grammar.
Page 131
Time: 5–10 minutes

> Many of the sentences in this exercise are paired to be quite similar. Compare the meanings of items to be sure students under the important differences.

Optional Vocabulary
junk mail
index

❏ EXERCISE 47. Let's talk: interview.
Page 132
Time: 15–30 minutes

• Arrange to do this activity during a class period when students can poll each other.
• Have each student make up his / her own list of questions, and encourage students to ask specific questions that will yield concrete answers.
• Give the students ample time — perhaps even overnight — to think of interesting questions.
• Have students use expressions of quantity when reporting back on their findings.

Expansion: Another possibility would be for your class to poll other classes in a language program and then report their findings. Taking a poll in, for example, a lower-intermediate level English class could be fun not only for your students but also for those in the other class, giving all the students a enjoyable opportunity for interaction.

❏ EXERCISE 48. Let's talk. Page 133
Time: 10–15 minutes

> The sentences in this exercise are <u>not true.</u> That's the point of this exercise; using expressions of quantity is important because unqualified statements are inaccurate. Discuss the importance of quantifying a generalization in order to make it accurate. The sentences in the text are examples of overgeneralizations that need expressions of quantity to make them reasonable, true, and supportable statements.

❏ EXERCISE 49. Let's talk. Page 133
Time: 15–30 minutes

• Give students additional controversial topics if they have trouble coming up with enough on their own, such as:

the welfare system	*legalization of recreational drugs*
gun control	*instituting uniforms in public*
socialized medicine	*schools*
abortion	*forbidding prayer in schools*
the death penalty	*mandatory military service*
the drinking age	*testing drugs on animals*
censorship	*genetic engineering*

Chapter 8
Pronouns

CHAPTER SUMMARY

OBJECTIVE: To become familiar with pronouns and their use.

APPROACH: This chapter reviews most aspects of personal pronoun use, with emphasis on the problem areas of agreement and the use of *other* as both a pronoun and an adjective. The chapter finishes with a summary of the material presented in Chapters 6–8.

TERMINOLOGY: A "possessive adjective" (for example, *my, your, her*) is a pronoun (a noun substitute) that functions as a determiner. Some grammars call it a "possessive determiner" or a "determinative possessive pronoun." The terminology may be confusing for students because a possessive adjective is indeed a pronoun, but the term "possessive pronoun" (for example, *mine, yours, hers*) is used in this text and most others refer to an independent possessive pronoun that is used alone as a noun substitute.

In an effort to minimize grammatical terminology, the text does not use the term "determiner," finding others ways to present these function words (such as *a / an / the, one, no, this / that / these / those, many, other, my / your / her, some / any*). If you are comfortable with the term "determiner" and find it useful, by all means introduce it to your class and explain that what this text calls a "possessive adjective" may be called a "possessive determiner."

❏ EXERCISE 1. What do I already know?
Page 135
Time: 5–10 minutes

> When appropriate, emphasize that mistakes with pronouns lead to ambiguity. Sometimes, as in item 1, this ambiguity (Did the speaker eat his friends?) can be humorous. Exploiting this humor can help students appreciate the importance of correct reference.

❏ EXERCISE 2. Warm-up. Page 135
Time: 10–15 minutes

> Give students plenty of time to complete both parts of the warm-up since they both elicit natural use of pronouns and can help students realize how much they already know about pronouns while also gaining speaking practice.
>
> You may want to put student in small groups for this exercise.

Part I
Expansion: Have a contest to see which student can repeat all the names of the other students in the class, using clauses starting with pronouns. For example, write on the board:

We are . . .
Our names are . . .
They are . . .
Their names are . . .
You are . . .
Your names are . . .

The student who is able to use one of the sentence starters to correctly name all of his/her classmates without making any mistakes at all wins.

Part II
Expansion: Write very specific questions on index cards or prepare a handout on the topic beforehand. You may want to make different sets of questions for different groups and then ask that the groups report back on the topic they were given.

Specific questions include:

Is it common for names in your culture to have specific meanings? Are these meanings abstract or concrete?

Is it common for children to be named for their parents, famous people, or saints? Are there any taboos related to giving children the same name as a dead relative in your culture? In the U.S., some people have the exact same name as a parent but with a number after it (III, IV) or the word "Junior." Is this common in your country?

Who decides the name of the child in your culture? Is it simply the parents, or is this honor given to an older member of the parents' families (for example, a grandparent or great aunt?)

Are there special naming ceremonies in your culture? If so, what are these ceremonies like? When do they occur and who is present?

Some cultures celebrate name days as well as birthdays. Is this true where you are from?

We all know that famous people often choose stage names or other names that they believe sound better than their own names. Students of languages sometimes do this too. If you were to pick a name in English for yourself, what would it be?

What are some of the most common names in your country? What do you think are some of the most common English names in the U.S.? What American names do you find strange or silly?

What kinds of names are given to pets in your country? Are farm animals given names or just house pets?

In some families in the U.S., children call their parents by their first names. Is this common in your country?

Most people have a nickname, and some people have many. Are nicknames common in your culture? Do you have one? How did you get it?

CHART 8-1. Personal Pronouns. Page 136
Time: 10–20 minutes

Most of this information should be familiar to students, but they can use the chart as a reference.

Note the definition of "antecedent" in (a). Keep students' focus on the importance of making sure they can identify which noun each pronoun refers to.

Pay attention to possessive pronouns vs. possessive adjectives, pointing out that adjectives occur <u>with</u> a noun, but possessive pronouns occur <u>without</u> a noun.

Give additional examples of *its* vs. *it's;* this is a frequent source of errors (for native speakers too.)

• Start by re-creating the list of pronoun categories at the top of Chart 8-1.
• Write on the board the following headings:

Subject Pronoun   *Object Pronoun*
Possessive Adjective   *Possessive Pronoun*

• Students will probably be quite familiar with the first two categories, so go through each person in a verb conjugation and have students give you both the subject and object pronoun as review. For example, say:

Okay, first person singular . . . The subject pronoun is ____.

(You can write a sample sentence leaving out the subject pronoun to help elicit it, e.g., ____ am a teacher.)

Students supply the subject pronoun *I*.

The object pronoun is ____.

(You can again write a sample sentence to elicit the appropriate object pronoun, e.g., Help ____ teach.)

Students provide the pronoun *me*.

• Explain that a possessive pronoun takes the place of a noun altogether and is not followed by a noun.

• Write a sample sentence to elicit the possessive pronoun for first person singular. For example,

These keys are ____.

Students supply the word *mine*.

• Follow this technique to elicit the possessive adjective. Remind students that the possessive adjective must also be followed by a noun. For example, write:

These are ____ keys.

• Continue completing the chart on the board, with your students giving you pronouns as appropriate.
• Draw students' attention to the special notes for (j)–(m).
• Write two sentences on the board — one that shows the use of *its* as a possessive pronoun and one that shows *it's* as a subject pronoun + verb contraction.

❏ EXERCISE 4. Looking at grammar.
Page 137
Time: 5 minutes

• Explain to students that object pronouns follow verbs but that as the note in the text states, even native speakers make mistakes with object pronouns after *and*.
• Remind your students that as in item 2, prepositional phrases are followed by the object form of the pronoun.
• Tell your students that one way to decide which form should come after *and* is to cover the first pronoun and conjunction to see if the sentence is correct. For example, in the sentence:

You and I / me like the same kind of music.

Have students cover up *You and*. Then have them decide which pronoun fits best in the sentence.
• Instruct students to try this approach if needed while they complete the exercise.
• Review answers as a class.

❏ EXERCISE 7. Let's talk. Page 138
Time: 5–10 minutes

• Model the example with one student.
• Continue to model each of the six items, and ask a different student to repeat each one, pointing and using the possessive pronouns correctly.

❏ EXERCISE 8. Looking at grammar.
Page 138
Time: 5 minutes

• Write *1. its* and *2. it's* on the board. (Since both words sound the same, instruct students to use either *number one* or *number two* when discussing the words.) Then ask a student or students to explain the difference between the two.
• Give students time to complete their answers individually.

- To review the answers, read through each item, pausing at each blank. Instruct students to call out *number 1* or *number 2* for their answers.

❏ EXERCISE 9. Looking at grammar.
Page 139
Time: 10 minutes

- Give students time to circle the correct form of the word in italics on their own first.
- Have students take turns saying the completed sentences aloud.
- Correct students' pronunciation as well as pronoun choice.
- Ask students some simple comprehension questions about the passage, such as:

  Where does the anhinga bird live?

  What does the anhinga bird eat?

  Where does it feed?

  Does it go under the water while eating the fish or just to catch it?

Optional Vocabulary

dive	pointed
spear	bill
prey	emerging

❏ EXERCISE 10. Listening. Page 139
Time: 10–15 minutes

- Explain that hearing pronouns in spoken English can be challenging because they are often unstressed and the /h/ sound is usually dropped.
- Model this for students by putting a few sentences on the board and then reading them as a native speaker would. For example:

  Is he a good singer?   *[Iz-ee a good singer?]*

  This is her notebook   *[This iz-er notebook.]*

  We saw him last night.   *[We saw-im last night.]*

- Play the audio through once without stopping.
- Play the audio a second time, stopping after each sentence.
- Have students compare their answers with a partner, and then review the answers as a class.
- Play the audio again so that students can hear the correct answers.

❏ EXERCISE 11. Warm-up. Page 140
Time: 5 minutes

- Ask students which sentence they find most clear.
- Because all are correct, students are welcome to debate the merits of each. You can let your students know that debates are encouraged within academic communities.

CHART 8-2. Personal Pronouns: Agreement with Generic Nouns and Indefinite Pronouns.
Page 140
Time: 10–15 minutes

The English language traditionally used only male pronouns when speaking of people in general, e.g., *A doctor treats **his** patients kindly,* as though no women were doctors (which, in fact, was true during certain periods of Western history). Language reflects social change; today women have more equal representation in language usage because they do in society in general. Now English speakers try to use *he or she, him or her, his or hers, etc.* The easiest way to avoid the question of which form to use is to use a plural rather than a singular generic noun so that *they / them / their* (which are neither masculine or feminine) may be used, for example, *Doctors treat their patients kindly.*

Not so long ago, it would have been unthinkable for an educated speaker to use *their* (a plural pronoun) to refer to *someone* (singular). Today it seems to have become the norm rather than the exception in spoken English, and it avoids a feminine/masculine pronoun problem. However, singular pronouns are still expected in formal writing. Discuss with your class guidelines for feminine / masculine and singular / plural pronoun usage.

- Tell the class that there are a number of options for indefinite pronouns when these must agree with a generic noun.
- Tell students you will need their help in showing these options, and that to that end, they should be prepared to give advice to a student studying American English, beginning with *A student should. . . .*
- Write their advice on the board, and underline indefinite pronoun options that reflect (c), (d), and (e) in the chart. Point out the different options (c), (d), and (e) as you record students ideas. For example:

  A student should not be afraid to use his English with strangers.

  A student should listen to English conversations.

  A student should read his or her favorite book or magazine in English before going to bed each night.

  Students should ask their teachers a lot of questions.

- Ask students to refer to points (f), (g), and (h) in the chart along with the list that precedes it.
- Remind students that the indefinite pronouns in the list have singular grammar even when the idea they refer to is certainly plural (for example, *everybody, everyone*).

Expansion: If your class is interested, take this opportunity to facilitate a discussion of language as a tool that both reflects and shapes society. Discuss some of the characteristics valued in language and ask students to prioritize them: clarity, brevity, accuracy, descriptiveness, thoroughness. While students are discussing these topics in small groups, circulate and correct pronunciation usage.

Possible discussion questions include:

How important is it to avoid having to use both a female and/or male pronoun? Is it too lengthy to use both?

Can you understand why some people may feel the exclusive use of the masculine pronoun is offensive?

Are there similar issues in your language that have changed the accepted grammar over time, the way the need to reflect women's roles and existence has fostered the use of "their" with singular nouns?

Many languages actually have masculine, feminine, and neutral nouns. Do you think this fact affects the way the cultures speaking those languages have developed?

❏ **EXERCISE 12.** Looking at grammar.
Page 140
Time: 10 minutes

Optional Vocabulary
manual
jury
lecturer

❏ **EXERCISE 13.** Looking at grammar.
Page 141
Time: 10 minutes

> The principal purpose of this exercise is to provide material for discussion of the usage problems in Chart 8-2. Students will want your advice.

• Write two sentences on the board.

 Every student needs their own notebook to keep track of new vocabulary.

 Every student needs his or her own notebook to keep track of new vocabulary.

• Ask your students which sentence they find more formal, and discuss why singular pronouns may seem more formal than their plural counterparts.
• Have students complete the exercise individually.
• Discuss and review as a class, and ask students which sentences and pronouns they find to be more formal.
• Because other languages have both formal and familiar pronouns, you may want to ask students about what parts of speech in their languages signify more and less formal terms of address.

Optional Vocabulary
effective
corporate
motivate

CHART 8-3. Personal Pronouns: Agreement with Collective Nouns. Page 142
Time: 5–10 minutes

> The speaker's view of the collective unit determines the grammatical usage of the words in this chart. The English language is somewhat flexible on this point. If the speaker wants to emphasize unity or wholeness, the collective noun will be singular, and this number will influence both the pronoun and the verb. On the other hand, if the speaker wants to emphasize the individuals within the group, the collective noun will be considered plural (but it will not add -s / -es).
>
> Other collective nouns not included in Chart 8-2: *army, community, company, crew, enemy, gang, herd, media, press.*

• Write the two example sentences (a) and (b) on the board showing that *family* can agree with both plural personal pronouns and singular ones.
• Highlight the singular personal pronoun used in (a) by underlining it in the same color as *My family* (singular, impersonal unit).
• Highlight the plural pronoun used in (b) by underlining it in the same color as *My family* (plural pronouns, indicating various members).

❏ **EXERCISE 15.** Looking at grammar.
Page 142
Time: 10 minutes

> The purpose of this exercise is to help students develop an understanding of the difference between singular and plural uses of collective nouns. In general, the singular usage is impersonal or statistical, while the plural usage emphasizes the actual people involved.

Optional Vocabulary
exceeded   motorcade
enthusiastically   overflowing
premier

❏ **EXERCISE 16.** Warm-up. Page 143
Time: 5–10 minutes

> If you wish, supply drawing paper and colored pencils or crayons. Reassure those students who believe they can't draw by first drawing a self-portrait of yourself — a drawing that is simple and funny, requiring no special artistic skills. The self-portraits should be a fun task.

• The questions in the book are simply suggestions for the teacher. You can also ask other questions to prepare students for the use of reflexive pronouns. For example:

 Have you ever cut your hair yourself?

 Have you ever taken photographs of yourself?

Do you travel to class by yourself or with friends?

How often do you look at yourself in the mirror?

How old are young adults in your country when they first live by themselves (not with their families)?

CHART 8-4. Reflexive Pronouns. Page 143
Time: 10–15 minutes

In informal English, reflexive pronouns are sometimes substituted for object pronouns, especially in prepositional phrases. To some degree, the reflexive pronoun adds emphasis. This use of reflexive pronouns is variously deemed to be incorrect, nonstandard, questionable, or perfectly acceptable.

Informal Usage:

*She gave the gift to Bob and **myself**.*

Preferred Usage:

*(a) She gave the gift to Bob and **me**.*

*(b) I gave a gift to **myself**.*

Other examples:

*What happened between my girlfriend and **myself** is no one's business.*

*No one on the bus spoke English except a few Italians and **ourselves**.*

In the vast majority of instances, reflexive pronouns cannot be substituted for personal pronouns as objects.

*I sit in the front row in class; Mustafa sits behind **me*** (not *myself*).

*When Tom arrived, Alice spoke to **him*** (not *himself*).

As with any other grammar structure, idiomatic use of reflexive pronouns develops as learners gain experience with the language. Grammar basics can be taught and provide a good foundation for growth, but idiomatic usage ability grows with time and exposure. Engaging in lots of reading, listening, and communicative interaction is essential for second language learners. The study of grammar is but a foundation and springboard; it is neither desirable nor possible to explain every possible structure in the English language. Students who believe they need to know a "rule" for every possible variation of an English structure should be disabused of that notion — and encouraged to go to a movie or make an English-speaking friend.

Some other exceptions are given in the chart footnote. The text focuses on the basic patterns of any given structure but also tries to anticipate questions students may have about exceptions that they note. The old saying about there being an exception to every rule is a good one for students of language to keep in mind.

- Contrast the example sentences (a) and (b) by writing them on the board.
- Make sure that students understand the mistake in (c) is not possible, and that *I saw me in the mirror* is ungrammatical.
- Explain that when *myself* is used for emphasis, it is usually because it is surprising that the actual subject (as opposed to another person) performed the action.

❑ EXERCISE 19. Looking at grammar.
Page 145
Time: 10–15 minutes

- Explain that certain phrases such as those in the list are often followed by reflexive pronouns.
- Give students time to complete the sentences. Remind them they will be choosing appropriate phrases from the list <u>and</u> adding reflexive pronouns.
- Review as a class, discussing the meanings of phrases from the list as needed.

Optional Vocabulary

shocked	encounter
supervision	careless
self-pity	impatient

❑ EXERCISE 20. Listening. Page 146
Time: 5–10 minutes

- Tell students that they will not hear the reflexive pronoun, so they will need to pay attention to the personal pronouns (subject pronouns) that they will hear at the start of each sentence.
- Play the audio through once without stopping. Then play it again, stopping the audio so that the class can provide the correct reflexive pronoun.

❑ EXERCISE 21. Looking at grammar.
Page 146
Time: 10–15 minutes

This exercise provides a cumulative review of subject-verb agreement (Chapter 6), nouns (Chapter 7), and pronouns (Chapter 8).

Optional Vocabulary

penguins	evolved	harsh
creatures	flippers	offspring
adapted	hatch	endurance

CHART 8-5. Using *You, One,* and *They* as Impersonal Pronouns. Page 147
Time: 10 minutes

Point out that when a speaker is using impersonal *you*, the *you* does not refer specifically to the listener. For example:

A: *What are some of the customs in your country about touching another person?*

B: *Well, **you** shouldn't touch someone else's head.*

Speaker B means "people in general" should not do this. She is not giving personal instructions to the listener; the *you* does not refer specifically and/or only to Speaker A.

- Elaborate on the background notes above by creating and eliciting examples your students can easily relate to. For example, ask your students:

What are some cultural rules or practices you have learned about the United States?

Possible answers may include (and if necessary, you can lead your students to the following):

You can eat in public.

You should arrive on time for most things.

You don't need to wear formal clothes most of the time.

- Explain that *one* is more formal and is becoming an increasingly less common impersonal pronoun than *you*.
- Tell students that *they* is used when the noun it refers to is understood. *They* is commonly used in reference to an organization or groups of people.

❑ **EXERCISE 23.** Looking at grammar.
Page 147
Time: 10–15 minutes

- Arrange students into small groups of three or four.
- Ask them to discuss the use of impersonal pronouns in Exercise 23, deciding which pronouns refer to one actual subject or listener, and which refer to an impersonal subject.
- Review this exercise as a class.

Optional Vocabulary
generosity
depleted

Expansion: While students are still in small groups, ask them to decide on the most important suggestions they can give future students who will be studying English in the same school/setting. They should use impersonal pronouns to write their suggestions.

Possible sentences/suggestions include:

Don't worry if you can't understand every word you hear. You will learn best if you try to listen for the main ideas when you are having conversations with native speakers.

Americans may seem rude or impatient sometimes, but they may just be nervous that they can't understand you. Also, they tend to work very long hours, so they are often very busy and rushed.

Alternatively, you can write up index cards with descriptions of challenging situations. Distribute one to each group. Together students need to come up with generalizations and advice about this situation, using impersonal pronouns as modeled in Chart 8-5. Remind students that they can use *you, one,* and *they* and that *they* will come in particularly handy when referring to others in each situation.

Possible situations include:

You have to meet your boyfriend's or girlfriend's family or parents.

You have a job interview.

You are traveling to a new place all by yourself.

You are going skiing, skating, sailing, swimming, etc., for the first time.

You have to make dinner for a special occasion, but you aren't an experienced cook.

You are going to babysit for a friend's child.

You are applying for a passport or visa and have to go the consulate or embassy.

❑ **EXERCISE 24.** Let's talk. Page 148
Time: 10 minutes

- In groups, have students try to guess the meaning of each of the common English sayings.
- Ask students whether they have similar expressions which convey similar "truths" in their languages. Write any on the board and discuss what they mean.

CHART 8-6. Forms of *Other.* Page 148
Time: 10 minutes

The use of forms of *other* is a common source of errors. Emphasize that *other* has a final *-s* only when it is used as a pronoun and never when it is used as an adjective. Point out that this is consistent with the fact that English adjectives never take a final *-s* when they come in front of plural nouns.

Point out that *another* is a combination of the article *an* with other, so *the* never precedes *another* (because it already has an article). *The* and *a/an* are never used together. (A common mistake is, for example, *I bought the another book.*)

- This point lends itself to a visual demonstration using the members of your class. First ask students to chat with each other about the weekend. Encourage them to stand and walk around if they like. You may want to play background music for a few minutes while they circulate.
- Stop the music and ask everyone to stay where they are. Some will still be standing, and some will probably be seated.
- Ask the students to look at you. Then write the following sentences on the board. (Of course, these sentences will need to be adapted to the configuration of your class.) Highlight the use of *others* and *another* by underlining or using another color. For example:

There are twenty students in this class.

Some are standing right now.

Others are sitting.

- Now refer to just two students by pointing to one area of the room. It is best if one student is standing near another who is sitting. If the students don't happen to be in an ideal position, use their clothing to distinguish one from another.
- Describe the stance or clothing of one by writing on the board:

On that side of the room, one student is sitting.

OR

On that side of the room, one student is wearing a black T-shirt.

- Now go on to write about an additional student's stance or clothing, using *another.*

Another is standing.

OR

Another is wearing a red T-shirt.

- Explain that when using the forms of *other* demonstrated above, the meaning is either one additional one (in the case of *another*) or some additional ones (in the case of *others*).
- Ask the three students, by name, to stand. Write a group of sentences to describe this on the board. For example:

  There are twenty students in this class.

  Ariane, Maki, and Jorge are standing.

  The others are sitting.

- Explain that in this case, *the others* refers to <u>all</u> of the additional ones, and we use a definite article because we know who these people are.
- Go over the chart, putting the sentences from the chart on the board if you feel your students require additional examples.

❏ **EXERCISE 26.** Looking at grammar.
Page 149
Time: 10 minutes

- Begin this exercise by having one student read item 1 aloud.
- Lead students through a discussion of items 2 and 3.
- In items 2 and 3, your students will use their hands to understand the difference between *another* and *the other.* Explain that in item 2, there is a finite, known number of fingers.
- To show your students how *another* is used in a series of items in an unknown, indefinite quantity you can go around the room saying (while pointing to or touching objects) *This is a book.* Then go on to each other book you see and say *This is another. This is another. This is another. This is another.*
- You can then go on to contrast this again with a series in a known, finite quantity.
- Ask five students to use their books to demonstrate. Stack textbooks on your desk, saying again *This is a book. This is another. This is another. This is another.* Before you stack the last book on top, emphasize that this final book (of the five) is *the* other (the remainder, rest, or last of a finite quantity.)
- Have students complete the remaining items as a class and discuss as a group.

❏ **EXERCISE 30.** Listening. Page 151
Time: 10 minutes

- Before playing the audio, have students read through the exercise and predict which form of *other* will be required in each item.
- Play the audio through once without stopping. Then play it once more, stopping after each item.
- Review as a class, and then listen once more so students can hear the correct answers.

CHART 8-7. Common Expressions with *Other.* Page 152
Time: 10–15 minutes

When the phrase *every other* means "alternate," the vocal emphasis is on *every*; for example, *I receive that magazine **every** other month.*

When *every* is used as an expression of quantity that happens to be followed by *other*, the stress is on *other*: for example, *George is the only student who missed the test; every **other** student took it last Friday.* In this instance, *every* has the meaning of *each* or *all: All of the other students took it last Friday.*

Forms of *other*, especially the reciprocal pronouns in (a), can be used to show possession, in which case an apostrophe is used; for example, *They enjoy each other**'s** company.*

- Ask a student to tell you someone who loves them. They may say a parent, spouse, or other family member. Then ask the student if they love this person in return. Write this information on the board using *each other,* and underline *each other.* For example:

  Rafaella and her mother love <u>each other</u>.

  Draw an arrow to show the connection between the subjects and *each other.*

- Then ask another student who he/she misses right now. Using the information the student gives you, involve the whole class in writing a similar sentence using the verb *miss* and the phrase *one another.* Underline *one another.* For example:

  Baek Jin and his girlfriend miss <u>one another</u>.

  Draw an arrow to show the connection between the subjects and *one another.*

- Ask a question that will lead to an answer with alternate times, such as:

  How often do you call your parents/spouse?

  How often do you check your personal email?

  How often do you weigh yourself?

  How often do you go to the gym?

  How often do you take cash out of an ATM?

- If an answer doesn't naturally present itself, offer one from your own life that involves alternate-day frequency. For example:

  I go running every other day.

  If your students need more demonstration, you can show them what it means to write on every other line, simply by drawing lines on the board and doing so.

- Explain the remaining expressions included in Chart 8-7. Whenever possible, ask questions that will elicit use of the expressions. Use students' lives to create examples and write these on the board.

❏ EXERCISE 32. Looking at grammar.
Page 152
Time: 10–15 minutes

Optional Vocabulary
cactuses
nearsighted
farsighted

❏ EXERCISE 33. Looking at grammar.
Page 154
Time: 5 minutes

Expansion: Have students write their complete sentences (including their chosen words in the appropriate places) on a separate sheet of paper. Tell students that they should try to be as creative as possible and use unusual nouns / verbs / adjectives whenever they can. Collect the sentences and read them aloud to the class. Ask the class to guess which set of sentences was written by which classmate, or have students vote on which sentence for each of the five options is the most creative.

❏ EXERCISE 35. Check your knowledge.
Page 154
Time: 10–15 minutes

Exercise 35 can be led as a game or worked through as a practice test, depending on the needs and preferences of your students.

- Game Approach: Divide the students into competing groups for this exercise, set a time limit (about five minutes for advanced classes and eight to ten minutes for intermediate students.)
- The group that identifies and corrects the most errors is declared the winner.
- Deduct one point for each error students overlook, for each word that they mistakenly identify as an error, and for each error that they correct in an unacceptable way. You may decide how to reward the winners.

❏ EXERCISE 36. Let's write. Page 155
Time: 15 minutes

One of the purposes of this kind of writing assignment is to reduce the students' hesitation to write freely by challenging them to write quickly on a broad topic. This sort of practice is especially good for those students who, unsure of themselves before now, have written only laboriously, wrestling with each word, afraid of making mistakes. Assure them that mistakes are not the end of the world and that even English teachers make changes in their own paragraphs. No one can write perfectly on the first attempt. All writers need to do their own proofreading ("error analysis"), rewording, and reorganizing.

In terms of grammar, the main purpose of this exercise is to let the students see if their old habits of singular-plural misuse remain in their writing. If so, they need to be especially aware of these problems when they monitor their writing and speech.

Many students tend to proofread another's writing more assiduously than they do their own; point out that they need to apply the same care and effort to their own writing. It is simply part of the writing process for everyone.

This type of exercise, designed to develop speed and fluency as well as to improve proofreading skills, can be repeated periodically throughout the term with topics of your or the students' choosing. You can set the time limit from two to ten minutes. In marking, you may choose to focus only on the target grammar points you have recently taught in class.

- Tell students to write as much as they can on the topic they choose, as quickly as they can. Ask students to try to write as many as 100 words in ten minutes, but tell them not to count their words as they write.
- When they finish, they should exchange their paragraphs or writing with classmates for peer correction.
- As the students correct each other's papers, ask them to look especially for errors in singular and plural usage.

❏ EXERCISE 37. Let's write and talk.
Page 156
Time: 15–30 minutes

This exercise is principally for fun, with a focus on pronoun awareness. The paragraphs should use the simple present tense. Probably there is no reason for you to mark them because the real test of their effectiveness is whether the class can identify the object described. You could spread this activity over several days.

- In order to get students started, prepare a sample paragraph to share with your class (either on a handout or on the board). The paragraph should describe your chosen object's characteristics (starting with more general ones and becoming increasingly specific).
- Have students guess what the object is, and give them further clues until they get it.
- Explain that they need to prepare such a paragraph for an object of their choosing. Give them time to do so in class and for homework.
- Students can correct each other's use of pronouns as these paragraphs are read aloud and discussed and the correct object is discovered.

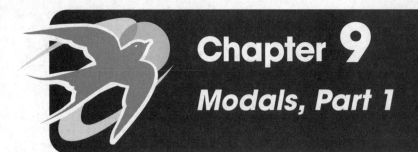

Chapter 9
Modals, Part 1

CHAPTER SUMMARY

OBJECTIVE: To review basic modal forms and gain mastery of the more advanced modal forms and meanings.

APPROACH: Modal auxiliaries are used in English to express attitudes, give advice, and indicate politeness. Mistakes with modal auxiliaries can, therefore, sometimes cause bad feelings or misunderstandings between speaker and listener. Students should become aware that a small change in a modal auxiliary can signal a large difference in attitudes and meanings.

Students using this textbook are probably familiar with the most common meanings of the modal auxiliaries. The focus at the beginning of the chapter is on the basic forms, and Exercise 1 calls attention to errors in form that should be avoided. The rest of the chapter takes a semantic approach, grouping together modals and other expressions that have similar meanings. Matters of pronunciation, spoken / written usages, and formal / informal registers are noted in the charts.

TERMINOLOGY: The terms "modal auxiliary" and "modal" are both used. Most modal auxiliaries are single words (for example: *must, should*); the exceptions are *ought to* and *had better.* Many have two- or three-word phrases with similar meanings (for example: *have to, be supposed to*) called "phrasal modals." Phrasal modals are also called "periphrastic modals" in some grammar books.

CHART 9-1. Basic Modal Introduction.
Page 157
Time: 15–20 minutes

A detailed discussion of the meaning of each modal is not necessary at this point since students should already know enough about modals to understand their basic meaning and use. Some general points you could make include:

1. There are differences in degrees of politeness (for example: *Can you open the door for me?* vs. *Could you open the door for me?*).

2. Use of modals sometimes depends on the relationship between the speaker and the listener (for example: the use of *had better* may indicate the speaker has a social role that is considered "above" or superior to that of the listener, such as a parent speaking to a child).

3. There may be differences in levels of formality / informality (for example, *may* vs. *can* for permission).

The chart mentions that each modal auxiliary has more than one meaning or use. These are presented throughout Chapters 9 and 10 and are summarized in Chart 10-10 (pp. 204–205). This may be a good time to point out this reference chart to the students. The text itself does not present this chart at the beginning of modal study for fear it will seem too intimidating; however, if students know they have two chapters to learn what's in the summary chart of modals, the task should seem less daunting.

If students want to get an idea of how varied the meanings of modals are, refer them to any standard dictionary and ask them to look up the meanings of *can, could, may,* or any of the others. Perhaps point out that this kind of information found in a dictionary is what their grammar text presents more fully and summarizes in Chart 10-10.

Students are sometimes not aware that *shall* and *should* have meanings as separate modals and are not simply the present and past forms of one modal. **Should** + *simple form* has a present / future meaning. Only in rare instances in the sequence of tenses of noun clauses does *should* represent the past form of *shall* (which makes it curious that in some dictionaries, the first definition of *should* is as the past form of *shall*).

- Personalize and tailor the sentences below as much as possible and write them on the board. Underline the modal in each sentence, and ask students to paraphrase the modal's function.

  Would you open the door, Makiko?
  (Elicit from students that *would* indicates a polite request.)
  You should open the door, Pedro.
  (Elicit from students that *should* expresses strong advice or instruction.)
  You may open the door, Byung Jin.
  (Elicit from students that *may* expresses permission given.)
  You could open the door, Miriam.
  (Elicit from students that *could* shows a possibility or opportunity but not instruction in the indicative voice.)
  You'd better open the door, Karim.
  (Elicit from students that *you'd better* shows urgent advice or instruction.)

CHARTS 9-2 and 9-3. Pages 158 and 159

The grammar in these two charts may be quite familiar to your students and can probably be covered quickly.

Before covering the charts, you may want to discuss how polite requests allow the speaker to show respect for the listener. A person who says *Give me your pencil* or *Pass the salt* seems to be too abrupt, aggressive, or unfriendly.

Point out the levels of formality and politeness in this chart and how modals express such subtleties. For example, a change from *may* to *can* usually signals a difference in the relationship between the people who are conversing.

The word *please* is frequently used in conversation. Using *please* is another way to show respect and friendliness.

Typical responses to requests, especially in informal American English are: *Okay, Sure,* and *No problem.*

CHART 9-2. Polite Requests with "I" as the Subject. Page 158
Time: 10–15 minutes

• Ask students to close their books for the following presentation so that they are not distracted by reading ahead.

• In order to introduce the various degrees of politeness, write three sentences on the left-hand side of the board.

  May I borrow $5.00?
  Can I borrow $5.00?
  Could I borrow $5.00?

• Tell students that the person asking each of these questions is a 21-year-old student. This same person is asking three <u>different</u> people the same question — his brother, his new roommate, and his supervisor at work.

• Ask students to decide which question goes with which listener and then have one student write his / her opinion on the board by writing either *brother, new roommate,* or *supervisor* to the left of each of the three sentences.

• Explain to students that different modals express different degrees of formality and politeness.

• Go over Chart 9-2 and review typical responses. Emphasize the differences in formality and politeness.

CHART 9-3. Polite Requests with "You" as the Subject. Page 159
Time: 10–15 minutes

• Ask students to do some simple tasks around the classroom, and write the requests on the board.

• Use students' names to personalize these requests. For example:

  Bertrand, can you open the door?
  Fernanda, will you tell me what time it is?

Marta, would you put your textbook on my desk?
Baek Eun, could you erase the board?

• Correct and refine your students' answers so that they are natural and represent typical responses.

• Have your students rank the above requests in order of politeness. As *would* and *could* are considered equally polite, students should rank these as a tie.

• As you work through Chart 9-3, be sure to provide typical affirmative and negative replies.

❏ EXERCISE 3. Let's talk. Page 159
Time: 10–15 minutes

• Model the example with a student, making sure his / her book is closed.

• Then have students work through the scenarios in pairs. If need be, elaborate on the roles and scenarios described in the book to ensure that students can easily imagine which modals are appropriate.

• As a review, ask particularly lively or amusing pairs to act out their scenario for the entire class.

CHART 9-4. Polite Requests with *Would You Mind.* Page 160
Time: 10–15 minutes

An alternative way of asking permission is <u>*Do you mind if I close the window?*</u> Using *would* is a bit more formal or polite than using *do.*

In casual conversation, the auxiliary and subject pronoun are often omitted and a present — not past verb is used: *Mind if I sit here?*

Another informal response is: *No. Go ahead,* or sometimes (somewhat illogically) even a positive response: *Sure. Go ahead.* Both mean "You have my permission to proceed."

Note that *No* as a response to *Would you mind* is a positive response, not a refusal. It means "No, I don't mind./It's no problem."

In (c): A gerund is used following *Would you mind.* Gerunds are not presented until Chapter 14. You may need to explain briefly that a gerund is the *-ing* form of a verb used as a noun.

Occasionally, one hears the form *Would you mind <u>my asking</u> a question?* This has the same meaning as "if I asked."

• Write the two headings from the chart on the board. The first heading on the left should read *Asking Permission,* and *Asking Someone to Do Something* should be on the right.

• Write the first target structure on the board:

  Would you mind + if I _____ -ed?

• Ask a few students permission by using the target grammar presented in the chart.

- Personalize the example requests, and underline the target grammar. For example:

  Chieko, would you mind <u>if I borrowed</u> your cell phone?
  Bruno, would you mind <u>if I moved</u> my desk closer to yours?
  Felicie, would you mind <u>if I put</u> my papers on your desk?

- Now move on to the second heading, *Asking Someone to Do Something.*
- Write the target grammar beneath this heading:

  Would you mind + _____ -ing?

- Model the target grammar with two or three personalized examples. For example:

  Yi-Feng, would you mind <u>putting away</u> your cell phone?
  Mikal, would you mind <u>reading aloud</u> the first example in the chart?

- You can even include a request to stop doing something, with *not*.

  Soo-Young, would you mind <u>not tapping</u> your pen on the desk?

- Once you have modeled the two target grammar categories, read through the rest of the chart and discuss the appropriate responses, as outlined under (b) and (d).

❏ **EXERCISE 5.** Looking at grammar.
Page 160
Time: 5 minutes

> This is essentially an exercise on verb forms. It also gives examples of typical situations in which *would you mind* is used.

- Explain that requests for permission start with *I want to* and that asking someone to do something starts with *I want you to*, etc.
- Have students write the correct transformations on the board, and correct these as a class.

❏ **EXERCISE 6.** Looking at grammar.
Page 161
Time: 10 minutes

Optional Vocabulary
personal question
It depends.
I didn't catch what you said.

❏ **EXERCISE 7.** Listening. Page 161
Time: 10 minutes

> Because students may not be used to the relaxed pronunciation they will hear in the audio, it is important to model it first.

- Read the example sentence using the relaxed speech pronunciation "ju" or "juh" in *would you.*
- Write on the board the relaxed speech pronunciation of *you: ju* or *juh.*
- Using this relaxed pronunciation, ask your students a few questions. For example:

  Would "juh" open your books, please?
  Would "juh" keep your cell phone off in class?

- Play the audio once through without stopping. Play it again and stop after each item. Review students' responses.
- Please see the front of this text for further suggestions on using listening exercises in class.

❏ **EXERCISE 9.** Looking at grammar.
Page 162
Time: 10 minutes

> These controlled-completion dialogues are a preparation for Exercise 10, where the students make up their own dialogues.

❏ **EXERCISE 10.** Let's talk: pairwork.
Page 163
Time: 10–15 minutes

> You may not want every pair of students to work on every item, so decide how to divide up the items before assigning pairs.

- Assign pairs or groups.
- Give each pair one or two items to prepare in a time limit of five to eight minutes.
- Ask each group or pair to "perform" its best dialogue for the other students.
- In discussion, ask the class to identify which modals were used and to comment on how appropriately and idiomatically they were used.

Expansion: You may turn this into a writing exercise for homework by asking students to choose one of the four situations presented to expand on. You may also provide additional scenarios and have students write a scripted dialogue for homework.

Additional scenarios include:

1. Bob's car battery has died while he is at a crowded shopping area. In order to start his car, he needs a battery "jump" from the driver of the car parked next to his, whose name is Marcia.
2. Bertrand has just arrived at your school and does not know how to register for classes. He asks Lara, who has been studying at your school for several months, how to enroll.

3. Xiao Min has never used a laundromat before coming to the United States. He asks his roommate, Juan, how to go about doing this and if Juan could help him carry his laundry to the laundromat.

4. Flora is sitting next to Xavier on a long-distance flight. Xavier keeps absentmindedly using Flora's headset to enjoy the in-flight entertainment.

5. Mikael has never used the type of computers that your school has in its computer lab before. He asks Julian, who has been using this type of computer for several months, how to start using email and save his documents to a file.

Alternatively, you can ask students to both come up with a situation and write the dialogue for it as homework. At the next class meeting, they can read or perform just the dialogue aloud, and classmates can guess the original situation from the actual spoken words.

❏ **EXERCISE 11.** Let's talk. Page 163
Time: 5 minutes

• To get students started on this exercise, have the class brainstorm two or three items, trying to think of as many requests as possible.

• Have pairs make up dialogues accordingly, and encourage students to take risks with vocabulary and idioms.

Expansion: You may want to assign roles to students and have them make up a dialogue extemporaneously. For example, for item 1, Student A is the teacher and Student B is a student. You could ask them what polite questions the teacher of this class has asked the students, what polite questions the students have asked their teacher, and what their typical responses have been.

You can expand on this exercise further by assigning your students to write down any requests that they hear — polite or not — during the coming week. Also, you can suggest that they write down any requests that they themselves make. At the end of the week, use the students' papers for discussion.

Additional locations include:

in a bookstore	in a library
in a bank	in the school office
at a post office	at a doctor's or dentist's office

CHART 9-5. Expressing Necessity: *Must, Have To, Have Got To.* Page 164
Time: 10–15 minutes

This chart contains information about pronunciation, formal/informal usage, spoken/written forms, and one past form. Students should note and discuss these points.

Note especially that *must* is used primarily with a forceful meaning. *Have to* and *have got to* are much more frequently used in everyday English.

Encourage students to practice (but not to force) conversational pronunciations. These are the most natural and frequent forms in spoken English. The phonetic representations of these pronunciations follow:

have to = /haeftə/ or /haeftu/

has to = /haestə/ or /haestu/

got to = /gadə/ or /gotə/

Have got to (necessity) is <u>not</u> the same as *have got* (possession). For example:

I've got to get some money. (I need money.)

I've got some money. (I have some money.)

• Write on the board the title *Must / Have To* — Necessity

• Under this, write example sentences using first *must* and then *have to.* Underline the modals in each example, and model sentences that relate to students and their lives. For example:

In order to learn English, students <u>must</u> practice speaking as much as possible.

In order to learn English, students <u>have to</u> practice speaking as much as possible.

• Tell students that *must* sounds both more formal and more urgent to most American English speakers, so *have to* is more commonly used.

• Explain that *must* is not often heard in spoken English but is found in written English, particularly in legal contracts, etc.

• Write examples on the board that are obviously more and less formal, respectively. Underline the modals. For example:

Jin Ho <u>has to</u> get to the airport early since he is flying standby.

All residents of the dormitory <u>must</u> return their keys to the manager in order to receive their housing deposits back.

• Introduce *have got to* as an informal variation of *have to.* Explain to students that in some cases, the use of *got* in this phrase exaggerates the necessity and is sometimes emphasized in speech.

• Write an appropriate example with *have got to* on the board and underline the modal phrase. For example:

Marietta <u>has got to</u> remember to call her parents. If she doesn't, they will be very worried.

• Explain that *had to* expresses past necessity for all of the following expressions: *have to, have got to,* and *must.* Explain that there is no past form of *must.*

The directions ask the students to practice usual spoken forms. Reinforce that it is by no means necessary for students to use contracted spoken English; clear enunciation of full forms is always good. Contracted speech can be practiced, but it doesn't need to be forced.

If you prefer not to put the emphasis on spoken forms (which you model), this exercise could be used for pairwork.

CHART 9-6. Lack of Necessity and Prohibition: *Have To* and *Must* in the Negative. Page 165
Time: 10 minutes

Need not (principally British) and *don't need to* are similar in meaning to *don't have to*.

- Write the headings *Lack of Necessity* and *Prohibition* on the board and underline them:
- Ask students to explain, in their own words, what each phrase means and write their explanations underneath each heading. Their explanations may take the following forms, but write whatever is closest in meaning:

Lack of Necessity	*Prohibition*
don't have to do something	*you can't do something*
your choice whether or not to	*something is forbidden*
something is not needed	*something is not permitted*

- Once you are sure that these two concepts are very clear to students, explain that *don't have to* is used to show lack of necessity while *must not* shows prohibition.
- To illustrate this, discuss with students the rules that organize your school or program.
- As a class, come up with sentences that fall under the *Lack of Necessity* heading and use *don't have to* to express these.
- Then come up with a few sentences that show prohibition, and write them under the *Prohibition* heading, using *must not.*
- You can encourage the use of either third person plural (*Students*) or first person plural (*We*) as a subject. For example:

Lack of Necessity	*Prohibition*
Students don't have to wear uniforms.	*Students must not behave violently.*
We don't have to use English names.	*We must not pull the fire alarm unless there is a fire.*

- Review the remainder of the chart.

- Allow time for students to think about the meaning of each item.
- As the context determines which answer is appropriate, help students understand the situational context of each item, perhaps by means of role-playing and discussion.

Optional Vocabulary
encounter   sense
growling

CHART 9-7. Advisability: *Should, Ought To, Had Better.* Page 167
Time: 10–15 minutes

Advice or a suggestion is usually friendly. It is often given by one's supervisor, parent, or friend. It is not as forceful as necessity. (Advice can also, of course, be not-so-friendly, depending upon the speaker's tone of voice and attitude.)

Note the special meaning of *had better.* It is used to give advice to a peer or to a subordinate but not to a superior.

- Write the heading *Advisability* on the board.
- Write *should* and *ought to* beneath the heading.
- Explain that *should* and *ought to* can be used interchangeably and can indicate a range of strength, from a simple opinion or suggestion to a statement about another's responsibility.
- With students, select a situation about which someone may need advice and co-create sentences advising the person with the dilemma. It may be easiest to use the second person singular (*You*) to address the advice to.

Possible situations include:
  you are homesick in the United States
  you want to find ways to practice your English outside of class

- Write the advice the class provides on the board, using both *should* and *ought to.* For example: You have a crush on a classmate . . .

  You should find out if the person has a boyfriend or girlfriend.
  You should sit next to him or her in class.
  You ought to offer to help him or her with homework assignments.
  You ought to introduce yourself to him or her.

- Now introduce *had better* under the heading of *Advisability,* but explain that this phrase shows more strength and urgency and is not used with someone in a superior position (e.g., a parent, boss, or teacher).
- Invent a situation in which there are negative consequences of a failure to act soon, and create *had better* sentences as a class. Write these on the board.

Possible situations:

You are failing a class and need to turn in another assignment late.

Your roommate is very angry that you borrowed his bike without asking.

You have twisted your ankle, and it is starting to swell up.

Possible *had better* sentences:

You <u>had better</u> talk to your teacher and explain the situation.

You <u>had better</u> apologize.

You <u>had better</u> go to the doctor right away.

• Go over the remainder of the chart.

❏ **EXERCISE 20.** Let's talk: pairwork.
Page 168
Time: 10 minutes

The intention of this exercise is to give short examples of situations in which modals of advice are frequently used, but expanding the examples can certainly be helpful. In later exercises, students are given fuller contexts as well as real-life contexts in which to practice giving advice.

Using this as a teacher-led exercise enables you to take advantage of the opportunities for leading a spontaneous discussion of the topics in some of the items.

If this exercise is teacher-led rather than done as pairwork, your book is open and the students' books are closed. You are Speaker A, in which case students probably would not want to use *had better* in some of the situations. An alternative to this teacher-led approach would be for one student to be the "teacher" and lead the exercise, or for several students to each present four or five items.

• Discuss who might be talking to whom when *had better* is used.
• Contextualize each item for the class by inventing who is talking to whom and embellishing the situation.
• Ask for two students to role-play each situation, with one of them saying the words in the text.

❏ **EXERCISE 23.** Looking at grammar.
Page 169
Time: 10 minutes

Students can write their answers as seat work, then discuss them in small groups or as a class. Your role is to ensure that students are engaged in discussion and to resolve disagreements.

Some of the items have fine distinctions in meaning which may be confusing for some students. Sometimes there is only a fine line between *should* and *must/have to,* but students should understand that the line does exist. In none of the items is the same meaning conveyed when both *should* and *must/have to* are used to complete the sentences.

CHART 9-8. The Past Form of *Should.*
Page 170
Time: 10 minutes

Sometimes students confuse the past form of modals with the present perfect tense because the <u>form</u> of the main verb is the same (**have** + *past participle*). If students ask about "tense," tell them that **have** + *past participle* here doesn't carry the same meaning as the present perfect tense; it simply indicates past time.

The information in Chart 9-12, example (f), page 178, says that the past form of *should* is also used to give "hindsight advice." Here you may want to introduce the concept of viewing something in hindsight: We use *should have done something* when we look at the past (for example, we look at something in hindsight), decide that what was done in the past was a mistake, and agree that it would have been better if the opposite had been done. Another way to introduce this concept is to talk about regrets.

The short answer to a question with the past form of should is simply *I should've* (British: *I should've done*). Note the pronunciation of *should've,* which is exactly like *should + of.* In fact, some people (native speakers and second language learners alike) mistakenly spell the contraction as if it were made from the words *should of.*

Also, students should be reminded to pronounce *should* like *good,* with no sound for the letter "l."

• Write the chart title on the board: *Past Form of Should.*
• Now write the word *regret* near the heading and discuss its meaning with students.
• You may want to model some of your own regrets, keeping the tone light but clearly explaining actions you should have taken. Write some of these on the board:

I should have learned a second language thoroughly.

I should have studied harder when I was in college.

- Using the example sentences, students should be able to create related sentences. Write each one on the board, directly beneath the regret expressed with *should have*.

  I should have learned a second language thoroughly.
  (*You didn't learn a second language thoroughly.*)

  I should have studied harder when I was in college.
  (*You didn't study hard enough when you were in college.*)

- Now go through Chart 9-8 with students, explaining the finer points as needed.

❏ **EXERCISE 27.** Let's talk. Page 171
Time: 10 minutes

- Have students work quickly in pairs since these items are straightforward and uncomplicated.
- Alternatively, have a student with clear pronunciation read the situation aloud (to the whole class or to other members of a small group). Then another student can give an opinion about it, using the past form of *should*.
- You may also choose to ask for volunteer responses and run through these items quickly as an extension of your presentation of the information in Chart 9-8.

❏ **EXERCISE 28.** Let's talk: pairwork.
Page 171
Time: 10–15 minutes

- With an advanced group, follow the direction line as presented in the text. With a less advanced group or if you sense students will struggle with this, instruct Speakers B to keep their books open.

❏ **EXERCISE 29.** Let's talk or write. Page 172
Time: 10–15 minutes

There are several options for effectively using this exercise, and it can be expanded into a writing assignment for homework. No matter what methodology you use, support students as they discuss what the various characters in each situation *should have done* differently. Help students be creative in their responses and also help them to employ passive vocabulary.

- If you want to work through this exercise quickly, lead it yourself and have students call out their responses. With an advanced group, students can keep their books closed.
- In pairs or small groups, have students discuss their opinions about each situation.
- If you want to include writing in the in-class part of the exercise, one person in each group can record the others' responses, and another person in each group can then read these aloud to the whole class, or you can ask that these be handed in.

CHART 9-9. Obligation: *Be Supposed To.*
Page 173
Time: 10–15 minutes

The important difference between obligation and necessity (Chart 9-5: *must, have to, have got to*) is that the notion of necessity can sometimes originate within oneself. Obligations, as the term is used here, come from outside, from other people; therefore, *be supposed to* is similar to passive verb phrases with no agent. *He is supposed to come* means "He is expected (by someone) to come."

An expression similar to *be supposed to* is *be to*. *Be to* has been included in previous editions of this text but is omitted here due to its relative infrequency of occurrence. (*Be supposed to,* by comparison, is a phrase every learner will need to know and use.) You may wish to introduce students to *be to* at this juncture. If alert students ever come across it, perhaps on standardized proficiency tests, they will find this structure curious. *Be to* is close in meaning to *must* but includes the idea of expectation, the idea that someone else strongly expects, demands, or orders this behavior. For example, if *be to* were used in example (c) — *I am to be* at the meeting — it would convey the idea that *My boss ordered me to be there. He will accept no excuses for my absence.*

- Write the heading *Obligation* on the board.
- Ask students to think about expectations that others have of them, whether in their family, work, or student lives. Model a sentence related to what they know of your life as their teacher on the board. For example:

  As your teacher, I am supposed to start my classes on time.
  I am supposed to know the grammar you are learning very well.

- Then, elicit student-generated examples:

  Juan: *I am supposed to present an ad campaign in English when I return to my job in Mexico next month.*
  Miyako: *I am supposed to phone my parents every Sunday morning.*
  Ivan: *I am supposed to get a 200 on the TOEFL test before I complete my Ph.D. application.*

- Now explain that to discuss past obligations, only the verb *be* changes, as *supposed to* is already a past participle form.
- Ask students if they have failed to carry out any obligations or expectations in the last week and to formulate sentences from their experiences. These sentences can also be about their expectations of others. For example:

  Maria: *I was supposed to email my sister about my travel plans.*
  Yao: *My friends were supposed to have sent me the photos from my going-away party, but I haven't received them.*

❏ **EXERCISE 31.** Let's talk. Page 173
Time: 10 minutes

> Remind students that there are many things that we "are supposed to do" or "are not supposed to do" in everyday life.

Optional Vocabulary
prior to
blaring

❏ **EXERCISE 32.** Looking at grammar.
Page 174
Time: 5–10 minutes

> This exercise compares the modal auxiliaries from Charts 9-5 through 9-9 and serves as a good way to review these charts.

Expansion: Have students create a context for each item and decide who the speakers are. For example, items 1–3 involve people who are riding in an airplane or automobile; they might be father and son, flight attendant and passenger, two business partners, etc. While students discuss and decide which sentence is stronger, they should also discuss the appropriateness for the context they have created. Some statements are naturally too strong between people of equal status and could cause the listener to become angry. Discussing the created context and the appropriateness of each statement enriches students' understanding of the subtleties of modal usage.

❏ **EXERCISE 33.** Let's talk or write. Page 174
Time: 10–15 minutes

• Have students make sentences about one or more of the occupations listed, using the various modals presented.

Expansion: Ask students to rank these occupations in terms of their difficulties and challenges and then discuss their rankings with other students, using modals in their justifications. For example:

I think a taxi driver is the most challenging job because you are supposed to know how to get to every part of a city. You have to be patient even when many of the people who get in your taxi aren't. You are not supposed to be rude to your customers, but they may sometimes be rude to you.

❏ **EXERCISE 34.** Let's write or talk. Page 174
Time: 10–20 minutes

> Students need to use their imagination in this exercise; most of them probably haven't had any experience in the roles described in the given situations. You could suggest other, more familiar roles of authority (for example, the teacher of this class), or students could invent their own authority roles.

• Discuss item 1 with the whole class. Have them contribute other answers, using all of the rest of the modals and similar expressions on the list.
• Assign students one, two, or all of the other topics to discuss, role-play, or write about.

Expansion: If you assign this as written work, have students write about one of the given situations as well as one of their own devising. They can try to disguise the authority role of their own devising and then read their sentences aloud, encouraging other class members to guess what the original authority role was.

CHART 9-10. Unfulfilled Intentions:
Was/Were Going To. Page 176
Time: 10 minutes

> Be sure students understand the meaning of the word *intention.*
>
> The important difference here between the future and the past use of *be + going to* is that the future indicates a strong possibility the action will be completed. In contrast, the past usually indicates that the action did not happen.

• Write the heading *Unfulfilled Intentions* on the board, and have students discuss the meanings of both words.
• Elicit as many related words and phrases as you can from students, and write these beneath the heading.
• Give students help in coming up with other descriptors of *unfulfilled,* such as *unrealized, unreal, never happened, unmet, failed, changed (his/her) mind,* etc.
• Lead students to think about *intentions* simply as plans, and write *plans* beneath the heading.
• Give students an example of your own unfulfilled intentions and write it on the board. For example:

  Last weekend, I was going to take a long bike ride, but it rained all day Saturday and Sunday.

• Elicit examples of unfulfilled intentions from students and write these on the board, underlining or highlighting the *was/were going to* part.

❏ **EXERCISE 36.** Looking at grammar.
Page 176
Time: 5–10 minutes

- Since these can be tricky, put students in pairs to work on them together.
- Ask three different pairs of students to write their sentences on the board, and discuss as a class.

CHART 9-11. Making Suggestions: *Let's, Why Don't, Shall I / We.* Page 177
Time: 10–15 minutes

These three expressions are followed by the simple (i.e., base) form of the main verb. For example: *Let's **be** careful: Why don't you **come** at six?, Shall I **be** your partner in this game?*

Shall is used only with *I* or *we*. It is not appropriate to ask, *Shall he, Shall you,* etc.

These suggestions are similar to polite requests but also may include both speaker and listener in the suggested activity.

In informal British usage, *Don't let's* is a possible alternative form of *Let's not*. *Don't let's* is also heard in American English but is considered nonstandard.

- Write the title *Making Suggestions* on the board.
- Explain that *Let's / Let's not* and *Why don't* + base form of the verbs are common ways of making suggestions for a plan or activity for the speaker and listeners present.
- Write the following formulas on the board:

  Let's / Let's not + base form of verb

  Why don't + subject + base form of verb

- With your students, make suggestions for the coming weekend and a hypothetical class outing or weekend trip. Tell students that money is no object and that they should call out any suggestions they have.
- Write the suggestions that you and your class co-create on the board. For example:

  Let's fly to Bali and learn to surf.

  Let's go to Vegas and stay at Caesar's Palace.

  Let's book cruises on the Queen Elizabeth and travel to the Canary Islands.

  Why don't we take the train to New York?

  Why don't we go on safari in Kenya?

  Why don't we see a Broadway musical?

- Now explain that *Shall I / Shall We* are considered slightly formal and old-fashioned and are used primarily as rhetorical devices in everyday speech. Explain that when *shall* is used, agreement is expected.
- Model a few *Shall I / Shall we* questions and write these on the board. For example:

  Shall I continue with the grammar lesson?

  Shall we become even better at using modals?

- Go over the remainder of the chart.

CHART 9-12. Making Suggestions: *Could vs. Should.* Page 178
Time: 10–15 minutes

Make sure that students understand that *could* refers to a present or future time here. Sometimes learners mistakenly think of *could* only as the past tense of *can*, but *could* has many uses and meanings. (See Chart 10-10, page 205, for a summary of other uses of *could*.)

Could is used to make suggestions when there are several good alternatives. It often occurs with *or*, as in *You could do this, or you could try that.*

- Explain to students that *could* is used when there are a number of suggestions, while *should* is used to give advice.
- Write two headings on the board: *Could vs. Should*
- Ask students for fun extracurricular suggestions to give a new student to the school, and write these under *Could*. For example:

  If you are in Boston, you could . . .

  A new student could rent a bike and ride by the Charles River.

  She could go to Cape Cod for the weekend.

  She could explore Boston by following the Freedom Trail.

- Now ask students to pick the one thing they recommend most for a new student at your school. Explain that because you have asked them to give you their strongest or main suggestion, it is strengthened by the use of *should*.
- Write students' *should* suggestions on the board under the appropriate heading.

  She should see a Red Sox game.

  She should go to Faneuil Hall.

  She should go on a whale watch.

- Finally, explain that *could have* + *past participle* is a past possibility, whereas *should have* + *past participle* expresses a regret about a past mistake.
- Model the differences with examples on the board:

  I could have visited Rome when I was in Italy. (I could have visited Rome among other Italian cities I did visit, such as Venice and Milan.)

  I should have studied harder in college. (I didn't study hard, and this was a mistake.)

- Review the remainder of the chart and answer any remaining questions.

❏ **EXERCISE 41.** Looking at grammar.
Page 179
Time: 15–30 minutes

The purpose of this type of exercise is to give additional examples of the structure for students to discuss and explore.

- Give students ample time to read through each of the three dialogues and understand the situation.
- Help students articulate that Speaker B is giving one piece of definitive advice (or hindsight advice), whereas Speaker C is simply listing alternatives.

❑ **EXERCISE 42.** Let's write: pairwork.
Page 179
Time: 15–30 minutes

- Explain the format and purpose of an advice column. Encourage students to include imagination and good humor in their letters.

- Have students brainstorm together in small groups and perhaps co-author a short sample letter before working on their own.
- To help students take imaginative risks and try out their passive vocabulary, tell them that they will only be graded on their use of modals and that you want them to be as playful as possible.

Expansion: Bring in newspaper or magazine advice columns. Have students read these in order to become familiar with the general format, typical phrases, terms of address, etc. You can collect the "advice" from the classroom columnists and read these aloud to the group. Students should then guess what specific complaints or problems provoked these particular responses.

Chapter 10
Modals, Part 2

CHAPTER SUMMARY

OBJECTIVE: To learn additional uses of modal auxiliaries, as a continuation of Chapter 9.

APPROACH: The first half of this chapter concentrates on using modals to express suppositions and logical conclusions and relates modals to matters of time and duration. Then attention is paid to a few additional modal uses. The chapter leads to a summary chart of the information presented in Chapters 9 and 10 and review exercises on modal usage.

TERMINOLOGY: The term "degrees of certainty" is used with those modals that express the strength of a speaker's belief in the sureness of what she / he is saying. In other grammar books, terms such as "logical possibility" or "degree of possibility" are used in discussions of these modal usages.

❑ **EXERCISE 1.** Warm-up. Page 180
Time: 5 minutes

• Explain to students that an important use of modals is in supposing (or guessing) what happened when you can't be 100% sure.
• Read the introductory paragraph about Ramon's guitar to your students before proceeding with the warm-up.

CHART 10-1. Degrees of Certainty: Present Time. Page 180
Time: 10 minutes

The percentages presented are, of course, not exact. They show the relative strength of one's certainty and can be very helpful to students.

Be sure to call students' attention to the note about *maybe* and *may be;* confusing the two is a common written error for both native and non-native speakers.

• Using the name of a student in your class, especially if someone happens to be absent, write on the board an example similar to the one in the chart.
• Ask students to make guesses about where their missing classmate may be and/or why their missing classmate isn't present.
• Write students' guesses on the board, using the appropriate modals as you do so and underlining the

modals in each sentence. For example:

Mi-Hong is a good student who comes to class regularly. Today she is not in class. No one knows where she is.

Mi-Hong must have a good reason.   95% certainty

(We think she has a good reason for not being here because she is a good student.)

Mi-Hong may be sick today.

Mi-Hong might be in another city.   50% or less certainty

Mi-Hong could be at home studying for the TOEFL test.

(We really don't know why she isn't in class today, so the three previous sentences express a weak degree of certainty.)

• Go over the rest of the chart with students and discuss the notes.

❑ **EXERCISE 3.** Let's talk. Page 182
Time: 10 minutes

This exercise can be teacher-led as a quick follow-up to the discussion of Chart 10-1. It presents simple, everyday situations in which to practice using *must* to express logical conclusions.

• Have a student pantomime the action in an item first, and then lead the students through making a best guess. For example, in item 1:
    You: *Oscar, please yawn.*
    Oscar: *(yawns)*
    You: *Oscar is yawning. Why do you think he is yawning, Abdul?*
    Abdul: *He must be sleepy.*

Optional Vocabulary
shivering
goose bumps
fans

❑ **EXERCISE 4.** Let's talk. Page 182
Time: 10 minutes

• Point out that the answers in this exercise express less certainty than the answers in Exercise 3.
• Model or lead the exercise by taking the role of Speaker A.

- Encourage students to be as imaginative as possible with their responses, and ask related questions to promote new and related guesses. For example, for item 3:

  Speaker A (You): *You all know I enjoy reading novels on my subway commute.*

  Speaker (student): *You <u>must have</u> a book with you.*

CHART 10-2. Degrees of Certainty: Present Time Negative. Page 183
Time: 10–15 minutes

> The percentages shown are not exact; they show only relative certainty.
>
> Note that while *could* indicates less than 50% certainty (Chart 10-1), *couldn't* indicates 99% certainty. You can sympathize with your students' frustration about language. This discrepancy demonstrates that language does not always have logical or predictable structure.

- Write four categories and their explanations on the board:

  100% sure = fact (no modal needed)

  99% sure = couldn't/can't (speaker has a lot of evidence but is not 100% sure)

  95% sure = must not (speaker has plenty of evidence but is less than 99% sure)

  50% sure = may not/might not (speaker doesn't have evidence — all possibilities have equal likelihood)

- Now using information about students and their lives, create sentences with your class to illustrate each of the above categories.
- Underline the modal used in each case. For example:

  There is an unpleasant ringing noise that everyone in class can hear.

  It isn't a fire alarm because the fire alarm is much louder.

  It <u>couldn't be</u> someone's cell phone because the noise is constant.

  It <u>must not be</u> a watch because a watch's noise is too faint.

  It <u>may not be</u> an alarm on someone's computer, but it could be.

- Go over the chart with students.

❏ EXERCISE 7. Let's talk. Page 183
Time: 5 minutes

- Work through this exercise as a group, having students take turns reading A and B parts.
- Help students identify the appropriate degree of certainty by articulating the "evidence" for each logical conclusion.
- For example, with item 1, first ask students what *flunked* means and ask them what alternatives they may offer for Yuko's chronic failure:

  You: *What are some other reasons that someone could repeatedly flunk quizzes or exams? Is it ever possible to study hard but still flunk tests? Are there other conclusions we can draw about Yuko?*

Possible alternative student responses:

  Yuko must not be very good at this subject.

  Yuko must not feel very satisfied with her progress.

  Yuko might not be very good at test taking.

CHART 10-3. Degrees of Certainty: Past Time. Page 186
Time: 10–15 minutes

> Note the parallels between the <u>affirmative</u> expressions in this chart and in Chart 10-1.
>
> Then note the parallels between the <u>negative</u> expressions here and in Chart 10-2.
>
> Point out to students that modal auxiliaries are very useful in communicating how one perceives situations for which 100% certain facts are not available. Other languages may use different kinds of expressions for these ideas, so English modals can be difficult to learn.
>
> Again, because students have already explored degrees of certainty in the Charts, 10-1 and 10-2, they should be able to participate fully and give you example sentences.

- Write two main headings on the board: *Past Time: Affirmative* and *Past Time: Negative.*
- Remind students to turn back to Charts 10-1 and 10-2 frequently as the foundation laid in each of those charts is expanded here in the past tense.
- Under *Past Time: Affirmative*, write three degrees of certainty:

  100% sure = fact = was

  95% sure = must <u>have been</u>

  50% sure = may / might / could <u>have been</u>

- Explain that the only difference in this modal form is that it is past, and that the modal itself is followed by *have been* + base verb.
- Write an example of 100% certainty on the board, and have students tell you what the corresponding 95% and 50% modals should be. For example, write:

  Pablo wasn't in class yesterday. The day before yesterday he was complaining of allergies.

  You: *If I know for a fact that the reason Pablo wasn't here was his allergies, what can I say?*

  Students: *Pablo was sick.*

- Write this on the board, underlining the verb, and then continue to elicit from the class:

  You: *Right, but if I am only 95% sure?*

  Students: *Pablo <u>must have been</u> sick.*

- Write this on the board as above.

  You: *Right, and what options do I have if I am really not sure why Pablo was out, and I hadn't overheard him complaining about allergies the last time he was in class? What can I say about Pablo's absence with 50% or less certainty?*

  Students: *Pablo <u>may have been</u> sick.*

  Pablo <u>might have been</u> sick.

  Pablo <u>could have been</u> sick.

- Write all these options on the board, and encourage students to come up with more creative responses. For example:

  He might have won a sudden trip to Las Vegas.

- Now follow the same approach for *Past Time: Negative.*
- Remember that there are four degrees of certainty with the negative and that the second category takes the form: *99% sure = couldn't have been / can't have been*
- Go over the remainder of the chart with students.

❏ EXERCISE 13. Let's talk. Page 187
Time: 10 minutes

- This discussion can be teacher-led or you can put students in pairs or groups.

  Have students take turns using modals to explain the likelihood that each one of the men got engaged.

  Expansion: Ask students questions about their culture and expectations around becoming engaged in preparation for marriage. Though this topic may not readily elicit targeted modal usage, it is one that students tend to be interested in. As a five or ten-minute discussion, it can provide a much-needed break from degrees of certainty and modal usage, which students can find a bit abstract and challenging.

  Possible questions include:

  At what age do most people get engaged?

  Do couples live with one another before becoming engaged?

  Does the man generally ask the parents' permission before proposing to the woman?

  In the United States, an engagement often includes a diamond ring and a romantic dinner for two. Is this also true in your country?

❏ EXERCISE 15. Let's talk. Page 187
Time: 10 minutes

If you lead this exercise, take an active role, helping each dialogue develop in a fairly natural way.

- Say the first line to the class, using the name of a student.
- Wait for several students to give some good guesses, and write these on the board, particularly for the first item or example exchange.
- Then pose the *What if* question and wait for new responses.

CHART 10-4. Degrees of Certainty:
Future Time. Page 189
Time: 10–15 minutes

Of course, no one can be 100% sure about future events. But we can make promises with *will* and confident predictions (as in Chart 4-2 using *will*).

This chart is titled "future time," but for convenience in section (b), the past forms *should have* and *ought to have* are included.

Compare *should have* meaning "unfulfilled expectation" with *should have* in Chart 9-8, meaning "hindsight advice." The forms are identical, but the contexts modify the meanings.

- You can use the academic setting your students are in or recent events in the news to co-create example sentences on the board. For example, if students have a midterm or final coming up, choose that upcoming test to create example sentences.
- Using suggestions from students, create sentences to demonstrate each degree of certainty presented, and write each on the board under the appropriate heading.

❏ EXERCISE 19. Looking at grammar.
Page 189
Time: 10 minutes

Learners may sometimes sound more assertive than they intend to if they use *will* instead of other "softer" modals. By pointing out the differences in degree and telling your students which modals a native speaker would use in various situations, you will help your students grasp these somewhat abstract uses.

- Discuss the fine line between *will* and *should / ought to,* as in item 2.

❏ EXERCISE 20. Looking at grammar.
Page 190
Time: 10 minutes

Expansion: Have students create their own situation and related modal cues by looking at the five situations in Exercise 20. This can be assigned as homework, and then students can exchange and complete one another's situations.

❏ EXERCISE 21. Listening. Page 192
Time: 10 minutes

Be sure to let students know that this exercise is a review of Chapter 9 and Charts 10-1 through 10-4.

- Before listening, model the reduced pronunciation of *may-uv, shouldn't-uv, could-uh, should-uh,* etc.
- With books closed, play the audio through once without stopping.
- Have students open their books and listen again as you pause after each sentence.
- Ask individual students to write their answers on the board, and discuss.
- Listen again to correct the answers.

CHART 10-5. Progressive Forms of Modals.
Page 193
Time: 10 minutes

> Every progressive form must contain both a form of **be** and a *verb + -ing*.
>
> Point out similarities and differences with other progressive verb forms:
>
> Chart 2-2: present progressive (*is sleeping* vs. *might be sleeping*)
>
> Chart 2-10: past progressive (*was sleeping* vs. *might have been sleeping*)

- Have students first think of someone in their lives who is not in the class. Possible examples are a student's parent, partner, spouse, child, or friend.
- Alternatively, you can pick one famous person for the whole class to discuss. Possible options are a famous movie star, political figure, athlete, or newsmaker.
- Ask students to imagine what the person *may be doing* or *must be doing*.
- Explain to students that if they have enough evidence, they can increase the level of certainty from **may** to **must** + **be** + **-ing**, and lead them through creating sentences. For example:

  You: *It is morning here in the United States. Think of a friend or family member who is in your country right now and decide whether to use* **may** + **be** + **-ing** *or* **must** + **be** + **-ing** *to describe what he or she is doing right now. Be prepared to explain why you chose* **may** *or* **must**.

  Students' responses:

  Maria: *It is 11:00 A.M. now in Boston, but is 4:00 P.M. in Spain right now, so my mother* <u>may be preparing</u> *food for dinner later.*

  Jin Baek: *It is midnight in Korea right now, and my father goes to sleep around 10:00 P.M., so he* <u>must be sleeping</u> *right now.*

- Write students' sentences on the board and underline or highlight the contrasting modals.
- Using the same approach, change the time from *right now* to *5:00 P.M. yesterday afternoon,* and have different students offer example sentences about a friend or family member.
- Explain that students need to change the modal forms to *may have been + -ing* or *must have been + ing* to reflect the degree of certainty about the past action in progress.

  Students' responses:

  Pierre: *When it was 5:00 P.M. yesterday afternoon here, it was already 10:00 P.M. in Paris, so my girlfriend* <u>could have been studying</u> *in her apartment or* <u>she might have been eating</u> *dinner at a restaurant.*

  Kiri: *When it was 5:00 P.M. yesterday afternoon here in Boston, it was 4:00 A.M. the next morning in Bangkok, so my mother* <u>must have been sleeping</u>.

- Review the chart with your class and answer any further questions.

❏ EXERCISE 24. Looking at grammar.
Page 193
Time: 10 minutes

- Call students' attention to the situations, and remind them that the progressive is necessary for all actions that either <u>are</u> in progress right now or <u>were</u> in progress at a specific point in time.

  Optional Vocabulary
  herd
  hitchhiking

❏ EXERCISE 27. Let's talk or write. Page 196
Time: 10 minutes

> You may be surprised at how many different conjectures your class can have about this picture. By giving students ample time to study it first, they will feel equipped to make guesses using modals. Encourage students to incorporate all factual information into their guesses and use as specific vocabulary as they can.

- Ask students leading questions regarding the illustration.

  Possible leading questions include:

  What is your guess about the man at the front of the line?
  What is he doing?
  What is inside the envelope?
  Why is the envelope so large?
  What do you think the man's profession is?
  Why is he at the post office at 3:00?
  What is the woman behind him doing?
  What do you think her profession is?

Expansion: Bring in photos depicting people in specific situations. Advertisements from business or travel magazines may be useful. The photos should have at least two or three people in the picture, and the context should be identifiable. Divide the class into groups of three or four and have each group write detailed conjectures about one of the photos. After they have done so, collect all the photos and tape them to the board or display them so that all students can see them easily. Now have each group read their set of conjectures, and have the other students identify which photo the piece describes.

❏ EXERCISE 28. Let's talk. Page 196
Time: 10 minutes

- Give students time to read through the dialogue.
- Have a pair perform the dialogue using dramatic expression and tone of voice to ensure a lively class discussion.
- Encourage students to come up with as many variations as possible in answer to questions 1–5.

This exercise reviews modals used to express degrees of certainty. Students should discuss their choices and reasoning process along the following lines.

- Have students complete the exercise in class.
- Then have students compare answers and justify their choices. For example, in item 1, the speaker is expressing a logical conclusion based upon the evidence that is available (i.e., that Jeff was offered a scholarship); the speaker believes that Jeff is a good student but does not know that with 100% certainty.

Optional Vocabulary
accurate
matter
settled
den

CHART 10-6. Ability: *Can* and *Could*.
Page 198
Time: 10–20 minutes

In (b): a common use of *can* is with non-progressive verbs of sense perceptions (see Chart 2-3, p. 15) that are <u>not</u> used in progressive tenses to express the idea of "in progress right now."

Compare:

CORRECT: *I can't hear (right now) the lecture.*

INCORRECT: *I am not hearing. I don't hear.*

Pronunciation notes:

Can't has two acceptable pronunciations. Most Americans say /kaent/. But along the northern Atlantic coast, the pronunciation may be similar to the British /kant/.

Can also has two pronunciations. Before a verb, it is usually /ken/. In a short answer (*Yes, I can.*) it is /kaen/.

In typical intonation, *can't* is stressed and *can* is unstressed.

The modal *could* can be confusing. It has many uses, most of which are close to one another in meaning.

Compare the following:

I could run fast if I wanted to. (present / future contrary-to-fact conditional)

I could run or *I could walk.* (50-50 possibility, present / future)

You could run to improve your physical condition. (present / future suggestion)

To further complicate things, *could* meaning "past ability / possibility" occurs mostly in the negative:

I couldn't go to the meeting yesterday afternoon. I had a doctor's appointment.

However, one does not normally use *could* in the affirmative to indicate past possibility.

INCORRECT: *I could go to the meeting yesterday afternoon. I'm glad I didn't miss it.*

Rather, one would use *be able to, manage to,* or just the simple past in this case.

CORRECT: *I was able to go to the meeting yesterday afternoon.*

In sum, if the speaker is talking about an ability to perform an act at one particular time in the past, *could* is not usually used in affirmative sentences. Compare:

INCORRECT: *Did you read about the mountain climbers? They could reach the top of Mount Everest yesterday.*

CORRECT: *They were able to reach the top yesterday.*

They managed to reach the top yesterday.

They reached the top yesterday.

In negative sentences, however, there is no difference between using *could* and *was / were able to*:

They couldn't reach / weren't able to reach the top yesterday.

For an idea of how complicated and varied the meaning and use of *could* is, look it up in a dictionary such as the *Collins Cobuild English Language Dictionary.* *Could* in all of its aspects can be difficult to explain to learners, and doing so (for most learners) is not particularly helpful or necessary.

- Ask students to think about their own and their classmates' skills and abilities and to write a few sentences.
- While they are working, write the heading *Abilty: Can and Could* on the board.
- Ask students to call out a few of their sentences, and put these sentences on the board under a subheading *present / future ability* and underline the modal. For example:

  Paulo can juggle four oranges.

  Martina can walk on her hands because she used to be a gymnast.

  Valentina can speak Finnish.

- Now ask students to describe possibilities and opportunities they have currently. Explain that *can* doesn't just describe a skill, per se, but is also used to express possibilities.
- Write their sentences on the board under the subheading *present / future possibility.* For example:

  I can attend English classes.

  In Boston, I can visit famous universities.

  Because I am not working these days, I can sleep late in the mornings.

- Explain that *can* is also used to indicate permission or agreement in informal situations, and write an example on the board. For example:

    You <u>can borrow</u> my cell phone.

- Explain the past form of *can* is *could*. Under a subheading *past ability*, transform a few of the sentences students gave you earlier into past, asking them to imagine that the people no longer possess these skills.

- Write the transformed sentences on the board and underline the *could* form. For example:

    Paulo <u>could juggle</u> four oranges.
    Martina <u>could walk</u> on her hands.
    Valentina <u>could speak</u> Finnish.

- Go over the remainder of the chart with students.

❏ EXERCISE 32. Let's talk. Page 199
Time: 15–20 minutes

> This exercise is a general review of the uses of *can* and *could,* comparing them with other modals. This speaking activity gives students plenty of opportunities to use the target grammar and discuss everyone's favorite topic, himself / herself, so allow students to take their time with this.

❏ EXERCISE 33. Let's listen and talk.
Page 200
Time: 10–15 minutes

> Prepare students for the exercise by asking them about their own abilities and telling them they will compare their abilities with the research presented in the audio.
>
> Note how the definition of *can* changes with the age groups discussed in the audio. The college students *can,* in a literal sense, *dance, sing,* and *draw* (just as small children can), but not many define *can* as having a special skill rather than simply an innate ability.
>
> There is no "correct" answer to the discussion questions. Responses will probably mention that children are less self-conscious than adults and more able to express themselves naturally through their movement.

- Prior to having students listen to the audio, ask them for a show of hands: *How many of you can dance? sing? draw?*

- Lead the discussion as it is intended: a short communication opportunity.

- Don't put too much emphasis on modal usage. If good modal usage occurs naturally and appropriately, that is great, but don't require or force it.

Expansion: You might also discuss how our innate artistic abilities to express ourselves may become suppressed as we get older. Explanations for this may include (and you can raise these if students don't themselves):

> We gain an enhanced awareness and sensitivity to others' judgments as we age.
>
> We set new standards for ourselves based on comparisons with others or adopted societal standards, etc.

CHART 10-7. Using *Would* to Express a Repeated Action in the Past. Page 200
Time: 10 minutes

> Compared to *used to,* "habitual *would*" is somewhat more formal. *Would* is often preferred in writing, whereas *used to* may be preferred in speech.
>
> Note the important limitation on *would:* it cannot express a situation, only an action.
>
> This use of *would* is unusual in British English.

- Write the following heading on the board: *Would (instead of Used to) for Habitual Past Action.*

- Now ask three students to tell you something they used to do as children. It may help to specify a particular time in childhood (elementary school years, teenage years). For example:

    You: *Pablo, what did you used to do after school when you were a teenager?*
    Pablo: *I used to play football every day.*
    You: *Because Pablo is describing a past action (not a past situation), we can substitute "would" for "used to."*

- Write the new *would* sentence on the board as students produce it and dictate it to you.

    Pablo <u>would</u> play football every day when he was a teenager.

- Go over the remainder of the chart with students.

❏ EXERCISE 35. Looking at grammar.
Page 200
Time: 15–20 minutes

Optional Vocabulary
anthropology
archeological
expedition
arrowhead
unearthed

CHART 10-8. Expressing Preference:
Would Rather. Page 201
Time: 10–15 minutes

> In a question, either the word *or* or the word *than* can follow *would rather*:
>
> *Would you rather eat fruit or candy?*
>
> *Would you rather eat fruit than candy?*
>
> In a negative question, only the word *than* is possible for a preference:
>
> *Wouldn't you rather eat fruit than candy?*

- Write the title of the chart on the board as a heading.
- Begin by asking students what activities they prefer or like better. For example:

  Would you rather study modals or math?
  Would you rather go out to eat than fix dinner at home?

- Write their answers on the board:

  Vicenzo *would rather study* modals than math.
  Fatima *would rather go* out to eat *than fix* dinner at home.

- In a similar fashion, illustrate past (*would rather have* + *past participle*) and progressive (*would rather* + *be* + *-ing*) form by using student-generated information.

❏ EXERCISE 37. Looking at grammar.
Page 202
Time: 5 minutes

> The contraction *'d* is often difficult to hear and may be difficult for some learners to pronounce. Sometimes students omit it because they don't hear it. Encourage students to use *'d* contractions in their spoken answers and correct their pronunciation.

❏ EXERCISE 38. Let's talk: interview.
Page 202
Time: 10 minutes

> In order to engage and support students, you might try a round-robin sequence like this:
>
> Teacher to A: *What would you rather do than go to class?*
>
> Speaker A: *I'd rather go bowling than go to class.*
>
> Teacher to B: *What would you rather do than go bowling?*
>
> Speaker B: *I'd rather play chess than go bowling.*
>
> Teacher to C: *What would you rather do than play chess?*

CHART 10-9. Combining Modals
with Phrasal Modals. Page 202
Time: 10–15 minutes

> Some other possible sequences in (c), with a phrasal modal combined with another phrasal modal are: *be supposed to be able to, have (got) to be able to, used to have to, used to be able to, didn't use to be able to, be going to have to, be supposed to have to.*

- Write the heading / chart title on the board.
- Explain to students that a modal cannot <u>immediately</u> be followed by another modal, and write on the board the incorrect example sentence (or one of your own devising, using students' information) from (a).
- Cross out the part that is incorrect and show that modals can be combined with other complete phrasal modals. For example:

  Wei-Hsuan won't ~~able to~~ be able to come to class tomorrow.

- Go over the chart with students.

CHART 10-10. Summary Chart of Modals
and Similar Expressions. Pages 204–205
Time: varies

> By the time students reach this chart, they should be familiar with its contents. It summarizes what they have been learning since the beginning of Chapter 9.
>
> The term *similar expressions* in the chart title refers to phrasal modals.

- Tell students that you are not going to present this summary chart on the board the way you typically do, but that this is a reference chart that they should look at often.

❏ EXERCISE 42. Let's talk. Page 206
Time: 10 minutes

> In addition to a review of grammar, this kind of exercise provides students with the opportunity to develop their speaking skills by explaining something they already know and understand. It challenges students to express themselves in spoken English. Encourage students to invent possible contexts as a way of explaining differences in meaning.
>
> In some items, there is no difference in meaning; in other items there are distinct differences in meaning. In still other items, there might be a subtle difference in politeness or in forcefulness.

- Tell students that all of the sentences in this exercise are grammatically correct.
- Ask leading questions to elicit student interpretations of meaning. Be prepared to rephrase your questions in many ways in order to prompt students' responses.

❏ EXERCISE 43. Looking at grammar.
Page 207
Time: 10–15 minutes

- Tell students that they only have to think of one possible answer and not all the possibilities.

Optional Vocabulary
spring break	accompanied
compulsory	chaperone
cautious	

❏ EXERCISE 47. Let's talk. Page 209
Time: 10–30 minutes

Sometimes students get rather excited about a particular topic and don't want to stop, so you may need to set a time limit. The given ideas are, for the most part, overstated generalizations of opinions that need to be qualified, explained, and supported. To conclude the exercise, you might ask the students to rewrite or expand on a sentence given in the textbook so that all members of the group agree with the idea, or you might have each group present several sides to the argument.

If these topics are unfamiliar or uncomfortable for your students, you might add some others that are closer to their immediate interests. Topics about their school, sports, clothing fashions, etc. may be productive. These topics can be used for a writing assignment.

Optional Vocabulary
influences
banned
censored
agencies

❏ EXERCISE 48. Let's talk or write. Page 210
Time: 10–15 minutes

- Explain that a short paragraph should contain five to eight sentences.
- Remind students to begin with a topic sentence and that subsequent sentences should support this introductory one.
- Set a time limit for students and collect their work.
- When marking these paragraphs, focus on modals and verb tenses, and weight these target structures more heavily than non-target ones.

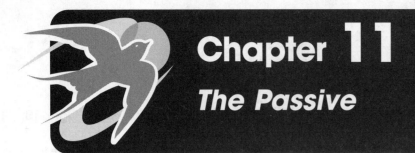

CHAPTER SUMMARY

OBJECTIVE: In speaking and writing, about one sentence in eight uses the passive structure. In scientific, academic, and informative reporting, usage increases to about one passive in every three sentences. The passive allows one to focus on actions and the receivers of actions, but it does not require identification of the agent because often it is not important or necessary to know who did something. Although the passive is a useful structure, learners should be encouraged to continue using active sentences for direct, forceful, or persuasive purposes when the agent is known.

APPROACH: Students are given plenty of practice in forming and using passive sentences throughout the chapter. Special attention is given to passive modals, the verb *get* as a passivizer, and the often confusing participial adjectives (e.g., *interesting* vs. *interested*). With the charts and tenses, students learn to use various tenses with the passive and to decide whether to use the passive or active form.

TERMINOLOGY: It is assumed that students understand the grammatical terms "subject," "object," and "(in)transitive verb." The term "*by*-phrase" is used for the prepositional phrase that includes the agent of the verb's action.

❏ EXERCISE 1. Warm-up. Page 211
Time: 5 minutes

- For clarity's sake, have students write the warm-up sentences on the board, and write the letters **S**, **V**, and **O** over the subject, verb, and object, respectively. For example, with item 1:

      S   V   O
  The girl hit the ball.

  And with item 2:

      S   V
  The ball was hit by the girl.

- Having identified these three basic parts of speech visually, and noticing the *by*-phrase, it should become apparent that item 6 is the incorrect one.

  Expansion: Before or after Exercise 1, you might want to demonstrate the passive in all the tenses. Ask students to assist you and then include their actions in your sentences. For example:

  (Omar) touches his book, then takes his hand from it.

    You: *Omar touched the book.*
    Students: *The book was touched by Omar.*

(You touch the book with your hand and do not take your hand from it.)

  You: *I am touching the book.*
  Students: *The book is being touched by you.*

Continue to work through all the verb tenses in this manner.

CHART 11-1. Active vs. Passive. Page 211
Time: 10–15 minutes

> Students must understand the difference between transitive and intransitive verbs; refer them to the Appendix if they need to review this. Some other languages use transitivity in very different ways, leading some students to make mistakes in English.
>
> INCORRECT: *The accident was happened.* OR *My shoe was fallen off.*

- Write the heading *Active vs. Passive* on the board.
- To both teach the form and demonstrate why the passive even exists, create a fictional sentence with the help of your students, using their names. Make sure the content involves one of them wronging another. For example: Say *Let's suppose . . .* and write:

  Hiroko punched Pablo.

- Now ask a student to come up to the board and identify the subject, verb, and object by writing **S**, **V**, and **O** over the appropriate words. For example:

     S   V   O
  Hiroko punched Pablo.

- Tell students that passive voice makes the object, or recipient, of an action the subject and de-emphasizes the role of the original doer of the action.
- Ask students *who* received the action, or was the object in the original sentence, and write this as the new subject.

     S
  Pablo

- Then explain that the passive is formed by using the helping verb *to be* in whatever tense is needed (in this case, it is past) and adding the past participle.
- Write the cues *helping verb + past participle* directly under the word *Passive* in the heading.
- Then have students give you the remainder of the new passive sentence and label it.

     S   V
  Pablo was hit.

- Tell students that one of the main reasons to use passive is to talk about the action without discussing who did it. Go back to the last sentence on the board and show that it is complete: We know what the action was and who received it — but the sentence can be complete without stating who did the hitting.
- Explain that the *by*-phrase can be added, if appropriate or desired, but that often it is not needed or wanted.
- To drive this point home, ask "Hiroko" whether she would like to add *by Hiroko* to the example on the board. Whether she does or doesn't, emphasize that responsibility for the action falls to her once we put in the *by*-agent. Without it, we don't know, and perhaps don't care, who did the hitting.
- Write the terms *Transitive* and *Intransitive* on the board.
- Write a sample sentence beneath each. You can illustrate transitive by drawing an arrow from subject to object and explain that the action of the verb is quite literally transferred from one to the other. For example:

    Transitive

    S   V   O

    Marta ate her lunch.

- Explain that intransitive verbs such as *come, die, happen, fall,* and *exist* cannot take an object and that as such, these verbs cannot have a passive structure.
- Write the following example:

    Intransitive

    S   V

    Hsing fell down.

- Again, draw an arrow, but make this arrow circle the subject itself. Explain that with intransitive verbs the action revolves only around the subject and doesn't get transferred anywhere.
- Go over the remainder of the chart.

❏ EXERCISE 3. Warm-up. Page 212
Time: 10 minutes

- Remind students that they need to be careful. The tense change is made is in the helping verb *to be,* and the participle itself remains the same.
- Go through the warm-up slowly.

CHART 11-2. Tense Forms of the Passive.
Page 213
Time: 10–15 minutes

The purpose of this chart is to allow students to see the transformation of each active tense to its passive counterpart. In reviewing these tense forms, you might have students change some of the statements into questions or negatives. This focuses their attention on the required use of the auxiliary *be* in every passive sentence.

- Before referencing this chart, enlist students to come up with an active sentence for each tense and form its passive versions. Doing so will reinforce the contents of Chart 11-1 and will highlight the necessary passive changes.
- Pick two students' names and create a simple present sentence "starring" these two students. Write the simple present sentence on the board. With the help of your students, transform each tense to passive voice.
- Remind students that they need to change each part of the helping verb to the appropriate tense but that the participle remains the same.
- Create a chart similar to Chart 11-2 on the board. Write the name of each tense on the far left and label both an *Active* and *Passive* column to the right.
- Underline the verb transformations. Highlight the *by*-phrase. For example:

	Active	*Passive*
Simple Present	*Tim loves Sue.*	*Sue is loved by Tim.*

- Go over the chart and make sure students understand how to create passive-voice questions.

❏ EXERCISES 4 and 5. Looking at
grammar. Page 213
Time: 10–15 minutes each

These two exercises can be done orally, in writing, or you can use a combination of both depending on the level of your class and how quickly they grasp the concept of passive voice.

For less advanced classes, it may be beneficial to have students transform some, if not all, of the sentences in writing first.

More advanced classes may benefit from transforming the sentences orally.

For Exercise 5, you may want to ask a student to remind the class what intransitive verbs are before you begin and write pertinent information on the board. For example:

Intransitive Verbs

action revolves around the subject

no object

no passive voice

CHART 11-3. Using the Passive. Page 214
Time: 10–15 minutes

Point out that a combination of factors determines when the *by*-phrase is omitted. It is not used:

—when it can easily be assumed who, in general, performs such an action (*Rice is grown "by farmers." Arithmetic is taught "by teachers," etc.*). In such cases, the *by*-phrase is implied.

—when the speaker doesn't know who performed the action. (*The house was built in 1890 "by some unknown people who engaged in house building." My shoes were made in Italy "by some unknown shoemakers," etc.*)

—when the focus is on the action, and it is not important to know who performed the action. (*This olive oil was imported from Spain "by people in a company that imports olive oil." It's not important to know who these people are. The focus is solely on the origin of the olive oil.*)

COMPARE: The active is usually used when the agent is specifically known. (*Mr. Lee grows rice on his farm. Ms. Hill teaches arithmetic in elementary school. My grandfather built our house. The Acme Trading Company imports olive oil from Spain.*)

The *by*-phrase is included (in other words, the passive voice is used even when there is an acceptable active equivalent with a known agent) when the speaker wants to focus attention on the <u>receiver</u> of the action, rather than the agent.

- Write the title *Using the Passive* on the board.
- Before looking at Chart 11-3, ask students what items are produced in their respective countries. These items can be food, building materials, electronics, etc.
- Ask students to come up with passive sentences to describe the items produced in their countries.
- They should come up with variations on the following, which you can write on the board. For example:

    Coffee is grown in Colombia.
    Electronics are manufactured in Korea.

- Ask students <u>who</u> grows the Colombian coffee, and emphasize that because the answer (*coffee plantation owners, etc.*) is not specific and can be assumed, there is no reason to add the *by*-phrase.
- Then ask students to give you a passive sentence in response to your question:

    Who writes books?

- Write their responses on the board.

    Books are written by writers / authors.

- Elicit whether the *by*-phrase is necessary in this case.
- Next, ask students who wrote their grammar book. They should give you a passive sentence and *by*-phrase as appropriate.
- Write their response on the board.

    This book is written by Betty Azar and Stacy Hagen.

- Explain that the *by*-phrase is meaningful when there is a specific actor or agent involved, and elicit more examples of appropriate *by*-phrase use from students.

❏ EXERCISE 7. Looking at grammar.
Page 214
Time: 5–10 minutes

- Have students read the sentences aloud and discuss why passive voice is appropriate in each case.
- Ask students leading questions about the sentences, such as:

    Why is the passive used here instead of the active?
    Who is the actor or agent?
    Can we even know who, specifically, did this action?
    Change the sentence to its active form; what's the difference in meaning or forcefulness?

Expansion: Have students look for 5–10 examples of passive voice outside of class and copy them onto a piece of paper. If it is possible to bring in the original text (for example, from a newspaper or magazine), they should do so. In any case, the original source for each passive sentence should be clear. Have students either write on the board or swap among themselves two or three of the passive sentences.

Based on each actual sentence, the remainder of the class has to guess its original source. You can then write three column headings on the board and have students discuss the source's rationale for passive structure.

Specific Agent not Known
De-emphasize Agent
Emphasize Process

Sample rationales:

If the sentence comes from a magazine article describing the building of hybrid cars, it is likely that the specific agents are not known.

If it is a scientific article discussing a new medical technique, the author wants to emphasize the process because the process itself is fascinating.

If it is a newspaper or internet article describing an unpopular civic action, the passive may be used to hide or obscure the fact that a particular government or organization is the one doing it.

❏ EXERCISE 8. Reading and grammar.
Page 215
Time: 15 minutes

Optional Vocabulary
rubbed	formulas
substances	synthetic
bark	

❏ EXERCISE 11. Looking at grammar.
Page 216
Time: 5–10 minutes

- Write on the board a real headline from the day's actual news.
- Ask students to identify which parts of speech are omitted in news headlines. Elicit from students the fact that helping verbs (which comprise passive verbs) and articles are regularly left out.

- Put students into groups to complete the exercise, and correct by having group members write full sentences on the board.

❏ EXERCISE 12. Game. Page 216
Time: 10–20 minutes

> This should be a fast-paced exercise. If you lead the exercise, you may want to add specifics that make the items relevant to your students' lives; for example:
>
> *Someone invited you to a reception for international students held at Berg Hall.* OR *Someone is televising the final match of the French Open on Channel 5 this coming Saturday.*
>
> As students speak, pay special attention to their pronunciation of -ed endings. Often they tend to omit them or add unnecessary vowel sounds.

- In order to heighten motivation, give each team a 45-second time limit for each item.
- Explain that the other team(s) should judge whether each sentence given is correct.
- If teams disagree about whether inclusion of the *by*-phrase is necessary, refer to Chart 11-3.

❏ EXERCISE 13. Let's talk. Page 217
Time: 10 minutes

- Have three students model the exercise format first to ensure that everyone understands the instructions. Emphasize that Student A changes the sentence to passive and Student B uses the information to answer the second question.
- Lead the exercise as directed in the text, having students keep their books closed and attention on the oral cues given by you.

❏ EXERCISE 16. Looking at grammar.
Page 219
Time: 10–15 minutes

> This exercise is a review of tenses in both active and passive voices.

- Give students time to complete the exercise individually before correcting as a class.
- In passive sentences, discuss why the passive is used and why it is preferable to the active.
- For the longer items 7, 8, and 9, you can also ask students to summarize without repeating verbatim from their books. Point out and praise proper use of the passive in the summaries.

Optional Vocabulary
ecology	exposed
test pilot	industrial
age discrimination	habitats

CHART 11-4. The Passive Form of Modals and Phrasal Modals. Page 220
Time: 10–15 minutes

> This chart assumes that students are familiar with the meanings of modal auxiliaries (Chapter 9).
>
> Remind students that a modal is always immediately followed by the simple form of a verb, in this case *be* and *have*.
>
> You might add examples relevant to your students' lives. Have them change passive sentences to active.
>
> Examples:
>
> *This room has to be cleaned.* → *Someone has to clean this room.*
>
> *Olga should be told about tomorrow's test.* → *Someone should tell Olga about . . .*

- Write the chart title on the board.
- Remind students that like transforming any other active sentence to passive, the important point is to ensure that the modal itself (which in this case is the main verb) is correct. Passive modals precede the verb *be* + the past participle, which remain constant.
- Ask your students to give you an active-voice sentence that refers to a context familiar to all in the class. For example:

    Our teacher has scheduled our final test for the last day of class.

- Now write all the modals from the chart on the board, and assist students as they create passive forms using each modal and the information included in the example sentence.
- Explain that the past-passive modal forms are simply the passive versions of past modals such as *should have, must have, could have,* and *ought to have.*
- Go over examples (i), (j), (k), and (l) in Chart 11-4. Have students transform those passive sentences to active sentences. Doing so will help them recognize that they have, in fact, worked with these complex, active modals before.

❏ EXERCISE 18. Looking at grammar.
Page 221
Time: 10–20 minutes

- Give students time to work through this exercise individually.
- As a class, compare similar items so that students can see the differences in pairs of sentences where one is passive and the other is active.
- Correct students' pronunciation carefully so that they clearly convey the tense and whether active or passive by enunciating verb endings.

Optional Vocabulary
spoil	personnel department
engineering firm	belated
competing	labor union
chores	

❏ EXERCISE 20. Let's talk. Page 223
Time: 10 minutes

- Have students work in pairs or groups to come up with two or three passive modals for each rule.

    Expansion: In groups, have students come up with rules or behavioral norms in passive modal format for a particular situation.

    Students should not say what setting the rules or norms are intended to control. After students have had a chance to make up a set of norms or rules, each group can then read their set of rules aloud to the class, and other groups can guess what the setting / situation is. For example:

    Liquids must not be brought in your handbag or backpack.

    Knives, sharp instruments, and/or weapons of any kind cannot be brought on board.

    Seat belts should be worn at all times unless a passenger is moving about the cabin.

    All electronic devices have to be turned off during takeoff and landing.

    The cockpit cannot be entered except by authorized personnel.

    What setting are these rules for?

    Flying on an airplane.

    Additional settings include:

    driving a car

    using a snow blower or lawn mower

    skiing

    riding a bike or motorcycle in traffic

    walking a dog in public

    visiting or being a patient in a hospital

    visiting an important public building

    taking a standardized test such as the TOEFL exam

    voting

    swimming in a public pool

    attending a live performance at a theater

    interviewing for a job

    passing through immigration while traveling

    dining in a fancy restaurant

    attending an English class

❏ EXERCISE 21. Looking at grammar.
Page 223
Time: 10–15 minutes

> Students may enjoy experimenting with various combinations here. Be prepared to explain in item 2 that in the U.S., by custom, a wedding ring is worn on the next-to-last finger of the left hand.

- Encourage more than one completion for each sentence, and give students time to come up with alternative completions.
- Review the expected and alternative completions as a class.

Optional Vocabulary

lap	serve
embarrass	endangered

❏ EXERCISE 22. Listening and grammar.
Page 224
Time: 15–20 minutes

Part I
- Make sure that students keep their books closed and focus on the content of the lecture.
- Then have students choose all the correct restatements in each set for items 1–7.

Part II
- Play the audio again and have students complete the cloze exercise. Correct as a class.
- As many of your students may remember or even have experienced such a natural disaster in recent history, you may want to discuss the content after you have completed the cloze.

    Expansion: After using the audio to spur a discussion of natural disasters and weather phenomena with your students, instruct them to come up with passive modals to protect people in such situations. For example:

    a hurricane

    People should be evacuated away from the coast or areas that flood easily.

    Windows ought to be reinforced in order to protect them from high winds.

    Big outdoor items (swing sets, picnic tables) should be tied down or brought inside.

❏ EXERCISE 23. Looking at grammar.
Page 225
Time: 15–20 minutes

> Be sure to point out during discussion that this passage illustrates a typical way in which the passive voice is advantageously and appropriately used. Passive voice is commonly used in a technical description in which information about the agents is unimportant and / or unknown.

- Have students identify why this passage lends itself to passive structure (no one knows precisely who does what action, and the agents are far less important than the processes.
- Each student can transform the sentences in each paragraph, or you may assign each paragraph to a different group.
- Discuss appropriate passive forms for each modal.
- For further discussion, you may want to ask the following questions:

    Will paper ever become outmoded?

    At some point in the future, will all written communication, including books, be composed, transmitted, received, and read electronically?

What are some of the pros of reading books made of paper versus reading books on a screen?

Expansion: Discuss the organization of the reading passage. It has an introduction (that announces the subject) leading to a thesis sentence: *Today people make paper from wood pulp by using either a mechanical or a chemical process.*

The second paragraph discusses one topic: the mechanical process.

The third paragraph is about the chemical process.

The fourth paragraph concludes the process of making paper from wood pulp.

The description of the process itself is in sequential order.

The last paragraph contains a conclusion, stating the general belief that this process is important to the modern world.

❏ **EXERCISE 24.** Let's write. Page 226
Time: 15 minutes

You might want to set a limit on the length of these of these compositions e.g., 10 to 15 sentences. Expect that your students will have some difficulty in trying to translate explanations from another language into English; tell them to use only English sources either from the internet or the library. If your students don't have access to the internet, they could interview a local expert, parent, or acquaintance about how some object is made.

Another possibility is for you to invite an expert such as a ceramicist, weaver, or carpenter to speak to the class. The students can take notes as the basis for their compositions.

Another alternative is for you to photocopy a description of a process. First, discuss the process, and analyze with the class the use of the passive in the passage. Then tell students to put the passage aside and write about the process in their own words.

You may choose to ask students to underline every example of a passive in their papers after they have finished writing and revising them. This helps you in marking their successes and errors. It also helps the students check their own use of the passive. Another possibility is for students to read each other's compositions and underline each instance of the passive.

You might assign the first topic as an in-class writing test and use the second topic as a homework assignment.

CHART 11-5. Non-Progressive Passive.
Page 227
Time: 10–15 minutes

The non-progressive passive is frequently used in both spoken and written English.

In Exercise 26, item 7 shows that the non-progressive passive can also describe an existing state in the past. As the chart itself only shows present-time examples, you may want to mention usage in past time in your discussion of the chart.

Example: *Tim tried to open the door (last night), but it was locked. = Someone had locked it prior to Tim's trying to open the door.*

- To demonstrate the difference between regular passive and non-progressive passive, close your book and say *I just closed my book.* Write this sentence on the board.
- Have your students change your original sentence to passive voice, and write this new passive version on the board.

    The book was closed by me. (describes an action)

- Then introduce a new sentence describing the condition or state of the book. Say and write: *Now the book is closed.* (describes an existing state)
- Lead students through another such explanation with a different classroom example.
- Have a student (Ali) break a piece of chalk or tear a piece of paper.

    Ali broke the chalk.
    The chalk was broken by Ali.
    Now the chalk is broken.

- Write the chart title on the board.
- Underneath the word *Non-Progressive,* write the words *state, condition.* Explain that when the past participle of a verb is used as an adjective to describe a state or condition, the form is called *non-progressive passive.*
- Go over the chart with students and explain that the non-progressive passive can also be used to describe an existing state in the past as well as in the present.

❏ **EXERCISE 27.** Looking at grammar.
Page 228
Time: 10–15 minutes

- Give students time to choose the correct verb for each item and to come up with the correct non-progressive passive form.
- Many students confuse *get married* with *be married,* so you may want to write the following on the board when reviewing item 10:

    Pablo and Hiroko <u>got</u> married one year ago. Now they <u>are</u> married, and they have been married for one year.

CHART 11-6. Common Non-Progressive Passive Verbs + Prepositions. Page 229
Time: 10 minutes

Choosing correct prepositions can be difficult for students; therefore, these phrases should be learned as whole units. The following exercises help in this process, but perfection at this stage of learning cannot be expected. The list in this chart is intended for reference, not for memorization, but learning styles do differ. Some students may set about memorizing the list on their own, while others will simply give it a minimal glance and put their learning emphasis into the exercises.

Learning prepositions is definitely worth students' time and attention, but it is not worth fretting over. Thus, the accompanying exercises are intended to help the students "educate their ears" so that eventually the correct prepositions will "sound right."

You may wish to try to explain the difference between *tired of* and *tired from*. *Tired of* is used to express that one has had enough of something, is now annoyed, and doesn't feel like doing it any longer. *Tired from* expresses that one is physically tired from doing a certain activity. For example: *I am pleasantly **tired** tonight **from** a good day's work in the garden.*

COMPARE:

*I'm **tired of** working in the garden* = I've been working in the garden and I don't want to do it anymore. I have had enough.

*I'm **tired from** working in the garden* = The reason that I am physically tired is that I worked (or I am still working) in the garden.

- Write the chart title on the board and illustrate the target structure with a few examples.

  Common Non-Progressive Passive Verbs + Prepositions

	Non-Progressive Passive	+ Preposition	
Ronaldo	is concerned	about	taking the TOEIC.
Miyuki	is interested	in	learning Swahili.

- Discuss with students the fact that all learners (no matter what their background) have difficulty learning preposition combinations.
- Explain that correct usage will come with time and experience and that they can use Chart 11-6 for reference.
- Reassure students that by doing exercises and reading and listening in English, in general, they will begin to hear which prepositions are right. Tell students that they will become familiar with the correct combinations over time.

❏ EXERCISES 29–34. Pages 229–232

Exercises 29–34 all deal with using prepositions correctly. The following are some suggestions for practicing and reinforcing preposition use.

1. Ask students to say the entire sentence, not just the preposition. This gives students a chance to say and hear the whole phrase in context.

2. At the end of an item, ask another student to repeat the information in the item without looking at the book by asking him/her to repeat the correct combination. Asking leading questions, such as (for Exercise 29, item 2), *What is Maya known for?*

3. At the conclusion of the exercise, review it orally with students' books closed, by reading an item up to the blank and prompting/asking the class to supply the preposition. For example (for item 3):

   Teacher: *She is interested . . .*

   Class: *in*

   Teacher: *She is interested **in** how children play with one another.*

4. Use the items in the exercise or chart and ask students about their lives: *Kyung Won, is there anything in your future that you are particularly excited **about**?*

5. Give one student a past participle to use in a question posed to another student. For example:

   Teacher: *accustomed*

   Speaker A: *Kim, are you accustomed **to** the food in the U.S.?*

   Kim: *No, I'm not accustomed **to** this kind of cooking.*

❏ EXERCISE 33. Let's talk. Page 231
Time: 5–10 minutes

Expansion: Have students formulate six interview questions, one for each of the non-progressive passives given. They can use the model from the book or come up with variations of their own. Have students interview six native speakers, using their interview questions and reporting the answers back to the class for further discussion.

CHART 11-7. The Passive with *Get*.
Page 233
Time: 10–15 minutes

Get has a meaning similar to *become;* in other words, it signals a changing situation or an altered state. Students at this level are generally quite familiar with this use of *get,* although they may not have recognized that it has a passive form, meaning, and use.

The passive with *get* is common, especially in spoken English. It is a somewhat informal structure, although it can, at times, be found even in formal writing.

- Write the chart title on the board and underneath the word *Get* write (*similar to "become"*).
- Create a sample sentence on the board with students, using the context at hand and focusing on the students' experience of learning grammar. For example:

  We are getting excited about the upcoming holidays.

  Sometimes students get anxious about prepositions, but they are not worth worrying about.

- To further discuss the meaning of *get,* have students make up their own sentences with **get** + *adjective* using the adjectives from the chart, almost all of which your students should know well. They may also use the past participles.
- Write some of their sample sentences on the board and highlight the correct use of *get.* For example:

  Tanya gets angry when her roommate borrows her clothes without asking.

  Victor got full before he could finish his meal.

  It's getting warm in here. Let's open a window.

- Explain that, as with the previous chart, they are not expected to learn all adjectives and past participles that are combined with *get* but rather, they should use this chart as a reference and the accompanying exercises to train their ears.

❏ **EXERCISE 38.** Let's talk: interview.
Page 235
Time: 10–20 minutes

- Have students get up and move around the room as they interview one another.
- Instruct them to take notes on one another's answers. Tell them that they will be asked to report back at least one specific response from another classmate.
- Circulate and participate in the interview as much as you feel appropriate. If students are shy or reluctant, you may need to help keep the conversation going.
- When students have gathered information, have each one report back to the class and describe what they learned about one another.
- In order to make sure that each student's information is discussed, you can lead the discussion by saying *Can someone tell me about a time that Juan Pablo got lost?* and continue in this way until each student has spoken and each student has been reported on.

CHART 11-8. Participial Adjectives.
Page 236
Time: 10 minutes

The active meaning of the present participle (the *-ing* form) is also observed in the progressive. (See Chapter 2.)

A frequent error learners make is the substitution of an active participle (for example, *interesting*), where a passive one is required.

This grammar point is dealt with in this chapter because it is a structure in which a passive meaning is compared with an active meaning.

- Write the chart title on the board.
- Write two sentences about your class using a student's name and containing active and passive participial adjectives. For example:

  Miguel is boring in grammar class.

  Miguel is bored in grammar class.

- Ask students which of the sentences above is a comment about you, the teacher, and which is a comment about Miguel, the student.
- Explain that if Miguel is boring, he causes others to be bored. In contrast, if he is bored, others cause him to feel that way.
- Go over the chart with students.
- Explain that the point of the chart is to highlight that both forms of the participial adjectives are possible.

❏ **EXERCISE 41.** Looking at grammar.
Page 236
Time: 10 minutes

This is a simple, straightforward exercise that helps students understand the basics of the information in the chart. One might say this exercise is "too easy," but something is easy only if one already knows how to do it. For some students, this is a difficult grammar point, and for many teachers not always an easy one to explain. This exercise allows you and your students to see how much they understand before proceeding.

Often, a person receives the emotion and is described with the passive participle. Similarly, a thing or event causes the feeling and is described by the active one, but this is by no means a strict rule.

- Encourage students to ask questions and discuss meanings during this exercise.
- Reiterate that the present participle has an active ("giving" or "causing") meaning, but that the past participle has a passive ("taking" or "receiving") meaning.
- Be ready to rephrase questions from the items. For example:

  Who is excited?

  What excites them?

❏ EXERCISE 42. Let's talk. Page 237
Time: 5–10 minutes

> This exercise is designed to reinforce students'
> understanding of the concepts underlying the use of
> participial adjectives.
>
> To review grammar in real contexts, ask students "real"
> questions, using the verbs in this exercise. For
> example:
>
> *Roberto, can you tell us about something you have*
> *found confusing?*
>
> *Ibrahim, have you ever been confused?*
>
> *Who has had an amazing experience? Tell us about a*
> *time you were really amazed.*
>
> *Etc.*

- You can be Speaker A for items 1–5 in order to
  effectively model the task at hand.
- After item 5, let pairs of students take over for the rest
  of the items. Make sure that students understand that
  they are to ask the question *How would you*
  describe . . . ? as the second part in each item.

❏ EXERCISE 44. Listening. Page 238
Time: 5 minutes

- Ask students to explain the meanings of *fascinating /*
  fascinated, thrilling / thrilled, shocking / shocked,
  delightful / delighted, and *confusing / confused* before
  playing the audio.
- Review the completions as a class.

❏ EXERCISE 48. Let's talk. Page 240
Time: 10–20 minutes

- Put students into groups and instruct them that each
  group member will report back to the class one piece
  of information about another member.
- Ask each group to also present which items they had
  similar responses to.

❏ EXERCISE 49. Let's talk or write. Page 240
Time: 10–15 minutes

- In groups, ask students to discuss all three topics and
  share opinions about them while keeping notes.
  Explain that this discussion should help them prepare
  for their written response.
- Have students write a response to one of the topics. If
  appropriate, share the written responses.

❏ EXERCISE 50. Check your knowledge.
Page 241
Time: 10–20 minutes

- To use this as an in-class review, give students time to
  correct all the errors they find independently.
- Review as a group, having students take turns reading
  the corrected items aloud.
- Because it is important that students hear the correct
  usage of non-progressive passive with prepositions
  and participial adjectives, have them read the entire
  sentence (not just the correction), and have them
  pronounce the correct endings of participial adjectives
  carefully.

Optional Vocabulary
convince
caterpillar

Chapter 12
Noun Clauses

CHAPTER SUMMARY

OBJECTIVE: One of the most common needs when speaking and writing is to report what was said by someone else. Another very common purpose is to express an opinion about, or reaction to, some situation. Therefore, speakers begin many sentences with "he / she / they said" and "I think" (or their equivalents) followed by a noun clause. The objective of this chapter is to learn to recognize and correctly form noun clauses, which, as stated above, are necessary to converse successfully. Learners should pay special attention in this chapter to <u>the order of words</u> in a noun clause.

APPROACH: The chapter focuses attention on the words that introduce noun clauses. It begins by focusing on the use of question words and the confusing similarity between noun clauses and questions. The students transform questions into noun clauses. Then many of the variations in the use of *that*-clauses are presented. Next, the students learn to punctuate quoted speech and then to make adjustments in verb forms and pronouns as they change quotes into reported speech. Added to the end of the chapter are two short sections, one on the subjunctive in noun clauses and one on words such as *whatever, whoever, whenever, etc.*

TERMINOLOGY: Noun clauses are referred to variously as "embedded sentences, embedded questions, indirect speech, nominal clauses" or certain kinds of complements. Words used to introduce noun clauses are labeled conjunctions in most dictionaries. Quoted and reported speech is also called "direct and indirect address / speech / discourse." Question words are also called *Wh*-words or "interrogatives (interrogative pronouns, interrogative adjectives, interrogative adverbs)." Information questions are also called "*Wh*-questions."

❏ EXERCISE 1. Warm-up. Page 242
Time: 5 minutes

- Before beginning, ask students to tell you what the parts of a complete sentence are, and write their ideas on the board.
- Put the term *Complete Sentence* in the middle of the board and write ideas and suggestions as spokes on a wheel.
- Tell students that the point of such brainstorming is to activate what they already know about complete sentences. For example, students may say any or all of the following:

    subject and verb
    clause

    starts with a capital letter and finishes with a period
    complete thought
    independent clause

- Then have students check those items that are complete sentences.

CHART 12-1. Introduction. Page 242
Time: 15 minutes

- Write the heading *Clause* on one side of the board and *Sentence* on the other.
- Write the following items (or some variation adapted to your students' lives) on the board:

    Suzanna left the room quickly.
    That Suzanna left the room quickly

- Ask a student to go to the board and label the subject and verb in the first item. Ask another student to do the same with the second item.

        S   V
    Suzanna left the room quickly.

            S   V
    That Suzanna left the room quickly

- Ask students which sentence sounds like a complete sentence. Almost all will say the first one, and that starting the second one with *That* makes the second item sound incomplete.
- Explain that clauses that can stand alone and don't require another clause to make sense are independent clauses, and they can be sentences.
- Go over the chart with students.
- Reiterate that a noun clause can take the place of an object or subject, and write your own example or those from the chart on the board.
- Illustrate the point clearly by replacing the noun with a noun clause in the examples you write on the board.
- Explain to students that a noun can be replaced with a noun clause.
- Write the following examples on the board:

    Pablo's dinner smelled delicious.
    <u>*What Pablo ate*</u> *smelled delicious.*

- In the second sentence, ask a student to mark the subject and verb of the noun clause by using small letters.

            s   v
    <u>*What Pablo ate*</u> *smelled delicious.*

- In the same sentence, ask a second student to find the main clause, and label the subject and the verb of the main clause using capital letters.

    S   V

    s   v

    <u>What Pablo ate</u> smelled delicious.

❏ **EXERCISE 3.** Looking at grammar.
Page 243
Time: 10 minutes

- Warn students they will find separate sentences as part of the same line of text, and they should be aware of this when adding punctuation and capitalization.
- Tell students to say each word silently to themselves (or to the class, if doing this as a group initially) so they can hear natural pauses and points of punctuation.

❏ **EXERCISE 4.** Looking at grammar.
Page 243
Time: 5–10 minutes

Expansion: Ask students (or pairs or groups) to make four more similar statements that other students can either agree or disagree with. Ask them to write these additional sentences on the board. When the board has 10 or 15 such sentences on it, go over each one, checking that the elements of a noun clause are there, that the word order is correct, and that the main clause is also correct. Possible new statements include (and there are infinitely more possibilities):

What politicians say is usually false.

What is happening to our planet is irrevocable.

What my friends believe influences my own beliefs.

What I do for work is extremely important to my future happiness.

I know what is best for me.

Other people know what is best for them.

How we live is damaging to the planet.

When we die is predetermined.

I can't support what my country does internationally.

I am in favor of what my country does internationally.

CHART 12-2. Noun Clauses Beginning with a Question Word. Page 244
Time: 15–20 minutes

It is often useful to substitute the pronoun *something* in the place of noun clauses. Then students replace this pronoun with a clause. For example:

Something *was interesting.*

What he said *was interesting.*

I heard **something**.

I heard **what he said**.

The main problem for most learners is word order. Also, they may try to use *do* or *did,* as in a question.

- Demonstrate when to use a noun clause introduced by a question word as follows:
- Ask one student to come to the front of the class, and tell him / her a secret "something." The "something" can be as mundane a message as *We are learning noun clauses* or as silly as you want to make it.
- Now write what you just did on the board.

    I just told Po-Han something. Po-Han now knows something.

- Explain that because the "something" is completely unknown, we can replace it with a noun clause beginning with a question word.
- Write the noun clause below *something,* and stress that the word order remains subject and then verb.

    Po-Han now knows something.
    what I said.

- Have a student label the main subject and verb with capital **S** and **V** and the subject and verb of the noun clause with a lower-case *s* and *v*.
- You should now have this on the board:

    S   V   *s   v*

    Po-Han knows what I said.

- Have Po-Han tell another student what you said, and then have the class come up with new sentences. Write these on the board.

    Silvia also knows what Martha said.
    Po-Han told Silvia what Martha said.

- Go over the chart and stress that noun clauses can take the place of both subjects and objects.

❏ **EXERCISE 6.** Looking at grammar.
Page 244
Time: 10–15 minutes

- Give students enough time to work through this exercise on their own first, and remind them to pay close attention to word order.
- Point out that if *who* is also the subject of the noun clause, the word order will be the same as the question.
- If your students seem to struggle with this exercise, write this two-step approach on the board:

    Step 1: *I don't know <u>something</u>.*
    Step 2: *I don't know <u>how old he is</u>.*
    Step 1: <u>*Something* was interesting.</u>
    Step 2: <u>*What he was talking about* was interesting.</u>

- Correct and review as a class by having students read and say the complete sentence, not just the noun clause, so that they can both say and hear the whole context.

Expansion: Ask students to write the complete sentences on the board and then use these to identify the noun clauses, discuss their grammatical function, and label the subjects and verbs in both dependent and independent clauses.

❏ EXERCISE 7. Looking at grammar.
Page 245
Time: 5–10 minutes

- Though students will be tempted to use question word order in the noun clause itself, keep reminding them that the only question they are asking is *Can you tell me . . . ?*
- Write the following prompt and model on the board as students make these transformations and say them aloud in turn.

  You: *Can you tell me . . . (noun clause)?*
  s   v

  Student(s): *. . . where Pietra lives?*

- Help students to self-correct, and make sure that everyone can hear each entire new question (containing a question-word noun clause).

❏ EXERCISE 8. Let's talk. Page 245
Time: 15 minutes

> This exercise has an uncomplicated pattern and can easily be used for pairwork.
>
> If you lead the exercise, you might want to change some of the items so that they are more directly related to experiences in your students' lives. This exercise can start slowly and get faster as students get accustomed to the pattern. There is no need to rush, however. Allow spontaneous interchanges to develop if students have interesting things they want to say. You may wish to select students at random instead of in a predictable order, or sometimes have the whole class respond in chorus to one or two items for a change of pace.
>
> Alternative format: Have students tell you to have someone else ask the question.
>
> You: *Where does Ali live?*
>
> Student: *I don't know. Ask him/Ali where he lives.*
>
> Or start a chain involving three students.
>
> You: *Maria, what is Ali's favorite color?*
>
> Student A (Maria): *I don't know. Roberto, ask Ali what his favorite color is.*
>
> Student B (Roberto): *Ali, what's your favorite color?*
>
> Student C (Ali): *Blue.*
>
> Write the pattern on the board:
>
> A: *I don't know. _____ , ask _____ .*
>
> B: *_____ , _____ ?*
>
> C: (answer) _____

- Tell students that though this pattern is easy, by repeating it and manipulating it, they will become used to the way noun clauses sound, and they will learn a bit about one another's lives.

- Explain that when asking more sensitive or personal questions, we often use the following phrases, which serve to soften the abruptness of such a direct question.

  Would you mind telling me . . .
  Do you mind if I ask . . .
  Could I ask you . . .

- Choose from the approaches above, and either lead the pattern or facilitate pairwork or small-group work.

❏ EXERCISE 10. Looking at grammar.
Page 247
Time: 5–10 minutes

> This exercise compares information questions and noun clauses that begin with a question word. The dialogues in this exercise give the students typical contexts in which noun clauses might be used, so be sure to point this out to your students.

CHART 12-3. Noun Clauses Beginning with *Whether* or *If.* Page 249
Time: 10 minutes

> The word *whether* always implies a choice — in this case, between *yes* and *no.*
>
> To avoid problems with the formal sequence of tenses in noun clauses, the main verbs in any material you might add or use for examples should not be put in a past form until the students reach Chart 12-7.

- Explain that *whether* and *if* noun clauses can be made from simple yes / no questions.
- Explain that *whether* and *if* clauses indicate that the noun clause may or may not be true, with equal likelihood in either case.
- Explain that *wonder* is commonly used with noun clauses in this way; it means, "I am considering both the yes and no versions of the noun clause."
- Model an example with students:

  I wonder whether (or not) the economy will improve (or not).
  I don't know if the economy will improve or not.

- Ask students to think of a question about the future that they really don't know the answer to and to put this in the form of a noun clause beginning with *whether.*
- Have two students write their sentences on the board. Now ask other students to identify the subjects and verbs of both the main clause and the noun clauses. For example:

  S V   s   v
  I wonder whether or not Colombia will beat England in the match on Saturday.

  S   V   s   v
  I don't know whether I will return to Boston or not.

Time: 5–10 minutes

> This exercise combines noun clauses that begin with question words and those that begin with *whether* and *if.*
>
> This exercise can be done rather quickly if you are the first speaker and a student merely gives the response. If, however, you set it up in the format below, the interactions will be more realistic, and students' responses will be a little less mechanical. For example:
>
> You: *Where is Yoko?*
>
> A to B: *I wonder where Yoko is.*
>
> B to C: *A wants to know where Yoko is. Do you know? What do you think?*
>
> C to B: *She's at home.* OR *I don't know where she is.*
>
> If students work in pairs, have them switch roles once or twice during the exercise.

❏ **EXERCISE 16.** Let's talk: interview.
Page 250
Time: 15–20 minutes

> Now that students have practiced noun clauses in a controlled way, they are prepared to learn more about the experiences of their classmates by using *Can / Could you tell me.*

Expansion: Have students make up their own additional questions and write them on an index card. They can then switch cards with another student before proceeding to ask questions.

You can also put students into rotating pairs as a fun way to give them the chance to have a new partner every few seconds.

CHART 12-4. Question Words Followed by Infinitives. Page 252
Time: 10 minutes

> This grammar point is an example of language flexibility — two ways to say exactly the same thing. The emphasis here is on the meaning of the infinitives in this structure.

• Create a sentence about one of your students in the following format:

  Diego can't decide what he should do about his roommate.

• Explain that the noun clause can be shortened by using an infinitive, and show this on the board.

                           to
  Diego can't decide what ~~he should~~ do about his roommate.

• Write another sentence about another student, and show the possible use of the infinitive:

                        to
  Mei doesn't know whether ~~she should~~ go hiking or not.

❏ **EXERCISE 22.** In your own words.
Page 252
Time: 10 minutes

• Give students the chance to work through the exercise on their own while you circulate and assist them as needed.

• Since students have come up with their own unique answers, ask multiple students to read aloud their answer for each item.

Optional Vocabulary
reception
dilemma

CHART 12-5. Noun Clauses Beginning with *That.* Page 253
Time: 15–20 minutes

> Using *that* in sentences such as the following is more common in formal writing than in everyday spoken English.
>
> *It was apparent **that** the suspect was lying.*
>
> Compare the uses of *that:*
>
> 1. *This is my coat. **That** coat / **that** one / **that** is yours.* (*That* is a demonstrative adjective/pronoun.)
>
> 2. *I don't have a coat. **That** is a problem in this cold weather.* (The demonstrative pronoun *that* refers to a whole sentence.)
>
> 3. *I bought a coat **that** has a hood. I showed my friend the coat (**that**) I bought.* (*That* is an adjective clause pronoun referring to the noun *coat.*)
>
> 4. *I think (**that**) Bob bought a new hat.* (**That** marks a noun clause and links it to the independent clause. It refers to nothing and has no semantic meaning. It is not a pronoun.)

• Write the chart title on the board and use the same approach as you did with Chart 12-2, substituting *something* for the noun clauses.

• Explain how *that* doesn't have to be included and it is often omitted in speaking.

• Make up two example sentences (one in which the noun clause replaces the subject and one in which it replaces the verb), using your students and their lives. Write the sentences on the board.

- It is easier for students to see the object noun clauses first, so start with:

  We hope <u>something</u>.

  We hope (<u>that</u>) Vilmar will bring us donuts again this morning.

- Now give students an example with a noun clause subject:

  <u>Something</u> is expected by all of us.

  (<u>That</u>) Maria had a great vacation is expected by all of us.

- Go over the rest of the chart, focusing on how to use *that*-clauses that follow the verb *be* and certain adjectives.

❏ EXERCISE 24. In your own words.
Page 254
Time: 10–15 minutes

> Students might produce some interesting personal responses to this exercise. If you think that they are shy about expressing their opinions in class, have them write their responses, to be seen only by you. Then you might also respond with your agreement or a differing point of view, in addition to marking errors in grammatical structures.

- In order to give students speaking practice, have students share their finished sentences in small groups.
- Go around to the different groups, facilitating, providing more sophisticated vocabulary if students are seeking such words, and helping make sure the noun clauses are in the right order.
- Tell students that though *that* is not as commonly used in speaking as in writing, using it may help them string all the parts of the noun clause together correctly.
- After students have spent some time discussing their completions in small groups, pick one or two completions for discussion as a class. Items 4 and 5 work particularly well for group discussion.

❏ EXERCISE 25. Let's talk: interview.
Page 254
Time: 10–15 minutes

- Ask students to try to remember (without writing notes) a classmate's answer for each of the seven items.
- Ask seven students to go to the board and write a classmate's response (or a near paraphrase of it).
- The rest of the class should correct the sentences written on the board.

❏ EXERCISE 26. Looking at grammar.
Page 254
Time: 10–15 minutes

- Before beginning this exercise, go through the words in the list and ask students to describe when they may use the words with *It is a. . . .*

- Make sure that students understand the appropriate use of the less familiar words and phrases such as *apparent, a pity, a shame, too bad,* and *unfortunate.*
- Review as a class.

Optional Vocabulary
abuse
ruin
entrance examination
principal

❏ EXERCISE 27. Game. Page 255
Time: 10–20 minutes

> **Expansion:** If you anticipate students enjoying this exercise, you may also want to prepare additional true and untrue trivia for students to work with. Having some Trivial Pursuit® cards on hand may help you expand upon this game with little preparation if appropriate.

❏ EXERCISE 29. Looking at grammar.
Page 255
Time: 5–10 minutes

- Have students make these changes on the spot, without prior preparation. (They have had, at this point, a fair amount of practice with this structure.)
- Correct students' pronunciation along with their use of the target grammar.

❏ EXERCISE 30. Let's talk. Page 256
Time: 10–15 minutes

> As students are working in groups, you may want to record some of the more memorable opinions and note who voiced them. You may be able to use these later in this chapter when presenting reported speech in Chart 12-7.

- Tell students that some of these statements will seem more factual, and others will seem more like opinions.
- Have students, in their small groups, explore and expand upon the facts and opinions. The statements should spur discussion, and you should encourage students to debate with one another, reminding them that being able to discuss such topics is a cultural expectation in the United States.
- Walk around and interact with groups as needed.

Optional Vocabulary
undeniable
aggressive
nurturing

❏ EXERCISE 31. Reading comprehension.
Page 256
Time: 10–20 minutes

Depending on the goals of your curriculum and whether students are also taking separate reading and writing classes, you may want to go over basic reading techniques of skimming and scanning, and set a time limit for students to focus on these skills.

Part I
- Remind students that, as discussed earlier in this section, *that* is more likely to be included in formal written English, such as this article.
- You can give students a chance to practice their sight-reading skills by having them take turns reading sentences or paragraphs.

Part II
- Go over the comprehension questions with the class, having students read the true/false statements aloud and choosing their responses.

Optional Vocabulary
avoid	stable
nutritious	transported
appealing	substance

CHART 12-6. Quoted Speech. Page 258
Time: 20 minutes

As an example of the importance of using quotation marks correctly, you might put the following sentence on the board and ask students to add punctuation marks:

My dog said Mary needs a new collar.

If the punctuation is incorrect, the dog might appear to be speaking:

INCORRECT: *My dog said, "Mary needs a new collar."*

CORRECT: *"My dog," said Mary, "needs a new collar."*

In the chart, *said* and *asked* are used as the reporting verbs. Additional reporting verbs are *cry, exclaim, mutter,* and *reflect.*

- Write the chart title on the board.
- Ask students how they are feeling, and quote them on the board, demonstrating correct punctuation. For example:

  Xavier said, "I feel tired."

  "I feel excited. My boyfriend will arrive this weekend," Paloma said.

  "How do I feel?" asked Kazumi.

- Stress the importance of using correct punctuation by adapting the example given in the background notes and writing it on the board.

- Go over the chart with students. Be prepared to explain the meaning of the various quote verbs included at the end of the chart.

❏ EXERCISE 33. Looking at grammar.
Page 259
Time: 10 minutes

To provide a focus for the class discussion, it is helpful to have students write the items on the board.

Make sure that students are writing the quotation marks above, not on, the line.

- Give students a chance to punctuate the items, and then ask for volunteers to write their answers on the board.
- Point out the exact placement of each punctuation mark while correcting.
- Model the punctuation points by reading each item aloud, pausing as needed and adding emphasis / inflection to the actual quotes themselves.

Expansion: Make a copy of a cartoon (or copies of several) from the newspaper with the speech and thought bubbles above the heads of each character removed. Distribute these to students and have them come up with their own dialogue, which they must then punctuate. If you have access to an overhead projector, you could project one cartoon strip (with all words removed) onto the board and have students independently create dialogue to quote. Alternatively, you could have students break into groups and have each group make up a dialogue to quote to the class.

❏ EXERCISE 35. Let's write. Page 260
Time: 10–15 minutes

Because not all students may be familiar with fables, be prepared to explain the genre and to give a few famous examples ("The Tortoise and the Hare," etc.). This fable shows a lazy grasshopper relaxing while ants are busily collecting food. Later, in the cold of winter, the grasshopper must beg for food from the industrious ants.

- Have students look at the illustrations, and ask them what the moral, or lesson, of the fable is.
- You can expect students to produce something along the lines of *It's important to work hard and prepare for the future.* OR *Those who don't take care of themselves must rely on the generosity of others.*

CHART 12-7. Reported Speech: Verb Forms in Noun Clauses. Page 261
Time: 15–20 minutes

> Changes in noun-clause verbs to a past form are sometimes called "the formal sequence of tenses in noun clauses."
>
> Tense usage in noun clauses is by no means as regular and consistent as this chart may indicate. Rules for sequences of tenses are helpful, but there are many exceptions. Encourage students to practice the sequence of tenses as presented in this chart, but accept any viable responses in the exercises.
>
> You might have Student A read a quoted speech sentence in the chart, then ask Student B (book closed) to paraphrase it in reported speech. Invite comments from the class about the grammatical differences.
>
> Point out the changes in modals (examples h–k) from quoted to reported speech, and note that in (l), *should, ought to,* and *might* do not change.

- Explain the general principal by stating that quoted speech represents the actual words and when they were actually said.
- Tell students that reported speech is a more conversational way to explain what someone else said. Reported speech also uses tense changes rather than quotation marks.
- Explain that the grammar of reported speech is that of a noun clause which is the direct object of the reporting verb.
- In order to show that the original speech occurred in the past (before the moment it is repeated to someone else), noun-clause verbs change to a past form.
- Write some basic notes on the board to show the differences between quoted and reported speech:

Quoted Speech	*Reported Speech*
quotation marks	no quotation marks
verbs in real time	noun clause used
no change in tense	verbs in past tense

- Demonstrate changing one simple present quoted speech sentence to a reported speech sentence by reporting something a student has recently said.
- If you use an example from a recent exercise in this chapter, remind your students of the context. For example:

  Okay, the other day when you were practicing using (that) noun clauses, I overheard Jun talk about what parents want for their children. First I am going to write it as quoted speech:
  Jun: "All parents want to have happy children."
  Now I will write it as reported speech. Notice what happens to the noun-clause verb.
  Jun said all parents want<u>ed</u> to have happy children.

- Go over the chart carefully, noting each verb change and focusing on the differences between immediate and later reporting.

❏ EXERCISE 37. Looking at grammar.
Page 262
Time: 10 minutes

> This exercise requires students to (1) form noun clauses and (2) adjust verb forms.

- Do this exercise as a class, with students taking turns reading aloud.
- Have the same student read both sentences included in each item.

❏ EXERCISE 38. Let's talk. Page 262
Time: 10 minutes

> This exercise gives students a chance to practice the formal tense sequence used in reported speech in a very controlled fashion. You may want to also discuss how immediate reporting differs, and you can even have students try both.
>
> As needed, you can slow the exercise down by having students write items on the board.

- Model the exercise clearly so that students know what is expected of them.
- Point out that they need to make tense changes, and correct any errors immediately.

❏ EXERCISE 39. Let's talk. Page 263
Time: 10 minutes

> Students can have fun with this exercise if they use their creativity. Speaker C, the "reporter," has to have a good memory.

Expansion: Prepare a short clip from a TV show or movie, choosing a scene where there is clear dialogue between two people or possibly among three. The clip should be very short if students are struggling with reported speech. Tell them that their task is to watch the clip and then afterwards paraphrase what they heard the characters say by using reported speech. Have one or two students write their versions on the board and compare.

❏ EXERCISE 41. Listening. Page 264
Time: 10 minutes

> Listening exercises are especially meaningful when studying reported speech. Strong listening skills are important in order to be able to make the necessary tense changes when reporting real speech to others.

- Have students complete the cloze as directed, focusing on the past tenses used.

- For an additional check, use the listening script to help students recreate what they originally heard.

Expansion: Play "Telephone" with your students. Break the class into two groups and ask them to line up. Explain that you are going to say the same sentence to each student at one end of each line and that that person should whisper it to the person in front of him, who should then whisper it to the person in front of him, etc. The last person in each line should write it down using reported speech. Then the two results (one from each group) can be compared.

To make it challenging, you may want to include a variety of tenses and / or modals in the original sentence. Make sure that students know to begin passing the message on saying *Our teacher said . . . / Martha said that . . .* and to keep the name of the original speaker throughout.

❏ **EXERCISE 42.** Looking at grammar.
Page 265
Time: 5–10 minutes

Optional Vocabulary

unexcused	obstacle
alternate	steppingstone

❏ **EXERCISE 44.** Check your knowledge.
Page 266
Time: 10–20 minutes

You might want to let students know that all of the items in this exercise come from the written work of students just like them, and that these errors are common. In language learning, an error in usage is a learning opportunity. Encourage students to feel good about their ability to spot and correct these typical noun-clause errors, and emphasize that self-monitoring is an important part of their own writing process.

- You can give students the choice of whether to use this exercise as an opportunity for independent work or to do it in class, taking turns going around the room.
- Because it is extremely helpful for students to hear themselves say noun clauses, make sure that they have a chance to read their answers aloud.

❏ **EXERCISE 45.** Let's talk. Page 267
Time: 5–10 minutes

As an ongoing activity over many classes, have one or two students per day give their one-minute speeches until everyone in the class has had an opportunity to speak. Allow writing time in class.

SUGGESTION: Give the written reports to the student who spoke and ask her/him to correct them. It is enlightening for a speaker to read what others think she / he said.

You may have to encourage reticent students to speak in front of the whole class and to speak clearly so that their classmates can take notes and report what was said. On the other hand, it will probably be difficult to keep some eager speakers within the one-minute limit.

If some students object to listening to each other's imperfect English, you might remind them that in future years they will probably use their English to communicate with people who, like them, are not native speakers.

- Because it can be very challenging to get started on a one-minute speech when the topic is both general and open-ended, prepare a handout of possible topics for students.
- You can also write each of the following questions / topics on separate slips of paper and have students choose one randomly. It may be challenging for students to simply accept whatever the topic is, but the limitation may jumpstart ideas. Here is a list of possible topics:

If you could have one wish, what would it be?

If you could take a cruise for a week, where would you go?

If you could have any animal in the world as a pet, what would it be?

If you could live anywhere in the world, where would you live?

If you could change your name, what would you change it to?

How would you define "courage"?

What aspect of your life makes you most proud?

Who is your role model?

Describe the best vacation place you've been.

What do you like to do more than anything in the world?

What is your favorite sport?

What is your favorite book?

If you could be a farm animal, which one would you be?

Tell about your favorite hobby.

What career do you want to have, or if you had to change careers now, what would you pick?

What is your favorite song and who sings it?

What do you like to do in your spare time?

What is your idea of a perfect job?

If you could be rich or famous, which would you choose?

If you could meet any celebrity, who would it be?

If you could meet anyone from the past, who would it be?

What is your favorite possession?

Who is / was your favorite teacher? (besides your current teacher, of course)

What is / was your favorite subject? (besides English, of course)

What is the scariest event that you've ever experienced?

If you could be anyone in the world, who would you be?

If you had to pick one food to eat for the rest of your life, what would it be?

❏ EXERCISE 46. Let's talk and write.
Page 267
Time: 15–20 minutes

> The person interviewed can be a family member, a community leader, a faculty or staff member, or a next-door neighbor — students enjoy interviewing native speakers of English.

- Whoever the interviewee is, prepare the students by giving them information about the person.
- Ask students to prepare questions before they come to class the day of the interview.
- Record the interview (on audio or video tape) so that the accuracy of quotations can be checked (and students can proudly hear their own public English).
- All students will interview the same person, so their written reports will be similar. Therefore, you might choose the best one for "publication."
- As an alternative, you could arrange for several people to be available for interviews and divide the class into groups. Then students' reports will differ, and you could publish more than one.

❏ EXERCISE 47. Let's talk and write.
Page 268
Time: 10–15 minutes

> This exercise uses meaningful, creative communication as the basis for written work to reinforce the grammar that students have been concentrating on.
>
> The topics are designed to engender different points of view and encourage open discussion. For example, not everyone will agree on what is most important in life or whether women can do all the same jobs that men can. Also, you or the class can provide other topics for discussion relevant to contemporary world events or issues in your city or school.
>
> Another possibility is to use the items as debate topics, assigning certain students to argue in favor of the statement and others against. Some students may find it hard to argue in favor of something they don't support, but this technique challenges students and gives them a great opportunity to practice their English.

CHART 12-8. Using -ever Words. Page 268
Time: 5–10 minutes

> These words are of fairly low frequency but deserve a moment's attention. Concentrate on meaning here. The text treats these words principally as vocabulary items because the underlying grammatical structures are complicated.
>
> Mention that *so* might be added with no change in meaning: *whosoever, whatsoever, wheresoever, howsoever.* This is more common in legal or religious contexts than in everyday speech or writing.

- Write the chart title on the board.
- Ask students what time they would arrive at a casual party or barbecue scheduled for 8:00 P.M., according to the norms of their culture. (This particular question works well for students of diverse cultural backgrounds, but you may have to improvise a different question when working with students from the same country.)
- Write their responses on the board in reported speech.

  Makiko said she would arrive by 8:15 P.M.

  Kristian and Ilsa said they would also arrive by 8:15 or 8:30.

  Juan and Beatriz said they would arrive sometime after 9:30 or 10:00.

  Marco said <u>he would arrive any time he wanted</u>.

- Explain that the noun clause in the sentence above can be rephrased as:

  Marco said he would arrive <u>whenever he wanted</u>.

- Go over the chart with students.

Chapter **13**
Adjective Clauses

CHAPTER SUMMARY

OBJECTIVE: To express more complex relationships between ideas than is possible in simple sentences alone. Even with a limited vocabulary, those who can employ dependent clauses can greatly increase their communicative competence in the new language.

APPROACH: The chapter begins with exercises on adjective clause pronouns used as the subject and then presents patterns of restrictive adjective clauses using subject pronouns, object pronouns, and possessive pronouns (*whose*). Then *where* and *when* are added, followed by a series of exercises that practice all these patterns. The use of commas in punctuating restrictive and nonrestrictive clauses is explained next, and then some less frequent uses of adjective clauses are explored. Finally, the reduction of adjective clauses to phrases is practiced.

TERMINOLOGY: A "clause" is defined as "a structure containing a subject and verb." Clauses can be either independent / main (like a simple, self-standing sentence) or dependent / subordinate (not meaningful by themselves). A "phrase" is defined as "a multiword structure that does not contain a subject-verb combination." There are many kinds of phrases.

The term "relative pronoun" is not used in the text. Relative pronouns (e.g., *who, whom, which*) are called "subject pronouns" to emphasize their connection with personal pronouns (e.g., *she, them, it*) in both meaning and grammatical function.

The terms "restrictive" and "nonrestrictive" are footnoted but otherwise not used. Restrictive / essential / identifying clauses are called "clauses that don't need commas," and nonrestrictive / nonessential / nonidentifying clauses are called "clauses that need commas."

The term "subordination" is not always easy to explain, but you may want to give students some background. In literature and academic publications, writers often construct complicated sentences with multiple clauses in order to highlight some information while putting other details in the background. Students don't need to produce such complex sentences, but they should understand the concept of subordination: that a dependent clause is subordinate in structure as well as in meaning to the independent clause. For intermediate students, the immediate task is to learn to control an independent clause with only one dependent clause closely attached to it. This can be quite challenging. For advanced students, the task is to review the basic forms of adjective clauses so that they can correct possible problems in their own usage.

❏ **EXERCISE 1.** Warm-up. Page 270
Time: 5 minutes

- Write the sentences on the board.
- Circle the pronouns and draw arrows back to their antecedents (or you can ask students to do this).

CHART 13-1. Adjective Clause Pronouns Used as the Subject. Page 270
Time: 10–15 minutes

The verb *modify* means "change" or "limit the meaning of." Point out that an adjective changes or limits the meaning of a noun slightly (*a friendly woman, an old woman, a tall woman*) and that an adjective clause likewise changes or limits the meaning of the noun slightly (*the woman who helped me, a woman I saw in the park, the woman the teacher was talking to*). Point out the useful functions of adjective clauses: adding details about a noun in the independent clause; i.e., expanding the amount of information in a sentence.

Stylistically and idiomatically, *who* is usually preferred to *that*, and *that* is preferred to *which* when they are used as subject relative pronouns. At this point, the students are being asked to learn all of the possible correct patterns.

Point out that the adjective clause follows immediately after the noun that it modifies. This may interrupt the main clause. Advise students that an adjective clause should be put as close as possible to the noun it modifies, but at times there may be an interrupting element, usually a modifying prepositional phrase:

*I didn't recognize the man **in the blue suit** who waved at me. The student **from Rome** who lives down the hall has invited me to a party.*

- Write the chart title on the board.
- Demonstrate the function of an adjective by writing sentences about your students or your class.

The tallest student is Marco.
The Thai students are so sweet and generous.
The level 8 grammar students are the most interesting in the school.
Our grammar text is the blue Azar book.

- Underline the adjective phrase in each sentence. Elicit from students that these phrases limit the noun and allow us to know which noun (among them all) the main clause is about.
- Then, use each adjective or adjective phrase to create a new adjective clause to be used as the subject. Write the restated sentences containing adjective clauses directly below the originals.

    The <u>tallest</u> student is Marco.

    The student <u>who / that is tallest</u> is Marco.

    The <u>Thai</u> students are so sweet and generous.

    The students <u>who / that are Thai</u> are so sweet and generous.

    The <u>level 8 grammar</u> students are the most interesting in the school.

    The students <u>who / that are in level 8 grammar</u> are the most interesting in the school.

    <u>Our grammar</u> text is the blue Azar book.

    The text <u>which / that we use in grammar</u> is the blue Azar book.

- Explain to students that sometimes it works better to use an adjective clause (particularly if the adjective phrase — like *level 8 grammar* — is a bit awkward to form).
- Go over the rest of the chart together.

❏ EXERCISE 3. Looking at grammar.
Page 271
Time: 10 minutes

- Give students time to complete the exercise on their own.
- For each item, have a student read both sentences aloud before subordinating the second one to the first.
- Correct target grammar deliberately and clearly. Write the complete, subordinated sentences on the board.

❏ EXERCISE 4. Let's talk. Page 271
Time: 5–10 minutes

Expansion: Provide students with additional and alternative sentence starters. Then have them circulate around the room, collecting more information from one another. Finally, have each student make a statement about another person's preferences.

Additional sentence starters:

I admire teachers who. . .
I want to work with people who. . .
I can respect a boss who. . .
I would vote for a politician who. . .
I would never marry someone who. . .
I look up to leaders in business who. . .

❏ EXERCISE 5. Listening. Page 271
Time: 10–15 minutes

Part I
- Tell students that the task is to expand the contracted form back to the full form and that they will hear the sentences just as they are written in the text (they will <u>not</u> hear the full, uncontracted form).

- When reviewing as a class, have students say the contracted form before giving the uncontracted one.

Part II
- Make sure students understand that though they will write the full form, they will not hear it.

Optional Vocabulary
protest march
retired

❏ EXERCISE 6. Warm-up. Page 272
Time: 5–10 minutes

- Have a student (or students) read parts of or the whole passage aloud.
- Discuss the term "stay-at-home" dad, and ask students whether this role is typical for fathers in their countries.
- Using items 1–8, have students create sentences containing adjective clauses describing the kind of job William is looking for.
- If time allows, have students write their sentences on the board.

CHART 13-2. Adjective Clause Pronouns
Used as the Object of a Verb. Page 273
Time: 10 minutes

Review the difference between "subject" and "object" if necessary, enlisting students' help to do so. Also, reiterate that the symbol Ø means "nothing" (no word is needed here).

Discuss informal vs. formal usage (e.g., informal = everyday conversation, a letter to a friend; formal = a business or school report, academic journal, encyclopedia, or reference source). Ask your students when or if they need to use formal English. The object form *whom* is used primarily in formal writing. Even in nonrestrictive clauses (Chart 13-8) *who* seems to be preferred to *whom* by most native speakers (e.g., *My best friend, **who** nobody else seems to like, needs to learn how to get along with people.*)

In everyday English, an object relative pronoun is usually omitted from a restrictive clause. Students should have control of all possibilities, however, so that they understand what they are omitting. Also, they will learn in Chart 13-8 that they cannot omit the object pronoun in nonrestrictive clauses.

Some languages connect clauses similar to these with a conjunction, not a pronoun. Those languages, therefore, keep the object pronoun in its normal position in the dependent clause. For some students, transferring this pattern may lead to an ungrammatical sentence in English. For example:

INCORRECT: *The book that I read ~~it~~ yesterday was enjoyable.*

INCORRECT: *I didn't know the man who(m) I spoke to ~~him~~.*

- Write the chart title on the board.
- Ask a student or students to first explain what the subject of a verb and object of a verb are, and where they usually appear. Write their responses on the board. For example:

  subject = noun or pronoun that does the action of the verb

  subject = usually the first noun in the sentence; comes immediately before the verb

  object = noun or pronoun that receives the action

  object = usually comes immediately after the verb

- Have students generate a simple example based on their lives and write it on the board, labeling the subject, verb, and object, respectively. (You will need to adapt your presentation to the actual sentence your students produce.) For example:

  Subject + Verb + Object
  Makiko assisted Hans with the homework.

- Leave the sentence on the board.
- Add to this information another sentence:

  The student was Hans.

- Explain that if we didn't know Hans's name or if we only knew that Makiko assisted him, we could define Hans as *the student who(m)/that/Ø Makiko assisted.*
- Write the options for defining Hans as separate sentences. For example:

  The student who(m) Makiko assisted was Hans.
  The student that Makiko assisted was Hans.
  The student (Ø) Makiko assisted was Hans.

- Go over the rest of the chart with students.

❏ **EXERCISE 7.** Looking at grammar.
Page 273
Time: 5 minutes

- Have student take turns reading items aloud and choosing all possible completions.
- Write correct completions on the board, and label the parts of speech and their functions as appropriate.

CHART 13-3. Adjective Clause Pronouns
Used as the Object of a Preposition. Page 274
Time: 10–15 minutes

Common problems:

1. repeating the preposition: . . . *the woman about whom I told you about*

2. omitting the preposition: . . . *the music that we listened last night*

Some older grammar books and style manuals stated that a preposition must never be the last word in a sentence. Today it is quite acceptable to end with a preposition, as in examples (b), (c), and (d), except in perhaps the most formal writing. The writer as stylist would have to make that determination, but grammatically there is no error in ending a sentence with a preposition.

- Write the chart title on the board.
- Explain that because some verbs require a preposition directing the action to the object (for example: *listen **to** music*), adjective clause pronouns can serve as the object of this preposition.
- Under the heading word *preposition,* write all of the prepositions that students can think of on the spot.
- With your students, create a few sentences that include verbs that are followed by prepositions, and write these on the board.
- Lead students into creating the following examples by first writing simple prompts on the board and setting a scene. For example, say:

  We all know Monique's birthday is coming up. We are planning a surprise party for her.

  Then write:

  Monique \ be \ student + We \ plan \ surprise party \ her.

- Help students complete/create the following examples by writing *Monique* on the board and giving them words as necessary. You may have to lead them through this rather deliberately.

  Monique is the student for whom we are having a surprise party.
  Monique is the student who we are having a surprise party for.
  Monique is the student that we are having a surprise party for.
  Monique is the student Ø we are having a surprise party for.

- Try the same approach with the following (or one more relevant to your class members) example. Say:

  Pablo and Ariane seem to be discussing some news. Apparently, Jana just told them about it.

- Now write the following cues on the board:

  Pablo \ Ariane \ discuss \ news + Jana \ tell \ them \ it.

- Help students come up with the following possibilities, and write them on the board.

  Pablo and Ariane are discussing the news about which Jana told them.
  Pablo and Ariane are discussing the news which Jana told them about.
  Pablo and Ariane are discussing the news that Jana told them about.
  Pablo and Ariane are discussing the news Ø Jana told them about.

- Go over the chart with your students.

❏ **EXERCISE 10.** Looking at grammar.
Page 274
Time: 5–10 minutes

- Have students complete the exercise aloud, taking turns.
- Correct them immediately and, if appropriate, write any incorrect choices on the board so that you can deliberately and visually correct the sentences by either crossing out repeated prepositions or adding in omitted ones.

- Ask students which is the most formal option and also which is the most natural for them to say. Students acquiring this structure are not always ready to omit the adjective clause pronoun until they have become used to the form.

□ **EXERCISE 14.** Check your knowledge.
Page 275
Time: 10–15 minutes

- Explain to students that this is a review of adjective clauses, but simple matters of agreement within the clause may also arise.
- Give students plenty of time to work through the exercise on their own before reviewing as a class.
- As part of correction, make sure to have students read the incorrect sentence first and then the corrected version aloud.

Optional Vocabulary
amateur   starvation
temper   malnutrition

□ **EXERCISE 15.** Looking at grammar:
pairwork. Page 276
Time: 10–15 minutes

> This exercise is intended to promote fluency and ease of usage.

- Model the examples clearly and carefully so that both Speaker A and Speaker B understand what is expected of them.
- Make sure that students understand the task before attempting it in pairs.
- Circulate, offering help especially to Speaker Bs, and ensure that both partners get equal time to practice with the forms.
- Review as a class by asking pairs of students to read their conversations aloud.

Optional Vocabulary
clerk
cash a check

CHART 13-4. Using *Whose*. Page 277
Time: 10 minutes

> *Whose* can be troublesome for students. It has a relatively low frequency, so most learners aren't as familiar with adjectives containing *whose* as they are with the ones in the preceding charts. Emphasize that *whose* functions as a possessive <u>adjective</u> and needs to be paired with a noun.

- Explain that *whose* has the same possessive meaning as any other possessive adjective pronoun (*his, her, our, my, its,* etc.) and that like these, it has to be followed by a noun.

- Ask students to remind you how we normally form a possessive adjective. Elicit *Add an apostrophe and an "-s."*
- Explain that we can't simply use an apostrophe + *-s* because of the confusion with *who's,* which is a contraction of *who* and *is.*
- Illustrate this further by showing students that *whose* truly is a possessive by reminding them of *it's* vs. the possessive *its.* Write the following on the board:

  who's = contraction of who + is

  whose = correct possessive form meaning belonging to or of who

- Using known information about the students in your class, create a couple of examples with the help of your students, and write these sentences on the board.

  The woman <u>whose hair</u> is extremely curly is Aranxa.

  The man <u>whose wife</u> is arriving from Saudi Arabia later today is Abdur Rhaman.

- Have two students go to the board and identify/mark the adjective clause, its subject and verb with a lowercase *s* and *v,* and the subject and verb of the main clause with a capital *S* and *V,* respectively.
- Go over the chart with your class.

□ **EXERCISE 18.** Looking at grammar.
Page 278
Time: 5–10 minutes

> Word order in this structure can be challenging for students. Take time with this exercise and use the board so that students can easily see patterns.

- Give students a few minutes to combine the two sentences, subordinating the second to the first with *whose.*
- Assign one item to each of five students, and have them write their combined sentences on the board.
- Those students remaining at their seats should correct the sentences on the board as part of the review.

□ **EXERCISE 20.** Let's talk: pairwork.
Page 278
Time: 5–10 minutes

> *There* in these sentences is spoken with emphasis, as if one were pointing at someone. This is very different from the form *There + be* (Chart 6-4), which is rarely followed by *the.* Make sure to model the correct emphasis given to *there* and explain the context to your students before they begin practicing.

Expansion: Give students an opportunity to create their own descriptions of one another utilizing this adjective clause format. Make a copy of the class roster to hand out (if the class is relatively small) and ask class members to come up with one descriptive sentence for each of their peers. If the class is too big for this, divide it into groups of four or five, and instruct each group member to write a sentence about every other member. Let students know that these sentences will be read aloud to the rest of the class, and the rest of the class will need to guess which student each sentence describes. This information should put them on notice to be both kind and professional in their descriptive sentences. Additionally, each sentence should be ambiguous enough to make the activity interesting and challenging. For example:

This student is the one whose favorite hobby is football.

This student is a Spanish woman whose passion is fashion.

❑ **EXERCISE 21.** Listening. Page 279
Time: 5–10 minutes

• Write all three possibilities on the board:

   whose   who is   who has

• Now ask students what kind of phrase they expect to follow each, and have students create a sentence for each category before having them listen to the audio. For example:

  whose
  I know someone whose hair is red.

  who is
  I have a friend who is an actor.

  who has
  I like any person who has integrity.

• Play the audio through once without stopping. Then play it again, stopping after each item.

• When reviewing answers as a class, point to the correct form of the answer on the board.

CHART 13-5. Using *Where* in Adjective Clauses. Page 279
Time: 5–10 minutes

Where (and *when*) substitute for prepositional phrases and serve as the link between an adjective clause and the noun that it modifies.

Note the special rules for the prepositions in all examples.

• Write the chart title on the board.

• Underneath the word *where*, write the reminder that this word modifies a place.

• If you feel confident that students are happy with the program or school where they are studying, use it as the main focus of the remainder of the presentation.

• Ask students to think about their school, and together you will create sentences describing it. For example:

Boston College is a place <u>where</u> students all over the world meet each other.

This is a school <u>where</u> the teachers and staff enjoy their jobs.

The school <u>where</u> we study English is located in Harvard Square.

• Go over the chart with students, spending extra time on the use of prepositions.

CHART 13-6. Using *When* in Adjective Clauses. Page 280
Time: 5–10 minutes

• Write the chart title on the board and have students contribute some examples of possible *when* situations.

• Write the time nouns on the board (under the word *when*) and help students to expand the concept as much as possible. For example:

  season
  weekend
  holiday / birthday / anniversary
  decade
  century
  times of life: infancy, childhood, adolescence, young adulthood, middle age
  events: meals, vacations, trips, weddings, parties, celebrations, elections, funerals, revolutions, coups, wars, etc.

• Together with your students, create a couple of sentences on the board. Use the context of their real lives to do so and, if needed, give them prompts so that they can come up with meaningful sentences. For example:

A birthday is a day <u>when</u> your family and friends celebrate you.

The most important time of Makiko's life was <u>when</u> she was home with her daughter.

• Go over the chart with students.

❑ **EXERCISE 26.** Looking at grammar. Page 280
Time: 5–10 minutes

• You may wish to review the use of prepositions (*in, at, on, during, after, before,* etc.) with particular time phrases or words.

• Write the prepositions *At, In, On* on the board, and have students go to the board and write time words that are preceded by each one. For example:

<u>At</u>	<u>In</u>	<u>On</u>
8:00 P.M.	a week	December 25, 1987
lunchtime	December	Halloween

❑ **EXERCISE 27.** Looking at grammar. Page 281
Time: 5–10 minutes

Optional Vocabulary
pastries
dominated
miser

Expansion: In order to give students some creative practice with using *where* and *when* in adjective clauses, you can play a version of the game Password with them. Prepare index cards with six or eight nouns / noun phrases on them. These can also be proper nouns, as long as you are sure they are familiar to each student. Nouns that work best are everyday items, holidays, places, and events — they shouldn't be difficult, nor should they be too basic. Ideally, each member of the class has a unique card, but that does take some preparation.

Distribute one card to each student, and have the students arrange themselves so they are directly facing the person they will play the game with.

Have students begin the game. Whoever is going first describes each noun on his card — using adjective clauses — until his/her partner can say the noun aloud. The student then moves on to the next noun until he / she has finished and then it is the partner's turn to describe. Alternatively, students can take turns rather than one person completing all the nouns on his / her card before the other student goes.

Possible sets of random nouns: These can be copied, printed, and glued onto index cards so that they can be used again. They also provide a sample which is easy to replicate.

dental floss	a nail salon
a brontosaurus	the Fourth of July
a presidential election	an SUV
rice	moisturizer
a closet	a clown
a remote control	paste

a combination lock	Paris
the Dark Ages	the 1960s
flour	a pediatrician
an attic	an office supply store
paperclips	pudding
a shovel	childhood

❏ **EXERCISE 30.** Let's talk. Page 282
Time: 15–20 minutes

The idea of this exercise is to engender as natural a conversation as possible while guiding the grammar structures used. It gives students the opportunity to practice what they have learned by combining free response with controlled structure use.

Given that this is a somewhat complicated exercise format, it might work best if it is teacher-led (in terms of time allotted especially). If time is available, give students the opportunity to take responsibility for the quality of their own practice by interacting in small groups. And this is a good point in the chapter for student-student interactive work.

If you lead the exercise, it is not necessary to use the exact words in the book. Use ideas and things that occur naturally in your classroom with your students. Encourage students to exchange real information or, if they prefer, to invent an interesting response.

- Model the exercise carefully, acting as the leader for the first example.
- You can set this exercise up with groups of three to four students, but it is important that one student be designated the leader to begin. If working with four students per group, students can rotate taking the roles of leader, Speaker A, and Speaker B.
- If you are not leading the exercise yourself, move around the room, ensuring that only the leader has a book open. Students may need you to step into each group and act as the leader briefly while establishing the pattern.
- Review as a class and choose some items to address to the whole class, encouraging students to answer using correct adjective clause formats.

CHART 13-7. Using Adjective Clauses to Modify Pronouns. Page 283
Time: 20 minutes

Discourage students from using adjective clauses to modify personal pronouns. Sometimes students get enthusiastic about gaining control of adjective clauses and want to use them everywhere, including following personal pronouns, for example, *I, who am a student from Malaysia, am studying English.* Explain that such structures, even though grammatically logical, rarely occur idiomatically.

This chart is included in the text because:

1. adjective clauses modifying indefinite pronouns are common and useful;

2. the patterns in examples (g) and (h), though less common, are also useful; and

3. the text seeks to point out that extending the use of adjective clauses to modify personal pronouns, while logical, is not common and should be avoided.

- Write the chart title on the board.
- Underline the word *Pronouns,* and discuss with students the types of pronouns likely to be modified by adjective clauses.
- In order to make it clear to students what kind of pronouns need modification, present indefinite pronouns by reminding students to think back to their first day in the class, before they knew the school, you, or their peers. Ask students to recall their very first impressions of one another, the school staff, or teachers.
- You may need to ask them specific questions to prompt the production of appropriate adjective clauses. Help students with this task by sharing your first impression of one of them. For example:

    When I first met this class, I noticed someone who was smiling a lot.

- Ask students the following questions, and lead them to come up with related sentences, using adjective clauses:

  Who did you first notice when you sat down in this class? What did you notice about this person?

  What was your first impression of your roommate?

  When you first arrived at the school, who helped you to enroll in classes? What is your memory of this person?

- Now carefully help students piece together sentences, and write them on the board, demonstrating this common use of the modification of indefinite pronouns. For example:

  When Chien-hui first entered this class, she saw someone who is very tall and very talkative. Who is it?

  Maia first noticed two Thai students who seemed to be very good friends already.

- Go over the rest of the chart.

❏ EXERCISE 32. Looking at grammar.
Page 283
Time: 10 minutes

Since using adjective clauses to modify indefinite pronouns is a very common pattern, it is assumed that the students are familiar with it and will have little difficulty with idiomatic responses for items 2–9. The pronouns to be modified in items 10–12 are specifically for advanced students and may seem unfamiliar to intermediate students.

Optional Vocabulary
powerless
term
intermission

CHART 13-8. Punctuating Adjective
Clauses. Page 285
Time: 20–25 minutes

The use of commas with adjective clauses can be rather challenging to learn. In fact, native speakers of English are often uncertain about this point.

You might point out that commas with adjective clauses are similar to parentheses ( ). They are placed before and after additional, but not essential, information.

This chart contains several important points, so you should plan to spend time discussing them and be ready to provide additional examples.

- Write the chart title on the board.

- Write the adjective clause category headings below on the board and demonstrate the difference between a necessary and unnecessary adjective clause by writing two closely related sentences about someone in your class.

Necessary Information	Extra Information
The student in our class who is tall is Mario.	Mario, who is tall, is in our class.
no commas	commas used — similar to parentheses
clause is necessary to understand who we are talking about	clause adds extra information — not necessary to understand who we are talking about

- Go over the chart carefully, and remind students repeatedly that if they need the adjective information to understand which noun is being modified, no commas are used.

❏ EXERCISE 35. Looking at grammar.
Page 286
Time: 10 minutes

- Give students time to complete the exercise alone.
- Read the first two items in the exercise aloud to students as examples for them to follow.
- Demonstrate to them how to pause and lower their voices between the two commas.
- Have students read the complete sentence aloud and then comment on the punctuation of each one, as illustrated in items 1 and 2.
- It is critical to make sure that students really understand the fundamental difference between necessary and unnecessary adjective clauses before moving on. Therefore, explain the meaning of each sentence.

Optional Vocabulary
staple   situated
tropical

❏ EXERCISE 40. Looking at grammar.
Page 288
Time: 10 minutes

This is a review exercise. Students should do it at home, where they have plenty of time to think. Then in class, you can lead a discussion of each item as classmates check their work. Group work is another option, where students can discuss the punctuation among themselves.

Optional Vocabulary
tusk   conduct
chiefly   chamber

❏ EXERCISE 41. Reading and grammar.
Page 289
Time: 20 minutes

Part I
- Before reading through the passage, ask students what famous names they know associated with the computer industry.
- Ask students the difference between a PC and a Mac computer.
- Have students take turns reading sentences from the passage aloud, and refine their pronunciation of adjective clauses as you go through the reading.

Part II
- Explain to students that they will be completing the sentences with both necessary and non-necessary adjective clauses.

Optional Vocabulary
operating system
program
acquire
the rights

CHART 13-9. Using Expressions of Quantity in Adjective Clauses. Page 290
Time: 5–10 minutes

Example (a) illustrates the pattern where *whom* is always used (not *who*), even in speech. This pattern is of low frequency, occurring typically in situations such as complicated journalistic sentences in which the most information possible is packed into a single sentence.

This chart needs minimal time and attention in class. Advanced students who find it of interest will get what they need from the text and a quick run-through of the exercises. It is a relatively formal written structure. Even in writing, students at this level can communicate their meaning clearly and accurately without ever using this structure.

- Write the chart title on the board. Explain that this structure is used primarily in writing, when the author wants to pack as many statistics into one sentence as possible.
- Look at your class and find some article or color of clothing that a number of your students are wearing. You can also focus on nationality and gender to provide you with easily observable examples of the structure.
- Come up with three or four sentences using expressions of quantity in adjective clauses.
- Write the sentence on the board and underline the expressions of quantity in each of the adjective clauses. For example:

  There are twenty-five students in this class, seventeen of whom are wearing blue jeans at this moment.

  There are twenty students in this class, roughly half of whom are South American.

There are twelve students in this class, six of whom are women.

- Go over the chart with the students, but remind them that the structure is not critical and they will master it with time and increased exposure to it.

CHART 13-10. Using *Which* to Modify a Whole Sentence. Page 291
Time: 5–10 minutes

Make sure that students understand that *this* and *that* are used here as demonstrative pronouns that refer to a whole sentence.

This pattern is fairly common in spoken English, especially when discussing ideas and opinions. *Which* is used as a connector of ideas. Often speakers pause before they add this kind of *which*-clause to what they have just said.

- Write the chart title on the board.
- Explain that this structure is very useful, especially when discussing ideas and opinions. In order to demonstrate, ask a student his/her opinion and another student to agree or disagree. It is best not to pick anything too controversial so that the structure can be the focus. For example:

  What do you think the best age to get married is, Peter?

  Mimi, do you agree with Peter's opinion?

- Now using your students opinions, transform them into one sentence using *which* to modify the whole sentence. For example:

  Peter thinks 32 is the perfect age to get married, which Mimi disagrees with.

- Review the chart with your students, giving them plenty of examples of times they may use this structure.

❏ EXERCISE 47. Looking at grammar.
Page 292
Time: 10 minutes

This exercise is a review of Charts 13-1 through 13-10. It illustrates adjective clause usage in formal written English.

- Give students time to combine the two sentences on their own, using correct subordination and punctuation.
- Review as a class by having students read their answers aloud, using correct pronunciation and intonation for non-necessary clauses.

Optional Vocabulary
raw   case studies
heredity   administrator
longevity

❏ **EXERCISE 48.** Reading and grammar.
Page 293
Time: 10 minutes

• Tell students that they will be identifying either whole sentences / ideas or noun phrases by the adjective clauses that modify them.
• Students can take turns reading each paragraph and identifying which whole clauses or nouns are modified.
• If there is time, students can take turns writing items on the board and drawing an arrow to the clause (sentence) or words being modified. Doing so will prompt both self-correction and correction by peers and can prompt further engagement of the topic.

Optional Vocabulary
ferry
blocks
reimburse

❏ **EXERCISE 49.** Let's talk or write. Page 293
Time: 10–15 minutes

• Explain to students that ideals are, by definition, somewhat unreal. They should imagine a type of person and not name someone they know.
• Ask students to expand their use of vocabulary in this exercise. By really imagining how they would like others to behave in an ideal world, they may be prompted to move beyond their "safety-zone" vocabulary.
• You may want to have students discuss these first in small groups and then have each student pick one item to expand into a paragraph, incorporating as many adjective clauses as they can.

CHART 13-11. Reducing Adjective Clauses to Adjective Phrases. Page 294
Time: 15–20 minutes

The structures in this chart are of relatively high frequency. Although these patterns may not seem immediately familiar to the students, encourage them to include these patterns in their everyday use. Certainly, students will hear these structures used in everyday conversation. Also understanding these structures is critical for reading comprehension. Readers need to be able to identify what nouns are being modified by which phrases and clauses in order to fully understand meaning.

Some other terms used for adjective phrases are:

• modifying participial phrases: *The man underline{talking to John}. . . The ideas underline{presented in that book}. . .*

• appositive: *George Washington, underline{the first president}, was. . .*

In these exercises, all of these types are simply called "adjective phrases."

• Write the chart title on the board.
• Write the words *Clause* and *Phrase* on the board and ask your class how these two words differ.
• You can expect students to remember what a *clause* is as they have discussed this term so often in this chapter. In any case, help them to come up with key words for both and write these definitions underneath the terms on the board. For example:

Clause	*Phrase*
has subject and verb	*doesn't have subject and verb*
expresses whole idea, with action	*group of related words*
independent clause can be a sentence	*can't be independent or a sentence*

• Now write a sentence containing an adjective clause that can be reduced on the board. Use your students' lives for the context of the sentence. For example:

The students who are studying in this class are some of the most intelligent people I have ever met.

• Have a student go to the board, underline the adjective clause, and label the subject and verb of both the adjective clause and the main clause.
• Explain that only those adjective clauses that have a subject pronoun (*who, which, that*) can be reduced.
• Show students that in the case of the above sentence both *who* and *is* can be omitted by crossing them out and having a student read the remaining, now reduced clause aloud.

The students ~~who are~~ studying in this class are some of the most intelligent people I have ever met.

• Review the rest of the chart with your students.

❏ **EXERCISE 53.** Looking at grammar.
Page 295
Time: 10 minutes

This exercise is the reverse of Exercise 51 and requires students to expand adjective phrases into complete adjective clauses.

• Tell students that when they read books and articles, it can be important for them to be able to determine what key structures have been omitted from a complicated sentence.
• Give students time to work on this independently, and then review as a class.

Optional Vocabulary
orbiting
monumental
tombs

Expansion: Give two students the same sentence including a reduced adjective phrase and have each expand it into a sentence on the board at the same time, without looking at one another's work. The seated students can correct the new sentences.

❏ EXERCISE 55. Looking at grammar.
Page 296
Time: 10–15 minutes

This exercise consists of appositives. The appositive is a useful and common structure in written English. An appositive usually consists of a noun phrase but functions grammatically as an adjective clause. It is equivalent to another noun phrase; it gives more information about a noun by describing it or defining it. Appositives are nonrestrictive, requiring commas; they give additional information about the head noun but are not essential to give meaning to the nouns. In Part II, item 1, Mount Everest is Mount Everest with or without the appositive; the appositive is nonrestrictive and nonessential, giving only additional clarifying information.

Optional Vocabulary

beam	industry
populous	lasers
seismographs	

❏ EXERCISE 56. Listening. Page 297
Time: 10 minutes

Optional Vocabulary

debated	vibrations
deserted	detected
barking	dismiss
howling	subtle

❏ EXERCISE 57. Looking at grammar.
Page 298
Time: 10–20 minutes

"Choppy" answers are short and not smoothly connected. This exercise gives students practice in constructing quite complex sentences, an important technique for communicating a lot of related information successfully and succinctly.

Optional Vocabulary
basin
bauxite
ore

❏ EXERCISE 59. Let's write. Page 300
Time: 15–20 minutes

At this point, students should feel relatively comfortable using adjective clauses and phrases in their own writing. You should assure your students that it is neither necessary nor appropriate to have such structures in _every_ sentence.

- Give students at least 15 minutes to write on the topic of their choice. You may want to set a limit on how long or short the essay(s) should be.
- When marking students' writing, reward and note their successful sentences, especially those with good adjective clauses or phrases.
- See the teaching suggestions in the front of this book for additional ideas for marking student writing.

Chapter **14**
Gerunds and Infinitives, Part 1

CHAPTER SUMMARY

OBJECTIVE: Gerunds and infinitives are common features of both spoken and written English (as the following underlines demonstrate). A person who tries <u>to speak</u> English without <u>using</u> gerunds and infinitives will produce very unnatural-sounding sentences. <u>Learning to understand</u> and <u>use</u> these structures fluently is important for students.

APPROACH: The chapter begins with gerunds and their functions, then introduces infinitives, then special groups of verbs followed by either a gerund or an infinitive. Throughout, the emphasis is on becoming comfortable with these structures through practice, not memorization. Reference lists are also included.

TERMINOLOGY: Like most traditional terms in grammar, "gerund" and "infinitive" were borrowed from analyses of the Latin language; they do not fit the description of the English language equally as well as they do the Latin one. In this text, the combination **to** + *simple form of a verb* is no indication of tense or number (for example, *be, fly*). A "gerund" is *verb* + *-ing* which functions like a noun (for example, *being, flying*).

CHART 14-1. Gerunds: Introduction.
Page 301
Time: 10–15 minutes

Students should learn that "gerund" is the name of a <u>form</u> based on a verb. A gerund may have the <u>function</u> of a subject or an object in a sentence.

In Chapter 1, students learned that some verbs (for example, *know, need, want*) usually have no progressive use and therefore, they may hesitate to use the *-ing* form of these verbs. Point out that these verbs can be used as gerunds:

INCORRECT: *I am knowing John.* (progressive form is not possible)

CORRECT: *Knowing John is a pleasure.* (gerund as subject)

CORRECT: *I insist on knowing the truth.* (gerund as object of a preposition)

Because a gerund is based on a verb form, it can have an object and can be modified by adverbial phrases.

I play games. = verb + object → *Playing games is fun.* = gerund + object

We play in the park. = verb + prepositional phrase → *Playing in the park is fun.* = gerund + prepositional phrase → *Playing games in the park is fun.* = gerund + object + prepositional phrase

A gerund with its associated object or modifier is called a "gerund phrase." In the above examples, *Playing games, Playing in the park,* and *Playing games in the park* are gerund phrases. (These are called "nominals" in some grammars.)

- Write the chart title on the board.
- Ask several students what they plan to do this coming weekend and/or after class and why they want to do those activities.
- Write the answers on the board in the following way:

  What?
  This weekend Tariq is going to play soccer with the students from his dorm.
  Why?
  Tariq likes sports.

- Now explain that we can talk about Tariq's information by making a gerund from *play soccer*. Tell students that every gerund is a form based on a verb but can have the same function as any noun. Write a corresponding note on the board, such as:

  gerund = verb form but noun function

- Ask students what functions nouns can have, and help them articulate that a noun can be either a subject or an object (of either a verb or a preposition).
- Returning to the above information provided by a student (for example, Tariq), write three new sentences on the board.

  Playing soccer is Tariq's plan.
  Tariq likes playing soccer.
  Tariq talked about playing soccer.

- Ask a student to go to the board to underline the new gerund form as subject.

  Playing soccer is Tariq's plan.

- Ask another student to go to the board, but this time ask the student to underline the gerund used as the object of a verb.

  Tariq likes playing soccer.

- Ask a final student to identify the gerund used as the object of a preposition.

  Tariq talked about playing soccer.

- One student may well be able to do all three of the above identifications, so adjust this presentation as needed.
- Go over the rest of the chart with your students.

CHART 14-2. Using Gerunds as the Objects of Prepositions. Page 302
Time: 10–15 minutes

A gerund can immediately follow a proposition, but an infinitive cannot.

The exception that proves the rule: There is one idiom in which a preposition is followed by an infinitive and not by a gerund — *be about*, meaning "ready for immediate action." For example:

I am *about to open* my book.

You may want to have students check off the phrases they already know in the list of common preposition combinations followed by gerunds. Doing so will remind them that they are already familiar with many of these combinations and will help them concentrate on expressions they haven't heard and / or don't know.

As you work through the many charts and lists in this chapter and the next, remind your students frequently that mastery of gerunds and infinitives will increase with actual use. Some students may be tempted to memorize lists and combinations, but reassure your students that they will learn these and other lists by using and hearing their contents frequently. For this reason, Chapters 14 and 15 contain numerous speaking exercises.

- Write the chart title on the board.
- Elicit from students a sentence containing a preposition preceding a gerund, and write this on the board. (You can use the last example sentence from your presentation of Chart 14-1, if appropriate.)

  Tariq talked *about playing* soccer.

- Choose a few common phrases that have prepositions and that precede a gerund from the list in Chart 14-1, and write these on the board. For example:

  be excited about

  be tired of

  be interested in

- Ask three students to go to the board and create a sample sentence using the above three phrases and three gerunds. For example:

  We are excited *about going to the party*.

  Some students are tired *of studying grammar*.

  My friends and I are interested *in hearing the latest news from Wall Street*.

- Explain to students that it can be challenging to learn the idiomatic and prepositional phrases that precede gerunds and that they should not attempt to memorize the list included in the chart.
- Tell students to refer to this list as often as they like.
- Go over the remainder of the chart, paying special attention to the negative form.

❏ EXERCISE 3. Looking at grammar.
Page 302
Time: 5 minutes

Explain to students that they should pay attention to whether certain combinations sound correct or not because chances are they have heard the correct prepositional combinations many times prior to this formal study.

❏ EXERCISE 4. Looking at grammar.
Page 303
Time: 5–10 minutes

- Have students complete the first situation individually and then have them take turns reading their completed sentences aloud.
- Correct any errors right away and check for comprehension of meaning.
- Complete Situation 2 as a class and increase the pace a bit, giving students a greater challenge.

Optional Vocabulary

blaming	prohibiting
excuse	accused
aisle	elderly
personnel	

❏ EXERCISE 6. Listening. Page 305
Time: 5–10 minutes

- Explain to students that in summarizing each dialogue, they are not reporting what they heard precisely but rather restating it.
- Prior to listening to the audio, give students a few minutes to guess which preposition will follow each verb.
- Play the audio through once without stopping. Then replay and stop after each item.
- Review answers as a class.

❏ EXERCISE 7. Let's talk: interview.
Page 305
Time: 5–10 minutes

- Tell students that they will be reporting on what they learned and that they should be prepared to expand on their answers if asked further questions.
- Have students get up and move around the room to conduct the interviews.
- Review as a class, having each student give information about the responses of at least one classmate. Correct any mistakes in target or non-target grammar as they arise.
- Ask further questions of either the student reporting or the student who gave the original information.

❏ EXERCISE 9. Let's talk. Page 306
Time: 5 minutes

Expansion: Prepare index cards before class. Each should have the question *How can you . . . ?* and list four or five different phrases describing various actions / tasks. Give one index card to each student. Have students stand up and move around the class, asking each other how they would perform the action or task described. When answering a question, they should use a ***by*** + *-ing* (***by*** + *gerund phrase*) to explain how they would perform the action or task described. Each student should collect the variety of answers he/she receives. Then have students return to their seats and ask a student to read aloud five to ten ***by*** + *gerund* responses that one of his/her actions prompted. Students then use this information to guess what the original task was. Possible index card tasks (and possible responses in italics) follow:

How can you . . .

get elected to public office?

By joining many committees, by attending community events, by meeting people and discussing their concerns, by campaigning energetically.

improve your health?

By limiting calories, by eating healthy foods, by getting enough sleep, by exercising.

have the career of your choice?

By being studious at the right time of life, by being open-minded to new opportunities, by working hard, by networking.

ensure you have a pleasant retirement?

By investing money wisely, by not getting deeply into debt, by keeping busy and in good health.

How can you . . .

expand your understanding of the global economy?

By reading international newspapers, by taking an Economics course, by traveling.

build upper body strength?

By lifting weights, by doing yoga, by carrying groceries.

keep your mind sharp?

By doing crossword puzzles, by taking up a challenging new hobby or language, by practicing a musical instrument.

❏ EXERCISE 10. Let's talk: interview.
Page 306
Time: 10–15 minutes

- First, ask students to model how certain emotions are shown in their cultures. You may want to begin this activity by modeling a few expressions yourself.
- As a class, write a list of specific facial movements on the board. For example:

  raise your eyebrow
  furrow your brow
  scowl
  frown
  clench your teeth
  set your jaw
  blink
  sneer
  smirk

- If students would like to share their drawings of faces expressing different emotions, they may do so or draw their faces on the board.

CHART 14-3. Common Verbs Followed by Gerunds. Page 307
Time: 10 minutes

This chart and the following exercises present just a few of the verbs that are followed by gerunds. Some students, depending on their learning style, may want to memorize the list, but remind them that it is far more effective to practice using the verbs orally and in writing until they begin to "sound right."

- Write the chart title on the board and explain that gerunds are the objects of certain verbs, many of which may already be familiar to your students.
- Have students put checks next to those verbs they already know. From those verbs, have students come up with a sentence describing their lives, likes, dislikes or other actions.
- Write two or three of the student-generated sentences on the board. For example:

  Lola doesn't mind taking care of her sister's children.
  François postponed leaving for the train station until the weather improved.
  Michiko mentioned having a Halloween party with her classmates.

- Now send three students to the board and have them identify the subject, verb, and object of each sentence. For example:

  S   V   O
  Lola doesn't mind taking care of her sister's children.

- Go over the rest of the chart with the class.

❏ EXERCISE 14. Looking at grammar.
Page 308
Time: 5–10 minutes

- Remind students that more than one gerund is possible as a completion for each sentence.
- Have students try this as seatwork first and then review as a class, discussing the appropriateness of various gerunds.
- Correct pronunciation and target grammar immediately and overtly.

CHART 14-4. Go + Gerund. Page 309
Time: 10 minutes

Some grammarians disagree about the nature of these *-ing* words; are they gerunds or participles? For your students, terminology is much less important than idiomatic use. We will call these structures "gerunds."

Definitions of some vocabulary items in the chart:

birdwatching = a hobby for people who enjoy identifying birds in natural habitats

bowling = a sport in which a heavy ball is rolled toward nine or ten wooden pins in order to knock them down (in as few rolls as possible)

camping = living in a tent or trailer/caravan for fun; "getting back to nature"

canoeing = floating/paddling on a river or lake in a small, simple boat called a *canoe*

hiking = walking vigorously in the mountains or countryside (possibly while also carrying equipment in a pack on one's back = *to go backpacking*

jogging = running somewhat slowly for exercise

sailing = traveling on a lake or sea in a boat that has a sail or perhaps a motor for power

sightseeing = touring; traveling to see a famous or beautiful place

sledding = in winter, going down a snowy hill using a sled, which is a wooden seat on metal bars or a plastic surface that can slide quickly over the snow

snorkeling = swimming underwater with a face mask and breathing tube in order to watch fish

window shopping = looking into shop windows but perhaps not intending to buy anything

A phrase similar in structure is *to go missing*, meaning "to disappear." For example: *In the mystery novel, a rich widow **went missing**, and Sherlock Holmes has to use all his powers of deduction to find her.* Go missing is principally British, but is also sometimes used in American English. Students may find it of interest.

- Have students look through the list and check off a few activities that they enjoy.
- Ask a few students to write sentences on the board about the activities they have done already or want to do in the near future.
- Ask a few other students to go to the board and identify the subjects, verbs, and objects. For example:

     S   V   O

  Dario and I went sailing on the Charles River last weekend.

- Remind students that by using these **go** + *gerund* combinations frequently, they will become more confident using them.

❑ EXERCISE 16. Let's talk. Page 309
Time: 5–10

- Ask these questions in a natural, conversational way while students are looking at Chart 14-4.
- Encourage students to respond with complete sentences.
- Encourage other students to ask for specific details by doing so yourself.

CHART 14-5. Special Expressions Followed by *-ing*. Page 310
Time: 10 minutes

In examples (a) and (b), the verb *have* means "to experience" something.

The *-ing* verbs are labeled "gerunds" in some grammar texts. The argument, however, for their being called "present participles" is strong. This text chooses simply to call them *-ing* forms.

Frankly, the grammar in this chart doesn't fit in neatly anywhere in this text. This chart is included in the unit on gerunds because this seems a logical place: certain verbs are typically followed by *-ing* forms, and the verbs and expressions in this chart share this characteristic.

- Write the chart title on the board.
- Explain to students that these *-ing* expressions originally come from clauses containing present participles. For example, *We had a good time while we were playing soccer* can be expressed in a reduced way as *We had a good time playing soccer*.
- Tell students that the name or classification of these expressions doesn't matter so much as the goal that students can use them easily.
- Ask students to go through the list and check off those expressions they are already familiar with.
- Write some of the most common expressions on the board, and then have students come to the board to complete each sentence with information that is true for them. For example:

  I had a good time <u>going out with my friends last night</u>.
  I had trouble <u>getting all my homework done before class today</u>.
  I had difficulty <u>phoning my parents in Turkey last night</u>.
  I spend a lot of time <u>reading books in English and writing emails to my English-speaking friends from all over the world</u>.
  I waste a lot of time <u>watching video clips on YouTube when I should be studying</u>.

- Go over the remainder of the chart and remind students again that, as with the other parts of the chapter, they will learn these expressions best by simply hearing and speaking them repeatedly.

❑ **EXERCISE 20.** Looking at grammar.
Page 311
Time: 10 minutes

> There may be more than one possible completion for these items, especially if one stretches one's imagination, but the items are constructed to produce one logical, typical completion.

Optional Vocabulary
indecisive
spoil

❑ **EXERCISE 21.** Let's talk: pairwork.
Page 311
Time: 10–15 minutes

Expansion: This activity can readily be turned into an impromptu game. Tell students that before they begin, they can either choose to tell the truth or lie, depending on their preference. If they lie successfully (and their partner does not challenge the response), they gain a point. If they lie unsuccessfully and their partner does question the truth of what the student is saying, the partner gains a point. Possible exchange between two students:

> Speaker A: In my free time, I have fun <u>riding and taming horses</u>.
>
> Speaker B: I don't think you are telling the truth.
>
> Speaker A: I am. My parents have a ranch and horse farm in Argentina.

CHART 14-6. Common Verbs Followed by Infinitives. Page 313
Time: 20–25 minutes

> Remind students that, as with gerunds, they have probably encountered the infinitive form many times before. (It is usually introduced with the base form, and most students use it to describe what they want or like to do.)
>
> The passive examples (f) and (g) assume that students are familiar with the basic passive forms in Chapter 11. If they aren't or they need to have their memories refreshed, you may need to review passive forms because they are used in Exercises 25 through 29.
>
> The alternative structures in the notes below this chart are important for the following exercise, and you should call your students' attention to these sentences.

• Write the chart title on the board.
• Write *verb + infinitive* on the board and tell your students that they will help you create example sentences for this structure.

• Choose six of the more common infinitives and write the beginnings of sentences about your students on the board. Use the verbs included in the chart. For example:

> Valeria hopes to _____
> Matteus promised to _____
> Ah-Ram plans to _____
> Viktor agreed to _____
> Lei-wen offered to _____
> Our teacher pretended to _____

• Ask six students to complete the sentences with particular information about their peers.
• Ask another six students to identify the parts of each sentence. For example:

> **S   V   + Infinitive**
> Valeria hopes to travel this weekend.

• Go over the first part of Chart 14-6, (a)–(c), especially noting the placement of *not*.
• Now write *Verb + Object + Infinitive* on the board and explain that most verbs that follow this pattern have to do with instructing or telling someone to do something.
• Write an example on the board and review (d)–(g) with your class. For example:

> Martha asked us to open our books.

• Identify the parts of speech (you can have your students say them while you mark them).

> **S   V   O + Infinitive**
> Martha asked us to open our books.

• If there is time, write more than one example, and have students identify parts of speech.
• Finally, write the heading *Verb + Infinitive / Verb + Object + Infinitive*
• Explain that verbs in this category can either be followed by an infinitive or can be followed by an object and then an infinitive. Explain that these verbs can have both the patterns described above.
• Write an example of both possibilities with the same verb on the board. For example:

> She asked to leave early.
> She asked John to leave early.

• Have a student go to the board to identify and contrast the differences. For example:

> **S   V   + Infinitive**
> She asked to leave early.
> **S   V   O + Infinitive**
> She asked John to leave early.

• Remind students that, as with gerunds, they will benefit most from using and hearing infinitives in real speech and that the exercises that follow the chart will help them to hear what sounds right.

❏ EXERCISE 26. Looking at grammar.
Page 314
Time: 10 minutes

The answers are in the form of reported (or indirect) speech. The cues are in quoted (or direct) speech. Chapter 12 contains charts on quoted and reported speech, but students probably don't need that lesson in order to complete this exercise. Students can understand that *verb + infinitive* is a way of reporting what someone has said. You may wish to point out the equivalency between modals / imperatives in quoted speech and *verb + infinitive* in reported speech. Or you may not wish to discuss the concept of quoted vs. reported speech at all.

• Show students how item 1 was produced by transforming the quote into a different *reporting verb + an infinitive*.
• Give students time to write their answers while you circulate, helping as needed.
• Review all your students' answers orally, as a class, with each student reading one answer aloud.
• Discuss those items that cause any difficulty right away and correct these target items overtly and immediately.

Optional Vocabulary
stern
valid

❏ EXERCISE 27. Let's talk. Page 315
Time: 10 minutes

• Because this exercise follows a pattern of production that students have seen before in this text, encourage them to personalize and make their responses as real as possible.
• Remind students that by using their own ideas to complete each sentence, they will be gaining meaningful practice of the structures presented in Chart 14-6.
• You may want to have a student quickly remind the class of changes that need to be made when changing from active to passive voice first.

CHART 14-7. Common Verbs Followed by Either Infinitives or Gerunds. Page 317
Time: 20–25 minutes

The complex history of the English language — elements from German, French, Norse, etc. — has produced the parallel forms in Group A. Learners should be confident that using the infinitive or gerund with these verbs causes no substantial change in meaning that would in any way interfere with communication.

However, you can let students know that native speakers don't always agree on their uses of the forms in Group A. The differences are mainly the result of regional or social variations in use.

In contrast, the differences in meaning with Group B verbs are substantial, and students need practice in order to understand and use these verbs appropriately. Using an infinitive instead of a gerund with one of these causes a significant change in meaning and students should be taught what these changes are.

Plan to spend ample time on this chart. These distinctions are important and not always easy for students to grasp. Before class, create multiple real-life examples for Group B that clearly illustrate the differences in meaning.

• Present the Group A verbs by writing on the board *Gerund or Infinitive: NO Difference.*
• Illustrate this with the verb *to like* by writing two examples on the board: one followed by a gerund and one followed by the same verb but in infinitive form. For example:

    Hye Won likes <u>skiing</u>.
    Hye Won likes <u>to ski</u>.

• Tell students that they may meet native speakers who argue that there is a difference, but tell them that if there is a subtle difference, it is too minimal for most people to be able to explain exactly what it is. Stress that for students' purposes, the usage and meaning is exactly the same with Group A verbs.
• Now introduce the Group B verbs by writing on the board *Gerund or Infinitive: BIG Difference.*
• An effective way to introduce this is by asking one student to volunteer to help you. Ask the volunteer to stand up, jump up and down, walk around, or do a particular physical action.
• Now ask the student to stop the previous action.
• Ask students to help you write on the board what they just observed. For example:

    Seiko stopped jumping up and down.

• Now ask another student to stand up and walk around the room. Tell him to stop walking. After he stops, ask him to pick up a book.
• With your students help, write on the board what they just observed in this second demonstration. For example:

    Alvaro was walking.
    Alvaro stopped walking.
    Alvaro stopped (walking)(in order) to pick up a book.

• Work through the other verbs in Group B, giving your students very specific examples for the verbs in Group B.
• Take the time to write sentences to illustrate the differences in meaning. Use key examples to make sure students understand these differences.
• Go over the chart, especially Group B, to reinforce those concepts.

❏ **EXERCISE 30.** Looking at grammar.
Page 318
Time: 10–15 minutes

> The answers to this exercise will probably raise many questions that need to be discussed briefly. Therefore, it is best to discuss the exercise with the whole class.

- Give students ample time to complete the exercise.
- Have students take turns reading answers aloud.
- Be extremely clear when correcting them and make frequent use of the board. You may need to come up with several examples of each new use in order to help students grasp the different uses.

❏ **EXERCISE 33.** Let's talk. Page 320
Time: 10 minutes

> This is a quick review that requires uncomplicated sentences.

- Explain the roles of Speaker A and B, and model the examples orally with a student.
- Give the pairs or small groups plenty of time to practice.
- Walk around the room helping students and participating / taking the role of Speaker A or B, respectively.

Expansion: After the pairwork, you could turn the exercise into a quiz, with the students writing sentences from your spoken cues. You could make up additional items for a quiz.

CHART 14-8. *It* + Infinitive; Gerunds and Infinitives as Subjects. Page 322
Time: 10–15 minutes

> You may need to point out that a gerund subject is singular and requires a singular form of the verb (for example: *Playing* games is fun.)
>
> The emphasis in Chart 14-8 and the exercises that follow is on the *it* + *infinitive* structure, a frequent pattern in both speech and writing.
>
> Of course, *it* + *gerund* is also possible, and students may produce some examples. Also, an infinitive can be the subject of a sentence. Commend students if they use these correctly, but return their attention to the more common *it* + *infinitive* and *gerund as subject* patterns in this lesson.

- Write the chart title on the board and tell students you will be looking at *it* + *infinitive* first.

- Ask students if they can think of any expressions with *it* + *infinitive* that they have used previously. They will probably be able to offer several. Write the phrases they provide on the board and develop them into sentences. For example:

  Carlo: *It is important . . .*
  You: *Great. It is important . . . how can you complete this? What is it important to do? It can be anything, in any context.*
  Carlo: *It is important to speak English as much as possible, outside of class.*
  Yaniv: *It is important to save money for future emergencies.*
  Lila: *It is important to tell the truth — most of the time.*

- Now turn to *Gerunds and Infinitives as Subjects.*
- Explain that using gerunds as subjects is a bit more common, but that both are possible. Tell students that using an infinitive as the subject may make their English sound more formal and less ordinary.
- Ask students to give you some infinitives and gerunds for common activities, and write these on the board. For example:

studying	to study
eating	to eat
sleeping	to sleep

- Ask students to go to the board and write sentences for each one.
- Go over the chart and discuss note (d) as this syntax can be quite challenging.

❏ **EXERCISE 38.** Looking at grammar.
Page 323
Time: 10 minutes

> This exercise has two purposes. One is to teach the correct location of the *for (someone)* phrase between the adjective and the infinitive. (For example, it is highly unusual or highly incorrect in English to say *For me it is important to go. / It for me is important to go. / It is for me important to go.*)
>
> The other purpose is to demonstrate the meaning and use of the *for (someone)* phrase. It limits the meaning of the general statement. For example, item 2, (*It's easy to speak Spanish.*) is not true for most people, so it's necessary to limit that statement to some person or group (*It's easy for Roberto to speak Spanish because it's his native language. It isn't easy for Mr. Wu to speak Spanish because his native language is Chinese and he's studied very little Spanish.*)

Expansion: Have students complete this exercise in groups. Then as a class, judge how creatively the groups have adapted the sentences. Give each group a chance to read (or write on the board) their best version of each expanded sentence and award points based on 1) grammatical accuracy, 2) level of vocabulary, and 3) creativity.

CHARTS 14-9 and 14-10. Reference List of Verbs Followed by Gerunds. Reference List of Verbs Followed by Infinitives.
Pages 324–325
Time: 10–20 minutes

These lists are for students to refer to, not for them to memorize. The exercises that follow, and the Workbook, provide a lot of practice, but learners don't need to learn the lists by heart. Some students, however, will sit down and try to memorize every word on the lists no matter what you say.

These lists are not exhaustive, but they do represent many of the most frequently used words that fall into these patterns.

- Tell students that they will gain the most from these lists by referring to them, and then trying to incorporate new vocabulary and the gerund or infinitive forms into their everyday speech.
- Ask and answer any questions about vocabulary. When you do so, give your students a whole sentence with a meaningful context rather than just a brief definition.
- Be sensitive to what works best for your students. Many students may need help understanding the words listed, but some may not. Do your best to challenge all of the students in your class by allowing the strongest ones to define vocabulary that not everyone is familiar with.
- Please see the front of this book for further suggestions on strategies for presenting grammar or patterns to a class as a whole. In particular, you will need to focus on keeping the interest of the most experienced students while being equally supportive of the less experienced ones.

Expansion: Create an oral exercise using these charts. Select some of the sentences at random and ask students to put the verbs in their proper gerund or infinitive forms. For example:

You: (choosing item 9 from the first section in Chart 14-10): *I don't care* (pause) *see that show.*

Student: *I don't care <u>to see</u> that show.*

You: (Perhaps repeat the correct answer. Then choose another item, for example, item 5 from Chart 14-9): *He avoided* (pause) *answer my question.*

Student: *He avoided <u>answering</u> my/your question.*

❏ EXERCISES 43 and 44. Looking at grammar. Page 327
Time: 10–15 minutes each

You may want to use these exercises as review quizzes. Students can write their answers on a piece of paper to hand in.

❏ EXERCISE 45. Let's talk. Page 328
Time: 20–30 minutes

- Once you have clearly explained and modeled the directions, move around the room making sure that the various groups have understood the activity.
- Encourage students to keep the list on the next page (page 329) handy so that they can refer to it as needed.
- If each group chooses a different story beginning, they can retell their stories later to the whole class.

Expansion: As a follow-up activity, have each group hand in a written summary of its story. All the infinitives and gerunds should be underlined. You could make copies for the whole class to read.

Alternatively, ask each student to come up with a new beginning of the story. Have students exchange new story beginnings or collect and redistribute. Each student then writes a new story as a homework assignment and hands it in.

Chapter 15
Gerunds and Infinitives, Part 2

CHAPTER SUMMARY

OBJECTIVE: To learn some special uses of gerunds, infinitives, and the simple form.

APPROACH: The chapter begins with the infinitives of purpose and common structures that require infinitives. Then passive forms are presented. Next, some classes of verbs that are accompanied by other simple or *-ing* forms are presented. Finally, a set of exercises provides a review of Chapters 14 and 15.

TERMINOLOGY: The traditional term "infinitive" is used for ***to*** + *a verb* in its simple (i.e., non-finite or uninflected) form. A "gerund" is defined as "a word that ends in *-ing* and functions as a noun."

CHART 15-1. Infinitive of Purpose: *In Order To.* Page 331
Time: 10 minutes

> Additional examples for the chart footnote:
>
> General: *An encyclopedia is used for locating facts and information.*
> Specific: *I used the encyclopedia to locate facts about India.*
>
> General: *Knives are used for cutting or slicing.*
> Specific: *My brother used a knife to cut his birthday cake.*

- Write the chart title on the board.
- Ask students where they went the previous weekend and why or what they went to this location *in order to do.*
- Write the simple *Why* question on the board and then immediately underneath it, write a restatement using *in order to.* For example:

    You: *Juan, why did you go to the airport this past weekend?*

    You: *Juan, what did you go to the airport in order to do?*

- Explain that this second question can be asked and answered without stating *in order,* and write the resulting question and answer on the board. Remind students that the infinitive of purpose follows a subject / verb clause. For example:

    You: *Juan, what did you go to the airport to do?*

    Juan: *I went to the airport to meet my sister.*

- Generate similar examples with students and have others go to the board to underline or highlight the infinitives of purpose. For example:

    Malaika went to the mall to buy a new pair of sunglasses.
    Pietro traveled to New York to spend time with his uncle.
    Ya-Yeng drove to the mountains to hike and relax.

- Explain that the preposition *for* is used before a noun, but it also expresses purpose.

❏ EXERCISE 2. Looking at grammar.
Page 331
Time: 5 minutes

> Though this exercise may appear basic, many students are used to expressing purpose with a translation of ***for*** + *a verb.* Remind students of why *for* must be followed by a noun object.

- Do this exercise aloud with students taking turns.
- Correct any mistakes immediately and give concrete reminders of the target structure. For example:

    You can't use "for" there because it precedes a verb.

❏ EXERCISE 4. Looking at grammar.
Page 332
Time: 5–10 minutes

- Instruct students to ask a *why*-question in each case to determine whether *in order* is possible.
- Review answers as a class by having various students read sentences aloud.

Optional Vocabulary
fertilizer
support herself
relief

❏ EXERCISE 6. Let's talk: interview.
Page 333
Time: 10–15 minutes

Expansion: Create six "Top Ten Reasons" lists (one for each item in the exercise) and write these on the board. Some of your students who have been exposed to U.S. culture may recognize these types of lists from popular television, but if not, writing these lists will give every student a chance to contribute their own findings. These lists are often presented with the tenth reason first and the top reason / number 1 reason last.

Sample Top Ten Reasons List:

Why People Go To Hawaii for Vacation

10. *Some people go to Hawaii to go to a luau.*
9. *Some people go to Hawaii to wear a grass skirt and a lei.*
8. *Some people go to Hawaii for the delicious seafood.*
7. *Some people go to Hawaii to see a volcano.*
6. *Some people go to Hawaii for the sunshine and beaches.*
5. *Some people go to Hawaii to have an "exotic" vacation without leaving the U.S.*
4. *Some people go to Hawaii to visit Diamond Head, Pearl Harbor, and Waikiki Beach.*
3. *Some people go to Hawaii to learn to hula.*
2. *Some people go to Hawaii to practice surfing.*

And the number 1 reason people go to Hawaii is . . . for their honeymoon or anniversary.

Possible Alternative Topics

What are two reasons why some people . . . ?

get married

have children

travel far from home

volunteer

climb Mount Everest

take risks

email (when they could phone)

phone (when they could email)

use alternative healthcare practices (acupuncture, herbal medicine, chiropractic)

eat frozen or fast food

give their children nontraditional names

become vegetarians

wear expensive labels/designer clothing

CHART 15-2. Adjectives Followed by Infinitives. Page 333
Time: 5–10 minutes

This list is not complete; other examples can be found in reference books on grammar. However, many of the most frequently used adjectives are included here.

Many of these adjectives can be followed by other structures. For example:

I was *happy about going* to the circus. (preposition + gerund)

I was *happy watching* the clouds float by. (present participle)

It is not necessary to mention these structures to the learners at this point as their focus should remain primarily on *adjective + infinitive*.

If students wonder why these particular adjectives, unlike others, are followed by infinitives, tell them it is a traditional pattern developed over time during the long history of the English language.

- Tell students they have already heard many of the adjectives followed by infinitives included in the chart's list.
- Ask students to scan the list and see which of the included phrases they already know. Some of the more common phrases follow:

  glad to

  happy to

  lucky to

  ready to

  sorry to

  surprised to

- Write one example on the board. For example:

  Han Na was <u>surprised to meet</u> *her neighbor from Seoul here.*

- Following this template, give five students one of the more common expressions above and ask them to come up with a sentence using the adjective expression on the board.
- Ask other students to identify the adjective followed by infinitive phrase.
- Go over the remainder of the chart with students and make sure to address any vocabulary questions they may have.

❏ **EXERCISE 8.** In your own words. Page 334
Time: 10 minutes

- Encourage a variety of completions using the adjectives listed in Chart 15-2.
- Have students take turns reading each item (as printed in the book), and then ask them to call out different completions.

Optional Vocabulary

expressway   desperately
family reunion   wayward
supportive

❏ **EXERCISE 9.** Let's talk. Page 334
Time: 5–10 minutes

- Give each group either one or both situations.
- Encourage students to come up with additional sentences to describe Mr. Wah's and the residents of Viewmont's feelings about their situations.
- Discuss answers as a whole class.
- Please see the front of this book for more suggestions on how to get the most from group work.

This exercise gives students more opportunities to communicate their own ideas. This exercise can be carried out in several ways described below.

Many of these items are deliberately open-ended and personal and are designed to stimulate discussion. You will want to correct the target structures, but do so in a supportive manner that in no way inhibits students' discussion.

Item 5 could serve as an opening for a fairly detailed discussion in which students can share their personal difficulties and frustrations in using English — if they are not too reluctant to try to express these in English.

As a teacher-controlled dialogue, read the questions aloud, pursuing interesting student responses, and encouraging students to expand on their answers. Spend more time on those questions that students become quickly engaged in and less time on those that students don't seem as excited by.

As an interview, have students get up, move around the room, and gather as many responses to each question as possible. Either ask students to focus on getting as many different answers as possible or to concentrate on asking related questions and delving deeper into each response.

Pairwork is also a possibility, but a larger number of speakers might produce a more interesting discussion.

Expansion: Whichever method you have chosen for Exercise 10, a writing assignment provides a nice follow-up. Ask students to provide a written response to four of the ten items. Let students know that they have the option of explaining their personal responses or sharing some of the responses that were publicly discussed in class. On their papers, note the accurate and meaningful production of the target structures, but also take the time to comment on the content they have chosen to share.

CHART 15-3. Using Infinitives with *Too* and *Enough*. Page 335
Time: 10 minutes

Learners of English often fail to understand that the word *too* before an adjective has a negative meaning (usually that something is excessive and that this causes a negative result). The speaker gives completely different information when using *very* or *too* followed by an infinitive.

• Write the following examples (or modify the ones here to make them more relevant to the members of your class) on the board:

Pedro enjoys listening to loud music <u>very</u> much.
Pedro enjoys listening to loud music <u>too</u> much.

• Explain that when we use the adverb <u>very</u> to modify an adjective or adverb, it strengthens the adverb or adjective.
• Explain that when we use the adverb <u>too</u> to modify an adjective or adverb, it does more than strengthen the adverb or adjective. It actually changes the meaning to the negative.
• Now add to the second example sentence on the board.

Pedro enjoys listening to loud music <u>too</u> much. → His eardrums have been damaged, and he has lost a bit of his hearing ability over the years.

• Now write the following reminders on the board:

very = a lot
Mr. Nagy is <u>very excited</u> to go to Paris.

too = negative
Mei is <u>too tired</u> to come with us. → Therefore, she will just stay home and rest.

• Check that students understand that *too* indicates a negative result.
• Explain that *enough* follows the adjective and does not indicate a negative result.
• Go over the chart.

❑ **EXERCISE 12.** Let's talk. Page 336
Time: 10 minutes

• In order to make sure that students understand the negative result indicated by the use of ***too*** + *infinitive*, ask them to explain <u>why</u> the ring can't be bought in item 1 (and why the meeting won't be attended in item 2).
• Give students time to go through Part I, generating the negative results for each item.
• Have students take turns reading their negative statements aloud.
• Correct and discuss the target structures students produce before going on to Part II.
• Follow the same steps for Part II and review as a class.

❑ **EXERCISE 13.** Let's talk. Page 336
Time: 10–15 minutes

This exercise intends to touch upon typical student misunderstandings in the use of *too* instead of *very* for example:
INCORRECT: *My country is too beautiful.*

• Ask students to close their books if you plan to work as a class.
• You may need to repeat a cue or add some brief contextual information to help students understand.
• If students are working in small groups or pairs, have the person asking the question keep his/her book open while the others keep theirs closed.
• Because these questions could lead to lively discussion, be ready to help students further engage one another (rather than only interacting with the teacher).
• Go over the answers to all the items and discuss.

CHART 15-4. Passive Infinitives and Gerunds. Page 338
Time: 5–10 minutes

> Chapter 11 presents the passive. You may wish to review the notions of "passive verb" and "*by*-phrase" with your students.
>
> Students may need to review the reference lists of verbs followed by infinitives or gerunds.

- Write the chart title on the board.
- Using what you know of your students' lives, create an example of a passive infinitive and write it on the board. For example:

  Yuval was surprised <u>to be given</u> such a big present.

- Now, with students' help, come up with an example of the passive gerund.

  Annika was worried <u>about being asked</u> to give a speech at the wedding.

- Go over the chart with your students.

❏ EXERCISE 18. Looking at grammar.
Page 338
Time: 10 minutes

> This exercise requires students to think about the meanings and forms of tenses, verbs that require infinitives or gerunds, and relationships in time. Be sure to allow plenty of time for them to prepare their answers.
>
> Sometimes a simple gerund can be used with a past tense main verb even though the gerund's action occurred earlier in time. This shows that the English language is changing — not everyone always uses these forms in the same way. But both forms are still in common use, so students need to learn their normal functions.

CHART 15-5. Using Gerunds or Passive Infinitives Following *Need*. Page 339
Time: 5–10 minutes

> British English can also use *want* in examples (c) and (d), but American English can only use *need* in those cases. For example:
>
> *The house wants painting* = BrE but not AmE.
>
> There are regional, dialectical differences in native-speaker preferences for using gerund vs. passive infinitive after *need*.

- Write the chart title on the board.
- Explain that using the passive infinitive after *need* is more widely accepted than using the gerund form.

- Present students with an example of the passive infinitive following *need* and write this on the board. For example:

  Those clothes need <u>to be washed</u>.

- Explain that in some parts of the world, it is quite common to use a gerund form after *need*. Illustrate this with the same sentence. For example:

  Those clothes need <u>washing</u>.

- Go over the chart.

❏ EXERCISE 22. Let's talk. Page 340
Time: 10 minutes

- You can discuss this as a class or in small groups. You can also assign this as a written exercise, requiring at least five sentences.

  Expansion: If working in small groups, assign a time limit (10 minutes or so) for each group to write as many sentences as possible. After 10 minutes, have one student from each group write his/her group's sentences up on the board. As a class, review all the sentences for both meaning and grammar. The group with the most correct sentences wins.

CHART 15-6. Using Verbs of Perception.
Page 341
Time: 10 minutes

> The five physical senses are sight, hearing, touch, smell, and taste. This chart deals with the patterns of complementary verb use with the list of "verbs of perception" that express four of the five senses — all but taste.
>
> Since both the simple form and the *-ing* form are correct and often interchangeable, it is sometimes difficult to explain that there can be a difference in meaning. The chart attempts to make the difference easier to grasp, but for some students the distinction may seem unnecessarily subtle.
>
> New users of English can't really make any sort of substantial communication error by using one form rather than another, so the grammar points in this chart are not crucial. However, for those interested in the subtleties of how form affects meaning and how choice of form can make meaning more precise, the information in this chart will be of interest.
>
> In the terminology used in this text, the "simple form" of a verb is the form that is usually listed in the dictionary, the form with no tense or endings, i.e, the uninflected form.
>
> SIMPLE FORM: *go, accept*
>
> SIMPLE INFINITIVE: *to go, to accept*

- Write the chart title on the board.
- Explain to students that you are going to present two ways of using verbs of perception.

- With your students' help, create sentences using verbs of perception followed by the simple form of the verb based on what they can actually observe in class at the moment. For example:

  Paulo is listening to his teacher explain the grammar.
  Susana sees Miguel take notes in class every day.

- Explain that it is also possible for these same verbs to be followed by the *-ing* form of the verb.
- Write the same observations from above but this time with the *-ing* form.

  Paulo is listening to his teacher explaining the grammar.
  Susana sees Miguel taking notes.

- Explain that the *-ing* use shows a subtle emphasis on duration.
- Illustrate this point by writing an example in which the *-ing* form is similar to a reduction of a *while*-clause. Write the following example on the board:

  Susana sees Miguel (while he is) taking notes.

- Explain that in some cases, given the actual context, it makes more sense to use either a simple or an *-ing* form.
- Explain that if an action is already in progress when the subject observes it, it may make sense to use the *-ing* form. Write an example of this on the board.

  When I arrived in my English class late, I saw my teacher handing out our final exam.

- Explain that if the emphasis is on perception of a complete action or performance, it makes most sense to use the simple form. Write an example of this on the board.

  Keiko saw the Rolling Stones perform last night.

- Go over the chart.

❏ **EXERCISE 25.** Let's talk. Page 341
Time: 5–10 minutes

> This item demonstrates a common use of verbs of perception in everyday life.

- Do item 1 with your class as a whole. Have individual students give you their descriptions orally.
- You can also have a student go to the board and write what he / she heard and saw for item 1.
- Break students into pairs or small groups for items 2 and 3, and circulate as they describe their classmates' actions to one another.

Expansion: Take the students to another place (outside the facilities, perhaps, or to another area of the class building) and ask them to describe their perceptions, encouraging them to observe closely and describe carefully what they see and hear.

You could also assign this extension as written homework. Have students describe their observations of any setting they choose. The more action they observe the better, so a crowded area (café, university library, gym, etc.) may work best. They can read their observations aloud without stating the venue and have others guess what the venue is. Students can write their assignment in the present tense and finish with "Where am I?"

For example (sample homework assignment):

  I hear weights being lifted onto machines. I see people stretching and lifting things repeatedly. I see other people running. I can smell sweat and Gatorade. Where am I? (The gym.)

❏ **EXERCISE 26.** Looking at grammar.
Page 341
Time: 10 minutes

> This exercise asks that students identify the verbs of perception in each item.
>
> Because the difference in usage of the simple or *-ing* form with verbs of perception is quite subtle in Part I, do your best to explain it clearly, but don't belabor it.
>
> In Part II, where the difference is more significant, this difference depends heavily on context, and it can be quite difficult for students to actually grasp it. Even in these cases, the line between the use of the two forms can still be too thin to easily discern. Don't let students dwell on this challenge. Do your best to reassure them that they will eventually grasp the differences by using the forms in particular situations.

- Explain that the items in Part I illustrate the fact that in many situations either form of the complementary verb is both correct and possible.
- Have students complete the sentences in Part I, bearing the above in mind and referring to the chart when reviewing as a class.
- Now explain that Part II presents situations where there is clearly a difference in meaning between the two forms.
- Have students complete Part II, and review as a class.

Expansion: Students can have fun demonstrating some of the situations in the entries, as if performing in a theater. Other students can describe the situation while you correct the target structures included in their observations. For example, for item 4, Carlos acts out being in an earthquake. Another student reports *Carlos could feel the ground shake / shaking.*

Optional Vocabulary
suspicious-looking
slammed
softball
auditorium
glanced
swatted

CHART 15-7. Using the Simple Form after *Let* and *Help*. Page 343
Time: 10 minutes

> The American English preference is (d), the simple form of a verb rather than an infinitive after *help*. The British English preference is (e), the infinitive after *help*.
>
> In the contraction *Let's* (c), the apostrophe indicates omission of the letter "u" in *Let us*. (See Chart 9-11). There is no other instance in English in which an apostrophe plus -s represents a contraction of *us*.

- Explain that *let* has the meaning "allow," and it is followed by first an object (usually a pronoun or proper noun) and then the simple form of the verb.
- Write the following pattern on the board:

  subject + *let/help* + *pronoun* + *simple verb*

- Ask students to help you think of a sentence about their classroom structure using *let*, and write this sentence on the board. For example:

  Our teacher lets us use our dictionaries.
  Our teacher lets us drink coffee in class.

- Explain to students that this pattern can also be used with the verb *help*. Refer to the pattern on the board.
- With students, come up with an example to illustrate *help* followed by the simple form. Write this example on the board:

  Jung Woo helped his mother wash her car.

- Briefly explain that example (e) is more commonly used in British English but that students will sometimes hear it in American English.

❏ EXERCISE 28. In your own words.
Page 343
Time: 5–10 minutes

> The purpose of this exercise is to accustom students to using simple forms after *let* and *help*.

- Ask students to complete the sentences on their own first.
- Have them take turns reading their completions aloud.
- Correct their production of the target structures as well as usage and vocabulary.

Expansion: For additional practice, you and your students can think of new sentences. One way to do so is to give students pieces of paper or index cards. Have students count off in groups of 3 (*1, 2, 3 . . . 1, 2, 3*). Ask all the 1's to write the name of a person or pronoun on their card or slip of paper. Ask the 2's to write the simple form of any verb. Now ask each 1 and 2 to give their cards to the number 3 person to their immediate right. This person should use the subject and verb he/she has been given to come up with a sentence using all the words and *let* or *help*. That student then must write his / her sentence on the

board, and the rest of the class will correct it. For example:

Index Card from #1	Index Card from #2
My mother	clean

Possible sentence to be created and written on the board by #3:

My mother helps my married sister clean her house every Saturday.

CHART 15-8. Using Causative Verbs: *Make, Have, Get*. Page 344
Time: 20–25 minutes

> A "causative" verb carries the meaning that something/someone produces (causes) a result. This may be a difficult concept in some cultures, and languages express the notion of causation in very different ways. Therefore, you may need to discuss the notion of causation with your students.
>
> The <u>method</u> of causation is expressed by choosing one of the three verbs:
>
> *make* = use force; *have* = request or order; *get* = use persuasion or perhaps trickery.

- Write the chart title on the board.
- Explain *causative* as a combination of active and passive. You can even say one half passive and one half active.
- Remind students that in a typical active sentence the subject both causes the verb to happen and also does, or performs, the action of the verb.
- Tell students that a causative-verb sentence is similar to an active sentence because the subject causes the verb to happen. Further explain that like a passive verb, the subject of a causative verb does not actually do/perform the action.
- Ask the class the following question:

  When you were a child, what was something your parents caused you to do?

- Write a list of their answers on the board. You may need to prompt them by supplying some examples such as:

  clean my room
  finish my chores
  do my homework

- Explain that we have three verbs we use for causative and that they have slight but important differences in meaning. Write the following on the board:

  make + simple form → no choice
  have + simple form → request
  get + infinitive → persuade

- Have students look at the list of tasks on the board again, and ask them:

  What was something your parents made you do that you had <u>no choice</u> about?
  What was something they <u>requested</u> you do?
  What was something they <u>persuaded</u> you <u>to</u> do?

- While students are thinking of their answers, model some correct forms by writing sentences about you on the board. For example:

When I was a child, my parents . . .

  made me go to bed at 8 P.M. every night.

  got me to eat my vegetables by promising me ice cream later.

- Elicit sentences from the class and write them on the board.
- These completions may spur some natural discussion of raising children and the different expectations parents have of small children across cultures. Encourage such conversation if it occurs, but reinforce the target grammar by writing the target structure on the board as it arises in discussion.
- Explain passive causatives by asking your students questions about everyday actions that they may cause to happen as subjects but that they may not actually do themselves. For example:

  Who decides that you need a haircut?

  Who actually cuts your hair?

- Tell students that a haircut is a perfect example of causative as the subject causes the action but (usually) does not do it him or herself.
- Explain that we use *have* and *get* to describe the typical action of going to a hairdresser, and write the following example on the board:

  Josefina had / got her hair <u>cut</u> last weekend.

- Go over the chart with students.

❏ EXERCISE 32. Let's talk or write. Page 345
Time: 10 minutes

- Though most students will already know most expressions, have them look through the list, and pre-teach any less familiar vocabulary.
- Have students make sentences for each of the items. If some tasks can't be performed at the shopping area nearest their homes, tell them to simply use a negative verb.
- Ask students to choose five items to make into a paragraph and turn in as homework. You can encourage students to expand on this by adding items that are not included in the original exercise.

❏ EXERCISES 35–39. Pages 347–350

These exercises are comprehensive reviews of Chapters 14 and 15. There are plenty of items in these exercises for additional practice of all the materials in Chapters 14 and 15. You might want to do the first few items of each as a whole class and then let students do the rest in small groups or as homework. Due to the number of items, you may choose to only discuss those items which caused difficulty.

❏ EXERCISE 36. Reading and listening.
Page 348
Time: 10 minutes

It is important that students understand the benefit of being able to guess meaning or vocabulary choices as the direction line instructs them to do when they first look at this passage. All autonomous language learners must be able to logically "fill in the blanks" both when they listen and read. Here they have practice with both skills.

- Explain to students the benefit of first trying to complete the cloze items without having listened to the audio: Using context to understand the correct vocabulary choices is something they have to do successfully to become active listeners and readers.
- After students listen to the audio, review and correct as a class.

Expansion: Have students close their texts, and ask them to paraphrase the paragraph as best they can. Ask students comprehension questions, or have them write what they understood in paragraph form. This topic may also lead to a general discussion, so some discussion questions are included below.

Possible comprehension questions:

1. *Roughly how much of the world's population is functionally illiterate?*
2. *What does it mean to be functionally illiterate?*
3. *What particular problem resulting from this illiteracy does the passage discuss?*
4. *What is one solution to this particular problem?*

Related discussion questions:

1. *Do you live in a country with a high or low rate of illiteracy?*
2. *There are many socioeconomic factors that contribute to illiteracy. What do you imagine these are?*
3. *There are many socioeconomic trends that are the result of illiteracy. What might these be?*
4. *The passage discusses the impact of illiteracy on health care. What are some other possible areas of a person's life that would be impacted by their inability to read?*
5. *What support exists in your country for those people who can't read?*

❏ EXERCISE 39. Let's talk and listen.
Page 350
Time: 10–15 minutes

Part I
- Have students discuss the questions in Part I for a few minutes with <u>their books closed</u>. You can also ask them to discuss other threatening weather they have experienced and to compare the relative violence of the weather they are used to.
- Play the audio.

Part II

- Have students open their books and complete the True / False section independently.

Part III

- Have students listen to the audio again, this time completing the cloze items.
- Discuss the completed passage with students, and encourage them to share personal stories and to ask questions.

- Draw attention to incorrect use of target structures, and encourage students to self-correct.

Optional Vocabulary

shelters	strike
fatal	conduct
bolt	plumbing
depression	
ditch	

Chapter **16**
Coordinating Conjunctions

CHAPTER SUMMARY

OBJECTIVE: This chapter gives students more choices for expressing related ideas. They will learn how English connects pieces of information that are in a relationship of equality.

APPROACH: Essentially, the chapter deals with the concept of parallelism. Two or more similar pieces of information should be expressed in similar grammatical forms, according to the preferred style of written English. The chapter introduces the use of coordinating conjunctions and related rules for punctuation.

TERMINOLOGY: A "conjunction" is a function word that serves as a connector or a linking word to join words, phrases, or clauses. This chapter deals with coordinating conjunctions, words that are used to create compound structures (e.g., compound subjects, compound verbs, compound sentences). In this text, correlative conjunctions (for example, *both . . . and*) are called "paired conjunctions." Subordinating conjunctions (e.g., *when, because, if*) are used to create complex sentences and are dealt with in the following chapter.

CHART 16-1. Parallel Structure. Page 352
Time: 15–25 minutes

Using parallel structure is an economical way to include several pieces of information in a single phrase or clause. The ability to use parallel structure is highly valued in spoken and written English because conciseness is a cultural value in English-speaking countries. Other cultures may have other values with regard to the expression of ideas in speaking and writing.

Problems with parallel structure are common in student writing.

To understand parallel structure, learners need to understand the idea of ellipsis: that certain words have been omitted from a sentence. The sentence can be understood without them because the omitted words are repetitive. English rhetoric does not value repetitiveness.

Wordy and repetitive: *Steve is coming to dinner and his friend is coming to dinner.*

In ellipsis, the repeated words (*be + coming to dinner*) are omitted and the verb is made to agree with the compound subject: *Steve and his friend are coming to dinner.*

- Write the chart title on the board.
- Introduce the concept of parallel structure by explaining that the English language has a stylistic preference for concise expression whenever possible.
- Next, write some intentionally repetetive sentences on the board, such as:

    The man is wearing a hat and the man is wearing a coat.
    The woman is wearing her hat and the woman is holding her coat.

- Ask a volunteer to go to the board and cross out any words that can be omitted without changing the meaning of the sentence. The improved sentences should look like this:

    The man is wearing a hat and ~~the man is wearing~~ a coat.
    The woman is wearing her hat and ~~the woman is~~ holding her coat.

- Explain to students that this concise approach is the grammatical source of the parallel structure they will now learn.
- A similar process that many students learned in school is balancing the equations that describe chemical reactions. Even if you can't remember how to balance an equation yourself, your students are likely to be familiar with the concept. It may help to write the following visual on the board:

    $2 H_2 + O_2 \rightarrow 2 H_2O$

- Explain that the task of creating parallel structure is similar to balancing an equation. Students using parallel structure need to account for each necessary word on either side of the conjunction.
- Write the following example on the board, and ask students to identify what seems unbalanced. You may need to read the sentence aloud so students can hear the error.

    Michael likes to eat pizza and drinking.

- Students should be able to identify that *and drinking* sounds unbalanced and doesn't match *eat pizza*.

    Michael likes to eat pizza and ~~drinking~~.

- Rewrite the above sentence in parallel structure by identifying the elements of parallel structure, as in the example below:

	infinitive + object		infinitive + object
Michael likes to eat	pizza	*and*	(to) drink soda.

- Go over the chart with students.

❏ EXERCISE 2. Looking at grammar.
Page 352
Time: 10 minutes

> At this early stage in recognition and production of the target material, it helps to be explicit when correcting students. For example, in item 1, if a student had chosen *C. kindness* as a possible answer, you should say:
>
> *Answer C. isn't possible because "friendly" is an adjective, and so we need another adjective, not a noun.*
>
> You may even want to write some simple equations on the board, such as:
>
> *noun + conjunction + noun*
>
> *adjective + conjunction + adjective*
>
> *verb + conjunction + verb*

- Remind students that their answers need to be the same part of speech as the word(s) to the left of the conjunction.
- Allow students time to complete the items on their own, and then review as a class.

CHART 16-2. Parallel Structure: Using Commas. Page 354
Time: 10 minutes

> In a series, the last item is preceded by a conjunction (usually *and* or *or*). Many people place a comma before that conjunction (e.g., *an apple, a banana, and a pear*), but the last comma is a matter of choice. This final comma is sometimes called an "Oxford comma," or "serial comma," and grammar books and style guides do not agree on whether that comma is required. This text uses the final comma so that students can see more clearly each element of a serial parallel structure. In addition, spoken English patterns usually have a pause before the conjunction in this instance, and the comma reflects the pause.

- Write the chart title on the board.
- Explain to students that certain uses of commas are grammatically required and that other uses are stylistic choices.
- Using your students' names and experiences, write a sentence on the board that uses *and* to connect two parts of a parallel structure. For example:

  Miguel and Kwong Min were late for class.

- Explain that if you add a third student, you would clearly separate all three by using commas.

  Miguel, Kwong Min, and Viktor were late for class.

- Tell students that the second comma in the example is not required, but it does reflect the necessary pause in the sentence. Say the sentence again, and exaggerate the pause so that students can hear it.

❏ EXERCISE 5. Listening and punctuation.
Page 354
Time: 5–10 minutes

> It is helpful to repeatedly remind students that grammatical and stylistic conventions (such as the use of the Oxford comma) are meaningful rather than arbitrary. The Oxford comma appropriately expresses the pause a speaker naturally includes before the final item in a series. Many students believe English punctuation practices are arbitrary, and thus it is up to teachers to emphasize the ways in which appropriate punctuation both clarifies and conveys meaning.

- Explain to students that they need to develop the ability to hear where commas and other punctuation marks belong, and that this exercise will help them do so.
- Play the audio through while students add commas as needed.
- To practice the pacing and appropriate pauses when listing elements of a series, ask students to take turns reading the items aloud.
- Ask students to paraphrase what is meant in item 10. They may want to discuss it briefly, and they may need you to expand on the irony of Twain's words.

Optional Vocabulary

snapped	bigotry
suspense	narrow-mindedness
prejudice	

❏ EXERCISE 6. Looking at grammar.
Page 354
Time: 10–15 minutes

- Ask students to explain the grammatical functions of the parallel words. For example, in item 1 the parallel words are both nouns.
- The class discussion may lead to a review of basic terminology of parts of speech (noun, verb, adjective, preposition, etc.) and how to recognize the various forms.
- Ask individual students to write their parallel sentences on the board for review. The class can then see whether all unnecessary words have been removed and check for correct punctuation and conjunction use.

Optional Vocabulary
generous
trustworthy

❏ EXERCISE 7. Looking at grammar.
Page 355
Time: 10 minutes

- Have students work in pairs for this exercise, and encourage them to be as creative as possible.
- Review answers for each item by asking several pairs to read their versions aloud.

❏ **EXERCISE 9.** Let's talk. Page 356
Time: 10–15 minutes

- Explain to students that as a group, they will need to discuss and reach agreement about possible answers.
- Tell students to first identify which part of speech is needed in each item.
- Assign each group an item to write on the board.
- Review as a class, and comment on content and meaning as well as parallel form.

CHART 16-3. Paired Conjunctions: *Both . . . And; Not Only . . . But Also; Either . . . Or; Neither . . . Nor.* Page 358
Time: 10–15 minutes

> There are two important grammar points here: (1) subject-verb agreement and (2) parallel structure. Both are practiced in the exercises following the chart.
>
> Some native speakers of English have trouble using these structures correctly (according to formal English preferences); learners can expect to be confused sometimes too. In actual usage of *neither . . . nor,* native speakers often use a plural verb with two singular subjects (e.g., *Neither my mother nor my sister **are** here. Neither my brother nor I **were** interested*). This usage is not presented in the text because it seems unnecessarily confusing for learners. You may wish to mention it, though, perhaps with the caveat "When in doubt, use formal English."
>
> Another point not mentioned in the text is that when there are two independent clauses connected by *not only . . . but also,* the first independent clause usually (but not always) has inverted subject-verb word order. (When a sentence begins with a negative, the subject and verb are often inverted.) Example: *Not only **does John go** to school full-time, but he also has a full-time job.* You may or may not wish to introduce this point to your students.

- Write the chart title on the board.
- Write the following sets of paired conjunctions on the board.

    not only . . . but also
    both . . . and
    neither . . . nor
    either . . . or

- Ask students whether they are already familiar with *either . . . or* and *neither . . . nor.* Many may already know how to use these and if so, you can ask them for sample sentences to write on the board.

    Pablo says he likes <u>neither</u> chocolate <u>nor</u> vanilla ice cream.

Mei-lin has been to <u>neither</u> France <u>nor</u> Italy.
Bernadette will <u>either</u> go to New York <u>or</u> stay at home this weekend.
Xiao-Ping is happy with <u>either</u> Italian <u>or</u> Vietnamese food, but she does not want to have Mexican food tonight.

- After you have written student-generated sample sentences similar to the ones above on the board, underline the phrases following each paired conjunction and note that the parts of speech are the same.
- Explain that these expressions always occur as paired conjunctions. When students see the first part of one (for example, *not only*), they should expect to see the completion (*but also*). For simplicity's sake, stress that these conjunctions always occur in pairs and that the second part must follow the first.
- Write some simple sentences on the board incorporating various paired conjunctions, such as:

    Not only the students but also _____ enjoy a day off from school.
    Both my mother and _____ love apple pie.

- Have students complete these sentences with similar nouns to establish the pattern.
- Explain that when there are two subjects introduced by paired conjunctions, the subject closer to the verb determines whether the verb is singular or plural.

❏ **EXERCISE 13.** Looking at grammar.
Page 358
Time: 10–15 minutes

> For an advanced class, you can conduct this as a teacher-led exercise with books closed.
>
> Group or pairwork is also possible, followed by a quick quiz using one item from each section.
>
> *Both . . . and* is used more frequently than *not only . . . but also.*
>
> *Not only . . . but also* tends to mean that something is especially interesting or surprising.
>
> Note that *Yes* is the required answer in the first three groups of items, but *No* is the answer with *neither . . . nor.*

- Write the first example on the board, and underline both the paired conjunctions and parts of speech that follow each conjunction.
- After students have completed each part, ask individual students to write their answers on the board.
- As a class, highlight both the paired conjunctions and the parts of speech in each sentence.

❏ EXERCISE 15. Looking at grammar.

Page 360
Time: 10 minutes

- Give students time to go through the items individually.
- Have students read their combinations aloud, using paired conjunctions.
- If there is a question about whether a certain structure is correct, write it on the board and evaluate it as a class.

Optional Vocabulary
deny
irreplaceable

❏ EXERCISE 16. Listening. Page 360

Time: 10 minutes

Part I

- To engage students in the topic, ask them for adjectives or nouns that they associate with bats, and write them on the board.
- Other possible questions to further the discussion:

  Why do some people seem to fear bats?

  What other animals do people fear and why?

- Before moving on to Part II, have students orally paraphrase the lecture, and write their simple restatements on the board.

Part II

- Remind students that in each word choice, they are creating parallel structure.
- Review answers by having students take turns reading aloud.

Optional Vocabulary

unreasoned	pollinating
tangle	overripe
carriers	flourish

CHART 16-4. Separating Independent Clauses with Periods; Connecting Them with *And* and *But*. Page 361

Time: 10–15 minutes

> Another term for a "run-on sentence" is a "comma splice" when a comma is used in place of (and when there should be) a period. Run-on sentences are a common problem in student writing (native and non-native alike).
>
> Advanced students may be interested to know that it is possible to use commas between independent clauses in a series: *Janet washed the windows, Bob swept the floor, and I dusted the furniture.* INCORRECT: *Janet washed the windows, Bob swept the floor.*

- Write the chart title on the board.
- Ask students to define *independent clause,* and write

the best parts of their definition on the board. For example:

independent clause = S + V;
         can stand alone as a sentence

- Explain that two independent clauses cannot be separated by only a comma.
- Write an incorrect example of this on the board, and then exaggerate crossing it out.

  INCORRECT: ~~Juan played tennis, Marco preferred golf.~~

- Now explain that the independent clauses can either 1) be separated by a period or 2) be joined by a conjunction (in this case, either *but* or *and* would work, depending on meaning).

  CORRECT: *Juan played tennis. Marco preferred golf.*
  CORRECT: *Juan played tennis, and Marco preferred golf.*
  CORRECT: *Juan played tennis, but Marco preferred golf.*

- Review the rest of the chart.

EXERCISE 18. Looking at grammar.

Page 361
Time: 5–10 minutes

- This exercise should be done quickly, so give students a time limit of five minutes to complete it individually.
- Assign an item to five different students and have them write their completed sentences on the board.
- Review the sentences and discuss the target structures.

❏ EXERCISE 20. Looking at grammar.

Page 362
Time: 10 minutes

Optional Vocabulary

intention	offspring
devastating	extended
crumbled	

Expansion: Prepare three or four sets of 21 index cards. Each set should have cards with the following:

9 index cards with 9 different independent clauses (These can be about any topic, but students do love to see their own names in print, so you may want to write simple clauses using your students as subjects.)

3 index cards with periods (only) on them

3 index cards with commas (only) on them

3 index cards with the conjunction *but* on them

3 index cards with the conjunction *and* on them

Put students into small groups, giving one set of cards to each group. Have them use the cards to come up with as many combinations of correctly punctuated sentences containing more than one clause as they can. Circulate and assist as needed. At the end, students can write some of their sentences on the board for the class to review and correct.

❏ EXERCISE 21. Listening and grammar.

Page 363
Time: 10–15 minutes

Part I
- To illustrate just how meaningful and grammatically necessary proper punctuation is, have students take turns attempting to read sentences from the passage (as it is written) aloud.
- You may want to ask students to predict where and what punctuation marks are needed.

Part II
- Play the audio and have students punctuate accordingly.
- Give students ample time to review what they have done before playing the audio a final time.

Part III
- Play the audio a final time, and ask students to correct their punctuation according to what they can hear.
- Be prepared to stop and clarify as needed.

❏ EXERCISE 22. Let's read and talk.

Page 363
Time: 10–15 minutes

Part I
- Have students read the introduction to Martin Luther King, Jr.'s, speech aloud.
- Ask students what they already know about Dr. King and what they know about the civil rights movement in the U.S. Write the information they give on the board.
- Ask them to compare Dr. King to anyone who has played a similar role in either their country or the world at large.
- Discuss Part I optional vocabulary.

Optional Vocabulary (Part I)
segregation
discrimination
assassinated
inspiring

Part II
- Put students into small groups.
- Read the direction line in the text aloud, and make sure that students can see how the instructions have been carried out in item 1.
- Discuss Part II optional vocabulary with students. Ask them to use their knowledge of parallel structure (and thus, their familiarity with parts of speech) to help them paraphrase unknown words.

Optional Vocabulary (Part II)
disciplined	oppression
nonconformists	retaliation
controversy	aggression
crucial	method

Expansion: Choose 5-10 famous quotes that exemplify parallel structure. Prepare index cards with one-half of a famous quote on each one. Put students into small groups and hand out a few incomplete quotes to each group. Using what they know about parallel structure, students can either complete the famous quote with their own words and see how close they can come to the real thing. Or, if that task is too difficult, you can give each group two halves of the quotation, and they simply have to match them up.

While engaging in this exercise, students can also discover who said the quote, what the context was, and what the quote means. Possible quotations:

"You can fool some of the people all of the time, all of the people some of the time, but you can't fool all of the people all of the time." —*Abraham Lincoln*

"Ask not what your country can do for you; ask what you can do for your country." —*John F. Kennedy*

"It is easier to love humanity as a whole than to love one's neighbor." —*Eric Hoffer*

"The danger of the past was that men became slaves. The danger of the future is that men may become robots." —*Erich Fromm*

"The only way to keep your health is to eat what you don't want, drink what you don't like, and do what you'd rather not." —*Mark Twain*

"Money may be the husk of many things, but not the kernel. It brings you food, but not appetite; medicine, but not health; acquaintance, but not friends; servants, but not loyalty; days of joy, but not peace or happiness." —*Henrik Ibsen*

"The love of liberty is the love of others; the love of power is the love of ourselves." —*William Hazlitt*

❏ EXERCISE 23. Let's write. Page 364
Time: 10–15 minutes

- If possible, have students write the first draft quickly in class. You may even want to give students a time limit of 10–15 minutes.
- Have students take their first draft home, tighten it up, and then return both the first and second drafts to you.
- Reproduce some of the more successful attempts at tightening writing style through good use of parallelism; discuss them with the class.
- Some students may not want to produce two versions of the same paragraph, but assure them that most people — even very experienced and skilled authors — use this method of improving their writing. Tell students that revision with an eye toward conciseness is an essential process in producing good writing in English.

Chapter 17
Adverb Clauses

CHAPTER SUMMARY

OBJECTIVE: Learning to use adverb clauses extends one's ability to communicate complex information and show relationships between ideas.

APPROACH: This chapter focuses on the common functions of adverb clauses to express relationships of (1) time, (2) cause and effect, (3) contrast, and (4) conditions (except for contrary-to-fact conditional sentences, which are covered in Chapter 20).

TERMINOLOGY: As noted in the footnote to Chart 17-1, in this text "subordinating conjunctions" (e.g., *when, because*) are called "words that introduce adverb clauses." Coordinating and correlative conjunctions (Chapter 16) link equal, parallel elements; subordinating conjunctions link a dependent structure to an independent one.

CHART 17-1. Introduction. Page 365
Time: 10–15 minutes

Students were introduced to adverb clauses in Charts 2-7 and 2-8 in conjunction with the presentation of simple past and past progressive. Chart 17-1 expands that presentation by defining the term "adverb clause," describing its form and focusing on some of its features in written English, such as punctuation and sentence completeness. You might note for the students that the comma usually reflects a pause in speaking.

The use of a comma in a sentence begun by an adverb clause is less common in British English than in American English. Even in American English, the comma may be omitted at times. This text focuses on providing a pattern that students can use as a guideline in their own production — without getting into too many refinements too soon.

Students have learned about two other kinds of dependent clauses: adjective clauses (Chapter 13) and noun clauses (Chapter 12). You might want to review the characteristics of dependent clauses: they must contain a *subject + verb;* they cannot stand alone as a sentence.

Incomplete sentences consisting of a single adverb clause are a common problem in student writing. INCORRECT: *He went to bed. **Because he was sleepy.***

However, such incomplete sentences are common in conversation in response to a *why*-question.

A: *Why did he go to bed?*

B: ***Because he was sleepy.***

- Write the chapter title on the board.
- Ask students what the characteristics of a dependent clause are, and write these on the board as a reminder.

  Dependent Clause
  must contain a subject + verb
  cannot stand alone as a sentence

- Remind students that they already use simple adverb clauses of time with the simple past and past progressive, and with *when* and *while.*
- Ask students to give you an example sentence using *when,* and write it on the board.

  When Juana arrived for class, the test had already started.
  The test had already started when Juana arrived for class.

- Ask students which part of each sentence is a dependent clause, and underline it.
- Explain that an adverb clause is always a dependent clause and that it cannot stand alone.
- Write the words *adverb clause* beneath the underlined section of the sentences on the board as follows:

  When Juana arrived for class, the test had already started.
      adverb clause
  The test had already started <u>when Juana arrived for class</u>.
          adverb clause

- Explain that adverb clauses have four main functions. List the functions on the board as column headings.

  Time   *Cause and Effect*   *Contrast*   *Condition*

- Then ask students to add words to each function, without looking at their text. If students have difficulty starting, you may want to provide one word for each function.
- Students are likely to be familiar with many words used to introduce adverb clauses, so have them try to exhaust their existing knowledge. After students have supplied a number of words for each category, add the following title above the list:

  Words Used to Introduce Adverb Clauses
  Time   *Cause and Effect*   *Contrast*   *Condition*

- Explain that the words in the list they just created typically come at the beginning of an adverb clause.
- Now have students open their text and compare the words on the board to the ones in chart 17-1.
- Go over the rest of the chart as necessary.

❏ EXERCISE 2. Looking at grammar.
Page 366
Time: 10 minutes

- Remind students that dependent clauses can't stand alone, and write a couple of dependent clauses on the board, such as:

  Because Keiko loves sushi

  Whenever Max calls his mother

- Explain to students that when they see or hear a dependent clause, they should look for the main clause to follow. Point out that the above clauses should seem unnatural because they are incomplete thoughts.
- Give students a few minutes to complete the exercise.
- Then add to the exercise by asking students to change or add to the incomplete, dependent clause and make them into complete sentences.
- Review the exercise as a class, having students read their newly created / corrected sentences for items 2, 3, 8, 9, and 11.

❏ EXERCISE 4. Looking at grammar.
Page 366
Time: 5–10 minutes

> Many of the items in this exercise require an understanding of the uses of periods and commas as presented in Chapter 16 "Coordinating Conjunctions."

- Give students time to add punctuation in their texts.
- Then lead a quick run-through of the items, or have pairs of students compare their work.

Optional Vocabulary
routine
hard of hearing
elderly
nearsighted

CHART 17-2. Using Adverb Clauses to Show Time Relationships. Page 368
Time: 10 minutes

- Write the chart title on the board.
- Ask students to come up with an all-purpose main clause to use with a variety of dependent time clauses, and write it on the board. It helps if the clause is humorous and reflects some joke specific to your class, as students will have more fun working with it. For example, the whole class knows that Yukiko loves to shop and always talks about going shopping. Yukiko freely and humorously admits to

this. An appropriate main clause could be based on this fact.

  Yukiko goes shopping.

- Elicit time words from the class and put them on the board.
- Ask students to come up with dependent clauses to follow the time words. Write one on the board and add the main clause. For example:

  After . . .
  After the sun rises in the morning, Yukiko goes shopping.

- Next, ask students to change the tense of the sentence, and write their response on the board.

  After the sun rose in the morning, Yukiko went shopping.

- Continue using the same main clause in combination with a variety of student-created time clauses.
- You may have to help students come up with specific dependent time clauses based on words or time phrases they haven't yet used, so be prepared to do this. For example:

  Before . . .
  Before Yukiko deals with anything else, she goes shopping.
  Before Yukiko dealt with anything else, she went shopping.

  When . . .
  When life gets stressful, Yukiko goes shopping.
  When life got stressful, Yukiko went shopping.

- You may want to spend extra time discussing the meaning of those time words in which the relationship between the two actions is more complex, (e.g. *as soon as, once, until,* and *as long as*).
- After the range of time words has been illustrated through student-generated sentences, review the chart as necessary. Point out to students that this chart serves as a reference tool and that they do not need to memorize it.

❏ EXERCISE 6. Looking at grammar.
Page 369
Time: 5–10 minutes

- Give students time to work through the exercise individually.
- Have students take turns reading their completions aloud.
- When there is any question over which part is the dependent adverb clause, have students write their completions on the board and put brackets around the adverb clause.

Optional Vocabulary
carrier
active volcano

❏ EXERCISE 7. Looking at grammar.
Page 369
Time: 5–10 minutes

- Give students time to combine the sentences on their own before reviewing as a group.

- Assign each item to a student and have him / her write it on the board.
- As a class, review the sentences on the board. For each item, ask the class to supply the alternate answer aloud. For example:

    (on the board)
    After I turned off the lights, I left the room.
    (alternate answer aloud)
    I left the room after I turned off the lights.

Optional Vocabulary

bites her nails   butterflies in my stomach
burst   promotions

❏ **EXERCISE 8.** Looking at grammar.
Page 370
Time: 5–10 minutes

> This exercise can be used as a quick, informal quiz. You can also put students into pairs or groups to determine the best completions. Whichever approach you choose, review the material by having students read the items aloud.

Optional Vocabulary

lottery   dent   fender

CHART 17-3. Using Adverb Clauses to Show Cause and Effect. Page 373
Time: 20–25 minutes

> There are differences among the ways to say "because". *Because* is used to make the most direct or explicit cause-and-effect statement. *Since* means "because it is a fact that" or "seeing that it is true that." For example: *Since you've done this before* (a known fact), *could you please show me how? Because,* but not *since,* can ask about an unknown cause. For example: *Did he stay home because he was tired? Now that* is special to present-time, known reasons. It indicates that a situation has recently changed.
>
> Punctuation follows the same guidelines with these adverb clauses as with others. (And they are only guidelines, not rules. There are wide stylistic variations in comma usage with adverb clauses. This text simply presents the most usual patterns.)
>
> Other cause-and-effect subordinating conjunctions you may wish to introduce in an advanced class are *as, as / so long as,* and *insomuch as.* They are similar to *since*: they express a cause that is a known fact.
>
> *As* has many uses. Students might be interested in knowing that one use is to express cause and effect. In their own writing, however, they might prefer to use *because, since* or *now that* in order to ensure clarity.
>
> *Inasmuch as* is generally only found in formal writing and is relatively infrequent.

- Write the chart title on the board and underline *Cause and Effect.*
- Have students explain *cause and effect* in their own words, and write their explanations on the board.
- Tell students that English has a number of words that can be used to show cause and effect.
- As a class, create two sentences that can be linked by cause-and-effect phrases and write them on the board. (The two sentences should be able to make sense with *now that* and *since,* as well as with *because.*)
- Identify the cause and the effect on the board. For example:

    Ahmed's company is opening a branch in London. = cause
    Ahmad needs to learn English. = effect

- Now have students put these clauses together with *because* and dictate the whole sentence to you while you write. Have students give you two sentences, one beginning with the adverb clause and one ending with the adverb clause.

    Because Ahmed's company is opening a branch in London, he needs to learn English.
    Ahmed needs to learn English because his company is opening a branch in London.

- Now demonstrate the same sentences using *now that.* You will need to explain that *now that* only makes sense with recent / present tense causes. Write the new sentences on the board.

    Now that Ahmed's company is opening a branch in London, he needs to learn English.
    Ahmed needs to learn English now that his company is opening a branch in London.

- Explain that when using *now that*, the speaker is saying that this cause is a present or recent development that is <u>now</u> a factor or cause.
- Ask students to explain or demonstrate the use of *since.* They should be able to explain that we use *since* with present perfect tense to describe an action that began in the past and continues in the present.
- Write a student-generated example of this time use on the board, such as:

    Jae has been studying English since he came to Boston.

- You may want to remind students that *since he came to Boston* is a time adverb clause and does not show cause and effect.
- Explain that *since* also has the cause-and-effect meaning of "because it is a fact that."
- Show this new meaning of *since* using the same example sentence.

    Since Ahmed's company is opening a branch in London, he needs to learn English.
    Ahmed needs to learn English since his company is opening a branch in London.

❑ EXERCISE 13. Looking at grammar.

Page 373
Time: 5–10

- Give students a few minutes to work through the items individually.
- Ask students to take turns reading their combinations aloud.
- You may want to ask for two different versions of the response for a few of the first items. This will allow students to show the use of a comma whenever the adverb clause precedes the independent clause.
- When questions arise, have students write their responses on the board and discuss as a class.

CHART 17-4. Expressing Contrast
(Unexpected Result): Using *Even Though*.
Page 374
Time: 10 minutes

The general category of "contrast" is defined as "unexpected result" here to help students compare *because* and *even though,* and also to help them understand the meaning of contrast (i.e., that something is in some way different from something else) as the term is used in the text.

Other forms of *even though* are *although* and *though* (see Chart 19-6.) The differences are negligible.

- Write the chart title on the board.
- As a class, create a simple cause-effect sentence using *because* and write it on the board. It will help if the cause-effect link is very obvious. For example:

  Because it was raining, Maria, Peng, and Diego decided to postpone the picnic.

- Highlight how normal and predictable this cause-effect relationship is — it is really not fun to go on a picnic in the pouring rain.
- Now change the main clause to show an "unexpected result" and use *Even though* in front of the adverb clause. Write the new sentence on the board.

  Even though it was raining, Maria, Peng, and Diego had a picnic.

- Underline the result clause and write *unexpected result* underneath it.

  Even though it was raining, Maria, Peng, and Diego had a picnic.   unexpected result

- Emphasize why this structure is used.

  Most people don't want to have a picnic in the rain.
  Maria, Peng, and Diego had a picnic in the rain.
  This action (result) is unexpected.

- As a class, create a few more sentences expressing contrast and write them on the board.
- Have students take turns going to the board and underlining / identifying the unexpected result. For example:

  Hiromi and Rolf had to take the TOEFL at 9:00 A.M. last Saturday.

They went out dancing until 4:30 A.M. the night before.
Even though Hiromi and Rolf had to take the TOEFL at 9:00 A.M. last Saturday, they went out dancing until 4:30 A.M. the night before.
unexpected result

- Have students switch the order (whether the adverb clause comes first or not) to ensure they have control over both forms.

❑ EXERCISE 17. Looking at grammar.

Page 375
Time: 5–10 minutes

Point out to students that the first six items are contrasting pairs, while the final four items are not related to each other.

Optional Vocabulary

newborn   commercial fishing operations
kangaroo   mammals
pouch

CHART 17-5. Showing Direct Contrast:
While. Page 376
Time: 5–10 minutes

When using *while* for contrast, it can appear at the beginning of either clause with no change in meaning.

While has two different meanings: (1) "at the same time" and (2) "whereas."

1. *While (he was) swimming, he got very tired.*

2. *While fire is hot, ice is cold.*

In British English, *whilst* is another form of *while*. *Whilst* is fairly formal.

- Write the chart title on the board.
- Using what you know about your students, create a simple sentence showing obvious contrast and using the conjunction *but* (which can be used to show contrast between two independent clauses). For example:

  Maria is a woman, but Francisco is a man.

- Explain that *while* can be used to introduce adverb clauses which show direct contrast. Explain that direct contrast indicates that the information in the adverb clause is exactly the opposite of what came before.
- Next, change the example by using *while* in place of *but*.

  Maria is a woman, while Francisco is a man.

- Explain that because *man* is considered the complete opposite of *woman*, it is appropriate to use direct contrast here.
- Go over the chart with students.

❏ EXERCISE 21. Let's talk. Page 377
Time: 5–10 minutes

This exercise works best as an interview activity with students out of their seats and mingling with each other. If you have a class that is too large or is reluctant to initiate conversation, then you can either put students in small groups or conduct the exercise as a teacher-led, whole-class oral activity.

The first four items are fairly straightforward. The last two items should generate very different answers. As such, you may want to ask four to six different students to write their sentences on the board.

CHART 17-6. Expressing Conditions in
Adverb Clauses: *If*-Clauses. Page 377
Time: 10 minutes

As with adverb clauses of time, it is incorrect to use the future tense (i.e., *will/be going to*) in an *if*-clause. An exception, however, occurs when the speaker is trying to arrange an exchange of promises: *If you'll do it, I'll do it.*

All of the examples and exercise items in this unit on "condition" (17-6 through 17-11) are in present or future time. Chapter 20 picks up on the use of other verb forms in conditional sentences.

• Write the chart title on the board.
• Elicit a student-generated example of an adverb clause with *when,* (which students can be reminded is <u>not</u> followed by future tense) and write it on the board. For example:

   When Rieko goes back to Japan, ____.

• Have students complete the sentence with a main clause that makes sense, and write the completion on the board.

   When Rieko goes back to Japan, <u>she will speak excellent English</u>.

• Now explain that *if*-clauses are formed in the same way (followed by simple present verbs) and are combined with main clauses that have future tense verbs. Write the following example:

   If Peter wins the lottery, he will give his mother a trip to Paris.

• Underline the tenses in both clauses.

   If Peter <u>wins</u> the lottery, he <u>will give</u> his mother a trip to Paris.

• Ask students *Will Peter win the lottery?* You should get a variety of responses from *possibly* to *maybe* to *I don't know.*

• Explain that the *if*-clause refers to a situation that hasn't happened yet but that might happen. It is a possibility. Write the word *possibility* under the *if*-clause, and write *result* under the main clause.

       possibility   result
   If Peter <u>wins</u> the lottery, he <u>will give</u> his mother a trip to Paris.

• Ask students to come up with a few *if + present tense* clauses and write them on the board, leaving a blank for the main clause. Underline the present tense in the adverb clauses. For example:

   If Cassandra <u>meets</u> the love of her life tomorrow, ____.
   If Sang Min and Knut <u>go skiing</u> for the first time this weekend, ____.

• Have other students go to the board and complete these *if*-clauses with main clauses in the future tense.

   If Cassandra meets the love of her life tomorrow, <u>she will get married immediately</u>.
   If Sang Min and Knut go skiing for the first time this weekend, <u>they will probably fall down a lot</u>.

• Go over the chart with students.

❏ EXERCISE 23. Looking at grammar.
Page 377
Time: 5–10 minutes

The main point of this exercise is to use present verbs in *if*-clauses. You could assign this as individual work or conduct the exercise as a quick oral activity by asking several students for answers to each item. In either case, encourage students to be creative or humorous.

Optional Vocabulary
predictions
global warming

Expansion: Divide the class into an even number of teams. Hand out blank index cards to all students: half of the teams should create *if*-clauses using simple present verbs and write these *if*-clauses on the cards. The other half of the teams will come up with main clauses and write the main clauses on their cards. Give students 10–15 minutes to circulate and try to come up with sentences that can be matched. Obviously this will lead to some pretty funny combinations. The rest of the class can give points for the most outrageous or nonsensical pairing, as long as the target grammar is correct.

If the expansion activity is too open-ended for your group, you can also prepare two sets of index cards yourself. One set should have meaningful *if*-clauses and the other should be a "matching" set of related result clauses. You can distribute them among students and give them the task of finding the best match.

CHART 17-7. Shortened *If*-clauses.
Page 378
Time: 5 minutes

Let students know that English has "shorthand" phrases that can take the place of a full *if*-clause and that these are commonly used in speaking and in writing (especially when giving directions).

Students may be familiar with the concept of a flowchart, and you can present shortened *if*-clauses as having the same function as an arrow in a flowchart.

- Write the chart title on the board.
- Write a question followed by *if*-clauses on the board. It is more meaningful if you can base these on some instructions you have recently given or will give students. For example:

   Did you finish the assignment?

   If you did finish the assignment, please turn to the next chapter.

   If you did not finish the assignment, please finish it now.

- Explain that the complete *if*-clauses can be replaced by abbreviated ones and illustrate this by writing these on the board.

   Did you finish the assignment?

   If you did finish the assignment, please turn to the next chapter.

   If so, please turn to the next chapter.

   If you did not finish the assignment, please finish it now.

   If not, please do so now.

- Go over the chart as necessary.

CHART 17-8. Adverb Clauses of Condition: Using *Whether or Not* and *Even If.* Page 379
Time: 10 minutes

Be prepared to explain that *Whether or not* is used when whatever the condition may be will have no effect on the result. You can ask or discuss with your students for examples of "unconditional" truths in their lives. For example, most parents love their children *whether or not* the children obey their parents, do well in school, etc.

Students sometimes wonder about the difference between *even though* and *even if.* *Even though* deals with an actual, present-time event or state; *even if* deals with possible future conditions. *Even though the weather is cold (today)* = the weather is cold. *Even if the weather is cold (tomorrow or in the future)* = the weather may be cold. In some cases, this distinction blurs a bit. *Even if you don't like pickles, you should try one of these.*

- Write the chart title on the board.
- Begin by asking your students for some aspect of their life that does not depend on any condition whatsoever.

- Write their feedback on the board using *whether or not* clauses. For example:

   Raul will marry his girlfriend <u>whether or not</u> her parents approve of him.

   Parents love their children <u>whether or not</u> those children are well behaved.

   Many people manage to achieve their dreams <u>whether or not</u> other people support them.

- Explain that *whether or not* can be placed before the clause entirely. Alternatively, the *or not* can be placed after the clause. Show this in writing on the board.

   Parents love their children <u>whether</u> those children are well behaved <u>or not</u>.

- Next, explain that *even if* is used in front of a possible future condition and not a current one.
- Using your students' lives as material, come up with a meaningful example and write it on the board. For example:

   <u>*Even if*</u> *he doesn't get a high score on the TOEFL this time, Seung Jin will stay in school and continue working toward his goals.*

- Go over the chart as a class.

❏ EXERCISE 28. Looking at grammar.
Page 380
Time: 5–10 minutes

You should read the situations to the class so that they understand each context.

It isn't necessary to use the exact words from the text. You can change the wording or expand on the situation as needed to make sure that students understand the situation.

CHART 17-9. Adverb Clauses of Condition: Using *In Case.* Page 381
Time: 5–10 minutes

In case is used to explain that something may possibly happen and that it is this possibility that is the rationale for other actions. For example: *I will take my purse with me in case we decide to stop at the store.* In other words, the reason I'm doing one thing (taking my purse) is that something else might happen (we may decide to stop at the store).

Some scientific and philosophical texts use *in case* to mean "in the specific circumstance or example." This is often followed by a *that*-clause.

- Write the chart title on the board.
- Ask students to explain why they bring umbrellas or rain jackets with them on cloudy days. They will probably explain (or they may need your help to do so) that though it may not rain, it also may rain. When people carry umbrellas, they are prepared *in any case.*

- Now illustrate this concept by writing an easily understood example on the board.

  People carry umbrellas <u>in case it rains</u>.

- Ask students for other examples of actions they do or precautions they take that can be explained using *in case.*

- Write their feedback on the board using the target structure. For example:

  Maria always brings her cell phone in the car <u>in case there is an emergency</u>.

  Tetsuo brings a book with him when he commutes <u>in case he gets bored</u>.

- Go over the chart as a class.

❑ **EXERCISE 31.** Looking at grammar.
Page 382
Time: 5–10 minutes

- Put students in pairs or small groups to complete the items.
- Encourage students to be as creative and comprehensive in their responses as they can be.
- Review as a class. You can have groups write their responses on the board to compare and discuss.

CHART 17-10. Adverb Clauses of Condition:
Using *Unless.* Page 382
Time: 5–10 minutes

Trying to distinguish between *until* and *unless* can be difficult for some students. *Unless* expresses a condition that is required for a particular result. *Until* expresses a time relationship — but also expresses a condition required for a result. It is no wonder that students may be confused when they encounter the following:

You can't drive unless / until you are sixteen.

Class can't start unless / until the teacher arrives.

I don't eat unless / until I am hungry.

The verb in the *unless*-clause is usually positive, but it could be negative. For example:

A: *Will I see you at the theater tonight?*

B: *Yes, unless I can't go.*

- Write the chart title on the board.
- Write the following note on the board:

  unless = if . . . not,

  and explain that *unless* is another way to say *if . . . not.*

- Write the following sentences, underlining the target structures.

  Paulo will go to a movie tonight <u>unless</u> he gets homework in grammar class.

  Paulo will go to a movie tonight <u>if</u> he doesn<u>'t</u> get homework in grammar class.

- Ask students to tell you something that they plan to do *unless* a particular condition is not met. Write their responses on the board.

- Help get students started by writing the following on the board:

  I will go out with my friends this weekend unless ____.

- Have students go to the board and write a few possible completions.
- Go over the chart as a class.

❑ **EXERCISE 33.** Looking at grammar.
Page 382
Time: 5–10 minutes

Expect that some students may have difficulties with *unless,* and schedule a little extra time for this first exercise to ensure comprehension.

- Explain to students that they are restating the idea in the original sentence, but that they will use *unless.*
- Write their answers on the board as visual reinforcement.

❑ **EXERCISE 34.** Looking at grammar.
Page 382
Time: 5–10 minutes

Because you will have done the preceding exercise very carefully with students, they should be ready to try this one without as much support from you.

- Give students time to work through the items either independently, in pairs, or in small groups.
- Encourage students to be creative and use advanced vocabulary (that they have control over) to complete each item.
- You can have different groups or pairs write their completions on the board for comparison.

CHART 17-11. Adverb Clauses of Condition:
Using *Only If.* Page 383
Time: 5–10 minutes

No commas are used when *only if / only when / only after / only in* clauses begin a sentence.

Some students may be familiar with the concept of "if and only if," which expresses the same idea in mathematics: Only one particular condition will result in a particular effect.

- Write the chart title on the board.
- Explain to students that in many ways, this concept is an easy one to understand. If this one condition is not met, the result will not take place.
- Write a simple sentence on the board to illustrate this. For example:

  Miyako will be able to buy a new car <u>only if she can find the money to do so</u>.

- Now explain that when the sentence begins with *only if*, the word order of the subject and verb in the main clause is inverted.
- Write an example of this case on the board, and highlight the inversion by underlining it.

    Only if Miyako can find the money <u>will she be able to buy</u> a new car.

- Go over the chart as a class.

❏ EXERCISE 36. Looking at grammar.
Page 383
Time: 5–10 minutes

- Help students see the original condition more clearly by writing on the board:

    If you want Saturday off, you must work Thursday.

- Point out that items 1 and 3 also restate the original *only if* condition.

❏ EXERCISE 37. Looking at grammar.
Page 384
Time: 10 minutes

Part I
- Set up the situation in each item so that students understand it. In order to ensure this, you may need to have students read each situation aloud and discuss it.
- It is not necessary that you or your students use exactly the same words that are in the text; just explain / discuss each situation briefly and naturally enough so that students understand it.
- You can make up similar items using students' names and situations.

Part II
- Give students ample time to come up with their own completions.
- Help them explain the situation they had in mind to other students if it is not obvious from their initial completions.

❏ EXERCISE 39. Looking at grammar.
Page 385
Time: 5–10 minutes

- Do this exercise orally as a quick review.
- One student can answer, and another can then indicate the necessary punctuation in the sentence.
- Every answer should contain the two given ideas about rain and the party (unless you wish to encourage more creativity).

Expansion: Put students into groups and have each group create another situation which is dependent on certain conditions. Have students in each group come up with sentences using the words in items 1–5, in Exercise 39 to describe what conditions must be met. However, students should be somewhat vague and deliberately ambiguous about what the situation is. They can then present the sentences using *whether or not, even if, in case, unless,* and *only if* to the class and have their classmates guess the original situation.

Possible sample sentences:

We will go on this trip <u>whether or not we are cold</u>.

We will carry out our plans <u>even if we are extremely cold and wet</u>.

<u>In case the conditions are not naturally ideal</u>, there will be snow-making equipment.

We will go <u>unless it rains or becomes unseasonably warm</u>.

<u>Only if we are ready to enjoy the outdoors and perhaps fall often</u> will we have a good time.

What are we going to do?

Answer: *Go skiing!*

❏ EXERCISE 40. Reading and grammar.
Page 385
Time: 10–15 minutes

Part I
- Have students read the passage individually and be prepared to discuss or restate the most important points.
- Ask students if they can relate the premise of this passage to their own experiences, particularly those as language and grammar learners.
- Discuss this with students.

Part II
- Have students complete the sentences individually.
- Ask various students to read their completions aloud.
- Ask students to write some of these completions on the board to allow for comparison of both sentence content and structure / punctuation, etc.
- Discuss as a group.

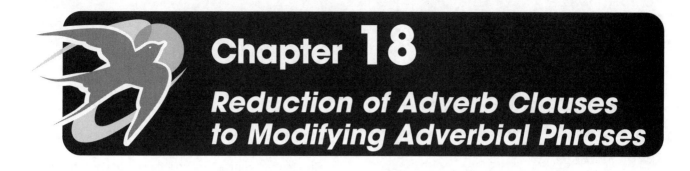

Chapter 18

Reduction of Adverb Clauses to Modifying Adverbial Phrases

CHAPTER SUMMARY

OBJECTIVE: To learn the meaning and use of adverbial phrases that modify the subject of a sentence. These phrases are primarily a feature of written English.

APPROACH: This chapter draws a parallel with Chapter 13, where adjective phrases are introduced. Adverb clauses and reduced adverbial phrases are illustrated and practiced with special attention to avoiding dangling modifiers.

TERMINOLOGY: A "dangling participle" is one type of dangling modifier.

Unsure of himself, *the right words stuck in Bob's throat.* = a dangling modifier (but not a dangling participle).

Being unsure of himself, *the right words stuck in Bob's throat* = a dangling participle that can also be called by the more inclusive term "dangling modifier."

CHART 18-1. Introduction. Page 387
Time: 10 minutes

Central to reducing adverb clauses to phrases is understanding that such reductions are only possible when the subject of the adverb clause and the subject of the main clause are one and the same.

The modifying phrases presented in this chart are often called "participial phrases" because the main word is a present participle (*-ing* form) or sometimes a past participle (*-ed* form, conveying a passive meaning). If the phrase doesn't modify the subject of the main clause, the unacceptable result is called a "dangling participle" — the participle has nothing to modify, and so it "dangles" (hangs) unattached to any other word. For example:

While walking by the lake, a fish jumped out of the water.

Obviously, the fish wasn't walking by the lake! But, in the above sentence, *walking* must refer to the fish, so the whole thing is ungrammatical (as well as unscientific and impossible).

- Explain that in order for an adverb clause to be changed to a modifying phrase, one main condition needs to be in place: The subject of the adverb clause and the main clause must be one and the same.
- On the board, write the following sentence:

  While Dmitry was studying with his classmates in Boston, his baby was being born in Minsk.

- Explain that the example sentence is correct, but that it cannot be reduced because it has two subjects.
- Ask student to identify the two subjects. Underline the subjects as the students call them out.
- Explain that if you try to reduce the first clause, you change the meaning of the second and render it incorrect and illogical.

  While studying with his classmates here in Boston, Dmitry's baby was born in Minsk.

- Ask students what is wrong with this second sentence. They should be able to articulate that the second sentence makes it sound as though the baby was born in front of Dmitry's classmates in Boston or that the baby was studying in Boston. Since we know the baby was being born in Minsk, the impossibility of this combination should be clear.
- Go over the rest of the chart with students.

❏ EXERCISE 2. Looking at grammar.
Page 388
Time: 5 minutes

- Give students a chance to work through the items individually.
- Have students take turns reading each item aloud and stating whether the sentence is grammatically correct or not.
- When a sentence is <u>not</u> grammatically correct, encourage students to explain why. For example, with item 1, a student can say that the fire alarm was not capable of sitting at a computer, etc.

CHART 18-2. Changing Time Clauses to Modifying Adverbial Phrases. Page 388
Time: 10 minutes

> In Chart 18-2, the word *since* has a time-related meaning, not a cause-and-effect meaning. Learners are sometimes confused about this. Just tell students that sometimes two different vocabulary items have the same spelling and sound the same, such as *fall (autumn)* vs. *fall (drop down)*.
>
> Call attention to example (f) in Chart 18-2 so that students see that a phrase may either precede or follow the main clause. Note the punctuation.

- Write the chart title on the board.
- Ask students to recall what main condition must be met in order to reduce an adverbial clause to a modifying adverbial phrase. They should be able to tell you that the subject of the adverb clause and that of the main clause must be the same. Write on the board:

  To change adverb clause to a modifying adverbial phrase:

  subject of the main clause = the subject of the adverb clause

- Using students' lives, co-create sentences which have the same subject in the adverb clause as in the main clause, and write these on the board. Ask students to make the adverb clauses about timed or sequenced events and base them on real events. For example:

  Since she came to the United States, Inez has kept up regular email correspondence with her family in Colombia.
  After Mikhail takes the TOEFL, he will apply to graduate school.
  While Birgitt has been studying here in New York, she has also been taking yoga classes.

- Now ask various students to go to the board to change the adverb time clauses to modifying adverbial phrases.
- The class can correct these transformations as a whole. For example:

     coming
  Since ~~she came~~ *to the United States, Inez has kept up regular email correspondence with her family in Colombia.*

- Go over the chart as a class.

❏ **EXERCISE 3.** Looking at grammar.
Page 388
Time: 5–10 minutes

> You can use the first few items in this exercise to reinforce the contents of Chart 18-2. Then turn the remainder of the exercise over to group work, encouraging students to teach each other as they correct each item.

❏ **EXERCISE 4.** Let's talk: interview.
Page 389
Time: 5–10 minutes

- Write a sample question on the board and model it with a third person answer. For example:

  Question: *What do you do before going to bed?*
  Answer: *I read for at least half an hour.*
  Reported answer: <u>Before going to bed</u>, (Martha) reads for at least half an hour.

- Give students ample time to interview one another and collect complete-sentence answers.
- Have students report what they have learned to the rest of the class, either orally or by writing it on the board.

Expansion: After students have had practice with interview questions, put them in groups and ask them to come up with some questions of a more philosophical nature. Have them use the same time words (e.g., *before, after, while*). Elicit reduced adverbial time phrases, but instruct students to try to "dig deeper" with their questions. Some sample questions you may want to write on the board include:

What is it important for you to do before dying?
Why do people often have regrets when facing the end of their lives?
What can a person do to avoid feeling regretful when facing the end of his/her life?
What do you think everyone should experience before getting married?
If you are going anywhere in the world, what do you absolutely have to do before leaving home?
When do you judge how valuable a learning experience or challenge is to you — before starting it, while facing it, or when reflecting on it?

Once they have come up with three to six questions as a group, have students write them down on an index card. Then have them pass the index card to another group so that each group is actually asking fresh and new questions. You can give the class 10–15 minutes to obtain new information about their classmates' ideas and plans before coming back together to review what they have learned as a class.

CHART 18-3. Expressing the Idea of "During the Same Time" in Modifying Adverbial Phrases. Page 389
Time: 5–10 minutes

> Compare using modifying participial phrases at the beginning of a sentence with using gerund subjects (sometimes a point of confusion for learners). Be sure to give students some examples of gerunds as subjects.
>
> ***Walking*** *that street alone at night* ***is*** *dangerous.*
>
> ***Hiking*** *through the woods* ***is*** *an enjoyable way to get exercise.*

- Write the chart title on the board.
- Leave the room and reenter, discussing the target grammar as you do so. When you get to the board, write:

    Entering the room, I described the use of modifying adverbial phrases.

- Explain that because you were both "entering the room" and "describing modifying adverbial phrases" at the same time, just the gerund phrase can be used at the beginning of the sentence when the subject is clear.
- Now ask students to create sentences about one another, and write these on the board. For example:

    Clicking his pen, Antonio concentrated on the new grammar structure.

    Sighing, Amalia listened to the explanation.

    Smiling, Franz asked Emile if he could borrow a piece of paper.

CHART 18-4. Expressing Cause and Effect in Modifying Adverbial Phrases. Page 390
Time: 10 minutes

The important point for learners to understand is that the grammatical structure itself (without function words) expresses a cause-and-effect meaning. In many cases, an initial modifying participial phrase combines the ideas of "during the same time" and "because" — as students will discover in Exercise 6.

To illustrate that *being* expresses cause-and-effect in this structure, have the students compare the meanings of the following two sentences:

1. *Chicago, a large city, has a crime problem.*

(*a large city* = an appositive, reduced adjective clause that gives identifying information about the noun: *Chicago, which is a large city, has . . . .*)

A cause-and-effect relationship may be implied, but it is not stated.

2. *Chicago, being a large city, has a crime problem.*

The use of *being* shows a clear cause-and-effect relationship.

- Write the chart title on the board, and explain that Charts 18-3 and 18-4 are being presented together because the difference in usage is not always distinguishable.
- Explain that the *-ing* phrase at the beginning of a sentence can show a cause-and-effect relationship.
- Demonstrate this by describing an observable student action and writing a *because*-clause sentence on the board. For example:

    Because Xavier was hungry, he went to the cafeteria for lunch.

- Then illustrate how the sentence can be reduced as follows:

    Being hungry, Xavier went to the cafeteria for lunch.

- Next, explain that to change the tense of the above sentence to the past, you reduce it by using **having** + past participle. Write the steps on the board, starting again with the *because*-clause.

    Because Tina has eaten at the cafeteria before, she doesn't want to eat there again.

    Having eaten at the cafeteria before, Tina doesn't want to eat there again.

    Having eaten at the cafeteria before, Tina didn't want to eat there again.

- Review the rest of the chart with students.

❏ EXERCISE 6. Looking at grammar.
Page 390
Time: 10 minutes

- Give students time to answer the questions on their own.
- Put students in pairs or small groups to discuss their answers. Encourage them to refer back to the explanations offered in the chart as much as possible.
- Review as a class, writing problem sentences up on the board for visual reference.
- Remind the class that very often the distinction between simultaneous action and cause-and-effect is not completely obvious.

Optional Vocabulary
widow
wander
dreadful

❏ EXERCISE 7. Looking at grammar.
Page 390
Time: 5–10 minutes

This exercise emphasizes that the modifying phrases convey a cause-and-effect meaning without the word *because*.

- In the example, call attention to the structure of the negative phrase and to the necessity of identifying the subject in the main clause.
- Point out that these phrases modify the subject of the main clause.
- Have students make the changes independently.
- Ask different students to write the new sentences (with modifying adverbial phrases) on the board.
- Review as a class, discussing any sentences in which the meaning of the adverbial phrase is not completely clear.

❏ **EXERCISE 8.** Looking at grammar.
Page 391
Time: 10 minutes

> This exercise is a summary of Charts 18-2, 18-3, and 18-4.

- Before starting the exercise, point out that the phrases in these three charts modify the subject of the main clause. Be prepared to repeat this as often as needed.
- Depending on your class, either give students time to complete the exercise individually or have students complete the items on sight by taking turns reading each item aloud and choosing the possible completions.
- Ask students to justify their answers and be able to articulate "why not" regarding the choices that are not possible completions.

Optional Vocabulary

formula	gaining	popped (ears)
terrain	union leader	

❏ **EXERCISE 9.** Looking at grammar.
Page 391
Time: 5–10 minutes

> In this exercise, the students have to make modifying phrases while being careful to avoid dangling participles. Strongly emphasize that such phrases modify the subject of the main clause.

- Have students work independently or in pairs to combine each pair of sentences correctly.
- Review as a class, discussing the implied meanings of the adverbial phrases *because, while,* and a blending of the two.

❏ **EXERCISE 10.** Game. Page 392
Time: 10–15 minutes

Expansion: Prepare index cards that contain two parts of a complex sentence. The first part should be a correctly formed modifying phrase, and the second part should be the main sentence. Hand out all the index cards, and have students find their "match" by discussing possible combinations with their classmates.

CHART 18-5. Using *Upon + -ing* in Modifying Adverbial Phrases. Page 393
Time: 5–10 minutes

> These phrases are more common in formal writing than in ordinary conversation.

- Write the chart title on the board.
- Explain that the structure students are learning is not common in speech and they are unlikely to encounter it outside of written texts.
- Ask students for some examples of age-related, rite-of-passage events common in their countries, and write sentences with *when*-clauses that can be changed to *upon + -ing* appropriately. For example:

  When Mexican girls turn fifteen, they are given a special party called a "quinceañera."

  When French boys turn eighteen, they have to serve in the military for two years.

- You can also offer a few examples of your own: getting a driver's license, registering to vote, etc. (These examples are useful because they also suggest an appropriate level of formality.) For example:

  When Jeff became eighteen, he registered to vote.

  When Anita turned sixteen, she got her driver's license.

- Write the *when*-clause sentences on the board before transforming them to *upon/on + -ing* adverbial phrases. Underline the target grammar.

  When Mexican girls turn fifteen, they are given a special party called a "quinceañera."

  Upon turning fifteen, Mexican girls are given a special party called a "quinceañera."

  When Anita turned sixteen, she got her driver's license.

  On turning sixteen, Anita got her driver's license.

- Go over the chart as a class.

❏ **EXERCISES 14–18.** Pages 394–396

> These five exercises review the entire chapter by practicing the four major skills of reading, writing, listening, and speaking.

❏ **EXERCISE 15.** Let's talk. Page 394
Time: 10–15 minutes

- Put students into groups.
- Ask students to be as creative, specific, and comprehensive as possible in making suggestions.
- Circulate while helping students to come up with ideas for the main clause of each sentence. Correct form and usage as necessary.
- Assign each group an item, and have them write on the board all possibilities they came up with.
- Use this process as a springboard for a class discussion of sound vs. unsound advice.

❏ EXERCISE 17. Reading and grammar.
Page 395
Time: 10–15 minutes

Part I
- In addition to underlining the modifying adverbial phrases, have students identify which noun each phrase refers to.
- Ask students to take turns reading the passage aloud so that they can hear themselves pronounce the target structures.

Part II
- Have different students read items 1–4 aloud and other students give their answers in order to involve everyone in the review.
- Ask students to be ready to cite the part of the passage which contains the True or False answer.

Optional Vocabulary
latest attempt
acid
rushed
revolutionary
practical application

Expansion for Optional Vocabulary

Have students close their books after completing Exercise 17. Write the optional vocabulary items on the board. Have students explain the meaning of each by referring (without opening their books) to the context of the passage. Since the vocabulary items are listed in chronological order, it should be easy to adapt this activity to text recall.

Chapter 19

Connectives That Express Cause and Effect, Contrast, and Condition

CHAPTER SUMMARY

OBJECTIVE: To practice combining ideas into compound and complex sentences using various connectives. This gives students flexibility in communicating complex information, especially in written English.

APPROACH: This chapter presents many ways to show relationships among ideas. This is a semantic approach as well as a grammatical approach focusing on the meaning of certain conjunctions. The first section deals with cause-and-effect relationships. Next is a section on contrasts. Finally, ways of expressing a condition and outcome are presented, a section that anticipates the focus of Chapter 20. Matters of punctuation are also included. At the end of the chapter, Chart 19-9 summarizes the structures and connectives presented in Chapters 16 through 19.

TERMINOLOGY: The term "connective" includes expressions that serve to connect independent clauses to other coordinate or subordinate structures. This broad term includes words and phrases that are variously called "adverbial transitions," "subordinating conjunctions," "subordinators," "coordinating conjunctions," "conjunctive adverbs," "logical connectors," and "conjuncts" of various types.

CHART 19-1. Using *Because Of* and *Due To*.
Page 397
Time: 10 minutes

A common error is for a learner to begin an adverb clause with *because of*.

INCORRECT: *He stayed home because of he was ill.*

A phrasal preposition is a phrase that functions as a single preposition.

Traditionally, a distinction has been made between *because of* and *due to*.

Because of is used adverbially — following the verb. For example:

  He stayed home because of illness.

Due to is used adjectivally and following the verb *be* or a non-progressive verb. For example:

  His absence is due to illness.

However, in current usage, *due to* is also used with and following action verbs. For example:

  He stayed home due to illness.

Because of is not used adjectivally following *be*.

INCORRECT: *His absence is because of illness.*

Owing to is used in the same ways as *because of* and *due to*, more in spoken than in written English.

Note that punctuation rules are the same for these phrases as for adverb clauses.

- Write the chart title on the board.
- Explain that *because* always introduces a clause, complete with a subject and a verb.
- Write a sentence on the board containing a *because*-clause and a main clause, and punctuate it. For example:

  Because we are studying advanced English grammar, we are learning ways to connect complex ideas.

- Remind students that just as prepositions always precede nouns, the phrasal preposition *because of* must also come before a noun.
- Then transform the *because*-clause on the board into a phrasal preposition.
- Have students help you change *we are studying English grammar* into a noun phrase, and write the resulting new sentence on the board. Highlight the new structure.

  Because of our advanced English grammar studies, we are learning ways to connect complex ideas.

- Now substitute *due to* for *because of* in order to demonstrate that these phrases are interchangeable in the example sentence.

  Due to our advanced English grammar studies, we are learning ways to connect complex ideas.

- Go over the remainder of the chart with the class.

❏ EXERCISE 3. Looking at grammar.
Page 398
Time: 5–10 minutes

> The key to choosing the correct answer is recognizing whether a clause or a noun phrase follows either *because* or *because of*.

- Give students five minutes to complete each item on their own.
- Review each item by having a student read the completed item aloud.
- Ask students to identify either the subject and verb of the clause that follows *because* or the noun phrase that follows *because of*.

Optional Vocabulary
driving conditions	sprained
chlorinated	emigrated
jogging	famine

❏ EXERCISE 4. Looking at grammar.
Page 398
Time: 10 minutes

- Explain that students need to create noun phrases (and not clauses) to complete each item.
- Tell them that they will have to use the noun form of adjectives in order to make new noun phrases.
- Circulate and assist students in coming up with appropriate phrases.
- Select some students to write their completed items (with new noun phrases included) on the board by way of review.
- As a class, assess whether the phrase is correct and clearly represents the idea of the sentence in parentheses. There may be a couple of correct possibilities for each item.

CHART 19-2. Cause and Effect: Using *Therefore, Consequently,* and *So.* Page 399
Time: 10 minutes

> This chart focuses on the fact that *therefore* and *consequently* are placed as transitions between sentences or in the second of two related sentences. This differs from the use of *so,* which is a conjunction.
>
> Students sometimes ask *Why are "therefore" and "consequently" used differently from "so" if they mean the same thing?* There is no satisfactory answer except that it is traditional in English to use them in this way. Languages develop patterns; certain words fit certain patterns, and certain words do not.
>
> Have students identify which of the related ideas in the example sentences is the "cause" and which is the "effect" — *not studying* is the cause and *failing* is the effect.

> If students are advanced and are interested in conventions of formal writing, you could include the use of the semicolon at this point. Otherwise, the semicolon can simply remain in the footnote to Chart 19-2 as a minor point of information for those who may be interested.

- Write the chart title on the board.
- Underneath *Therefore, Consequently* write:

  <u>Transitions:</u> *Transitions come between or in the second of two related sentences.*

- Underneath *So* write:

  <u>Conjunctions:</u> *Conjunctions connect two independent clauses*

- Explain that all three are used to show cause and effect, and write this on the board as well.
- Now take an example based on your students' lives and demonstrate the use and placement of the transitions (*therefore, consequently*) and conjunction (*so*).
- Write the sentences you create (with the help of your class) on the board.
- As you write, highlight the different options for placement of the transitions and the use of *so* as a conjunction. For example:

  <u>Transitions: Therefore / Consequently</u>
  Pablo was late for his doctor's appointment.
  <u>Therefore / Consequently</u>, *the doctor couldn't see him.*
  The doctor, <u>therefore / consequently</u>, *couldn't see him.*
  The doctor couldn't see him, <u>therefore / consequently</u>.

  <u>Conjunction: So</u>
  Pablo was late for his doctor's appointment, <u>so</u> *the doctor couldn't see him.*

- Go over the rest of the chart.

❏ EXERCISE 6. Looking at grammar.
Page 399
Time: 5 minutes

Expansion: Put students into groups and have them compose three or four cause-and-effect sentences using *because.* Each group then exchanges their set of sentences with another group. Instruct each group to rewrite one sentence using *therefore,* one using *consequently,* and one using *so.* When finished, have them swap the new sentences back with the original group, who then corrects the sentences. At any point, you may want to have different students go to the board and demonstrate the use of the target words by writing a sample.

Even advanced students don't always understand that correct punctuation and capitalization are necessary for a sentence to be grammatical. Often students think of these matters as extra or decorative rather than essential. Conducting this exercise as instructed below will illustrate for students the need for correct punctuation and capitalization.

Student-to-student dictation is often challenging for both parties, but it is particularly beneficial in this situation. It forces the person dictating to state punctuation and capitalization changes clearly, bringing more attention to the importance of the target grammar. It also provides impromptu practice in both speaking / direction-giving and listening.

- Give students a few minutes to complete the exercise on their own.
- Ask one student to go to the board.
- Ask another student to randomly choose one of the items and read it aloud for the first student to write on the board. The student who is dictating should use pauses to indicate punctuation and should not say *comma* or *period*.
- As a class, decide if the sentence on the board is correct, and make any necessary changes.
- Have the student who dictated now go to the board, and ask another student to dictate a different item.
- Take time to review any questions students may have, as the placement of the transitions can often be challenging for students.

CHART 19-3. Summary of Patterns and Punctuation. Page 400
Time: 15–20 minutes

Students are learning structural distinctions in the use of coordinating conjunctions, subordinating conjunctions, adverbial prepositional phrases, and conjunctive adverbs by using cause-and-effect sentences as models. The patterns and terminology ("conjunction," "adverb clause," "preposition," "transition") they are learning here will transfer to the following sections on opposition and condition. The term "conjunction" in this chart is used to refer to "coordinating conjunctions"; include the term "coordinating" in your discussion if you think it helps students make distinctions among the differing patterns.

A wall chart, cards, or a transparency of the patterns and punctuation may prove useful not only here but also for the charts and exercises in the rest of the chapter. For example:

Adverb clause, ____.   Prepositional phrase, ____.
____, adverb clause.   ____, prepositional phrase.
____. Transition, ____.   ____, conjunction ____.
____. ____, transition.
____. ____, transition, ____.

When some students discover the semicolon, they tend to use it everywhere. You might point out that it is not often used, even by professional writers. (If students overuse it, tell them to look at any English text and see how many semicolons they can find. Chances are they will find very few.) Many native speakers are unsure about its correct use. A period (full stop) is usually acceptable or even preferable.

You might call attention to the relationship between a comma in written English and a slight pause in spoken English. (*Riddle:* What's the difference between a cat and a comma? *Answer:* A cat has claws at the end of its paws, and a comma is a pause at the end of a clause.)

- Write the chart title on the board.
- Because this chart is a summary, have students give you examples of each item presented in the chart.
- Begin by writing *Adverb Clauses* on the left side of the board and elicit from students an example of an adverb clause beginning with *because*.
- After you write the sentence under the heading on the board, ask another student to move the *because* clause and rewrite the sentence.
- With students' help, write any important notes or reminders to the right of the examples.
- The above step-by-step instructions can be used to elicit all the patterns and the punctuation options presented in the chart. (By calling on students to give you the examples you need, you will engage them in using recently acquired grammar and learn where further clarification is needed.) For example:

  Adverb Clauses
  Because Emi loves baseball, her father took her to a game.
  (If the adverb comes first, use a comma.)
  Emi's father took her to a game because she loves baseball.

- Once students have successfully demonstrated their knowledge of the patterns, go over anything from the chart that you have not yet discussed.

- Assign each item to a different student. Have the students write all of the possible patterns for their assigned items on the board.
- Insist on perfect punctuation and capitalization. (Include the semicolon only if it seems appropriate for your class.)
- Have the rest of the class offer suggestions and corrections.
- If students think they see an error, let them go to the board and correct it.
- Another option is to have the students work in small groups to produce one set of sentences that everyone in the group agrees is perfect, and then correct it as a class.

☐ **EXERCISE 11.** Looking at grammar.
Page 401
Time: 10 minutes

- Give students adequate time to combine each pair of sentences on their own.
- Remind students that correct punctuation is necessary for grammatical accuracy, and encourage them to look at Chart 19-3 as much as needed.
- Have students take turns reading their combined sentences aloud. Ask students to be as clear as possible when they pause to indicate punctuation.
- Review and correct each item, using the board as much as needed.

Optional Vocabulary

severe	slaughtered	ventured
stubborn	ruthlessly	forth
opinionated	conceivably	

☐ **EXERCISE 12.** Warm-up. Page 401
Time: 5–10 minutes

- Ask a student to read the situation aloud and then discuss the scenario as a class, pre-teaching any vocabulary (*utterly, exhausted*) students may struggle with.
- Ask students about their experience either being or observing new parents. Ask them to imagine all that is involved (tiredness, joy, amazement, etc.) being tripled.
- Once you have discussed the scenario enough to ensure students' understanding, move to the numbered items and use of *such / so that*.
- Be prepared to help students articulate the cause-and-effect nature of *so / such that*.

CHART 19-4. Other Ways of Expressing
Cause and Effect: *Such. . .That* and *So. . .That.*
Page 402
Time: 10 minutes

Often in conversation we don't add a clause with *that* after using *so*. The word *so* then seems to mean "very" with additional emphasis. For example:

A: *Did you enjoy that book?*

B: *Yes, it was* **so** *interesting.*

This implies a clause with *that*, such as . . . **so** *interesting* **that** *I couldn't stop reading until I finished the whole book.* Other examples:

I'm **so** *tired. I've never been this tired before.*

I'm **so** *glad to meet you.*

Everyone was **so** *relieved when the hurricane changed course and went back out to sea.*

This colloquial use of *so* is not appropriate in most expository writing.

Such can also be used to mean "very": It's such a beautiful day today! = It's a very beautiful day today.

- Write the chart title on the board.
- Using what you know of your students' interests and habits, write a cause-and-effect sentence on the board using *because.* For example:

  Because Elisa enjoys skating a lot, she is planning to attend the winter Olympics.

- Explain to students that you can express the same general idea by using *such / so that* and making different word choices.
- Compose *such / so . . . that* versions of the example on the board.
- In order to clearly show the transformation, draw an arrow from the first sentence (with *because*) to the new one.
- Start with *such . . . that,* and tell students that they need to find a way to describe the *because*-clause as a combination of adjective and noun. For example:

  Elisa is such a / an ____ that she is planning to attend the winter Olympics.

- Ask students what nouns are used for a person who really enjoys a certain sport, music, or activity.
- If they can't come up with *fan* or *enthusiast,* you may need to supply this word. For example:

  Elisa is such a / an skating fan *that she is planning to attend the winter Olympics.*

- Tell students that you also need an adjective because *such . . . that* encloses a modified noun.
- Once students have come up with a suitable adjective, complete the sentence on the board with it:

  Elisa is such a / an committed / enthusiastic / huge skating fan *that she is planning to attend the winter Olympics.*

- Now go through the same process with *so . . . that.* This may be easier for students since they can keep the same verb and add *much* to restate the original idea. For example:

  Elisa enjoys skating so much that *she is planning to attend the winter Olympics.*

- Go over the whole chart together as a class.

☐ **EXERCISE 14.** Let's talk. Page 402
Time: 10 minutes

- Model this exercise for students first. You may need to add to the example under the direction line and / or write the example on the board, underlining the target structure. Exaggerate to model the rhetoric as well as the structure.
- Break students up into small groups and have them work through the exercise while you circulate.
- Explain to students that they should be creative with this exercise and exaggerate as much as they like.
- Tell them that exaggerating with this form is a common use of *so / such . . . that,* often for a humorous effect.

Expansion: While students are in groups, have each group come up with a *so / such . . . that* sentence or prediction that characterizes one group member. You can model the task first by describing yourself with a suitable sentence that will allow your student to know who the sentence is about.

This person loves grammar so much that she reads the phrasal verb dictionary in her spare time.

The sentences could also take the form of a prediction.

This person is always so late he will miss his own funeral.

Together, the group should come up with and refine sentences for each member. Then they should write each sentence on a separate piece of paper. You should then collect all the sentences, shuffle them, and redistribute them. Each student then reads the sentence or prediction aloud, and the rest of the class guesses who the sentence describes. Students particularly enjoy it when they happen to receive the sentence that describes them.

CHART 19-5. Expressing Purpose: Using *So That.* Page 404
Time: 10 minutes

> In conversation, it is common for a dependent *so that*-clause to be used in answer to a *why*-question:
>
> A: *Why did you cut class yesterday morning?* (cut class = not go to class)
>
> B: *So (that) I could cram for a test in my afternoon class.* (cram = study hard at the last possible moment)
>
> In writing, a dependent clause must never stand alone; it must be joined grammatically to an independent clause: *I cut class so that I could cram for a test.*
>
> The word *that* does not have full pronunciation as a conjunction. (This is perhaps why it is so often omitted.) It is said very quickly and with a lower voice. The vowel is reduced to a very short sound /thət/.
>
> The difference between the coordinating conjunction *so* and the subordinating conjunction *so (that)* is a little tricky to explain. Students generally don't confuse the two in their own production. To avoid unnecessary confusion, the text does not compare the two; some students get so involved in trying to distinguish "purpose" from "cause and effect" that general confusion results, at least in the experiences of the writers of this text. Other teachers may have more productive results in comparison of these two uses of *so*.
>
> Advanced students may want to know that *so as to* is a more formal and less frequent alternative to *in order to*. Example: *The law was changed so as to protect people more equitably.*

- Write the chart title on the board.
- As discussed in the notes above, students may be confused about the difference between the concept of cause-and-effect and purpose. Demonstrate this distinction briefly in the following way, but don't worry if students can't access this distinction.
- Write the following explanation on the board (in columns and side-by-side), asking students to contribute information as much as possible.

Cause and Effect	vs.	Purpose
		I went to bed early in order to sleep.
Because I was tired, I went to bed early.		*I went to bed early so (that) I could sleep.*

- Now using your students' experiences, ask them about their recent activities and what the purpose in each was.
- Write sentences on the board using both *in order to* and *so (that)*. For example:

  Olivia is traveling to New York City this weekend in order to / so that she can take the TOEFL test.

  Bengt is going to the mall after class in order to / so that he can buy a birthday present for his mother in Sweden.

  Layla took her niece to the zoo in order to / so that she could show her the baby panda.

- Go over the remainder of the chart as a class.

❏ EXERCISE 19. Warm-up. Page 405
Time: 5 minutes

> Before beginning the warm-up, discuss the concept of *expected behavior*. Also, talk about the fact that expected behavior may vary from culture to culture, but the kinds of behaviors in this exercise are universally expected or unexpected.

CHART 19-6. Showing Contrast (Unexpected Result). Page 406
Time: 10–15 minutes

> This chart presents a number of synonyms. Point out their semantic similarities and grammatical differences. It is assumed that the students understand these structural differences and the grammatical labels from their study of Chapters 16 and 17 as well as Chart 19-3.
>
> A common error is the use of both *although* and *but* to connect two ideas within a sentence.
>
> INCORRECT: ***Although** it was raining, **but** we went to the zoo.*
>
> The text does not mention that *though* can be used as a final-position adverb:
>
> *I was hungry. I didn't eat anything though.* Advanced students may be curious about this usage. It is used mainly in spoken English.
>
> *Nonetheless* is not frequently used.

- Write the chart title on the board.
- Tell students that there are four different ways / means to express an unexpected result and that they should use <u>one</u> of these ways per idea.
- Because students will already be familiar with showing unexpected result by using adverb clauses and conjunctions, write those categories on the board first, and ask students to give you examples.

For example:

| _Adverb Clause_ | _Although I am hungry, I am not going to eat anything now._ |
| _Conjunction_ | _I am hungry, but I am not going to eat anything now._ |

- Ask students to look back at Chart 19-3.
- Remind them that the placement / location between or within sentences of transitions and prepositions (respectively) is the same as what they learned in Chart 19-3.
- Reiterate that the <u>function</u> of the transitions and prepositions (to show unexpected result rather than cause and effect) is different, but that the <u>placement</u> is the same.
- Explain that the transitions _nevertheless, nonetheless,_ and _however . . . still_ are placed between sentences just the way other transitions (_e.g., therefore_) are, but that they show unexpected results.
- Explain that the prepositions _despite, in spite of, despite the fact that, and in spite of the fact that_ are placed in front of noun phrases or clauses the same way _because of_ is, but they have an inverse meaning.
- With students' help, follow the pattern on the board:

| _Transition_ | _I am hungry. Nevertheless, I am not going to eat anything now._ |
| _Preposition_ | _Despite my hunger, I am not going to eat anything now._ |

- Review the chart as a class.

❏ EXERCISE 20. Looking at grammar.
Page 406
Time: 5–10 minutes

- Reiterate the direction line to students and write the words _inside_ and _outside_ on the board.
- Ask students to explain an expected result for weddings and weather, and write this on the board in a flowchart fashion, just to ground students in a common expectation.

good weather ⇒ _wedding outside_

- Have students take turns completing each item aloud.

❏ EXERCISE 21. Looking at grammar.
Page 406
Time: 10 minutes

- Have a student read the direction line aloud.
- Remind students that this exercise is very similar to the preceding one and that they need to identify which words determine whether _am_ or _am not_ is correct.
- Give students a few minutes to complete the exercise on their own before reviewing aloud.
- Have students take turns reading the items aloud. Correct students immediately, and ask students to self-correct on the spot by finding the determining words in each item.

❏ EXERCISE 24. Looking at grammar.
Page 408
Time: 5–10 minutes

Expansion: Prepare index cards with additional pairs of sentences. Each index card should have five pairs on it, and ideally they will all differ from one another so each group of students can have a unique set. Using these extra sets, have students continue the work on Exercise 24, combining sentences with the words given.

Possible index cards / sentence sets:

He is not in love with his fiancée. He is going to marry her.

The politician is notoriously corrupt. He was re-elected to public office.

The actress is extremely rude to her fans. She has a huge fan base.

Smoking is known to cause cancer. Smoking is on the rise among young people.

Jacqueline is in debt. She continues to make purchases on her credit card.

The weather in Scotland is very rainy. Scotland is a popular tourist destination.

Children suspect Santa Clause is not real. They write letters to Santa Clause at Christmas.

Many people are afraid of flying but not of driving. Driving is statistically much more risky.

Pit bulls are an aggressive breed of dog. Pit bulls are very popular.

Tornado chasing is extremely dangerous. More people chase tornadoes every year.

Most cars function well for at least ten years. Most Americans purchase new cars every three years.

Acupuncture is a very old medical treatment. Acupuncture is called a "new age" therapy.

CHART 19-7. Showing Direct Contrast.
Page 408
Time: 10 minutes

Students may need support and clarification about exactly what "direct contrast" means.

Students may notice that _however_ is included in both Chart 19-6 and 19-7. _However_ can express "unexpected result" as in Chart 19-6. It is also used to express direct contrast and has the same meaning as _on the other hand._ (A look in a dictionary would show students that there are still more uses of _however._)

- Write the chart title on the board.
- Illustrate the concept of direct contrast, emphasizing that in order to use this structure, the context has to call for a complete contrast. For example, the following verbs are too close in meaning to support direct contrast:

   INCORRECT:

   Martha loves going to the movies, while Maria likes it.

- Show how to use direct contrast by using complete opposites and correcting the example.

   Martha loves going to the movies, while Maria hates it.

- Then go on to demonstrate using both conjunctions and transitions with the same content. For example:

   Martha loves going to the movies, but Maria hates it.

   Martha loves going to the movies. Maria, on the other hand / however, hates it.

- Review the chart as a class.

❏ **EXERCISE 26.** Looking at grammar.
Page 409
Time: 5–10 minutes

- Explain that either transition is possible for each item and that various placements are also possible.
- Remind students of how to punctuate the various placements of the transitions.
- Have different students write their answers on the board.
- Make sure that you have six items written on the board so that each transition is used for each item.
- Correct as a class.

❏ **EXERCISE 27.** Looking at grammar.
Page 409
Time: 5 minutes

- Have students complete these on sight and encourage students to provide a variety of responses to each one.
- Write some of the completions on the board and highlight the target grammar.
- Explain to students that depending on which part / word they focus on, different completions can be correct. For example, both of the following completions are correct for item 3:

   While my desk always seems to be a mess, my sister's apartment is always neat.

   While my desk always seems to be a mess, my closet is always carefully organized.

❏ **EXERCISE 28.** Let's talk or write. Page 409
Time: 15–20 minutes

   Part I
- Put students into small groups to have them discuss the list of general characteristics of introverts and extroverts.
- Have groups try to add their own ideas to the two lists.

- Ask a student from each group to write one or two of their sentences on the board.

   Part II
- Encourage students to use some of the sentences that were written on the board to help them start their writing.
- Give students time to complete sentences in class. For homework, ask them to expand this into a longer writing assignment.

❏ **EXERCISE 29.** Let's talk. Page 409
Time: 5–10 minutes

In this exercise, you could focus primarily on the grammar and go through the items rather quickly, or you could develop the exercise into an activity designed to encourage the sharing of information about the students' countries in comparison with the United States.

Some options for making the most of this exercise include:

1. Ask for volunteers for each item, concentrating on how to express direct opposition.

2. Assign each student one item to present orally to the class to initiate open discussion of that topic.

3. Assign national groups to make oral presentations.

4. Have the students discuss all of the items in small groups.

5. Open all of the items for a brainstorming class discussion; follow with a composition that compares and contrasts the U.S. and the student's country. (You might point out that almost any one of these items alone could be the topic of an entire composition.)

6. In a multinational class, open discussion could also be followed by a short composition in which the students write about what they have learned and heard, both about the U.S. and about other countries represented in the class.

If students are not familiar with contrasts between their country and the U.S., they could choose two other countries or perhaps different regions within their own country.

Expansion: The following items lend themselves to comparison contexts as well.

rural and urban areas within their country

Eastern and Western culture in general

their countries today vs. 100 years ago

their country today vs. a utopian society of the future

CHART 19-8. Expressing Conditions: Using *Otherwise* and *Or (Else)*. Page 410
Time: 10 minutes

> As a transition, *otherwise* is common in contrary-to-fact conditional sentences. Its use is discussed again in Chapter 20 (Conditional Sentences and Wishes).
>
> *Otherwise* can also function as an adverb meaning "differently" (e.g., *John thinks that Mars is inhabited. I believe otherwise.*). *Otherwise* can also mean "except for that/other than that" (e.g., *I have a broken leg, but otherwise I'm fine*). The text asks students to focus on the use of *otherwise* only as a conjunctive adverb, but advanced students might be curious about these other uses.

- Write the chart title on the board.
- Remind students that they have studied previous charts that compare the uses of adverb clauses, transitions, and conjunctions to perform the same function in a sentence, and that what they will study next is also in this format.
- Write the following simplification on the board:

  otherwise / or else = if not

- Now write *Adverb Clause* and add a sentence beginning with *If I don't*. Ask students to help you complete the sentence starter. For example:

  Adverb Clause   If I don't drink coffee in the morning, ...

  If I don't drink coffee in the morning, <u>I feel sleepy in class</u>.

- Then introduce the transition *otherwise* by restating the example sentence on the board.
- Encourage students to come up with the right form of the remaining idea.

  Transition   I always drink coffee in the morning. Otherwise, I . . . .

  I always drink coffee in the morning. Otherwise, <u>I feel sleepy in class</u>.

- Finally, introduce the conjunction *or (else)*. Add *Conjunction* to what you have on the board and restate the two sentences already discussed. Write the new sentence using *or else* with the help of students.

  Conjunction   I always drink coffee in the morning, or (else) . . . .

  I always drink coffee in the morning, or (else) <u>I feel sleepy in class</u>.

- Remind students that they have now discussed the three ways of expressing, *If not, then . . . .*
- Go over the chart as a class.

❏ EXERCISE 31. Looking at grammar.
Page 410
Time: 5–10 minutes

- Have students work through each item on their own first, writing as many options using structures presented in Chart 19-8 as they can.

- Ask two different students to go to the board for each item. Instruct one to write a sentence using the transition *otherwise* and the other with the conjunction *or (else)*.

CHART 19-9. Summary of Connectives: Cause and Effect, Contrast, and Condition. Page 411
Time: 5–10 minutes

> Congratulate students on knowing how to use all of these expressions. Make them aware of how much they have accomplished.
>
> By way of review, you can have students provide you with the parts of this chart while they keep books closed. Because students have studied all of these structures recently, they should be able to complete the chart with a little prompting from you and help from their peers.

- Write the chart title on the board and ask students to close their books.
- Write the function categories down the left side of the board (*Cause and Effect, Contrast, and Condition*), and write the structure or form categories (*Adverb Clause Words, Transitions, Conjunctions, Prepositions*) across the top from left to right.
- Ask students to give you an example of an adverb clause showing cause and effect, and write it in the appropriate space.
- Keep your book open and fill in each category with a student-generated example until you have a complete replica of Chart 19-9 on the board.
- Praise students for their accomplishment and go over Chart 19-9 as a comparison point.

❏ EXERCISE 32. Looking at grammar.
Page 411
Time: 5–10 minutes

- Do the first few items with the whole class to show everyone how to proceed.
- Then have students work in pairs or small groups.
- Walk around the room and give assistance as needed. Suggest to students where they may look in the text to find or confirm their answers.
- As a final step, open the exercise for class discussion, answering any questions and settling any disputes.

❏ EXERCISE 34. Game. Page 412
Time: 10–20 minutes

> The class should have fun with this exercise and be impressed with their own recently acquired skills in using these words and structures.

- Break students up into groups or teams and have them sit or stand with their teammates.
- Explain the direction line and the scoring for the game to students before they begin.
- Write the name of each team on the board so that you can keep score.
- Work through the items in turn. If a team fails to combine the two ideas correctly, give the option to the next team and give that team a point if it succeeds.
- When there is any doubt about whether a combined sentence is correct, have a team member write it on the board while the rest of the class votes on its correctness.

❏ **EXERCISE 35.** Reading. Page 413
Time: 10 minutes

Part I
- Have students read the passage silently or aloud, taking turns.
- Ask students to identify or underline the adverb clauses, transitions, conjunctions, and prepositions that appear in the reading and that they have studied in this chapter.

Part II
- Ask students to try to restate the information using their own words when completing the sentences.

Optional Vocabulary

expression	tendency
tend	reframe
string of bad events	gradually
attributes	
trait	

❏ **EXERCISE 37.** Check your knowledge.
Page 414
Time: 15–25 minutes

This is a summary review exercise containing grammar covered in Chapters 1 through 19. It intends to challenge the grammar knowledge and proofreading skills that students have acquired during the course. Students need time, in or out of class, to edit the sentences prior to discussion.

Some errors are in spelling.

All of these items are adapted from student writing.

- Explain to students that the items in this exercise are adapted from student writing and that, having studied Chapters 1–19, they are equipped to correct them.
- Let students know that some of the errors may be in spelling.
- Give students time in class or as homework to make all necessary corrections.
- Ask students to be prepared to explain what is wrong and why it is wrong as they offer their corrections.
- When students have questions or disagreements about the correct versions, have them write the sentences on the board and correct as a class.
- Take ample time to review this as a class and emphasize the comprehensiveness of the exercise with students as they are responsible for a lot of material in this one exercise.

Chapter 20
Conditional Sentences and Wishes

CHAPTER SUMMARY

OBJECTIVE: Conditional sentences are among the most useful forms for communicating suppositions about events or situations that are contrary to reality. Students who learn to form these clauses correctly will add a very important dimension to their ability to understand and use English in order to communicate complex information in both speech and writing.

APPROACH: Since verb forms are used for distinctions of meanings in conditional sentences, the chapter begins with a summary of their use in presenting factual and contrary-to-fact information. Then variations in conditional sentences are introduced, including the use of *as if* and *as though*. The chapter ends with a unit on expressing wishes. Many of the exercises in this chapter provide opportunities for students to communicate their own ideas.

TERMINOLOGY: An *if*-clause is also called a "clause of condition."

CHART 20-1. Overview of Basic Verb Forms Used in Conditional Sentences. Page 416
Time: 10–15 minutes

This chart summarizes the information in the next three charts. It is helpful to have a wall chart or transparency of these verb forms for you to point to and for students to refer to during discussion of the exercises. When information about using progressives and other modals is introduced in later charts, this basic chart can be expanded to include them.

It is assumed that students are somewhat familiar with conditional sentences. You might introduce this chapter with an oral exercise in which you ask leading questions:

What would you do if there were a fire in this room?

What would you have done if you hadn't come to class today?

What would you do if I asked you to stand on your head in the middle of the classroom?

If you were a bird / cat / mouse, etc., how would you spend your days? Etc.

Some students may think that conditional sentences are odd and unimportant. Assure them that conditionals are extremely common in daily conversation as well as in writing. Mastering conditionals will help students communicate in a variety of situations, and you should emphasize their everyday use with your students (even by modeling, using conditionals as content: *If you don't learn to use conditionals, you will be unable to speak naturally in everyday situations.*) Conditionals are the only way to express some ideas. You might mention that one situation in which they are especially common is sports broadcasting. For example:

If the catcher hadn't struck out, the Red Sox would have won the World Series.

- Write the chart title on the board.
- Tell students that understanding and using conditionals is extremely important for their general use of English, particularly when speaking.
- Explain that much of what we humans like to talk about is "unreal." People love to talk about what will happen in certain cases, what could happen in the future, and what could have happened but didn't. Stress that without understanding and being able to use conditionals, students can't participate in these natural speech functions.
- Remind students that they have probably already studied and used very simple conditionals, and write an *if*-clause on the board that they can turn into a full sentence, such as:

  If I learn English very well, I ____.

- Ask students for a variety of completions in the correct tense (*will* future), and write some of the completed sentences on the board.

  If I learn English very well, I will be eligible to apply for a new job.

  If I learn English very well, I will attend university in the U.S.

  If I learn English very well, I will travel to Australia.

- Because conditionals will be review for some students, write the basic headings of Chart 20-1 on the board, and ask students to give you examples of the conditionals they already know.
- After replicating as much of the chart as possible by eliciting information from students, review the chart in the book as a class.

❏ EXERCISE 2. Looking at grammar.
Page 416
Time: 5–10 minutes

- You and / or a volunteer can read the situation in each item aloud.
- Ask different students to complete the conditional sentences that follow each situation.
- Referring back to the chart, focus students' attention on the true / untrue distinction.
- Point out the verb tense in each type of clause and then, as you lead the exercise, relate these tenses to the time phrases in the exercise.

❏ EXERCISE 3. Warm-up. Page 417
Time: 3–5 minutes

- Ask students which tenses are referred to in the items and how the use of these tenses may change the meaning of the sentence.
- Discuss the difference between a general statement and one referring to a specific time.

CHART 20-2. True in the Present or Future.
Page 417
Time: 15 minutes

Conditional sentences have a sort of "truth value" in the mind of the speaker. The *if*-clause contains a condition under which, in the speaker's opinion, an expected result might or might not occur. The result clause can state the speaker's prediction of an outcome.

Like adverb clauses of time, an *if*-clause usually does not contain a future tense verb, *will* or *be going to*. This is a fact about English usage that must be learned, even though it might seem illogical to some students. A language is not a logical set of scientific formulas or rules; it is a complex, flexible instrument of communication based on traditions and preferences. Students should understand this point by the time they complete this text.

In everyday conversation, the subjunctive use of *were* instead of *was* with singular subjects is more typical of American than British English. Favoring formal usage, the text encourages the use of *were,* but either is correct. (See examples (b) and (c) in Chart 20-3.)

You may want to incorporate the following sentence, which some learners find fun, into your lesson: *I would if I could, but I can't, so I won't.* It captures the distinction between the conditional and the factual.

- Write the chart title on the board.
- Start by reviewing time clauses using *when* and the fact that these clauses are followed by the simple present tense.
- With students' help, write a *when* time clause on the board.

    When Fabiana returns to Brazil, she will work in her mother's business.

- Explain that *if*-clauses function in the same way. Elicit an *if*-clause from students and write it on the board.

    If Juana stays up too late, she ____ tired.

- Point out to students that this is a general statement and it has no specific time frame.
- Tell students that the result clause has varied possible verb forms. With students' help, use an appropriate version of *become* in order to complete the sentence on the board.

    If Juana stays up too late, she becomes tired.

- Change the sample sentence to show a specific time frame and write it on the board.

    If Juana stays up too late tonight, she ____ tired tomorrow.

- Put the appropriate variations of the verb *become* on the board, and illustrate the possible result clause tenses when a specific time has been determined.

    If Juana stays up too late tonight, she will / could / may become tired tomorrow.

- Go over the rest of the chart as a class.

❏ EXERCISE 4. Let's talk. Page 418
Time: 5–10 minutes

Students should be encouraged to look at the chart if necessary. There are a lot of rules for students to keep in mind and master. Remind them that the form of the answer is included and modeled in each question.

❏ EXERCISE 5. Looking at grammar.
Page 418
Time: 5–10 minutes

- Have students read the items aloud, choosing the correct form of the verb as they go.
- Either verb form works for items 3–5, so ask students to describe the subtle differences in meaning attached to the use of both possible verb forms.

CHART 20-3. Untrue (Contrary to Fact) in the Present or Future. Page 419
Time: 10–15 minutes

Untrue does not mean that the speaker is lying, of course. It means that he or she is speaking of some situation that does not or cannot truly exist. The situation is hypothetical and not real. *Untrue* is defined as "contrary to fact" or "the opposite of what is true and real."

- Write the chart title on the board.
- Start by making a statement about yourself that lends itself to this structure. Write on the board a statement describing an action you won't take or a plan you won't carry out, such as:

    I won't take a teaching job in Bangkok.

- Elaborate on this by saying under what conditions you would complete this action even though you know this condition will not occur. Write this as an *if*-clause conditional.

    If I had a friend to accompany me, I would take a teaching job in Bangkok.

- Explain to students that the *if*-clause in this case is in the past and the result clause is formed with **would** + *base form* of the verb.

- Highlight the verb forms in both the *if*-clause and the result clause.

- Write the true situation, in two sentences, beneath the conditional.

    If I had a friend to accompany me, I would take a teaching job in Bangkok.

    I don't have a friend to accompany me.

    Therefore, I won't take a teaching job in Bangkok.

- Now ask students to think about dreams they would like to realize if the right conditions <u>were</u> present. Encourage them to be imaginative.

- Write an example on the board, using the same steps as above.

- Highlight the *if*-clause and result clause, and reiterate the true situation beneath the new conditional sentence. For example:

    If Consuela was the president of the United States, she would create a universal health care plan.

    Consuela is not the president of the United States.

    Therefore, she won't create a universal health care plan.

- Give other students a chance to write about their wildest dreams in this way, and write them on the board.

- Review the rest of the chart as a class.

❑ EXERCISE 8. Looking at grammar.
Page 419
Time: 5–10 minutes

> Because pairs of items in this exercise are related, showing true and untrue conditional statements, you may want to have students work on two items at a time.

- After giving students time to work on this exercise alone, lead them in a discussion of the correct forms and the differences in meaning.

- Explain that the speaker communicates an opinion about the truth value by his / her choice of verb forms. For example, if the *if*-clause is thought to be untrue or contrary to fact, the speaker will use the past tense.

- In order to help students understand the truth value, ask leading questions about this throughout the exercise, such as:

    Am I going to bake an apple pie?

    Do I have enough apples to do this?

    Do I know if I have enough apples?

    Do I want to bake an apple pie?

❑ EXERCISE 9. Let's talk. Page 419
Time: 10–15 minutes

- Write the terms *ethics* and *ethical dilemma* on the board. Ask students to explain both terms to you if they can.

- Explain that this exercise deals with ethical decisions, and discuss the fact that sometimes different circumstances influence whether a situation is 100 percent right or wrong.

- After you have discussed this point, divide the class into small groups for discussion, or review each item as a class.

- If working in small groups, give students sufficient time to work through the items.

- Then have different students write their conditional sentences on the board.

- As a class, first check the grammar in each sentence, and then vote on whether the conditions are "sufficient" to justify doing something normally considered wrong.

Expansion: You can expand on this activity further by offering students other ethical dilemmas and asking them to explain what they would do in various situations. Remind students to start each response with *if* by writing the following on the board:

    If ____, I would ____.

For each situation below, students should use a conditional to explain under exactly what conditions they would take certain actions.

Possible situations:

    A homeless person asks you for money on the street. You have extra money on you and you can afford to give it to this person.

    A friend tells you he / she lost the expensive camera you just lent him / her.

    At the movies, the people next to you talk loudly during the film, and you and your friends can't hear properly.

    A guest in your house opens the refrigerator and helps himself / herself to food without asking you if it is okay to do so.

    In a park, a babysitter slaps the child she is looking after.

    You are at a party when the host says something very offensive or racist about a friend of yours.

    You have been waiting in a line for ten minutes. Someone cuts in front of you.

    You have seen your best friend's boyfriend or girlfriend on a date with someone else.

    You are on a very crowded bus, and you are standing. An old person who can barely stand gets on the bus, but no one offers him / her a seat. You see a very young person continuing to sit comfortably while the elderly person is standing.

You are preparing for a math exam and accidentally come across the answers to it.

❏ EXERCISE 11. Let's talk: interview.
Page 420
Time: 10–15 minutes

- Model the example with one student. You may want to add to the example in the text and write possible answers on the board.
- Students can begin with *But if . . . .* Demonstrate how to add appropriate emphasis to the first auxiliary.
- Anticipate that students may not agree that item 6 is a fact, and encourage them to refine the fact as they see fit.

CHART 20-4. Untrue (Contrary to Fact) in the Past. Page 421
Time: 10–15 minutes

> Looking back at past times, we know whether events really occurred or not. Using conditional sentences, we can talk about hypothetical past events and results that would have or could have occurred had certain conditions been present.
>
> It is possible to use *would* in *if*-clauses.
>
> *If you'd try harder, you'd learn more.*
>
> *If you would've told me about it, I could've helped you.*
>
> The text does not teach this usage because it is not possible in all situations and is generally considered nonstandard, especially in formal written English.

- Write the chart title on the board.
- Write on the board the expression "Hindsight is 20/20." Ask students to guess what this means. You may need to breakdown *hindsight* and discuss how vision is assessed.
- Ask students if they often think about how their life would be different now if they had had more information at the time of making a big decision. Specifically, ask what would have happened if the conditions had been different.
- Ask a few students to share an example from their own lives. If no one feels comfortable doing so, share one from your life or write one that is considered to be general knowledge. For example:

    If I had known there was going to be a test today, I would have studied more last night.

- Write the verb tenses used under the *if*-clause and result clause of this conditional. Make sure students understand that both the first clause and the second are contrary to fact.

    If I had known there was going to be a test today,
    (past perfect tense)

    I would have studied more last night.
    ("would have" + past participle)

- Reiterate that both parts of this sentence are in the past. Write the true situation beneath each clause.

    If I had known there was going to be a test today,
    (I didn't know.)

    I would have studied more last night.
    (I didn't study very much last night.)

- Have students share some similar conditionals and write them on the board, following the steps taken above.
- Go over the chart as a class.

❏ EXERCISE 14. Looking at grammar.
Page 421
Time: 5–10 minutes

- Remind students that another way of thinking about whether a condition is true is to consider whether it is still possible.
- In the example, item 1, *If the weather is warm* is still possible.
- In item 2, *If the weather were warm* is still not possible, and by using *were,* the speaker is telling us it isn't true.
- Give students a few minutes to work through the items on their own.
- Review the exercise as a class, taking time to make immediate corrections, and review any item students find particularly challenging by writing it on the board.

❏ EXERCISE 16. Looking at grammar.
Page 422
Time: 10 minutes

> In this exercise, three similar sentences are grouped together up to item 10. Lead students in a discussion of the differences in form and meaning among the grouped sentences.

❏ EXERCISE 18. Let's talk. Page 423
Time: 10–15 minutes

> This is a pattern practice, with controlled responses, so students can easily check on one another's verb form usage and work out the answers together if need be. You could, of course, choose to lead the exercise yourself if you think it is too difficult for students.
>
> Often speakers add emphasis to the word *had* in the *if*-clause in responses that begin with *but if.*

Expansion: While students are in pairs, have them come up with their own versions of the items included in Exercise 18 and write complete conditionals from them, starting with *If I had ____, ____.* For example:

If I had known how upset Nancy was, I wouldn't have made that joke about her cat.

Hand out two index cards to each pair, and instruct each member of the pair to write either the *if*-clause or the main clause on his / her card. For example:

If I had known how upset Nancy was,

I wouldn't have made that joke about her cat.

Once these index cards have been completed, shuffle them and redistribute one card to each student. Instruct the students to read aloud what is on the index card they have just received. (It is important students read these aloud rather than simply show their card to other students in order to gain oral practice.) By reading what is on their card aloud and discussing the *if*- or main clause with other students, they should be able to find the original match. When everyone has found their match, have each new pair read the complete sentence to the class, and the "author pairs" can correct and approve the matches as appropriate.

❏ **EXERCISE 21.** Looking at grammar.
Page 425
Time: 10–15 minutes

These items are past, present, and future. Remind students that they must identify the time and also the truth value first, and then use appropriate verb forms.

❏ **EXERCISE 23.** Looking at grammar.
Page 426
Time: 10 minutes

Substituting an auxiliary for a verb phrase to avoid unnecessary repetition isn't explained in the text, as it is assumed students are familiar with these patterns. However, some students may have difficulty with this exercise. Its purpose is to prepare for the next oral exercise, so you should now take time for discussion of the patterns.

In speaking, the word in each blank should be given emphasis followed by a slight pause.

- Have a student read the first three completed example items aloud while you write each full sentence on the board.
- Underline the auxiliary in each one and ask students when, in their studies of English, they have used just the auxiliary (without the full verb) before.
- Many of them will recall using the auxiliary in simple short answers, but to remind them and reinforce the pattern, write a simple example of it on the board. For example:

  Has Hiro ever visited Turkey? ⇒
  Short Answer: / Yes, he has.

- Tell students they can use this same pattern with *but if . . .* and that they should complete the exercise using this verb form.

- Model and even exaggerate the spoken emphasis given to the auxiliary when it is used as a substitute for the complete verb form.
- Review as a class.

CHART 20-5. Using Progressive Verb Forms in Conditional Sentences. Page 427
Time: 10 minutes

If students are unclear about the function and meaning of progressive verb forms, you might conduct a review of the relevant parts of Chapters 1 through 3. A "progressive situation" is one in which an activity is (was / will be / would be) in progress during or at a particular time.

- Write the chart title on the board.
- Elicit an example of the form to write on the board. A simple way to do this is to first ask students what they are doing right now (e.g., sitting in English class, learning about conditionals, etc.) and then ask them what they would be doing right now <u>if they were not sitting in class</u>.
- Write the starter sentence on the board and have various students complete it. For example:

  If I were not sitting in English class right now, I ____.

- Explain to students that they can complete this with a simple form of what they would do or a progressive form that describes what they <u>would be doing</u>.
- Write some examples on the board.

  If I were not sitting in English class right now, I <u>would go</u> to the movies.

  If I were not sitting in English class right now, I <u>would be sleeping</u> at home.

- As you write such sentences on the board, reiterate the "truth value" by asking students what they are actually doing right now.
- Explain that *were not + -ing* is used to make the present conditional untrue and that *had not been + -ing* is used to make the past conditional untrue.
- Review the rest of the chart and practice making sample sentence with the past conditional with students. Write their examples on the board. For example:

  If Max had not been leaving town yesterday, I would have asked him to help us move.

  If Xiao Ping had not been studying for the TOEFL test last weekend, I would have asked her to join us for dinner.

❏ **EXERCISE 26.** Looking at grammar.
Page 427
Time: 10 minutes

- Model the first item and place emphasis on the first auxiliary.
- Have students go around the room taking turns completing each item aloud.

- Correct students immediately, and make sure they place appropriate emphasis on the first auxiliary. Doing so will help them both be understood and understand this structure when they hear it.

❏ **EXERCISE 28.** Warm-up. Page 428
Time: 3–5 minutes

> After students have read and you have discussed their choices, explain that sometimes particular situations require the use of "mixed" tenses to truly represent when a realization linked to a condition actually happens.

CHART 20-6. Using "Mixed Time" in Conditional Sentences. Page 428
Time: 10 minutes

> Most books don't point out this usage, but it is very common in both speech and writing. It is assumed that at this point, most students have control of the basic conditional verb forms outlined in Chart 20-1 and are ready to practice variations that are common in actual usage: progressive verb forms, mixed time, use of other modals, omission of *if*, implied conditions.

- Write the chart title on the board.
- Start by writing half a conditional sentence on the board and having students complete the information with an expected main clause. For example:

  If I had studied last week, <u>I would have been prepared for the exam</u>.

- Under both clauses, write *past time* to indicate that the "time" / tense for the condition has already passed and so has the "time" / tense for the result.

past time	*past time*
If I had studied last week,	<u>*I would have been prepared for the exam*.</u>

- Clarify by asking if the opportunity for studying is over (yes) and then asking if the exam is also over, (yes).
- Introduce *Mixed Time* by asking students to imagine that they have no more time to study but haven't yet taken the test and are just about to.
- Explain that in order to represent this actual situation, the *if*-clause is still in the past, but the main clause is in conditional present.
- Transform the structure on the board into this new mixture of tenses, and show this transformation by writing it step-by-step on the board.

past time	*past time*
If I had studied last week,	<u>*I would have been prepared for the exam*.</u>

  <u>*Using Mixed Time*</u>

past time	*present time*
If I had studied last week,	<u>*I would be prepared now*.</u>

- Go over the rest of the chart with students.

❏ **EXERCISE 29.** Looking at grammar.
Page 429
Time: 10 minutes

> **Expansion:** Put students into pairs. Have one student make a statement about his/her past activities. Have the other student use that information to make a mixed time conditional sentence. For example:
>
> Speaker A: *I ate dinner at the student cafeteria last night.*
>
> Speaker B: *If I were you, I would have eaten at Luigi's Restaurant on 5th Street. OR If you hadn't eaten at the student cafeteria last night, your stomach would feel better now.*

CHART 20-7. Omitting *If*. Page 429
Time: 10 minutes

> Of the three examples in this chart, the one with *had* (b) is the most commonly used in both conversation and writing.
>
> The example with *should* (c) is somewhat formal and uncommon usage.
>
> The example with *were* (a) is less frequent than the others, especially in conversation. *Was* is not substituted for *were* in this pattern.

- Write the chart title on the board.
- Write a complete conditional on the board in which you can replace the *If*-clause with *had*, which is the most commonly used form of these omission. For example:

  If I had known English was so easy, I would have studied it years ago.

- Cross out the *If I had* to show how the inversion takes place.
  ~~*If I had known*~~ *English was so easy, I would have studied it years ago.*

  Had I known English was so easy, I would have studied it years ago.

- Go over the rest of the chart.

❏ **EXERCISE 31.** Looking at grammar.
Page 429
Time: 10 minutes

> This is a simple transformation exercise designed to help students become familiar with the pattern.

- Give students a few minutes to work individually.
- Have one student read the original item aloud and then ask another to transform it into the new pattern.

- Make sure that students have inverted subject and verb appropriately as they omit the *if*. Make any corrections by writing the new pattern on the board as needed.

CHART 20-8. Implied Conditions. Page 430
Time: 10 minutes

These examples show one of the most common uses of conditional verb forms. A result clause does not always come neatly attached to an *if*-clause. Many of the uses of *would* and *could* in daily conversation express results of implied conditions. In writing, one condition expressed near the beginning of a composition can affect word forms throughout.

- Write the chart title on the board.
- Underline the word *implied* and ask students to describe its meaning.
- Use this as an opportunity to explain that in many cases, the condition is present but isn't overtly tied to an actual *if*-clause that we can see.
- Have students read the examples (a), (b), and (c) aloud in turn, or you can make up three new examples using students' lives.
- For each example, ask students to restate the original as a typical conditional sentence, and write these on the board as students read them to you. For example:
    - (a) Sylvie would have come to the party, but she had to meet her mother at the airport.

      If Sylvie hadn't had to meet her mother at the airport, she would have come to the party.
    - (b) I couldn't have done it without you.

      If I didn't have you, I couldn't have done it.
    - (c) Leo took a cab. Otherwise, he would have been late for work.

      If Leo hadn't taken a cab, he would have been late for work.

❏ EXERCISE 34. Looking at grammar.
Page 431
Time: 5–10 minutes

An understanding of implied conditions expands students' communicative repertoire.

- Give students time to make the implied conditionals into actual *if*-clause conditionals and complete sentences.
- Review as a class, and write any particularly challenging items on the board to highlight the correct and required forms together.

❏ EXERCISE 36. Looking at grammar.
Page 431
Time: 10 minutes

- Inform students that this exercise reviews all of the charts in this chapter, and invite them to look back at previous charts as needed.
- Encourage the use of contractions (for example, *wouldn't, hadn't*), especially in dialogues.
- Give students time to complete this individually before reviewing as a class.

❏ EXERCISE 38. Let's talk. Page 433
Time: 10–15 minutes

The purpose of this exercise is to prompt spontaneous, interactive use of conditional sentences. The exercise can be done in pairs and small groups, but it also works very well as a teacher-led activity, with you prompting a variety of responses.

You should set up situations that students will respond to. It isn't necessary to use the exact words that you find in this exercise. Feel free to alter each item or use alternative contexts that are more familiar to students.

CHART 20-9. Verb Forms Following *Wish*.
Page 434
Time: 10–15 minutes

Noun-clause verbs following *wish* are in a past form. The past form signifies "contrary to fact" — just as it does in conditional sentences in *if*-clauses. You may want to discuss verb relationships.

"true" situation	"wish" situation
simple present	simple past
present progressive	past progressive
simple past	past perfect
present perfect	past perfect
will	*would*
am / is / are going to	was / were going to
can	could
could + simple form	could have + past participle

Wish can also be followed by an infinitive, for example: *I wish to know the results of the test as soon as possible.* In this instance, *wish* is usually a more formal way of saying *want* or a more direct (possibly impolite or imperious) way of saying *would like.* This use is rare.

The subjunctive use of *were* instead of *was* with *I / he / she / it* is considered formal by some but standard by others. Students who will take the TOEFL exam need to recognize and be able to work with the subjunctive using *were.*

Some teachers like to compare *hope* and *wish.* See notes in this Teacher's Guide for Chart 20-10.

- Write the chart title on the board.
- Explain that the verb forms following *wish* are noun clauses and that the general pattern changes the tense in the clause to past time.
- You can point out that (or ask if) students have seen a similar pattern when learning reported speech, which is also formed from noun clauses.
- Write a simple sentence about a truth in the future on the board.

    Dana will return to India at the end of this month.

- Underline the future *will* and write the word *future* beneath the sentence.

                        future
    Dana <u>will</u> return to India at the end of this month.

- Now show the new pattern by writing a new *wish* sentence, using *would*.

    I wish (that) Dana <u>would not return</u> to India next month.

- Continue with this step-by-step presentation for wishes about the present and wishes about the past, writing on the board to clearly show the changes made as you go.
- You may wish to remind students again of the similarities with reported speech tense changes, as they have mastered these already.
- Review the rest of the chart as a class.

❏ EXERCISE 40. Looking at grammar.
Page 434
Time: 10 minutes

This exercise is a quick check of the students' understanding of Chart 20-9. If students seem to be having difficulty, make up additional items to illustrate verb-form usage in noun clauses following *wish*.

❏ EXERCISE 41. Let's talk. Page 435
Time: 10–20 minutes

- Have half the class (Group A) close their books. Have the other half (Group B) keep their books open to bring with them as they interview the other students.
- Explain that Group B will be interviewing Group A. Encourage Group A students to give detailed answers and Group B students to ask follow-up questions.
- After ten minutes or so, switch roles. Tell Group B to close their books while Group A retrieves their books and begins interviewing.
- As a class, review the questions. Ask students to call out some of the answers they heard using complete sentences, such as:

    Maria wishes she could sing well.

❏ EXERCISE 42. Looking at grammar.
Page 435
Time: 10 minutes

Only an auxiliary (helping verb) verb is required in each item. Note that British and American English differ somewhat in usage. For example:

1. *I can't sing well, but I wish I could.* (AmE) vs. *I can't sing well, but I wish I could do.* (BrE)
2. *I didn't go but I wish I had.* (AmE) vs. *I didn't go but I wish I had done.* (BrE)
3. *He won't . . . , but I wish he would.* (AmE) vs. *He won't, but I wish he would do.* BrE

CHART 20-10. Using *Would* to Make Wishes about the Future. Page 436
Time: 10 minutes

When speakers want something to happen in the future and think it is possible, they usually use *hope* to introduce their idea: *I hope they (will) come.* When they want something to happen but think it is probably not possible, they'd probably use *wish*: *I wish they would come.*

A common mistake is the use of *will* in the noun clause following *wish*:

    INCORRECT: *I wish they will come.*

- Write a situation on the board that the students, in general, wish to change, such as:

    We are facing a problem with global warming right now.

- Explain that when they want to make a wish about the future, which is not simply a restatement of the opposite of the current truth, they should use *would* to do so.
- Elicit a new wish about the future, based on the example on the board, and write the new wish on the board. Underline *would*.

                    present
    We have a problem with global warming right now.
    I wish the global warming situation <u>would improve</u>.

- Go over the chart as a class.

❏ EXERCISE 46. Let's talk. Page 437
Time: 15–20 minutes

This exercise works best if you set up the questions so that students are eager to share their wishes and dreams. If you need to change any of the wording to make it more interesting or appropriate, do so.

Encourage students to elaborate on their answers, and help them to interact with one another as they offer responses.

Index

Student Book Answer Key

Exercise 1, p. 1.

Sample questions:
1. What is your name?
2. How do you spell your (last/first) name? / How do you spell that?
3. Where are you from?
4. Where were you born?
5. Where do you live? / Where are you living?
6. Why did you come here?
7. How long have you been living here? How long are you going to be living here? / How long do you plan to be here?
8. What is your major? / What is your field of study? / What do you do?
9. What do you like to do in your free time? What hobbies do you have?
10. How do you like living here? How do you feel about living here? What do you think about living here?

Exercise 2, p. 1.

Questions to ask:

Partner A:
1. What do you do every day before you leave home?
2. What have you done / have you been doing since you got up this morning?
3. What are you doing right now?
4. What were you doing at (this exact time) yesterday?
5. What had you done by the time you got here today? (*also possible:* What did you do . . . .)

Partner B:
1. What did you do last night?
2. What are you going to do / will you do tomorrow?
3. What have you been doing for the past five minutes?
4. What will you be doing at (this exact time) tomorrow?
5. What will you have done by the time you go to bed tonight?

Exercise 4, p. 2.

1. cooked
2. bought
3. get
4. will be
5. am going to watch

Exercise 6, p. 3.

1. was sleeping
2. am thinking
3. will be sitting
4. will be watching
5. was watching

Exercise 8, p. 4.

1. have done
2. had done
3. will have done
4. have studied
5. had studied

Exercise 11, p. 6.

1. studies
2. is studying
3. studied
4. was studying
5. will study / is going to study
6. will be studying / is going to be studying
7. has already studied
8. had already studied
9. will already have studied
10. has been studying
11. had been studying
12. will have been studying

Exercise 12, p. 8.

2. The speakers are discussing an activity that began and ended in the past. Tense: simple past.
3. The speakers are discussing an activity that is happening (is in progress) at the moment of speaking. Tense: present progressive.
4. The speakers are discussing an activity in progress at a particular time in the past. Tense: past progressive.
5. The speakers are discussing activities that have occurred (or not occurred) "before now," at unspecific times in the past. Tense: present perfect
6. The speakers are discussing what will happen at a specific time in the future. Tense: simple future.
7. The speakers are discussing the duration of an activity that has already started and will end at a specific time in the future. Tense: future perfect progressive.
8. This question concerns the duration of an activity that started in the past and is still in progress. Tense: present perfect progressive.
9. This question concerns an activity that started and ended before another time in the past. Tense: past perfect.

Exercise 14, p. 9.

1. Does Pedro **walk** to work every morning?
2. What **are you** talking about?
3. Did you **finish** your work?
4. My friend doesn't **like** her apartment.
5. **Are you working** for this company? / **Do you work** for this company?
6. What time **did your plane arrive**?
7. How long have you **been living** in this city? / How long have you **lived** in this city?
8. Ali **won't be** in class tomorrow.

1

Exercise 15, p. 9.

1. hoped
2. stopped
3. waiting
4. sitting
5. started
6. happened
7. planning
8. enjoyed
9. worried
10. studying

Exercise 16, p. 10.

Part I.

dating	putting	enjoying
dining	stopping	happening
grading	winning	staying

Part II.

answered	controlled
listened	permitted
offered	planned
opened	preferred

Exercise 17, p. 11.

Part I.

2. hiding
3. running
4. ruining
5. coming
6. writing
7. eating
8. patting
9. lying
10. beginning
11. earning
12. flying

Part II.

2. planning, planned
3. raining, rained
4. taping, taped
5. tapping, tapped
6. entering, entered
7. preferring, preferred
8. translating, translated
9. dying, died
10. employing, employed
11. burying, buried
12. admitting, admitted
13. visiting, visited
14. waiting, waited

Exercise 18, p. 12.

1. are renting
2. preferred
3. destroyed
4. visited
5. gained
6. 'm planning
7. 'm taking
8. am replying
9. replied

Chapter 2: Present and Past; Simple and Progressive

Exercise 1, p. 13.

2. **I don't know** Sam's wife.
3. My roommate usually **watches** television, **listens** to music, or **goes** out in the evening.
4. When I turned the key, the car **started**.
5. Air **consists** of oxygen, nitrogen, and other gases.
6. The children **drew** some pictures in school this morning.
7. Right now Sally **is** in the kitchen eating breakfast.
8. While **I was** driving home last night, I **heard** a strange noise in the engine.
9. A: What **are you** talking about?
   B: I **am** talking about the political situation in my country.

Exercise 2, p. 13.

1. (*Answers will vary.*)
2. (*Answers will vary.*)
3. No. (The earth revolves around the sun.)
4. Sentence 3 is a general truth.
5. Sentence 1 is a daily habit.
6. Sentence 2 is something that is happening right now.

Exercise 3, p. 14.

Sample sentences:
The earth revolves around the sun.
Air contains nitrogen and oxygen.
The human heart beats 72 times per minute (on average).
Snowflakes have six sides.
The average person sleeps eight hours a night.
Hybrid cars use less gas.

Exercise 4, p. 15.

2. washes
3. usually sits . . .
   is sitting
4. am trying
5. Do you always lock
6. am still waiting
7. is shining
8. shines . . . wakes

Exercise 5, p. 15.

1. right now
2. in the winter, every April
3. every year
4. right now, today
5. every summer, in the spring
6. this week

Exercise 7, p. 16.

1. b
2. b
3. a
4. a

Exercise 8, p. 17.

1. a. *smell* describes a state that exists, i.e., the flowers have a smell and that smell is good.
   b. *is smelling* describes the action of using one's nose.
2. a. *think* means "believe" in this sentence and describes a state.
   b. *am thinking* is an action; thoughts are going through the speaker's mind.
3. a. *see* describes a perception that exists right now as a result of the speaker using his/her eyes.
   b. *is seeing* a doctor means "is going to a doctor for help," a general activity in progress at present.
   c. *are seeing* means they are dating each other, a general activity in progress at present.
4. a. *looks* means "appears or seems to be" and describes an apparent state that exists: Astrid is apparently cold.
   b. *is looking* describes the action of using one's eyes.
5. a. *is feeling* describes the action of using one's sense of touch. Sue is using her hands to touch the cat's fur. The activity is in progress at the present moment.
   b. *feels* describes a state that exists, the state of the cat's fur; i.e., it is soft.
   c. *am not feeling* describes the speaker's physical feelings of illness, in progress at the present. [*Note:* The simple present is also possible here with little difference in meaning (*I don't feel well today*) to describe a state that exists.]
   d. *feel* means "think or believe" in this sentence and describes a state.
6. a. *remember* describes a state that exists.
   b. *is remembering* describes an activity in progress: memories are going through Aunt Sara's mind.

7. a. *be* describes a state that exists.
   b. *being* describes a temporary behavior: the children are acting awfully quiet.
8. a. *is appearing* describes the action of performing on stage in a theater, general activity in progress at present
   b. *appears* means "seems" and describes an apparent state that exists.

Exercise 9, p. 18.
2. a   5. a
3. b   6. a
4. b

Exercise 10, p. 18.
1. is beginning . . . don't have . . . don't own . . . is wearing . . . wear
2. is doing . . . is being . . . doesn't want . . . is always
3. am looking . . . looks . . . has . . . isn't having
4. A: do you like . . . Does it need
   B: tastes . . . reminds
5. A: are you looking
   B: look
   A: Do you think . . . resemble
   B: see
6. am looking . . . is writing . . . is biting . . . is scratching . . . is staring . . . seems . . . is thinking . . . do you think . . . is doing

Exercise 12, p. 22.
1. lost
2. forgot
3. made
4. wrote
5. took
6. did
7. understood
8. brought
9. got
10. knew
11. began
12. spoke
13. gave
14. spent
15. told
16. taught
17. sang

Exercise 13, p. 23.
1. Yes, I found a pet store.
2. Yes, I bought a parrot.
3. Yes, I took it out of its cage.
4. Yes, I had some trouble with it.
5. Yes, it bit me.
6. Yes, I left the pet store.
7. Yes, I went to the doctor.
8. Yes, I drove to the doctor's office.
9. Yes, she put a bandage on my finger.
10. Yes, I paid her.

Exercise 14, p. 23.
1. swam
2. stood
3. fell
4. ran
5. lay
6. wore
7. dug
8. built
9. wrote
10. drew
11. hid
12. sang
13. stung
14. saw

Exercise 15, p. 24.
1. Yes, I had a great trip.
2. Yes, I came back feeling rested.
3. Yes, I met many people.
4. Yes, I hung out with local people.
5. Yes, I did a lot of tourist activities.
6. Yes, I stood on the Acropolis.
7. Yes, I spent time in museums.
8. Yes, I bought some Greek sandals.
9. Yes, I spoke a little Greek.
10. Yes, I ate in typical Greek restaurants.
11. Yes, I got your emails.
12. Yes, I brought you a present.
13. Yes, I sent you a postcard.
14. Yes, I was sad to leave Greece.

Exercise 16, p. 24.
1. woke
2. caught
3. hurt
4. took
5. had
6. felt
7. kept
8. lay
9. slept
10. dreamt
11. ate
12. spoke
13. took
14. read

Exercise 17, p. 25.
Note: The pronoun *he* is being used for these answers.
1. Yes, he woke me up a lot.
2. Yes, I heard a lot of noise.
3. Yes, his cell phone rang many times.
4. Yes, he fought with someone.
5. Yes, he put on a CD.
6. Yes, he sang loudly.
7. Yes, he made breakfast at midnight.
8. Yes, he ground some coffee beans first.
9. Yes, he fed the neighbor's cats.
10. Yes, he swept the floor afterwards.
11. Yes, he knew I was awake.
12. Yes, he meant to wake me up.
13. Yes, he upset me.
14. Yes, I was upset.

Exercise 18, p. 25.
1. happy, good about my decision
2. two classes, at night
3. the car with gas
4. with colored pencils, several faces, for several hours
5. in the woods, some money
6. from the math class, some money from the bank
7. my hand, some rice
8. these jeans, my shirt
9. at the sad ending, when the play finished
10. over the fence, very quickly, in a sunny spot

Exercise 19, p. 25.
Part I.
1. F   4. T
2. F   5. F
3. F   6. F

Part II.
1. had
2. burst
3. broke
4. woke
5. heard
6. shook
7. hid
8. heard
9. sped
10. saw
11. ran
12. got
13. caught
14. felt
15. upset

Exercise 20, p. 26.
1. different
2. same
3. different
4. same
5. different
6. same
7. same
8. same
9. different

Exercise 21, p. 27.
1. /t/
2. /d/
3. /əd/
4. /d/
5. /əd/
6. /t/
7. /d/
8. /t/
9. /əd/

Exercise 22, p. 27.
1. blinked/t/ . . . yawned/d/ . . . stretched/t/
2. mopped/t/ . . . vacuumed/d/ . . . dusted/əd/
3. started/əd/ . . . ended/əd/
4. jumped/t/ . . . yelled/d/
5. departed/əd/ . . . landed/əd/
6. asked/t/ . . . suggested/əd/

Exercise 23, p. 28.

/t/	/d/	/əd/
chased	believed	accepted
fixed	complained	needed
missed	died	requested
pushed	played	
thanked	rained	
worked	worried	

Exercise 24, p. 28.
combed/d/
brushed/t/
cooked/t/
waited/əd/
walked/t/
washed/t/
typed/t/
worked/t/

exercised/d/
talked/t/
surfed/t/
translated/əd/
added/əd/
cleaned/d/
listened/d/

Exercise 25, p. 28.
1. Rita stood under a tree when it began to rain.
2. Rita was standing under a tree when it began to rain.

Exercise 26, p. 29.
1. a
2. b
3. a
4. a

Exercise 27, p. 30.
2. called . . . wasn't . . . was studying
3. didn't hear . . . was sleeping
4. was shining . . . was blowing . . . were singing
5. were arguing . . . walked
6. opened . . . found
7. was reading . . . fell . . . closed . . . sneaked/snuck
8. A: Did you hear
   B: wasn't listening . . . was thinking
9. was snowing . . . was shining . . . were shoveling . . . was lying

Exercise 28, p. 31.
1. A: was waiting
   B: Did they call
2. A: did you break
   B: slipped . . . was crossing

3. B: was looking
   A: Did you find
   B: parked
4. A: Did you ask . . . saw
   B: was working . . . looked . . . decided
5. B: happened
   A: got . . . was driving . . . wasn't paying . . . didn't see . . . kept

Exercise 29, p. 32.
1. found
2. was
3. were speaking
4. were sitting
5. looked
6. walked
7. stopped

Exercise 33, p. 33.
All the sentences are correct. *Always* can also be used with the present progressive.

Exercise 34, p. 33.
Sample sentences:
2. He's always leaving his dirty dishes on the table.
3. He's constantly borrowing my clothes without asking me.
4. He's always trying to show me he's smarter than me.
5. He's forever bragging about himself.
6. He's constantly cracking his knuckles while I'm trying to study.
7. He's always forgetting to give me my phone messages.

Exercise 35, p. 33.
Sample sentences:
1. playing the music too loud.
2. talking on the phone.
3. leaving her clothes on the floor.
4. inviting friends over for parties.

Exercise 36, p. 34.
In A, the focus is on the activity. In B, the focus is on the place.

Exercise 37, p. 34.
3. in his bedroom watching TV.
4. watching TV in his bedroom.
5. taking a nap on the couch in the living room.
6. on the couch in the living room taking a nap.
7. attending a conference in Singapore.

Exercise 38, p. 35.
1. Breakfast is an important meal. I always **eat** breakfast.
2. While I was working in my office yesterday, my cousin **stopped** by to visit me.
3. Yuki **stayed** home because she **caught** a bad cold.
4. My brother **looks** like our father, but I **resemble** my mother.
5. Jun, are you **listening** to me? I am **talking** to you!
6. While I was surfing the internet yesterday, I **found** a really interesting Web site.
7. Did you **speak** English before you **came** here?
8. Yesterday, while I was working at my computer, Shelley suddenly **came** into the room. I **didn't know** she was there. I was **concentrating** hard on my work. When she suddenly **spoke**, I **jumped**. She **startled** me.

Chapter 3: Perfect and Perfect Progressive Tenses

Exercise 1, p. 36.
Questions: Have you ever . . .
1. bought a boat?
2. broken a window?
3. hidden from the police?
4. taught English?
5. made ice cream?
6. won a contest?
7. ridden an elephant?
8. flown an airplane?
9. caught a butterfly?
10. left your umbrella at a restaurant?
11. dug a hole to plant a tree?
12. driven a school bus?
13. drawn a picture of yourself?
14. built a house?
15. forgotten your own name?
16. fallen off a ladder?
17. held a poisonous snake?
18. stolen anything?
19. eaten a duck egg?
20. swung a baseball bat?
21. fed a lion?
22. split wood with an axe?
23. hit a baseball?
24. read a play by Shakespeare?
25. grown tomatoes from a seed?
26. torn a page out of a library book?

Exercise 2, p. 37.
1. written
2. lost
3. climbed
4. given
5. told
6. sung
7. ridden
8. drunk
9. taken
10. shaken
11. helped
12. slept
13. driven
14. had
15. studied
16. played

Exercise 4, p. 39.
1. since
2. for
3. for
4. since
5. for
6. since
7. for
8. since

Exercise 7, p. 40.
Present perfect verbs:
1. 've had
2. 've missed
3. haven't eaten
4. hasn't finished
5. have met . . . haven't
6. I've eaten
7. haven't read . . . haven't had

Time frame:
1. from the beginning of the week to now (Wed.)
2. from the beginning of the term to now
3. from the time speaker got up to now
4. from right after dinner to now
5. unspecified time
6. unspecified time
7. from the time she/he got the book up to now

Exercise 11, p. 42.
1. is
2. has already left
3. have already left
4. have you been
5. has she done
6. has come
7. have lived
8. is planning
9. have you been
10. has been
11. is
12. has been
13. have finished
14. has read

Exercise 13, p. 44.
1. has never seen
2. saw
3. had . . . went
4. haven't had
5. has been
6. was
7. has just occurred . . . occurred
8. have gotten . . . saw . . . am also getting
9. have already taken . . . took
10. have known
11. knew

Exercise 14, p. 45.
1. Have you ever broken something valuable? What did you break?
2. Have you ever lost something important? What did you lose?
3. Have you ever stayed up all night? Why did you stay up all night?
4. Have you ever traveled to an interesting place? Where did you travel to?
5. Have you ever been in a car accident? When were you in a car accident?
6. Have you ever played a team sport? Which sport did you play?

Exercise 15, p. 45.
1. a, c
2. a, c

Exercise 16, p. 47.
2. is reviewing . . . has been reviewing
3. is standing . . . has been standing
4. has been playing
5. have been practicing
6. have been sleeping

Exercise 17, p. 47.
Possible sentences using the present perfect progressive:
1. He has been cooking some food.
2. He has been fixing the table.
3. He has been memorizing vocabulary.
4. He has been planting flowers.
5. He has been vacuuming.
6. He has been washing the windows.

*Using **yesterday** plus the simple past:*
1. He cooked some food yesterday.
2. He fixed the table yesterday.
3. He memorized vocabulary yesterday.
4. He planted flowers yesterday.
5. He vacuumed yesterday.
6. He washed the windows yesterday.

*Using **just** plus the present perfect:*
1. He has just cooked some food.
2. He has just fixed the table.
3. He has just memorized vocabulary.

4. He has just planted flowers.
5. He has just vacuumed.
6. He has just washed the windows.

Exercise 18, p. 48.
1. have you been
2. I've been taking
3. haven't been working
4. how are
5. haven't seen
6. They're doing
7. They're traveling
8. have they been
9. It's been
10. they've been traveling
11. They've been staying
12. spending
13. they're enjoying

Exercise 19, p. 48.
4. has been waiting
5. have liked
6. has been watching
7. has been teaching / has taught
8. have been playing . . . has been playing / has played

Exercise 20, p. 49.
1. has been waiting . . . 9:00 A.M.
2. has owned . . . one month
3. has not decided
4. has been sitting . . . 7:00
5. have been playing . . . three hours

Exercise 22, p. 49.
First events:
1. Someone had knocked . . . .
2. The teacher had written . . . .

Exercise 23, p. 51.
2. felt . . . took
3. had already given . . . got
4. was . . . had stopped
5. roamed . . . became / had become . . . appeared
6. had never seen . . . visited
7. had left/left
8. looked . . . had left . . . had forgotten. . . offered
9. saw . . . had not seen . . . didn't recognize . . . had lost
10. emigrated . . . had never traveled . . . settled . . . grew . . . went . . . had always wanted

Exercise 24, p. 52.
Past perfect verbs:
1. had forgotten . . . had called . . . had rushed (Fiction writing uses more past perfect.)
2. no past perfect verbs (Spoken English uses more past tense.)
3. had had . . . had passed away . . . had grown (Fiction writing uses more past perfect.) [Note: moved could be either had moved or moved. If past perfect, the second had does not need to be repeated.]

Exercise 25, p. 52.
1. we-əd   3. l-əd
2. movie-əd   4. roommate-əd

Exercise 26, p. 53.
1. We had . . .   4. (no reduction)
   He had . . .   5. flood had
   They had   6. Where had
2. children had   7. I had (1st sentence)
3. roommates had

Exercise 27, p. 53.
2. had   4. had   6. would   8. is . . . has
3. has   5. had   7. have

Exercise 28, p. 54.
1. had already eaten   5. hadn't called
2. she'd been   6. she'd forgotten
3. she'd had   7. It'd been
4. there'd been

Exercise 29, p. 55.
1. a   3. b
2. b   4. a

Exercise 30, p. 55.
3. have been studying   5. had been daydreaming
4. had been studying   6. have been sleeping

Exercise 31, p. 56.
Sample answers:
2. had been talking   5. had been looking
3. had been playing   6. had been drawing
4. had been dancing   7. had been studying

Exercise 32, p. 57.
2. Mr. Sanchez   6. Mr. Fox
3. Alice   7. Dan
4. Carlos   8. Ken
5. Jane   9. Robert

Exercise 33, p. 58.
1. a   4. a
2. b   5. b
3. b

Exercise 34, p. 58.
1. Since I came to this country, I **have learned / have been learning** a lot about the way of life here.
2. I **arrived** here only a short time ago. I **have been** here since last Friday.
3. How long **have** you been living here? I **have** been here for almost two years.
4. Why **haven't you** been in class for the last couple of days?
5. I **have been** coaching a soccer team for the last two months.
6. My grandfather **lived** in a small village in Italy when he was a child. At nineteen, he **moved** to Rome, where he **met** and **married** my grandmother in 1957. My father **was** born in Rome in 1960. I **was** born in Rome in 1989.
7. I **have been** living in my cousin's apartment since I arrived here. It **is** very small, and we are sharing the bedroom. I **need** my own place, but I **haven't found** one so far.
8. When I was a child, I **lived** with my grandmother instead of my parents. Grandpa **had died / died** before I **was** born, so I never knew him. Grandma raised me alone.

Chapter 4: Future Time

Exercise 1, p. 60.
1. future
2. future
3. present
4. future
5. future
6. present
7. present
8. future
9. future
10. present

Exercise 2, p. 60.
1. Marie will **cook** some chicken and rice for dinner tonight.
2. Where **will you** be tomorrow morning?
3. I **won't / will not** ride the bus to work tomorrow.
4. Marco will **probably call** us this evening.
5. I **am** going to look for a new apartment.

Exercise 3, p. 61.
1. no
2. yes
3. yes
4. no
5. yes
6. yes
7. yes
8. no

Exercise 5, p. 62.
1. You will need
2. We will review
3. test will have
4. There will be
5. You will have
6. nobody will finish
7. It will be
8. results will be

Exercise 6, p. 62.
1. going to
2. gonna
3. going to
4. gonna

Exercise 8, p. 63.
1. b
2. a . . . d
3. c

Exercise 9, p. 64.
1. c
2. a
3. A: c
   B: b
4. a
5. b
6. c

Exercise 10, p. 64.
1. willingness
2. plan
3. prediction
4. plan
5. willingness
6. prediction
7. willingness
8. plan

Exercise 11, p. 65.
3. B: 'll do
   C: 'll do
4. 's going to erase
5. B: 'll meet
   A: 'll see
6. 'm going to meet
7. won't tell
8. won't open

Exercise 12, p. 66.
1. a
2. b
3. a
4. b
5. a

Exercise 14, p. 67.
2. [After the rain <u>stops</u>,] I'm going to sweep the front porch.
3. I'm going to start making dinner [before my wife <u>gets</u> home from work today.]
4. I'm going to wait right here [until Sonya <u>comes</u>.]
5. [As soon as the war <u>is</u> over,] there will be new elections.
6. Right now the tide is low, but [when the tide <u>comes</u> in,] the ship will leave the harbor.
7. [While I<u>'m driving</u> to work tomorrow,] I'm going to listen to my Greek language CD.

Exercise 15, p. 67.
2. eat . . . will probably take / am probably going to take
3. get . . . will give / am going to give
4. watch . . . will call / am going to call
5. will wait / am going to wait . . . comes
6. stops . . . will walk / am going to walk
7. graduate . . . intend . . . will go / am going to go . . . get
8. will listen / am going to listen . . . am sleeping

Exercise 16, p. 68.
1. What are you going to do after you wake up tomorrow?
2. What are you going to do as soon as class ends today?
3. Before you go to bed tonight, what are you going to do?
4. What are you going to do when you have free time this weekend?
5. When you finish school, what are you going to do?

Exercise 17, p. 68.
All the sentences have a future meaning.

Exercise 18, p. 69.
4. in the future
5. in the future
6. now
7. in the future
8. habitually
9. in the future
10. in the future
11. habitually
12. A: now
    B: now
    A: in the future
13. A: in the future
    B: in the future
    A: in the future

Exercise 19, p. 70.
Sample answers:
2. am taking / am catching
3. am stopping / am quitting
4. am seeing
5. are driving

Exercise 21, p. 71.
All the verbs take a progressive form (present, past, future).

Exercise 22, p. 72.
1. is going to be studying / will be studying . . . am going to be finishing / will be finishing
2. is going to be seeing / will be seeing . . . is going to be doing / will be doing . . . is going to be talking / will be talking

Exercise 23, p. 72.
1. arrive . . . is going to be waiting / will be waiting
2. get . . . is going to be shining / will be shining . . . are going to be singing / will be singing . . . is still going to be lying / will still be lying

3. B: am going to be enjoying / will be enjoying
   A: am going to be thinking / will be thinking
4. will be / am going to be in Chicago visiting
5. will be / am going to be working

Exercise 24, p. 73.
All the verbs are in a form of the perfect.

Exercise 25, p. 73.
1. have been . . . had been . . . will have been
2. get . . . will have already arrived . . . will already have arrived
3. got . . . had already arrived
4. have been sitting . . . had been sitting . . . will have been sitting
5. will have begun . . . will have been teaching
6. will have been driving
7. get / will have taken
8. will have been running
9. will have been

Exercise 26, p. 74.
2. He will shave, shower, and then make a light breakfast.
3. After he eats breakfast tomorrow, he will get ready to go to work.
4. By the time he gets to work tomorrow, he will have drunk three cups of coffee.
5. Between 8:00 and 9:00, Bill will answer his email and (will) plan his day.
6. By 10:00 tomorrow, he will have called his new clients.
7. At 11:00 tomorrow, he will be attending a staff meeting.
8. He will go to lunch at noon and have a sandwich and a bowl of soup.
9. After he finishes eating, he will take a short walk in the park before he returns to the office.
10. He will work at his desk until he goes to another meeting in the middle of the afternoon.
11. By the time he leaves the office, he will have attended three meetings.
12. When Bill gets home, his children will be playing in the yard.
13. They will have been playing since 3:00 in the afternoon.
14. As soon as he finishes dinner, he will take the children for a walk to a nearby playground.
15. Afterward, the whole family will sit in the living room and discuss their day.
16. They will watch television for a while, and then he and his wife will put the kids to bed.
17. By the time Bill goes to bed tomorrow, he will have had a full day and will be ready for sleep.

Chapter 5: Review of Verb Tenses

Exercise 1, p. 76.
1. I **have been** studying here since last January.
2. By the time Hassan returned to his country, he **had been** away from home for more than three years.
3. After I **graduate**, I **am** going to return to my hometown.
4. By the end of the 21st century, man will **have** discovered the cure for the common cold.
5. I want to get married, but I **haven't met** the right person yet.
6. I have **seen** that movie three times, and now I **want** to see it again.
7. I **don't** like my job. My brother wants me to quit. I **think** he is right.

8. While I**'m studying** tonight, I'm going to listen to classical music.
9. We washed the dishes and **cleaned** up the kitchen after our dinner guests **left**.
10. My neighbors are Mr. and Mrs. Sanchez. I **have known** them ever since I **was** a child.
11. Many scientists believe there **will be** a major earthquake in California in the near future.

Exercise 2, p. 76.
1. is studying . . . is also taking . . . begin
2. had already eaten . . . left
3. always eats . . . goes . . . goes . . . will eat / is going to eat
4. called . . . was attending
5. will be attending
6. got . . . was sleeping . . . had been sleeping
7. is taking . . . fell . . . has been sleeping
8. eats . . . is going to go / will go . . . will have eaten . . . goes
9. started . . . hasn't finished . . . has been reading
10. has finished . . . is reading . . . has been reading . . . intends . . . has read . . . has ever read

Exercise 4, p. 78.
Part I.
1. F   3. F
2. T   4. T

Part II.
1. got   8. didn't see
2. took   9. saw
3. put   10. had been trying
4. didn't open   11. apologized
5. tried   12. went
6. knocked   13. felt
7. opened   14. had done

Exercise 6, p. 79.
1. got
2. have been trying
3. have been
4. have had / 've had
5. has been staying
6. have been spending / have spent / are spending
7. have been
8. went
9. watched
10. have barely had
11. is
12. am sitting
13. have been sitting
14. leaves / is going to leave / will leave
15. decided / have decided
16. am writing
17. am getting
18. am going to take / will take
19. get
20. are you getting
21. are your classes going

Exercise 8, p. 80.
1. a   3. b   5. b
2. a   4. a   6. b

Exercise 9, p. 80.

1. has experienced
2. will experience / is going to experience
3. began
4. have occurred
5. causes
6. have developed
7. hold / are holding
8. moves
9. waves
10. know
11. happened
12. struck
13. were sitting
14. suddenly found
15. died
16. collapsed
17. sent
18. will the next earthquake occur / is the next earthquake going to occur
19. have often helped
20. are studying
21. also appear
22. seem
23. have developed
24. will be / are going to be
25. strikes

Exercise 13, p. 82.

1. I haven't been in this town very long. I **came** here just two weeks ago.
2. Dormitory life is not quiet. Everyone **shouts** and **makes** a lot of noise in the halls.
3. My friends will meet me when **I arrive** at the airport.
4. Hasn't anyone ever **told** you to knock on the door before you enter someone else's room? Didn't your parents **teach** you that?
5. The phone **rang** while I **was** doing the dishes. I **dried** my hands and **answered** it. When I **heard** my husband's voice, I **was** very happy.
6. I **have been** in the United States for the last four months. During this time, I **have** done many things and **seen** many places.
7. When the old man started to walk back to his hut, the sun **had** already **hid / hidden** itself behind the mountain.
8. While I **was** writing my composition last night, someone **knocked** on the door.
9. Why did you **write** a children's book?
10. I'm really glad you **are going to / will** visit my hometown next year.
11. While I was **visiting** my cousin in Los Angeles, we went to a restaurant and **ate** Thai food.
12. When I was a child, I viewed things from a much lower height. Many physical objects around me **appeared** very large. When I **wanted** to move something such as a chair, I **needed** help.
13. When I was in my country, I **was** afraid to come to the United States. I thought I couldn't walk outside at night because of the terrible crime. But now I **have** a different opinion. I **have lived** in this small town for three months and **(have) learned** that there is very little crime here.

Chapter 6: Subject-Verb Agreement

Exercise 1, p. 84.

2. My **parents** visit many countries when they travel in Europe.

3. Robert **sings** when he **takes** a shower.
4. **Chickens**, **ducks**, and **turkeys** lay **eggs**.
5. Anna **wears gloves** on her **hands** when she **works** in her garden.
6. She **scratches** her chin when it **itches**.

Exercise 2, p. 84.

2. plural, noun
3. singular, verb
4. plural, noun
5. singular, verb
6. plural, noun

Exercise 3, p. 85.

2. writes/s/
3. robs/z/
4. rugs/z/
5. sleeps/s/
6. locks/s/
7. wishes/əz/
8. pages/əz/
9. months/s/

Exercise 4, p. 86.

4. bushes/əz/
5. hats/s/
6. rises/əz/
7. seasons/z/
8. develops/s/
9. touches/əz/
10. coughs/s/
11. methods/z/
12. languages/əz/

Exercise 5, p. 86.

1. Cats sleep . . . hours
2. shapes . . . sizes
3. practices . . . sentences
4. cafeteria . . . serves . . . sandwiches
5. teacher . . . encourages
6. coughs . . . sneezes

Exercise 6, p. 86.

1. Opera singers sing. An opera singer sings.
2. Teachers teach. A teacher teaches.
3. Butterflies fly. A butterfly flies.
4. Balls bounce. A ball bounces.
5. Doors open and close. A door opens and closes.
6. Mosquito bites itch. A mosquito bite itches.
7. Hungry babies cry. A hungry baby cries.
8. Students ask questions. A student asks questions.
9. Snakes hiss. A snake hisses.
10. Dogs say "arf-arf" in English. A dog says "arf-arf" in English.

Exercise 7, p. 87.

1. The verb agrees with the subject: In sentence a., the subject is singular, so the verb is singular. In b., there is a plural subject, so the verb is plural.
2. In a., there is a plural subject, so the verb is plural. In b., *every* is followed by a singular noun, so the verb is singular.
3. In a. and b., the subjects *fruit* and *apples,* not the prepositional phrases that follow, determine agreement.
4. In a., *vegetables* is the plural subject, so the verb is plural. In b., the gerund *eating* is the subject, not *vegetables.* Gerunds require a singular verb.

Exercise 8, p. 87.

1. is
2. are
3. astounds
4. are
5. is
6. agree
7. approves
8. has
9. are . . . is
10. is
11. do
12. was
13. were
14. Is
15. is

Exercise 9, p. 88.
1. know
2. know
3. knows
4. knows
5. knows
6. know
7. knows
8. knows

Exercise 10, p. 88.
In most expressions of quantity, the verb is determined by the noun that follows *of* (items 1, 2, 3, 4). Exceptions: *one of* and *each of* take a plural noun but a singular verb (items 5, 6).

Exercise 11, p. 89.
2. apples . . . are
3. movie . . . is
4. movies . . . are
5. students . . . are
6. money . . . is
7. students . . . are
8. clothing . . . is
9. one . . . is
10. Each . . . has
11. Each . . . has
12. Every one . . . is
13. animals . . . are . . . All . . . are
14. A number . . . are
15. The number . . . is
16. One . . . is
17. Do . . . students
18. Does . . . homework
19. were . . . students
20. was . . . one

Exercise 12, p. 90.
2. are
3. is
4. are
5. is
6. is
7. is
8. is
9. are
10. are
11. is
12. is
13. are
14. is
15. is
16. is
17. are
18. is
19. is
20. are

Exercise 14, p. 91.
1. aren't
2. isn't
3. are
4. is
5. are
6. isn't
7. was
8. is
9. are
10. has been
11. have been

Exercise 15, p. 91.
1. There are
2. there is
3. There are
4. There is
5. Is there
6. Are there
7. there are
8. Is there

Exercise 17, p. 92.
1. is
2. is
3. are
4. are
5. are

Exercise 19, p. 94.
2. is
3. is
4. seeks
5. is
6. are
7. is
8. is
9. do
10. are
11. is
12. are
13. is
14. commute
15. is . . . isn't it
16. are
17. want
18. depends . . .
   are . . . have

Exercise 20, p. 94.
2. Linguistics is
3. Diabetes is
4. English is
5. are . . . Canadians
6. 70 percent . . . is . . .
   one percent . . . is
7. is 256
8. The Netherlands is
9. Fish are

Exercise 22, p. 95.
1. are
2. is
3. are
4. are
5. is
6. are
7. is
8. are
9. are
10. is
11. is
12. is

Exercise 23, p. 96.
1. His ideas are interesting.
2. Some of the people are friendly.
3. One of the girls is absent.
4. Italian is a Romance language.
5. Two-thirds of the food is gone.
6. The clothes in that store are expensive.
7. The clothing in those stores is inexpensive.
8. Most of the stores in tourist towns are overpriced.

Exercise 24, p. 96.
1. has
2. is
3. need
4. needs
5. is
6. is
7. is
8. are

Exercise 25, p. 96.
3. I, are
4. C
5. C
6. I, are
7. C
8. I, has
9. I, work
10. C
11. I, are
12. C
13. C
14. I, contain

Exercise 26, p. 97.
2. are
3. keeps
4. makes
5. is
6. is
7. Does
8. Do
9. is
10. are
11. are
12. Are
13. is
14. is
15. appears
16. are
17. is
18. provides

Exercise 27, p. 98.
3. A lot of the people in my class **work** during the day and **attend** class in the evening.
4. Many of the satellites orbiting the earth **are** used for communications.
5. *(no errors)*
6. Studying a foreign language often **leads** students to learn about the culture of the countries where it is spoken.
7. One of the most common names for dogs in the United States **is** "Rover."
8. *(no errors)*
9. Most of the mountain peaks in the Himalayan Range **are** covered with snow the year round.
10. *(no errors)*
11. Seventy-five percent of the people in New York City **live** in upstairs apartments, not on the ground floor.
12. *(no errors)*
13. Unless there **is** a profound and extensive reform of government policies in the near future, the economic conditions in that country will continue to deteriorate.
14. While I was in Paris, some of the best food I found **was** not at the well-known eating places but in small out-of-the-way cafés.

Chapter 7: Nouns

Exercise 1, p. 100.
2. branches
3. mice
4. enemies
5. valleys
6. shelves
7. beliefs
8. women
9. echoes
10. photos
11. zeros/zeroes
12. crises
13. curricula
14. offspring

Exercise 2, p. 100.
2. potatoes
3. fish
4. sandwiches
5. carrots
6. vegetables
7. kangaroos
8. geese
9. donkeys
10. deer
11. wolves
12. sheep

Exercise 4, p. 102.
-s

beliefs
chiefs
clouds
kilos

memos
photos
videos
zoos

-es

heroes
boxes
classes
matches

potatoes
tomatoes
fishes (*possible, but rare*)

-ves

knives
leaves
lives
loaves

scarves
shelves
wolves

no change

deer
fish
sheep

Exercise 5, p. 103.
3. men
4. attorneys
5. discoveries . . . laboratories
6. boxes . . . oxen
7. beaches . . . cliffs
8. pianos
9. phenomena
10. media

Exercise 6, p. 104.
(1) **Bacteria** are the smallest living **things**. They are simple **organisms** that consist of one cell.

(2) **Bacteria** exist almost everywhere. They are in the air, water, and soil, as well as in the **bodies** of all living **creatures**.

(3) There are **thousands** of **kinds** of **bacteria**. Most of them are harmless to human **beings**, but some cause **diseases** such as tuberculosis and pneumonia.

(4) **Viruses** are also microscopic **organisms**, but **viruses** live in the **cells** of other living **things**. By themselves, they are lifeless **particles** that cannot reproduce, but inside a living cell they become active and can multiply **hundreds** of **times**.

(5) **Viruses** cause many **diseases**. They infect human **beings** with such **illnesses** as influenza, the common cold, measles, and AIDS (Acquired Immune Deficiency Syndrome).

(6) **Viruses** are tiny. The virus that causes AIDS is 230 million times smaller than the period at the end of this sentence. Some viral **infections** are difficult or impossible to treat.

Exercise 7, p. 104.
1. 2
2. 1
3. 1
4. 2
5. 2
6. 1

Exercise 8, p. 105.
2. boy's
3. boys'
4. children's
5. child's
6. Sally's
7. Bess's/Bess'
8. today's
9. month's
10. Jack and Larry's

Exercise 9, p. 105.
3. My uncle is my **father's** brother.
4. I have four aunts. All of my **aunts'** homes are within walking distance of my **mother's** apartment.
5. Esteban's **aunt's** oldest son is a violinist.
6. **Bill's** wife is a factory worker.
7. I walked into my **boss's/boss'** office.
8. I borrowed the **secretary's** pen to fill out the application form.
9. Five astronauts were aboard the space shuttle. The **astronauts'** safe return to earth was a welcome sight to millions of television viewers.
10. It is the **people's** right to know what the city is going to do about the housing problem.
11. Quite a few diplomats are assigned to our city. Almost all of the **diplomats'** children attend a special school.
12. A **diplomat's** work invariably involves numerous meetings.

Exercise 10, p. 106.
2. Psychologists have developed many different kinds of tests. A "personality test" is used to evaluate an **individual's** personal characteristics, such as friendliness or trustworthiness.
3. Many mythological stories tell of **heroes'** encounters with giants or dangerous animals. In one story, the **hero's** encounter with a dragon saves a village from destruction.
4. **Children's** play is an important part of their lives. It teaches them about their environment while they are having fun. For instance, they can learn that boats float and can practice ways to make boats move across water. Toys are not limited to children. Adults have their own toys, such as pleasure boats, and children have theirs, such as miniature boats. **Adults'** toys are usually much more expensive than **children's** toys.

Exercise 11, p. 106.
1. computer error
   computer screen
   computer skills
2. airplane passenger
   airplane pilot
   airplane ticket

Exercise 12, p. 107.
2. flowers . . . flower
3. beans . . . bean
4. babies . . . baby
5. children . . . child
6. salads . . . salad
7. mosquitoes/mosquitos . . . mosquito
8. two-hour . . . two hours
9. ten years old . . . ten-year-old
10. three-letter . . . three letters

Exercise 14, p. 108.

1. taxi, drivers
2. drivers, taxis
3. office, managers
4. managers, offices
5. airplanes, seats
6. airplane, seats
7. schools, activities
8. school, activities

Exercise 15, p. 108.

1. a, b, c
2. a, c, d

Exercise 16, p. 109.

2. jewelry (NC)
   rings (C)
   bracelets (C)
   necklace (C)
3. mountains (C)
   fields (C)
   lakes (C)
   scenery (NC)
4. Gold (NC)
   iron (NC)
   metals (C)
5. iron (C)
6. car (C)
   engine (C)
   furniture (NC)
   refrigerator (C)
   junk (NC)

Exercise 17, p. 111.

3. trees, bushes, grass, dirt, flowers
4. advice, suggestions
5. words, vocabulary
6. glasses, water
7. Windows, glass
8. glasses, eyesight
9. time, homework, assignments
10. times, time
11. smoke, dust, monoxide, substances, pollution
12. literature, novels, poetry, essays, poets, poems
13. seasons, weather
14. happiness, patience, rewards
15. stars, grains, sand
16. *(no change)*

Exercise 19, p. 112.

2. rivers
3. symphonies, music
4. trucks, traffic
5. computers, equipment
6. problems, homework
7. vocabulary, definitions
8. this information
9. advice
10. progress

Exercise 20, p. 113.

1. Tom uses *the* because he and Anna are talking about the same specific cat.
2. Tom uses *a* because Anna doesn't know the cat he's talking about. The speaker and listener are not thinking of the same specific cat.
3. Tom and Anna are talking about any and all cats in general.

Exercise 21, p. 115.

4. Ø Tennis
5. A
6. An
7. Ø Gold
8. A
9. Ø Health
10. An
11. A
12. Ø Water
13. Ø Knowledge
14. Ø Homework
15. Ø Grammar
16. A
17. Ø English
18. Ø Air
19. Ø Fruit
20. An
21. Ø Iron
22. An
23. A
24. Ø Basketball

Exercise 22, p. 116.

5. an
6. some
7. a
8. some
9. some
10. some
11. a
12. some
13. an
14. some
15. a
16. some
17. a
18. some
19. Some
20. some
21. an
22. some

Exercise 23, p. 117.

1. Ø
2. an
3. Ø
4. a
5. an
6. a
7. Ø
8. Ø

Exercise 25, p. 117.

1. Oh, look at **the** moon! It's beautiful tonight.
2. I saw a cat and a bird outside my window. **The** cat was trying to catch **the** bird, but it didn't succeed. **The** bird flew away.
3. **Birds** have **wings**. Many insects have wings too.
4. We all look **for happiness**.
5. I have **a** book.

Exercise 26, p. 118.

3. a
4. the
5. B: the
   A: a
6. a
7. the . . . the
8. A: The . . . a . . . the
   B: the
9. A: The
   B: a . . . a
   A: the
   B: a . . . the . . . the
   A: the
   B: an

Exercise 27, p. 119.

4. Ø
5. A . . . an
6. Ø Hats . . . Ø
7. The
8. Ø . . . Ø
9. the
10. an
11. the . . . the . . . an . . . the

Exercise 28, p. 120.

1. a
2. a
3. Ø Cell . . . Ø
4. a
5. the
6. Ø Jewelry . . . Ø . . . Ø
7. an
8. Ø Beings . . . the
9. Ø
10. The
11. The

Exercise 29, p. 120.

1. a
2. the
3. Ø (**People**) . . . Ø . . . Ø . . . Ø . . . Ø . . . Ø
4. Ø . . . Ø . . . Ø . . . a
5. a . . . an . . . a . . . a . . . the . . . the . . . the . . . the
6. Ø . . . Ø . . . Ø . . . an . . . Ø
7. a . . . the . . . the . . . the

Exercise 30, p. 121.

1. a
2. a
3. a
4. a
5. a
6. The
7. a
8. the
9. an
10. the
11. a
12. a
13. the
14. the
15. a

Exercise 31, p. 121.

Deleted words/expressions:

9. too much
11. a little
13. a great deal
16. two
17. a couple of
18. both
19. several
23. too many
25. a few
27. a number of

Exercise 32, p. 123.

Deleted words/expressions:

6. too many
7. a few
9. a number of
17. too much
20. a little
22. a great deal of

Exercise 33, p. 123.

3. much
4. many letter**s**
5. is . . . much
6. much
7. many side**s**
8. much
9. many
10. much
11. is . . . much
12. much
13. many patient**s**
14. many t**eeth**
15. isn't much

Exercise 34, p. 124.

2. stamps, rice, stuff, things
3. Ø, salt, equipment, Ø
4. Ø, loaves of bread, Ø, jars of honey
5. novels, Ø, poems, Ø
6. orange juice, light bulbs, hardware, computer software
7. sleep, information, facts, help
8. women, movies, scenes, Ø
9. shirts, Ø, pens, Ø
10. patience, wealth, Ø, Ø
11. money, advice, time, Ø
12. ideas, theories, hypotheses, Ø

Exercise 36, p. 125.

1. a
2. b

Exercise 37, p. 126.

3. A little
4. (very) little
5. a few
6. (very) few
7. a few
8. a little
9. (very) little

Exercise 38, p. 127.

3. (very) few
4. a few . . . a few
5. a few
6. (very) few . . . (very) little
7. a little
8. a little . . . a little

Exercise 39, p. 128.

1. b
2. a
3. b
4. a
5. a
6. b
7. b

Exercise 41, p. 128.

1. country
2. countries
3. country . . . country
4. countries

Exercise 42, p. 129.

2. girls
3. children
4. child
5. member
6. members
7. student
8. students
9. student
10. students

Exercise 43, p. 129.

3. The teacher gave **each student** / **each of the** students a test paper.
4. *(no change)*
5. Spain is one of the **countries** I want to visit.
6. Every **piece of** furniture / **All the** furniture / **All of the** furniture in that room is made of wood.
7. One of the **machines** / One of the **pieces of** equipment / One **piece of** equipment / **Some** of the equipment in our office is broken.
8. I gave a present to **each woman** / each of the **women** / **all of the women** in the room.
9. One of my favorite **places** in the world is an island in the Caribbean Sea.
10. *(no change)*
11. It's impossible for one human being to know every **language** in the world.
12. I found each of the **errors** / **each error** in this exercise.

Exercise 44, p. 130.

3. Ø
4. of
5. of
6. of
7. of
8. Ø
9. of
10. of
11. of
12. of
13. of
14. of

Exercise 45, p. 131.

3. Ø . . . Ø
4. of
5. of
6. of
7. Ø
8. of
9. Ø
10. of
11. Ø
12. of
13. of

Exercise 50, p. 134.

1. That book **contains** many different **kinds** of **stories** and **articles**.
2. In my country, there **are a lot** of schools.
3. She is always willing to help her friends in every possible **way**.
4. In the past, horses **were** the principal **means** of transportation.
5. He succeeded in creating one of the best **armies** in the world.
6. There **is** a lot of **equipment** in the research laboratory, but undergraduates are not allowed to use **it**.
7. I have a **five-year-old** daughter and a **three-year-old** son.
8. Most of **the** people in my **apartment** building **are** friendly.
9. Everyone **seeks happiness in life**.
10. Writing compositions **is** very hard for me.
11. Almost **all** of the students / **Almost all** students / **Most (of the)** students in my class are from Asia.
12. It's difficult for me to understand English when people **use** a lot of **slang**.

Chapter 8: Pronouns

Exercise 1, p. 135.
1. My friends and I ordered Indian food at the restaurant. I wasn't very hungry, but I ate most of **it**.
2. When we were in school, my sister and **I** used to play tennis after school every day.
3. If you want to pass **your** exams, you had better study very hard for **them**.
4. A hippopotamus spends most of **its** time in the water of rivers and lakes.
5. After work, Mr. Gray asked to speak to Mona and **me** about the company's new policies. He explained **them** to us and asked for **our** opinions.
6. My friends asked to borrow my car because **theirs** was in the garage for repairs.

Exercise 3, p. 137.

pronouns	*antecedents*
2. they . . . they	monkeys
3. she	teacher
them	papers
4. her . . . She	Nancy
it	apple
5. it	dog
6. She . . . She	cat
His (poss. adj.) . . . him	Yuri
They	dogs
him	Yuri

Exercise 4, p. 137.
1. me
2. me
3. him
4. her
5. me

Exercise 5, p. 137.
2. She
3. her . . . her
4. Her
5. She . . . her . . . her
6. her
7. She . . . her
8. I
9. me
10. me
11. my
12. mine . . . me

Exercise 6, p. 138.
2. mine . . . yours
3. their . . . hers . . . his
4. Our . . . our . . . ours . . . theirs

Exercise 8, p. 138.
2. its
3. Its . . . It's . . . It's
4. its
5. it's

Exercise 9, p. 139.
It . . . dives . . . spears . . . its . . . its . . . it . . . tosses . . . catches . . . it . . . swallows . . . it . . . It's . . . them

Exercise 10, p. 139.
1. A: him
   B: he's
   C: him
   D: his
   E: his . . . he's . . . he'll
2. A: Does she
   B: Is she
   C: they

D: their . . . he's
E: them
F: it's (it is) . . . mine . . . it's (it has)

Exercise 12, p. 140.
3. (**All**) students in Biology 101 **have** to spend three hours per week in the laboratory where **they do** various experiments by following the directions in **their** lab manual**s**.
4. Citizens **have** two primary responsibilities. **They** should vote in **all elections** and **they** should serve willingly on juries.
5. *(no change)*

Exercise 13, p. 141.
Most common answers:
2. they (informal) . . . want
3. his or her
4. them (informal)
5. their (informal)
6. his or her
7. his or her

Exercise 14, p. 141.
1. *Team* refers to individual players.
2. *Team* refers to a single, impersonal unit.

Exercise 15, p. 142.
2. it . . . consists
3. It
4. they
5. They
6. It was
7. They are . . . their . . . them
8. It is

Exercise 17, p. 144.
2. herself
3. himself
4. themselves
5. ourselves
6. yourself
7. yourselves
8. himself/herself/oneself

Exercise 18, p. 144.
2. herself
3. themselves
4. myself
5. themselves
6. yourself
7. yourselves
8. myself
9. yourself . . . himself . . . myself . . . ourselves . . . themselves

Exercise 19, p. 145.
2. enjoy himself
3. proud of yourselves
4. pat yourself
5. killed himself
6. entertained themselves
7. introduced myself
8. feeling sorry for yourself
9. talking to yourself
10. laugh at ourselves
11. promised herself
12. angry at himself

Exercise 20, p. 146.
1. yourself
2. myself
3. ourselves
4. himself
5. themselves
6. herself

Exercise 21, p. 146.
1. Penguins . . . creatures . . . birds . . . they
2. Millions . . . years . . . wings . . . These . . . their
3. Penguins' . . . was . . . fish . . . wings . . . flippers . . . them

4. spend . . . water . . . eggs . . . land
5. habits
6. lays . . . egg . . . ice . . . returns
7. takes . . . He covers . . . his . . . it hatches
8. This . . . takes . . . weeks . . . this . . . doesn't
9. hatches . . . goes . . . himself . . . offspring
10. Penguins . . . environment . . . They . . . need

Exercise 22, p. 147.
Mrs.: you = Mr. Cook
Mr.: I = Mr. Cook . . . He = Jack Woods . . . it = car
Mrs.: it = car
Mr.: they = people in general . . . you = people in general . . .
you = people in general
Mrs.: One = people in general . . . one = people in general

Exercise 23, p. 147.
3. people in general
4. Alex
5. people in general
6. Sonya
7. people in general
8. people in general
9. the orchestra
10. They = airline company;
you = people in general

Exercise 25, p. 148.
1. Picture B
2. Picture A

Exercise 26, p. 149.
2. Another . . . Another . . .
Another . . . the other
3. The other
4. another
5. Others
6. Other
7. The other
8. The others

Exercise 27, p. 149.
1. Helen
2. Mai
3. Susie's
4. Thursday

Exercise 28, p. 150.
2. Another . . . The other
3. others
4. other
5. other
6. others
7. another
8. Another . . . Others
9. others
10. Another . . . Others . . . other
11. the other
12. the others
13. another
14. another

Exercise 30, p. 151.
1. another
2. the other
3. the others
4. the other
5. Others
6. another

Exercise 31, p. 151.
1. T
2. F
3. F
4. T

Exercise 32, p. 152.
2. Another . . . other
3. each other
4. the other

5. other . . . other
6. other
7. others . . . others . . . others
8. each other . . . each other . . . each other . . . other
9. other
10. other
11. another

Exercise 34, p. 154.
1. a
2. b
3. b
4. a
5. b

Exercise 35, p. 154.
2. My cousin and her husband moved to **another** city because they don't **like cold** weather.
3. I like to travel because I like to learn about **other countries** and **customs**.
4. Collecting stamps is one of my **hobbies**.
5. I came here three and a half **months** ago. I think I have **made good** progress in English.
6. When I lost my passport, I had to apply **for another** one.
7. When I got to class, all of the **other** students were already in their seats.
8. English has borrowed quite a few **words** from **other** languages.
9. There **are** many **students** from **different** countries in this class.
10. **Thousands** of **athletes** take part in the Olympics.
11. Education is one of the most important **aspects** of life. **Knowledge** about many different things **allows** us to live fuller lives.
12. All of the **students'** names were on the list.
13. I live in a **two-room** apartment. **It's** too small for my family.
14. **Many people** prefer to live in small towns. Their attachment to their communities **prevents** them from moving from place to place in search of **work**.
15. **Today's** news is just as bad as **yesterday's** news.
16. Almost **all** of the students in our class **speak** English well.
17. The teacher gave us several homework **assignments / some** homework to hand in next Tuesday.
18. In today's world, **women** work as **doctors**, **pilots**, **archeologists**, and many other **things**. Both my mother and father are **teachers**.
19. Every **employee** in our company **respects** Mr. Ward.
20. A child needs to learn how to get along with **other** people, how to spend his or her time wisely, and how to depend on himself or herself. OR
Children need to learn how to get along with **other** people, how to spend **their** time wisely, and how to depend on **themselves**.

Chapter 9: Modals, Part 1

Exercise 1, p. 157.
2.–4. She can **see** it.
5. Can **you pass** the rice, please?
6. **Can you** see it?
7. They **can't** go there.
8. They aren't able **to** pay their rent.

Exercise 2, p. 158.
1. I
2. you
3. I
4. you
5. I
6. you
7. you

Exercise 4, p. 160.
1. B
2. A

Exercise 5, p.160.
2. a. Would you mind speaking with John?
   b. Would you mind if I spoke with John?
3. a. Would you mind if I turned on the air conditioner?
   b. Would you mind turning on the air conditioner?

Exercise 6, p. 161.
2. if I stayed
3. if I opened / opening
4. if I asked
5. if I smoked
6. speaking
7. if I changed / changing

Exercise 7, p. 161.
1. b
2. b
3. b
4. a
5. b

Exercise 9, p. 162.
Sample answers:
2. you give us a little more time
3. I get a ride
4. rescheduling / if I reschedule / if we reschedule
5. you take a look
6. if we moved

Exercise 12, p. 163.
1. a
2. b
3. a

Exercise 14, p. 165.
Sentences 2 and 3.

Exercise 15, p. 165.
2. must not
3. don't have to
4. doesn't have to
5. must not
6. don't have to
7. don't have to
8. doesn't have to

Exercise 17, p. 166.
1. must
2. don't have to
3. must not
4. must
5. don't have to
6. must not

Exercise 18, p. 166.
Advice possibilities: 1, 2, 4, 5
[*Note:* Item 6 is not advisable unless his cousin is a dentist.]

Exercise 22, p. 168.
1. b
2. b
3. a
4. a
5. b
6. a

Exercise 23, p. 169.
3. must/have to
4. have to/must (*have to* is preferred because the situation is not urgent or formal)
5. should
6. should (*also possible:* have to/must)
7. should OR must/have to (*if it's a requirement of the school*)
8. must/has to
9. should
10. must

Exercise 24, p. 169.
1. a
2. a, b
3. a, b
4. b

Exercise 25, p. 170.
Jim

Exercise 26, p. 170.
1. b
2. a, b
3. a
4. a, b

Exercise 27, p. 171.
Sample answers:
1. He shouldn't have left the door (to his house) open.
2. You should have gone (to the meeting).
3. She should have seen a doctor.
4. He should have read the contract (more) thoroughly.

Exercise 28, p. 171.
Possible answers:
1. I should have worn a coat.
2. I should have returned his call.
3. I shouldn't have opened the window.
4. I should have gone to the grocery store.
5. I shouldn't have bought her candy.
6. He should have married her.
7. He shouldn't have married her.
8. I should have gone out.
9. I shouldn't have lent her my car.
10. I should have set my alarm clock.

Exercise 29, p. 172.
Sample answers:
1. Kazu should have talked with Julie first.
   He shouldn't have accepted the job immediately.
   He should have thought about the offer before accepting.
   He should have known Julie would be upset.
2. Donna shouldn't have lent Hugo nearly all of her savings.
   Hugo shouldn't have spent her money so carelessly.
   Donna shouldn't have trusted Hugo.

Exercise 30, p. 172.
2. We're not **supposed** to open that door.
3. I have a meeting at seven tonight. I **am supposed** to be there a little early to discuss the agenda.
4. I'm **supposed** to be at the meeting. I suppose I'd better go.
5. Where have you been? You were **supposed** to be here an hour ago!

Exercise 31, p. 173.
Sample answers:
1. You're supposed to contact the police / fill out an accident report / call your insurance company.
2. You're supposed to put on your seat belt.
3. They are supposed to exercise.
   They are not supposed to eat unhealthy foods.
4. You're supposed to pull over (onto the shoulder).
5.–8. *(Answers will vary.)*

Exercise 32, p. 174.
1. a
2. a
3. a
4. b
5. b
6. a

Exercise 35, p. 175.
1. yes
2. yes (plan not completed)
3. no
4. yes (plan not completed)
5. no
6. yes (plan not completed)

Exercise 36, p. 176.
1. I had planned to stay home . . . .
   I was intending to stay home . . . .
2. I had planned to surprise you . . . .
   I was intending to surprise you . . . .
3. I had planned to reply . . . .
   I was intending to reply . . . .

Exercise 37, p. 176.
Sample answers:
1. I overslept
2. I got lost
3. I had to work
4. I couldn't get time off
5. we decided they wouldn't know anyone
6. I had the wrong date
7. we missed it

Exercise 40, p. 178.
Roberto's

Chapter 10: Modals, Part 2

Exercise 1, p. 180.
1. b
2. c
3. a

Exercise 2, p. 182.
Possible answers:
2. must have the wrong number.
3. may/might/could be at a meeting.
4. may/might/could fit Jimmy.
5. must miss them very much.

Exercise 5, p. 182.
1. 50% sure
2. 95% sure
3. 99% sure
4. 100% sure

Exercise 6, p. 183.
1. Rob
2. Linda and Hamid
3. Lucy

Exercise 7, p. 183.
Sample answers:
2. be home
3. be thirsty
4. like nuts
5. have many friends

Exercise 9, p. 184.
1. may be
2. can't be
3. don't run
4. could be
5. must be
6. might be
7. may be
8. couldn't be
9. could be
10. might be
11. I'll go
12. 's

Exercise 11, p. 185.
1. might have left
2. couldn't have left
3. must have left

Exercise 12, p. 186.
2. couldn't have been
3. must have been
4. must not have gotten
5. may/might/could have gotten

Exercise 13, p. 187.
Sample answers:
2. It may have been David because he met with his girlfriend's parents two nights ago.
3. It must have been Dylan because he took a diamond ring with him.
4. It couldn't have been Dick because he is going to wait to get married until he has a better job.
5. It must not have been Doug because he isn't sure if he's ready for marriage.

Exercise 14, p. 187.
Sample answers:
1. She (Laika) must have felt scared. He (Yuri) may have felt excited.
2. It must have been caused by the fireworks.
3. It might have been a mouse. It couldn't have been a burglar.

Exercise 16, p. 188.
2. must not like
3. must have been
4. must have been
5. must not speak
6. must be
7. must have hurt
8. must mean
9. must have been

Exercise 17, p. 188.
1. 50%
2. 100%
3. 50%
4. 90%
5. 50%

Exercise 18, p. 189.
1. Ned
2. Marco
3. Linda

Exercise 19, p. 189.
3. must
4. should/ought to/will
5. should/ought to
6. will
7. must
8. should/ought to/will
9. should/ought to/will
10. must be
11. should have/ought to have
12. must have

Exercise 20, p. 190.
4. Beth
5. Ron
6. Stacy
7. Barb
8. a rat
9. a cat
10. a mouse
11. Mark
12. my neighbor
13. Carol
14. Janet
15. Stephanie
16. Bob
17. Andre

Exercise 21, p. 192.

1. should ask
2. shouldn't ask
3. may have upset
4. should try
5. shouldn't have stayed
6. 'd better have
7. could have told
8. must have known

Exercise 23, p. 193.

1. no
2. no
3. yes
4. yes

Exercise 24, p. 193.

3. must be burning
4. may/might/could be talking . . . may/might/could be talking
5. must be playing
6. may/might/could be staying . . . may/might/could be staying
7. should be studying/ought to be studying
8. must be joking
9. may/might/could have been joking
10. must have been joking

Exercise 26, p. 195.

2. must be waiting
3. shouldn't have left
4. might have borrowed
5. must have been watching . . . must have forgotten
6. may have been attending (*also possible:* may have attended)
7. must have left
8. might be traveling
9. must not have been expecting
10. must have been daydreaming . . . should have been paying . . . shouldn't have been staring

Exercise 29, p. 197.

2. b	6. a	10. b
3. a	7. b	11. b
4. c	8. c	12. b
5. b	9. a	

Exercise 30, p. 198.

1. b
2. d
3. a
4. c

Exercise 31, p. 199.

1. can	6. Can't
2. can't	7. can
3. can	8. can't
4. can	9. can't
5. can't	10. can

Exercise 33, p. 200.

1. a group of four-year-olds
2. a college class of (twenty-five) students in their late teens and early twenties
3. How many of you can dance? How many of you can sing? How many of you can draw?
4. all
5. Fewer hands were raised in the second group (about 1/3 for the first question; fewer for the next question; two for the last question).

6. When children are young, they generally have the feeling that they can do anything. As they grow older, they become more cautious because they don't want to look foolish, especially around their peers.

Exercise 34, p. 200.

The sentences have the same meaning.

Exercise 35, p. 200.

2. would give
3. used to be
4. used to be . . . would start
5. would take
6. used to live . . . would go . . . would wake . . . would hike . . . would see
7. used to be . . . would get . . . would spend . . . would find . . . would gather

[*Note:* The directions ask you to use *would* for repeated actions in the past, but in general, *used to* is also correct for repeated actions in the past.]

Exercise 39, p. 202.

Correct sentences: 3, 4, 5, 6

Exercise 40, p. 203.

1. will you be able to get
2. are going to have to take
3. am not going to be able to attend

Exercise 41, p. 203.

2. have to be able to
3. must not have been able
4. would rather not have to
5. should not have to

Exercise 43, p. 207.

2. could / would you hand (can / will you hand)
3. don't / won't have to go
4. can already say / is already able to say
5. must / have to attend
6. had to wait
7. could / might go
8. must not have seen
9. can't / couldn't / must not be . . . may / might / could belong (must belong)
10. can't / must not / may not go
11. shouldn't have laughed
12. could / might / may be

Exercise 44, p. 208.

1. a	4. a
2. b	5. a, b
3. a, b	

Exercise 45, p. 208.

1. If you have a car, you can **travel** around the United States.
2. During class the students **must sit** quietly.
3. When you send for the brochure, you should **include** a self-addressed, stamped envelope.
4. A film director must **have** control over every aspect of a movie.
5. When I was a child, I **could** climb to the roof of my house and **see** all the other houses and streets.
6. We need to reschedule. I won't **be able to** see you at the time we scheduled for tomorrow.
7. I **broke** my leg in a soccer game three months ago.

8. **Would / Could / Will** you please help me with this?
9. Many students would **rather study** on their own than **go to** classes.
10. We **are** supposed to bring our books to class every day.
11. You can **have** a very good time as a tourist in my country. My country has many different climates, so you **had** better plan ahead before you **come**.
12. When you visit a big city in my country, you **must pay** attention to your wallet when you are in a crowded place because a thief **may / might / could** try to steal it.

Chapter 11: The Passive

Exercise 1, p. 211.
1. A
2. A
3. B
4. B
5. A
6. *(grammatically incorrect)*

Exercise 2, p. 212.
3. A
4. A
5. P
6. P
7. A
8. P
9. A
10. A

Exercise 3, p. 212.
2. is being opened
3. has been opened
4. was opened
5. was being opened
6. had been opened
7. will be opened
8. is going to be opened
9. will have been opened
10. Was . . . opened
11. Will . . . be opened
12. Has . . . been opened

Exercise 4, p. 213.
2. Customers are served by waitresses and waiters.
3. The lesson is going to be explained by the teacher.
4. The farmer's wagon was being pulled by two horses.
5. Yoko will be invited to the party by Toshi.
6. That report is being prepared by Alex.
7. The book had been returned to the library by Kathy.
8. Several public buildings have been designed by Miriam.
9. I won't be fooled by his tricks.
10. That note wasn't written by me. Was it written by Jim?
11. Is that course taught by Prof. Shapiro? No, it isn't taught by him.
12. Those papers haven't been signed by Mrs. Andrews yet. Have they been signed by Mr. Andrews yet?
13. Anwar gave the speech.
14. The teaching assistant is going to correct our assignments.
15. Did Thomas Edison invent the electric light bulb?
16. Most drivers don't obey the speed limit on Highway 5.
17. Has the building manager informed you of the rent increase?

Exercise 5, p. 213.
3. *(no change)*
4. That theory was developed by Dr. Ikeda.
5. The small fishing village was destroyed by a hurricane.
6. *(no change)*
7. *(no change)*
8. After class, the board is always erased by one of the students.

9. *(no change)*
10. *(no change)*
11. *(no change)*
12. The dispute is going to be settled by a special committee.
13. Was the thief caught by the police?
14. *(no change)*

Exercise 8, p. 215.
Early Writing Materials

The chief writing material of ancient times was papyrus. It was used in Egypt, Greece, and other Mediterranean lands. Parchment, another writing material that was widely used in ancient times, was made from the skins of animals such as sheep and goats. After the hair had been removed, the skins were stretched and rubbed smooth to make a writing surface. Paper, the main writing material today, was invented by the Chinese.

Ink has been used for writing and drawing throughout history. No one knows when the first ink was developed. The ancient Egyptians and Chinese made ink from various natural substances, such as berries, soot, and tree bark. Through the centuries, thousands of different formulas have been developed for ink. Most ink today is made from synthetic chemicals.

1. Papyrus and parchment were used for writing.
2. Parchment was made from the skins of animals such as sheep and goats.
3. The hair was removed, and the skins were stretched and rubbed smooth.
4. The Chinese first used paper.
5. No one knows when ink was first used.
6. Natural substances, such as berries, soot, and tree bark, were used for ink.
7. Synthetic chemicals are in ink today.

Exercise 9, p. 215.
2. A package was delivered to our apartment yesterday.
3. Maria taught her son to read when he was three.
4. When I was in elementary school, we were required to wear uniforms.
5. As we watched, the airplane disappeared into the clouds.
6. I agreed with your decision yesterday.
7. Timmy dropped a plate after dinner last night.
8. The plate fell to the floor with a crash.
9. What happened yesterday?
10. Something very sad happened yesterday.
11. My cat was hit by a speeding truck.
12. She was killed instantly.
13. She died instantly.

Exercise 10, p. 216.
1. a
2. b
3. b
4. a
5. b
6. b

Exercise 11, p. 216.
1. were killed by tornadoes
2. will be announced / is going to be announced
3. are consumed
4. have been recalled
5. will be delayed / are going to be delayed

Exercise 12, p. 216.
1. I was invited to a party.
2. Rice is grown in many countries.
3. The tennis match is being televised.
4. I was told to be here at ten.
5. Dinner is going to be served at six.

6. A mistake has been made.
7. *(no change)*
8. That picture was drawn by Ivan's daughter. This picture was drawn by my son.
9. The applicants will be judged on their creativity.
10. *(no change)*
11. Is that course being taught by Professor Rivers this semester?
12. The mail had already been delivered by the time I left for school this morning.
13. When are the results of the contest going to be announced?
14. After the concert was over, the rock star was surrounded by hundreds of fans outside the theater.

Exercise 14, p. 218.
2. is surrounded
3. is spelled
4. is going to be / will be built
5. was divided
6. is worn
7. was caused
8. was ordered
9. was . . . killed
10. was reported
11. was surprised
12. was offered
13. were frightened
14. was confused
15. is expected

Exercise 15, p. 219.
1. is made
2. have been roasted
3. is pressed
4. is called
5. contains
6. is separated
7. has been done
8. is left
9. is known
10. is ground
11. will be added

Exercise 16, p. 219.
2. is produced
3. is being treated
4. are controlled . . . are determined
5. was informed . . . was told
6. is exposed . . . affects
7. have been destroyed
8. was recognized . . . was asked . . . took
9. knew . . . multiplied . . . came

Exercise 18, p. 221.
4. must be kept
5. must keep
6. couldn't be opened
7. couldn't open
8. may be offered
9. may offer
10. may have already been offered / may already have been offered
11. may have already offered / may already have offered
12. ought to be divided
13. ought to have been divided
14. have to be returned
15. has to return . . . will have to pay
16. had better be finished
17. had better finish
18. is supposed to be sent
19. should have been sent
20. must have been surprised

Exercise 19, p. 222.
1. a. Many lives will be saved with the new medical procedure.
   b. The procedure will save many lives.

2. a. Shoppers can look for product information on the internet every day.
   b. Product information can be found on the internet.
3. a. People should check smoke alarm batteries once a month.
   b. Smoke alarm batteries should be tested once a month.
4. a. The typhoon may have killed hundreds of villagers yesterday.
   b. Hundreds of villagers may have been killed in the typhoon yesterday.
   c. Hundreds of villagers may have died in the typhoon yesterday.
5. a. Medical supplies had better be delivered soon.
   b. Villagers had better receive medical supplies soon.

Exercise 20, p. 223.
Sample answers:
1. Cell phones must be turned off.
   Cell phones have to be turned off.
2. Computers must be used for schoolwork only.
   Only schoolwork may be done on computers.
3. Computer games may not be played.
   Computer games cannot be played.
4. Music cannot be downloaded from the internet.
   Music must not be downloaded from the internet.
5. The printer must be used for schoolwork only.
   The printer cannot be used for any work except schoolwork.

Exercise 21, p. 223.
Sample answers:
2. must be married
3. must / have to be written
4. must have been left
5. should / ought to / must be encouraged
6. cannot be explained
7. may / might / could / will be misunderstood
8. must have been embarrassed
9. should / ought to have been built
10. must / should be saved

Exercise 22, p. 224.
Part I.
2. a
3. b, d
4. b, c
5. a, c
6. a, b
7. a

Part II.
1. were hit
2. were changed
3. was measured
4. has ever been recorded
5. was followed
6. were destroyed
7. were swept
8. died
9. were killed
10. were left
11. continued
12. could have been lessened
13. exists
14. doesn't reach
15. have been working
16. will not experience

Exercise 23, p. 225.
(1) Throughout history, **paper has been made** from various plants such as rice and papyrus, but today wood is the chief

source of paper. In the past, **paper was made** by hand, but now **most of the work is done** by machines. Today **paper is made** from wood pulp by using either a mechanical or a chemical process.

(2) In the mechanical process, **wood is ground** into small chips. During the grinding, **it is sprayed** with water to keep it from burning from the friction of the grinder. Then **the chips are soaked** in water.

(3) In the chemical process, first **the wood is washed**, and then **it is cut** into small pieces in a chipping machine. Then **the chips are cooked** in certain chemicals. After **the wood is cooked**, **it is washed** to get rid of the chemicals.

(4) The next steps in making paper are the same for both the mechanical and the chemical processes. **The pulp is drained** to form a thick mass, **(is) bleached** with chlorine, and then **(is)** thoroughly **washed** again. Next **the pulp is put** through a large machine that squeezes the water out and forms the pulp into long sheets. After the pulp sheets go through a drier and a press, **they are wound** onto rolls. These rolls of paper are then ready for use.

(5) The next time you use paper, you should think about its origin and how **it is made**. And you should . . . .

Exercise 26, p. 227.
2. is shut
3. are turned
4. is not crowded
5. is finished
6. is closed
7. was closed
8. is set . . .
   are done . . .
   are lit
9. is gone
10. is torn

Exercise 27, p. 228.
2. is . . . crowded
3. is scheduled
4. am exhausted
5. am confused
6. is stuck
7. are turned off
8. are divorced
9. are . . . qualified
10. am married
11. is spoiled
12. is blocked
13. is located
14. was born
15. Is . . . plugged in

Exercise 29, p. 229.
2. for
3. in
4. with
5. of
6. to
7. in/with
8. about

Exercise 30, p. 230.
1. of
2. with
3. to
4. in
5. for
6. to
7. about
8. with

Exercise 31, p. 230.
1. to
2. with
3. with
4. to
5. of
6. to
7. with
8. A: to
   B: of/by
9. A: with
   B: in
   A: to

Exercise 32, p. 231.
2. is finished with
3. is addicted to
4. am satisfied with
5. is engaged to
6. is divorced from
7. Are . . . related to
8. is dedicated to
9. is dressed in
10. is committed to
11. prepared for
12. done with

Exercise 33, p. 231.
1. about
2. about
3. to
4. with/by
5. to
6. to

Exercise 34, p. 232.
2. filled with
3. protected from
4. connected to
5. addicted to
6. dressed in
7. exposed to
8. gone from
9. qualified for
10. located in

Exercise 35, p. 232.
1. dirty
2. lost
3. wet
4. dressed
5. hungry
6. hurt

Exercise 36, p. 233.
2. b
3. a, b
4. c, d
5. a, b, d
6. b
7. c

Exercise 37, p. 234.
2. got wet
3. get nervous
4. is getting dark
5. is getting better
6. Get well
7. get accustomed
8. get done
9. got depressed
10. Did . . . get invited
11. get paid
12. got hired
13. got fired
14. got engaged . . . got married . . .
    got divorced . . . got remarried

Exercise 39, p. 235.
1. boring
2. bored

Exercise 40, p. 236.
1. B
2. A
3. A
4. neither
5. neither
6. B

Exercise 41, p. 236.
3. exciting
4. excited
5. surprising
6. surprised
7. frightened
8. frightening
9. exhausting
10. exhausted

Exercise 43, p. 237.
1. missing
2. satisfied
3. frightened
4. marrying
5. scary
6. finished

Exercise 44, p. 238.
1. thrilling
2. thrilled
3. shocked
4. shocking
5. delightful
6. delightful
7. confused
8. confusing

Exercise 45, p. 238.

2. embarrassing
3. injured
4. challenging
5. expected
6. printing
7. Experienced
8. growing . . .
   balanced
9. spoiled
10. sleeping
11. thrilling
12. abandoned
13. Polluted
14. furnished
15. dividing
16. elected
17. amazing

Exercise 46, p. 239.

Questions:
2. What are you tired of?
3. What (or who) are you pleased with?
4. What do you get really nervous about?
5. What do you want to be remembered for?
6. What is exciting to you?
7. What do you get excited about?
8. What is confusing to students?
9. What are you confused by?
10. What is confusing to children?

Exercise 47, p. 239.

Part I.
1. F
2. F
3. T

Part II.
1. began
2. were established
3. were allowed
4. were not even permitted
5. was
6. were not invited
7. was crowned
8. could be placed
9. Winning
10. were treated
11. brought

Exercise 50, p. 241.

2. Two people got **hurt** in the accident and were **taken** to the hospital by an ambulance.
3. The movie was so **boring** that we fell asleep after an hour.
4. The students **were** helped by the clear explanation that the teacher gave.
5. The winner of the race hasn't been **announced** yet.
6. When and where **was** the automobile invented?
7. My brother and I have always been **interested** in learning more about our family tree.
8. I **do not/don't** agree with you, and I don't think you'll ever convince me.
9. It was late, and I was getting very **worried** about my mother.
10. Many strange things **happened** last night.
11. I didn't go to dinner with them because I **had already eaten**.
12. In class yesterday, I was **confused**. I didn't understand the lesson.
13. When we were children, we **were** very afraid of caterpillars. Whenever we saw one of these monsters, we **ran** to our house before the caterpillars could attack us. I still get **scared** when I **see** a caterpillar close to me.
14. One day, while the old man was cutting down a big tree near the stream, his axe **fell** into the river. He sat down and **began** to cry because he **did** not have enough money to buy another axe.

Chapter 12: Noun Clauses

Exercise 1, p. 242.

Complete sentences: 2, 4, 6, 8

Exercise 2, p. 243.

Noun clauses:
3. where Tom went
4. Where Tom went
5. *(no noun clause)*
6. what Nancy wants

Exercise 3, p. 243.

3. What does Alex need? Do you know?
4. Do you know <u>what Alex needs</u>?
5. <u>What Alex needs</u> is a new job.
6. We talked about <u>what Alex needs</u>.
7. What do you need? Did you talk to your parents about <u>what you need</u>?
8. My parents know <u>what I need</u>.

Exercise 5, p. 244.

1. a
2. b

Exercise 6, p. 244.

2. What he was talking about
3. where you live
4. Where she went
5. when they are coming
6. which one he wants
7. what happened
8. who opened the door
9. Why they left the country
10. What we are doing in class
11. who those people are
12. whose pen this is

Exercise 7, p. 245.

Can you tell me . . .
1. how this word is pronounced?
2. what this means?
3. what my grade was?
4. who I am supposed to talk to?
5. when our next assignment is due?
6. how much time we have for the test?
7. when classes end for the year?
8. where our class is going to meet?

Exercise 9, p. 246.

2. Why is he coming? Please tell me why he is coming.
3. What/Which flight will he be on? Please tell me what/which flight he will be on.
4. Who is going to meet him at the airport? Please tell me who is going to meet him at the airport.
5. Who is his roommate? Please tell me who his roommate is.
6. Where does he live? Please tell me where he lives.
7. Where was he last week? Please tell me where he was last week.
8. How long has he been working for Sony Corporation? Do you know how long he has been working for Sony Corporation?
9. What kind of computer does he have at home? Do you know what kind of computer he has at home?

Exercise 10, p. 247.

2. A: is my eraser
   B: it is
3. A: didn't Franco lock
   B: he didn't lock
4. A: has he been
   B: he has been
5. A: are we supposed
   B: we are supposed

Exercise 11, p. 248.

1. a
2. b
3. a
4. b
5. a
6. b
7. b

Exercise 12, p. 248.

1. Do you know how many minutes (there) are in 24 hours? (1,440 minutes)
2. Do you know when the first man walked on the moon? (1969)
3. Do you know who won the Nobel Peace Prize last year? / . . . who the winner of the Nobel Peace Prize was last year?
4. Do you know where Buddha was born? (northern India — which is now part of Nepal)
5. Do you know how far it is from the earth to the sun? (about 93 million miles / 149 million km.)
6. Do you know how long it takes for the moon to rotate around the earth? (about a month — 27 days, 8 hours)

Exercise 13, p. 248.

I wonder <u>whether the mail has arrived</u>.
I wonder <u>whether or not the mail has arrived</u>.
I wonder <u>whether the mail has arrived or not</u>.
I wonder <u>if the mail has arrived or not</u>.
Whether, if, and *or not* are added to yes/no questions.

Exercise 14, p. 249.

1. Let me know if the financial report is ready.
2. Let me know if it will be ready tomorrow.
3. Let me know if the copy machine needs paper.
4. Let me know if someone is waiting for me.
5. Let me know if we need anything for the meeting.
6. Let me know if you are going to be there.
7. Please check whether they got my message.
8. Please check whether the copy machine is working.
9. Please check whether there is any paper left.
10. Please check whether this information is correct.
11. Please check whether the fax came in.
12. Please check whether we are going to have Monday off.

Exercise 15, p. 249.

I wonder . . .
1. where Tom is.
2. whether/if we should wait for him.
3. whether/if he is having trouble.
4. when the first book was written.
5. what causes earthquakes.
6. how long a butterfly lives.
7. whose dictionary this is.
8. whether/if it belongs to William.
9. why dinosaurs became extinct.
10. whether/if there is life on other planets.
11. how life began.
12. whether/if people will live on the moon someday.

Exercise 17, p. 250.

1. I don't know where you left your keys.
2. I don't know where you put your shoes.
3. I don't know where your other sock is.

4. I don't know what you did with your briefcase.
5. I'll find out where he's (he is) from.
6. I'll find out what he does.
7. I'll find out where he works.
8. I'll find out if he'd (he would) like to come to dinner.
9. Let's ask where the bus station is.
10. Let's ask how much the city bus costs.
11. Let's ask if the city buses carry bikes.
12. Let's ask if this bus schedule is correct.
13. We need to figure out how far it is from here to town.
14. We need to figure out how much it costs to take a taxi from here to downtown.
15. We need to figure out where we get our money changed.

Exercise 18, p. 250.

2. No one seems to know when **Maria will** arrive.
3. I don't know **what that means**.
4. I wonder **if/whether** the teacher **knows** the answer.
5. I'll ask her **if/whether she would** like some coffee or not.
6. Be sure to tell the doctor **where it hurts**.
7. Why **I am** unhappy is something I can't explain.
8. Nobody cares **if** we stay or leave.
9. I need to know **who your** teacher **is**.
10. I don't understand **why the car is** not running properly.
11. My young son wants to know **where the** stars go in the daytime.

Exercise 19, p. 251.

Sample answers:
1. Do you know if/whether the restaurant is open yet?
2. Could you tell me what the homework was?
3. I'll find out what the date is.
4. I haven't heard if/whether it is supposed to be sunny.
5. Could you tell me how many days I have to return the coat?
6. I don't care if/whether we go to a movie or get a DVD.
7. I'd like to know why I have a late fee on my bill.
8. It doesn't matter to me if/whether you bring your dog.

Exercise 20, p. 251.

b. to do
d. to get

Exercise 21, p. 252.

2. The plumber told me how to fix the leak in the sink.
3. Please tell me where to meet you.
4. Robert had a long excuse for being late for their date, but Sandy didn't know whether to believe him or not.
5. Jim found two shirts he liked, but he had trouble deciding which one to buy.
6. I've done everything I can think of to help Andy get his life straightened out. I don't know what else to do.

Exercise 22, p. 252.

Sample answers:
2. to live in a dorm . . . to get an apartment
3. to repair a bicycle
4. to get my sister
5. to take a job with low pay that he would enjoy . . . (to) take a job with higher pay that he wouldn't enjoy
6. to stay . . . to travel cheaply

Exercise 23, p. 253.

Correct sentences: 2, 3

Exercise 26, p. 254.

Sample answers:

2. It's too bad that Tim hasn't been able to make any friends. OR That Tim hasn't been able to make any friends is too bad.
3. It's a fact that the earth revolves around the sun. OR That the earth revolves around the sun is a fact.
4. It's true that exercise can reduce heart disease. OR That exercise can reduce heart disease is true.
5. It's clear that drug abuse can ruin one's health. OR That drug abuse can ruin one's health is clear.
6. It's unfortunate that some women do not earn equal pay for equal work. OR That some women do not earn equal pay for equal work is unfortunate.
7. It's surprising that Irene, who is an excellent student, failed her entrance examination. OR That Irene, who is an excellent student, failed her entrance examination is surprising.
8. It's a well-known fact that English is the principal language of business throughout much of the world. OR That English is the principal language of business throughout much of the world is a well-known fact.

Exercise 27, p. 255.

3. It's a fact that . . . .
4. It isn't true that . . . . (It's sunlight.)
5. It's a fact that . . . .
6. It isn't true that . . . . (It's about 55–78%, depending on body size.)
7. It's a fact that . . . .
8. It isn't true that . . . . (It went online in 1992 and was developed by British computer scientist Tim Berners-Lee.)
9. It's a fact that . . . . (The average pregnancy is 22 months.)
10. It isn't true that . . . . (They were made out of tree trunks — 3500 B.C.)
11. It's a fact that . . . .

Exercise 28, p. 255.

2. The fact that Rosa didn't come made me angry.
3. The fact that many people in the world live in intolerable poverty must concern all of us.
4. I was not aware of the fact that I was supposed to bring my passport to the exam for identification.
5. Due to the fact that the people of the town were given no warning of the approaching tornado, there were many casualties.

Exercise 29, p. 255.

2. The fact that traffic is getting worse every year is undeniable.
3. The fact that the city has no funds for the project is unfortunate.
4. The fact that the two leaders don't respect each other is obvious.
5. The fact that there were no injuries from the car accident is a miracle.

Exercise 31, p. 256.

1. T
2. T
3. T
4. F
5. F

Exercise 32, p. 257.

1. "Watch out!" Mrs. Brooks said.
2. "Are you okay?" she asked.
3. "You look like you're going to fall off the ladder," she said.

The punctuation is inside the quotation marks. A comma is used at the end of a quoted statement.

Exercise 33, p. 259.

1. Henry said, "There is a phone call for you."
2. "There is a phone call for you," he said.
3. "There is," said Henry, "a phone call for you."
4. "There is a phone call for you. It's your sister," said Henry.
5. "There is a phone call for you," he said. "It's your sister."
6. I asked him, "Where is the phone?"
7. "Where is the phone?" she asked.
8. "Stop the clock!" shouted the referee. "We have an injured player."
9. "Who won the game?" asked the spectator.
10. "I'm going to rest for the next three hours," she said. "I don't want to be disturbed." "That's fine," I replied. "You get some rest. I'll make sure no one disturbs you."

Exercise 34, p. 259.

When the police officer came over to my car, he said, "Let me see your driver's license, please."

"What's wrong, Officer?" I asked. "Was I speeding?"

"No, you weren't speeding," he replied. "You went through a red light at the corner of Fifth Avenue and Main Street. You almost caused an accident."

"Did I really do that?" I said. "I didn't see a red light."

Exercise 36, p. 260.

The reporting verbs (*said, told*) are simple past. This means that the noun clause verbs that are present in quoted speech change to the past in reported speech.

Exercise 37, p. 262.

2. if/whether I needed a pen.
3. what I wanted.
4. if/whether I was hungry.
5. (that) she wanted a sandwich.
6. (that) he was going to move to Ohio.
7. if/whether I enjoyed my trip.
8. what I was talking about.
9. if/whether I had seen her grammar book.
10. (that) she didn't want to go.
11. if/whether I could help him with his report.
12. (that) he might be late.
13. that I should work harder.
14. she had to go downtown.
15. why the sky is blue.
16. where everyone was.
17. (that) he would come to the meeting.
18. if/whether he would be in class tomorrow.
19. he thought he would go to the library to study.
20. if/whether Omar knew what he was doing.
21. if/whether what I had heard was true.
22. the sun rises in the east.
23. someday we would be in contact with beings from outer space.

Exercise 40, p. 264.

1. was scheduled
2. was snowing
3. needed
4. had applied
5. could come
6. was going to continue

Exercise 41, p. 264.

2. couldn't lend . . . was
3. was wearing . . . was giving
4. would meet . . . promised

5. was considering . . . thought . . . should do
6. were going to be . . . had to

Exercise 42, p. 265.

2. that she was excited about her new job and that she had found a nice apartment.
3. that he expected us to be in class every day and that unexcused absences might affect our grades.
4. that Highway 66 would be closed for two months and that commuters should seek alternate routes.
5. that every obstacle was a steppingstone to success and that I should view problems in my life as opportunities to improve myself.

Exercise 43, p. 265.

Possible answers:

1. Alex asked me what I was doing. I replied that I was drawing a picture.
2. Asako asked Cho if she wanted to go to a movie Sunday night. Cho said that she would like to but that she had to study.
3. The little boy asked Mrs. Robinson how old she was. She told him that it was not polite to ask people their age. He also asked how much money she made. She told him that was impolite too.
4. My sister asked me if there was anything I especially wanted to watch on TV. I replied that there was a show at 8:00 that I had been waiting to see for a long time. She asked me what it was. When I told her that it was a documentary about green sea turtles, she wondered why I wanted to see that. I explained that I was doing a research paper on sea turtles and thought I might be able to get some good information from the documentary. I suggested that she watch it with me. She declined and said she wasn't especially interested in green sea turtles.

Exercise 44, p. 266.

1. Tell the taxi driver **where you** want to go.
2. My roommate came into the room and asked me why **I wasn't** in class. I said (that) I **was** waiting for a telephone call from my family. OR I told him (that) . . . .
3. It was my first day at the university, and I **was** on my way to my first class. I wondered who else **would** be in the class **and what** the teacher would be like.
4. He asked me **what I intended** to do after I **graduated**.
5. What **a patient tells** a **doctor is** confidential.
6. What my friend and I **did was** our secret. We didn't even tell our parents what **we did**. (*also possible:* **had done**)
7. The doctor asked **if/whether** I felt okay. I told him that I **didn't** feel well.
8. I asked him what kind of **movies he liked. He said to me / He told me that he liked** romantic movies.
9. "**Is it** true you almost drowned**?**" my friend asked me. "Yes," I said. "I'm really glad to be alive. It was really frightening."
10. **The** fact that I almost drowned makes me very careful about water safety whenever I go swimming.
11. I didn't know where **I was** supposed to get off the bus, so I asked the driver **where the science museum was**. She **told** me the name of the street. She said she **would** tell me when **I should** get off the bus.
12. My mother did not live with us. When other children asked me **where my mother was**, I told them (that) she **was** going to come to visit me very soon.
13. When I asked the taxi driver to drive faster, he said **he would** drive faster if **I paid him** more. OR When I asked the taxi driver to drive faster, he said, "I will drive faster if

you pay me more." At that time I didn't care how much **it would** cost, so I told him to go as fast as he **could**.
14. My parents told me **it** is essential to know English if I want to study at an American university.

Exercise 48, p. 268.

1. any place that
2. at any time that
3. anything that
4. in any way that

Exercise 49, p. 269.

2. whenever
3. whatever
4. whatever
5. Whoever
6. however
7. whoever
8. wherever
9. whatever . . . wherever . . . whenever . . . whoever (*also possible, but rare:* whomever) . . . however

Chapter 13: Adjective Clauses

Exercise 1, p. 270.

1. a. He = man
   b. who = man
   c. that = man
2. a. It = computer
   b. which = computer
   c. that = computer

Pronoun choice: *who* = person; *that* = person, thing; *which* = thing.

Exercise 2, p. 271.

2. b, c
3. a, b
4. b, c

Exercise 3, p. 271.

2. The girl who/that won the race is happy.
3. The student who/that sits next to me is from China.
4. The students who/that sit in the front row are from China.
5. We are studying sentences that/which contain adjective clauses.
6. I am using a sentence that/which contains an adjective clause.

Exercise 5, p. 271.

2. who is
3. who has
4. who are
5. who have
6. who had
7. who would
8. will be
9. would like
10. is giving
11. has traveled
12. are planning
13. have worked
14. had been taking

Exercise 6, p. 272.

Note: which can be used in place of that.

1. He is looking for a job that leaves him free on weekends.
2. He is not looking for a job that requires him to work on weekends.
3. He is not looking for a job that includes a lot of long-distance travel.
4. He is looking for a job that has minimal travel requirements.
5. He is not looking for a job has a long commute.
6. He is looking for a job that is close to home.

7. He is not looking for a job that demands sixteen-hour work days.
8. He is looking for a job that has flexible hours.

Exercise 7, p. 273.
2. b, c, f
3. a, b, e, f
4. b, c, f
5. a, b, e, f

Exercise 8, p. 273.
2. I liked the woman who/that/whom/Ø I met at the party last night.
3. I liked the composition that/which/Ø you wrote.
4. The people who/that/whom/Ø we visited yesterday were very nice.
5. The man who/that/whom/Ø Ann brought to the party is standing over there.

Exercise 9, p. 274.
In the a. sentences, the preposition comes at the end of the adjective clause.
In the b. sentences, the preposition comes before *whom/which* (at the beginning of the adjective clause).

Exercise 10, p. 274.
1. a, b, c
2. a, b, d, f

Exercise 11, p. 274.
1. The man who I was telling you about is standing over there.
   The man whom I was telling you about is standing over there.
   The man that I was telling you about is standing over there.
   The man I was telling you about is standing over there.
   The man about whom I was telling you is standing over there.
2. I must thank the people who I got a present from.
   I must thank the people whom I got a present from.
   I must thank the people that I got a present from.
   I must thank the people I got a present from.
   I must thank the people from whom I got a present.
3. The meeting that Omar went to was interesting.
   The meeting which Omar went to was interesting.
   The meeting Omar went to was interesting.
   The meeting to which Omar went was interesting.

Exercise 12, p. 275.
2. who, whom, that, Ø
3. that, which, Ø
4. who, that
5. that, which
6. who, whom, that, Ø

Exercise 13, p. 275.
Adjective clauses:
2. which I had borrowed from my roommate
   that I had borrowed from my roommate
   I had borrowed from my roommate
3. I hadn't seen for years
   who I hadn't seen for years
   whom I hadn't seen for years
   that I hadn't seen for years
4. she knew very little about
   which she knew very little about
   that she knew very little about
   about which she knew very little
5. who keeps chickens in his apartment
   that keeps chickens in his apartment

Exercise 14, p. 275.
1. In our village, there were many people **who/that** didn't have much money.
2. I enjoyed the book that you told me to **read**.
3. I still remember the man **who taught** me to play the guitar when I was a boy.
4. I showed my father a picture of the car I am going to **buy as** soon as I save enough money.
5. The woman about **whom** I was **talking suddenly** walked into the room. OR The **woman whom** I was talking about suddenly walked into the room. I hope she didn't hear me.
6. The people **who/that** appear in the play are amateur actors.
7. I don't like to spend time with people **who/that lose** their temper easily.
8. While the boy was at the airport, he took pictures of people **who/that were** waiting for their planes.
9. People who **work** in the hunger **program estimate** that 45,000 people worldwide die from starvation and malnutrition-related diseases every single day of the year.
10. In one corner of the marketplace, an old **man was** playing a violin.

Exercise 16, p. 277.
Correct sentences: 1 and 2

Exercise 17, p. 277.
3. whose
4. who
5. who
6. whose
7. whose
8. who

Exercise 18, p. 278.
2. Mrs. North teaches a class for students whose native language is not English.
3. The people whose house we visited were nice.
4. I live in a dormitory whose residents come from many countries.
5. I have to call the man whose umbrella I accidentally picked up after the meeting.
6. The man whose beard caught on fire when he lit a cigarette poured a glass of water on his face.

Exercise 19, p. 278.
1. who's
2. who's
3. whose
4. who's
5. whose
6. who's
7. who's
8. whose

Exercise 20, p. 278.
3. There is the girl whose mother is a dentist.
4. There is the person whose picture was in the newspaper.
5. There is the woman whose car was stolen.
6. There is the man whose daughter won a gold medal at the Olympic Games.
7. There is the woman whose keys I found.
8. There is the teacher whose class I am in.
9. There is the author whose book I read.
10. There is the student whose lecture notes I borrowed.

Exercise 21, p. 279.
1. who is
2. whose
3. who has
4. whose
5. who is
6. whose
7. who has
8. who is

Exercise 24, p. 280.
1. The city where we spent our vacation was beautiful.
   The city in which we spent our vacation was beautiful.

The city which/that/Ø we spent our vacation in was beautiful.
2. That is the restaurant where I will meet you.
   That is the restaurant at which I will meet you.
   That is the restaurant which/that/Ø I will meet you at.
3. The office where I work is busy.
   The office in which I work is busy.
   The office which/that/Ø I work in is busy.
4. That is the drawer where I keep my jewelry.
   That is the drawer in which I keep my jewelry.
   That is the drawer which/that/Ø I keep my jewelry in.

Exercise 26, p. 280.

1. Monday is the day when they will come.
   Monday is the day on which they will come.
   Monday is the day that/Ø they will come.
2. 7:05 is the time when my plane arrives.
   7:05 is the time at which my plane arrives.
   7:05 is the time that/Ø my plane arrives.
3. 1960 is the year when the revolution took place.
   1960 is the year in which the revolution took place.
   1960 is the year that/Ø the revolution took place.
4. July is the month when the weather is usually the hottest.
   July is the month in which the weather is usually the hottest.
   July is the month that/Ø the weather is usually the hottest.

Exercise 27, p. 281.

3. A café is a small restaurant where people can get a light meal.
4. Every neighborhood in Brussels has small cafés where customers drink coffee and eat pastries.
5. There was a time when dinosaurs dominated the earth.
6. The house where I was born and grew up was destroyed in an earthquake ten years ago.
7. The miser hid his money in a place where it was safe from robbers.
8. There came a time when the miser had to spend his money.

Exercise 29, p. 281.

1. a, b	3. b	5. b
2. a, c	4. c	6. b

Exercise 31, p. 282.

2. somebody <u>who speaks Spanish</u>

3. Everything <u>the Smiths do</u>

4. one <u>who really understands me</u>

Exercise 33, p. 284.

1. who is	5. who is
2. that are	6. that sounded
3. whose	7. that I heard
4. whose wife	

Exercise 34, p. 285.

The adjective clause in sentence 1 can be omitted without changing the meaning.
The commas are used to set off additional information.

Exercise 35, p. 286.

3. additional: Rice, which is grown in many countries, is a staple food throughout much of the world.
4. necessary: The rice which we had for dinner last night was very good.
5. necessary: The newspaper article was about a man who died two weeks ago of a rare tropical disease.
6. additional: Paul O'Grady, who died two weeks ago of a sudden heart attack, was a kind and loving man.
7. additional: I have fond memories of my hometown, which is situated in a valley.
8. necessary: I live in a town which is situated in a valley.
9. necessary: People who live in glass houses shouldn't throw stones.
10. additional: In a children's story, Little Red Riding Hood, who went out one day to visit her grandmother, found a wolf in her grandmother's bed when she got there.

Exercise 36, p. 286.

1. Did you hear about the man who rowed a boat across the Atlantic Ocean?
2. My uncle, who loves boating, rows his boat across the lake near his house nearly every day.
3. Tea, which is a common drink throughout the world, is made by pouring boiling water onto the dried leaves of certain plants.
4. Tea which is made from herbs is called herbal tea.
5. Toys which contain lead paint are unsafe for children.
6. Lead, which can be found in paint and plastics, is known to cause brain damage in children.

Exercise 37, p. 287.

3. The Mississippi River, which flows south from Minnesota to the Gulf of Mexico, is the major commercial river in the United States.
4. A river **that** is polluted is not safe for swimming. *(no commas)*
5. Mr. Trang, whose son won the spelling contest, is very proud of his son's achievement. The man whose daughter won the science contest is also very pleased and proud.
6. Goats, which were first tamed more than 9,000 years ago in Asia, have provided people with milk, meat, and wool since prehistoric times.
7. She's furious at the goat **that** got on the wrong side of the fence and is eating her flowers. *(no commas)*

Exercise 38, p. 288.

3. a	5. a
4. b	6. b

Exercise 39, p. 288.

1. b	3. a
2. a	4. b

Exercise 40, p. 288.

1. *(no change)*
2. We enjoyed Mexico City, where we spent our vacation.
3. *(no change)*
4. One of the most useful materials in the world is glass, which is made chiefly from sand, soda, and lime.
5. You don't need to take heavy clothes when you go to Bangkok, which has one of the highest average temperatures of any city in the world.
6. Child labor was a social problem in late eighteenth-century England, where employment in factories became virtual slavery for children.
7. *(no change)*

8. *(1st sentence: no change)* The research scientist, who was wearing protective clothing before she stepped into the special chamber holding the bees, was not stung. *(3rd sentence: no change)*

Exercise 41, p. 289.
Sample answers:
1. developed QDOS.
2. Tim Paterson worked for.
3. meant "quick and dirty operating system."
4. was developing a personal computer.
5. was looking for an operating system, bought Tim Paterson's.
6. became known as MS-DOS.

Exercise 42, p. 290.
1. b
2. b

Exercise 43, p. 290.
2. Last night the orchestra played three symphonies, one of which was Beethoven's Seventh.
3. I tried on six pairs of shoes, none of which I liked.
4. The village has around 200 people, the majority of whom are farmers.
5. That company currently has five employees, all of whom are computer experts.
6. After the riot, over 100 people were taken to the hospital, many of whom had been innocent bystanders.

Exercise 45, p. 291.
1. The soccer team worked very hard to win.
2. Some of the athletes in the class cheated on the final exam.
3. final exam

Exercise 46, p. 292.
2. She usually came to work late, which upset her boss.
3. So her boss fired her, which made her angry.
4. She hadn't saved any money, which was unfortunate.
5. So she had to borrow some money from me, which I didn't like.
6. She has found a new job, which is lucky.
7. So she has repaid the money she borrowed from me, which I appreciate.
8. She has promised herself to be on time to work every day, which is a good idea.

Exercise 47, p. 292.
2. The blue whale, <u>which can grow to 100 feet and 150 tons</u>, is considered the largest animal that has ever lived.
3. The plane was met by a crowd of 300 people, <u>some of whom had been waiting for more than four hours</u>.
4. In this paper, I will describe the basic process <u>by which raw cotton becomes cotton thread</u>.
5. The researchers are doing case studies of people <u>whose families have a history of high blood pressure and heart disease</u> to determine the importance of   heredity in health and longevity.
6. At the end of this month, scientists at the institute will conclude their AIDS research, <u>the results of which will be published within six months</u>.
7. According to many education officials, "math phobia" (that is, fear of mathematics) is a widespread problem <u>to which a solution can and must be found</u>.

8. The art museum hopes to hire a new administrator <u>under whose direction it will be able to purchase significant pieces of art</u>.
9. The giant anteater, <u>whose tongue is longer than 30 centimeters (12 inches)</u>, licks up ants for its dinner.
10. The anteater's tongue, <u>which can go in and out of its mouth 160 times a minute</u>, is sticky.

Exercise 48, p. 293.
(2) 6:00 . . . parking lot . . . bus
(3) reports
(4) coffee
(5) commuting for an hour and a half

Exercise 51, p. 295.
2. The scientists researching the causes of cancer are making progress.
3. We have an apartment overlooking the park.
4. The photographs published in the newspaper were extraordinary.
5. The rules allowing public access to wilderness areas need to be reconsidered.
6. The psychologists studying the nature of sleep have made important discoveries.
7. Antarctica is covered by a huge ice cap containing 70 percent of the earth's fresh water.
8. When I went to Alex's house to drop off some paperwork, I met Jacob, his partner.
9. Many of the students hoping to enter this university will be disappointed because only one-tenth of those applying for admission will be accepted.
10. Kuala Lumpur, the capital of Malaysia, is a major trade center in Southeast Asia.

Exercise 52, p. 295.
1. a
2. b
3. a, b
4. a

Exercise 53, p. 295.
2. Corn was one of the agricultural products that/which was introduced to the European settlers by the Indians. Some of the other products that/which were introduced by the Indians were potatoes, peanuts, and tobacco.
3. Mercury, which is the nearest planet to the sun, is also the smallest of the planets which/that orbit our sun.
4. The pyramids, which are the monumental tombs of ancient Egyptian pharaohs, were constructed more than 4,000 years ago.
5. Any student who/that doesn't want to go on the trip should inform the office.
6. Be sure to follow the instructions that/which are given at the top of the page.

Exercise 54, p. 296.
(2) Walt Disney, the creator of Mickey Mouse and the founder of his own movie production company, once was fired by a newspaper editor because he had no good ideas.
(3) Thomas Edison, the inventor of the light bulb and the phonograph, was believed by his teachers to be too stupid to learn.
(4) Albert Einstein, one of the greatest scientists of all time, performed badly in almost all of his high school courses and failed his first college entrance exam.

Exercise 55, p. 296.

2. , the capital of Iraq.
3. , sensitive instruments that measure the shaking of the ground.
4. , the lowest place on the earth's surface,
5. , the capital of Argentina.
6. , devices that produce a powerful beam of light.
7. , the northernmost country in Latin America,
8. , the most populous country in Africa,
9. , the largest city in the Western Hemisphere, . . . , the largest city in the United States,

Exercise 56, p. 297.

Part I.
1. F
2. T
3. F
4. T

Part II.
1. Whether or not
2. reported that
3. that scientists
4. that were
5. something which
6. who followed
7. is that they
8. that begin
9. is that
10. and that
11. believe that
12. who have
13. are certain that
14. and that

Exercise 57, p. 298.

2. Disney World, an amusement park located in Orlando, Florida, covers a large area of land that includes lakes, golf courses, campsites, hotels, and a wildlife preserve.
3. Jamaica, the third largest island in the Caribbean Sea, is one of the world's leading producers of bauxite, an ore from which aluminum is made.
4. Robert Ballard, an oceanographer, made headlines in 1985 when he discovered the remains of the *Titanic,* the "unsinkable" passenger ship that has rested on the floor of the Atlantic Ocean since 1912, when it struck an iceberg. (*also possible:* Oceanographer Robert Ballard made headlines . . . .)
5. The Republic of Yemen, located at the southwestern tip of the Arabian Peninsula, is an ancient land that has been host to many prosperous civilizations, including the Kingdom of Sheba and various Islamic empires.

Exercise 58, p. 299.

1. Baseball is the only sport in which I am interested. OR Baseball is the only sport (**which**) I am interested in.
2. My favorite teacher, **Mr. Chu**, **was** always willing to help me after class.
3. It is important to be polite to people who **live** in the same building.
4. My sister has two children, **whose** names are Ali and Talal.
5. He comes from Venezuela, (**which is**) a Spanish-speaking country.
6. There are some people in the government (**who are**) trying to improve the lives of the poor.
7. My classroom is located on the second floor of Carver Hall, **which** is a large brick building in the center of the campus.
8. A myth is a story **expressing** traditional beliefs. OR A myth is a story **which/that expresses** traditional beliefs.
9. There is an old legend (**which/that is**) **told** among people in my country about a **man who lived** in the seventeenth century and saved a village from destruction.
10. An old **man fishing** (OR **who/that was fishing**) next to me on the pier was muttering to himself.
11. The road that we **took through** the **forest was** narrow and steep.

12. There are ten universities in Thailand, seven of **which are** located in Bangkok, (**which is**) the capital city.
13. At the national park, there is a path **leading** to a spectacular waterfall. OR At the national park, there is a path **which/that leads** to a spectacular waterfall.
14. At the airport, I was waiting for some relatives **who / that / whom / Ø** I had never **met before.**
15. It is almost impossible to find two persons **whose opinions** are the same.
16. On the wall, there is a colorful poster **which/that consists** of / **consisting** of a group of young people (**who are**) dancing.
17. The sixth member of our household is Pietro, **who** is my sister's son.
18. Before I came here, I didn't have the opportunity to speak with people **whose native tongue is English.** OR . . . people **for whom English** is their native tongue.

Chapter 14: Gerunds and Infinitives, Part 1

Exercise 1, p. 301.
a. sentence 2
b. sentence 1
c. sentence 3

Exercise 2, p. 302.
Each verb ends in *-ing.*

Exercise 3, p. 302.
2. about going
3. in going
4. about going
5. on going
6. to going
7. from going
8. from going

Exercise 4, p. 303.
2. to being
3. about flying
4. for spilling
5. about having
6. for being
7. for flying
8. from getting
9. of stealing
10. for taking
11. for doing
12. from taking
13. of listening
14. in convincing

Exercise 5, p. 304.
2. of doing
3. to having
4. for helping
5. on knowing
6. in being
7. of living
8. for not going
9. in searching
10. for making
11. to going
12. from running
13. to going
14. of clarifying
15. to wearing

Exercise 6, p. 305.
2. in finishing the project early/in getting the project done.
3. about doing housework.
4. for helping (out).
5. for not finishing his report.
6. to eating spicy food.
7. from going away for the holiday weekend.

Exercise 7, p. 305.
Questions:
2. What are you not accustomed to doing?
3. What are you interested in finding out about?

4. Where are you looking forward to going on your next trip?
5. What is a good reason for not doing your homework?

Exercise 8, p. 305.
1. Yes, I thanked him/her for helping me carry heavy boxes. OR No, I didn't thank him/ her for helping . . . .
2. Yes, I'm looking forward to visiting/going to visit my friends in another town this weekend. OR No, I'm not looking forward to visiting/going to visit . . . .
3. Yes, I had a good excuse for not coming to class on time. OR No, I didn't have a good excuse for not coming to class on time.
4. Yes, I'm accustomed to living in a cold/warm climate. OR No, I'm not accustomed to living . . . .
5. Yes, I'm excited about going to a tropical island for vacation. OR No, I'm not excited about going . . . .
6. Yes, she apologized for interrupting me while I was talking to the store manager. OR No, she didn't apologize for interrupting me . . . .
7. Yes, all of the students in the class participated in doing role-plays. OR No, all of the students in the class didn't participate in doing . . . .
8. Yes, I know who was responsible for breaking the window. OR No, I don't know who was responsible for breaking . . . .
9. Yes, I am used to having my biggest meal at lunch. OR No, I am not used to having . . . .
10. The hot/cold weather prevents me from . . . .
11. Yes, they complain about having to do a lot of homework. OR No, they don't complain about having . . . .
12. Yes, I blame him for taking my wallet. OR No, I don't blame him for taking . . . .
13. Instead of studying grammar last night, I . . . .
14. In addition to studying last weekend, I . . . .

Exercise 9, p. 306.
Sample answers:
2. By talking to native speakers. / By watching TV., etc.
3. By eating.
4. By drinking.
5. By looking it up in a dictionary.
6. By coming to work late.
7. By wagging their tails.
8. By saying, "Excuse me."

Exercise 13, p. 308.
2. hoping
3. working
4. going
5. doing
6. leaving

Exercise 14, p. 308.
Sample answers:
2. closing
3. studying
4. going
5. cleaning
6. making
7. going
8. taking
9. being

Exercise 17, p. 309.
2. go fishing
3. go sailing
4. went swimming
5. went biking
6. going dancing

Exercise 19, p. 310.
Verbs: understanding, asking, trying, looking, feeling
Form: -ing

Exercise 20, p. 311.
Sample answers:
2. understanding
3. doing
4. waiting
5. taking
6. listening
7. going
8. making
9. watching
10. eating

Exercise 22, p. 312.
1. remembering his children's birthdays
2. hiding his report card
3. eating her breakfast
4. learning foreign languages
5. sitting in traffic
6. singing songs on the bus trip
7. studying in the library
8. waiting in line to buy movie tickets [*Note:* Some speakers of American English say "on line."]

Exercise 23, p. 312.
Questions:
1. What do you have difficulty remembering?
2. What do you have a hard time learning?
3. What do you have a good time playing?
4. What English sounds do you have a hard time pronouncing?
5. What do people waste money doing?
6. What do people waste time doing?

Exercise 24, p. 312.
1. b
2. a
3. b, c

Exercise 25, p. 314.
4. to leave
5. to leave/me to leave
6. to leave
7. to leave/me to leave
8. me to leave
9. to leave
10. to leave
11. to leave
12. me to leave
13. to leave/me to leave
14. me to leave
15. me to leave
16. me to leave
17. to leave
18. to leave

Exercise 26, p. 314.
Sample answers:
2. Roberto reminded me to take my book back to the library.
   I was reminded (by Roberto) to take . . . .
3. Mr. Chang encouraged me to take singing lessons.
   I was encouraged (by Mr. Chang) to take . . . .
4. Mrs. Alvarez warned the children not to play with matches.
   The children were warned (by Mrs. Alvarez) not to play . . . .
5. The Dean of Admissions permitted me to register for school late.
   I was permitted (by the Dean of Admissions) to register . . . .
6. The law requires every driver to have a valid driver's license.
   Every driver is required (by law) to have . . . .
7. My friend advised me to get some automobile insurance.
   I was advised (by my friend) to get some automobile insurance.
8. The robber forced me to give him all of my money.
   I was forced (by the robber) to give him (the robber) . . . .
9. My boss told me to come to the meeting ten minutes early.
   I was told (by my boss) to come . . . .

Exercise 27, p. 315.

Questions:
1. What did a family member remind you to do recently? (*also possible:* present perfect tense with "recently" questions)
2. Where did a friend ask you to go recently?
3. What does the government require people to do?
4. What do doctors advise people to do?
5. What do teachers expect students to do?
6. What did our teacher tell you (us) to do recently?
7. What do the laws not permit you to do?
8. Where do parents warn their kids not to go?
9. What does our teacher encourage us to do to practice our English?

Exercise 28, p. 315.

Sample answers:

3. to give
4. opening
5. to be . . . talking
6. to know
7. to be
8. being
9. to touch
10. to have
11. to take
12. to finish
13. getting . . . to wait
14. to look for
15. to look for
16. looking for
17. looking for
18. walking
19. understanding
20. going

Exercise 29, p. 316.

1. same
2. different
3. same
4. different
5. different

Exercise 30, p. 318.

2. playing
3. doing
4. to do
5. to do
6. watching
7. to do
8. biting
9. to get
10. driving

Exercise 31, p. 318.

1. b
2. a
3. b
4. b
5. a

Exercise 32, p. 318.

2. lecturing/to lecture
3. seeing/to see . . . watching/to watch . . . reading/to read
4. moving/to move . . . racing/to race . . . to move . . . to race
5. driving . . . taking
6. to drive . . . (to) take [*Note:* See Chart 14-7 fn., p. 317.]
7. to inform
8. not listening
9. to explain
10. crying . . . holding . . . feeding . . . crying/to cry . . . burping . . . changing

Exercise 34, p. 320.

Questions:
1. What do you enjoy listening to?
2. What are you interested in learning?
3. What are you used to having for breakfast?
4. What time do you prefer going to bed?
5. What can't you stand watching/to watch?
6. Why did you decide to study English?

Exercise 35, p. 320.

2. to help . . . (to) paint
3. quitting . . . opening
4. to take
5. looking . . . to answer
6. watching . . . listening [*Note:* See Chart 14-7 fn., p. 317.]
7. to take . . . to pay
8. not to wait . . . to make
9. talking
10. to water
11. going skiing
12. not to smoke
13. not to know/not knowing
14. to renew
15. to tell . . . to call . . . going . . . swimming
16. to ask . . . to tell . . . to remember . . . to bring
17. doing
18. convincing

Exercise 41, p. 326.

1. to do it.
2. to do it.
3. to do it.
4. to do it.
5. to do it.
6. doing it.
7. doing it.
8. to do it.
9. doing it.
10. doing it.
11. to do it.
12. to do it.
13. to do it.
14. doing it.
15. to do it.
16. to do it.
17. to do it.
18. to do it.
19. doing it.
20. to do it.
21. doing it.
22. doing it.
23. doing it
24. to do it.
25. to doing it.
26. doing it.
27. to do it.
28. doing it.
29. to do it.
30. doing it?
31. doing it.
32. to do it.
33. to do it.
34. to do it.
35. doing it.
36. to do it.
37. to do it.
38. doing it.
39. doing it?
40. doing it.
41. doing it.
42. to do it.
43. doing it.
44. to do it.
45. to do it.
46. doing it?
47. to do it.
48. doing it?
49. doing it.
50. to do it.

Exercise 43, p. 327.

1. to bring
2. pronouncing
3. to eat
4. to lift
5. to know
6. being
7. to do
8. to be
9. to pass
10. getting/to get
11. seeing/to see
12. losing

Exercise 44, p. 327.

2. to have
3. being
4. worrying
5. to play
6. leaving
7. to return . . . (to) finish
8. hoping . . . praying
9. promising to visit
10. telling
11. to persuade . . . to stay . . . (to) finish
12. to race

Exercise 46, p. 328.

1. I don't mind **having** a roommate.
2. Most students want **to** return home as soon as possible.
3. Learning about another **country is** very interesting.
4. I tried very hard **not to make** any mistakes.
5. The task of **finding** a person who could tutor me in English wasn't difficult.
6. All of us needed to **go** to the ticket office before the game yesterday.
7. I'm looking forward **to going swimming** in the ocean.
8. **Skiing** in the **Alps was** a big thrill for me.
9. Don't **keep asking** me the same questions over and over.
10. During a fire drill, everyone is required **to leave** the building.
11. I don't **enjoy playing** card games. I prefer to spend my **time reading** or **watching** movies. OR **I prefer spending** my **time reading** or **watching** movies.
12. **It is** hard for me **to** understand people who speak very fast.
13. When I entered the room, I found my young son **standing** on the kitchen table.
14. When I got home, Irene was lying in bed **thinking** about what a wonderful time she'd had.

Chapter 15: Gerunds and Infinitives, Part 2

Exercise 1, p. 331.
Sentences that answer "Why": 3, 4, 6

Exercise 2, p. 331.
3. for
4. to
5. to
6. to
7. for

Exercise 4, p. 332.
3. Ø
4. in order
5. in order
6. Ø
7. in order
8. in order
9. Ø
10. Ø

Exercise 5, p. 333.
2. Helen borrowed my **dictionary to** look up the spelling of *occurred*.
3. The teacher opened the window **to let** some fresh air into the room.
4. I came to this school **to learn** English.
5. I traveled to **Osaka to** visit my sister.

Exercise 7, p. 333.
The *be* verb comes before the adjectives; infinitives come after the adjectives.

Exercise 11, p. 335.
Negative idea: sentences 1, 4

Exercise 14, p. 336.
1. b
2. b
3. a
4. b
5. a
6. a

Exercise 16, p. 338.
1. being seen
2. to be seen

Exercise 17, p. 338.
2. to be invited
3. to be invited
4. being invited
5. being invited
6. to be invited

Exercise 18, p. 338.
3. being understood
4. to be written
5. to be called
6. being elected
7. telling
8. to be loved . . . needed

Exercise 21, p. 339.
2. to be changed / changing
3. to be cleaned / cleaning . . . to clean
4. to be ironed / ironing
5. to be repaired / repairing
6. to take . . . to be straightened / straightening
7. to be picked / picking
8. to be washed / washing

Exercise 24, p. 340.
They take the simple or gerund form, not the infinitive.

Exercise 26, p. 341.
Part I. Sample answers:
2. singing/chirping OR sing/chirp
3. going/walking OR go/walk
4. shaking/moving OR shake/move
5. knock OR knocking
6. take off . . . land OR taking off . . . landing

Part II.
2. slam
3. snoring
4. playing
5. call
6. walking
7. land
8. calling

Exercise 27, p. 342.
Correct sentences: 1, 3, 4

Exercise 29, p. 343.
a. 2
b. 1
c. 3

Exercise 30, p. 344.
1. c
2. a
3. b
4. a
5. b
6. c

Exercise 31, p. 345.
3. cashed
4. to go
5. shortened
6. fixed
7. cry
8. to do
9. take . . . taken

Exercise 34, p. 346.
2. I asked my roommate to let **me use** his shoe polish.
3. I heard a car **door open** and **close**.
4. I had my **friend lend** me his car.
5. You should visit my country. It is **very** beautiful.
6. I went to the college bookstore **to get** my books for the new term.
7. One of our fights ended up with me having **to be sent** to the hospital **to get** stitches.
8. Lilly deserves to be **told** the truth about what happened last night.

9. Barbara always makes me **laugh**. She has a great sense of humor.
10. Stop telling me what to do! Let **me make** up my own mind.
11. I went to the pharmacy **to have** my **prescription filled**.
12. You shouldn't let children **play** with matches.
13. When Shelley needed a passport photo, she had her picture **taken** by a professional photographer.
14. I've finally assembled enough information **to begin** writing my research paper.
15. Omar is at the park right now. He is **sitting** on a park bench **watching** the ducks swimming in the pond. The sad expression on his face makes **me feel** sorry for him.
16. The music director tapped his baton **to begin** the rehearsal.

Exercise 35, p. 347.

2. a, c	5. a	8. c
3. a	6. c	9. a
4. c	7. b	10. c

Exercise 36, p. 348.

1. able to read
2. being
3. to read
4. to be understood
5. to solve
6. using

Exercise 37, p. 348.

2. thinking
3. to have . . . to know . . . to handle
4. having . . . adjusting
5. sipping . . . eating
6. being forced to leave/to be forced to leave . . . (in order) to study . . . having
7. have . . . join
8. coming . . . leaving
9. chewing . . . grabbing . . . holding . . . tearing . . . swallow
10. to force . . . to use . . . to feel . . . (to) share
11. to commute . . . moving . . . (in order) to be . . . to spend . . . doing . . . doing

Exercise 38, p. 350.

1. play/playing . . . joining
2. (in order) to let . . . run
3. staying . . . getting
4. to get . . . running . . . having . . . sprayed
5. feel . . . to get . . . feeling . . . sneezing . . . coughing . . . to ask . . . go

Exercise 39, p. 350.

Part II.

1. F	3. T	
2. T	4. F	

Part III.

1. to know how to stay
2. in order to protect
3. surprised to hear
4. likely to attract
5. to make
6. Crouching down or curling up
7. Finding
8. Being inside
9. being outside
10. Be careful to stay
11. to stay
12. to take
13. avoid touching
14. begin counting

15. need to seek
16. has passed
17. to stay

Chapter 16: Coordinating Conjunctions

Exercise 1, p. 352.

2. noun, and
3. adverb, and
4. gerund, or
5. adverb, but

Exercise 2, p. 352.

2. c	5. a, c	7. a
3. b, c	6. b	8. b
4. b		

Exercise 3, p. 353.

2. vegetables
3. rudely
4. strong
5. sped

Exercise 4, p. 353.

Correct sentences: 2, 3, 4

Exercise 5, p. 354.

Note: 2nd comma optional in items 2, 4, 6, 8, 10; 3rd comma optional in item 7.

2. The price of the meal includes a salad, a main dish, and dessert.
3. *(no change)*
4. Elias waited for his son, wife, and daughter.
5. *(no change)*
6. Susan raised her hand, snapped her fingers, and asked a question.
7. Red, yellow, gold, and olive green are the main colors in the fabric.
8. I love films full of action, adventure, and suspense.
9. *(no change)*
10. "Travel is fatal to prejudice, bigotry, and narrow-mindedness."

Exercise 6, p. 354.

2. Molly is opening the door and (is) greeting her guests.
3. Molly will open the door and (will) greet her guests.
4. Linda is kind, generous, and trustworthy.
5. Please try to speak more loudly and (more) clearly.
6. He gave her flowers on Sunday, candy on Monday, and a ring on Tuesday.
7. He decided to quit school, (to) go to California, and (to) find a job.
8. I am looking forward to going to Italy and eating wonderful pasta every day.
9. The boy was old enough to work and (to) earn some money.
10. I should have finished my homework or cleaned up my room.
12. I have met his mother but not his father.
13. Jake would like to live in Puerto Rico but not in Iceland.

Exercise 7, p. 355.

Sample answers:

2. the noise
   I dislike living in a city because of the air pollution, (the) crime, and (the) noise.

3. flowers
   Hawaii has a warm climate, beautiful beaches, and many interesting tropical trees and flowers.
4. is a good leader
   Mary Hart would make a good president because she works effectively with others, has a reputation for integrity and independent thinking, and is a good leader.

Exercise 8, p. 356.
Sample answers:
2. fair
3. greeted her students
4. lying on the sofa
5. get ready for work
6. Hiking in the mountains
7. sleeping under the stars

Exercise 10, p. 357.
1. By obeying the speed limit, we can save energy, lives, and **money**.
2. My home offers me a feeling of security, **warmth**, and love.
3. The pioneers hoped to clear away the forest and **plant** crops.
4. When I refused to help Alice, she became very angry and **shouted** at me.
5. When Nadia moved, she had to rent an apartment, make new friends, **and find** a job.
6. All plants need **light**, **a suitable climate**, and an ample supply of water and minerals from the soil.
7. Slowly **and cautiously**, the firefighter climbed the burned staircase.
8. On my vacation, I lost a suitcase, broke my glasses, **and missed** my flight home.
9. With their keen sight, fine hearing, **and refined** sense of smell, wolves hunt elk, deer, moose, and caribou.
10. When Anna moved, she had to rent an apartment, make new friends, **and find** a job.
11. The Indian cobra snake and the king cobra use poison from their fangs in two ways: by injecting it directly into their prey **or** (**by**) **spitting** it into the eyes of the victim.

Exercise 11, p. 357.
Agreement is determined by the noun that directly precedes the verb.

Exercise 12, p. 358.
2. is   5. is   7. are
3. is   6. are   8. are
4. are

Exercise 13, p. 358.
2. Yes, both the driver and the passenger were injured.
3. Yes, both wheat and corn are grown in Kansas.
4. Yes, the city suffers from both air and water pollution.
6. Yes, not only his cousin but also his mother-in-law is living with him.
7. Yes, I lost not only my wallet but also my keys.
8. Yes, she not only goes to school, but also has a full-time job.
10. Yes, I'm going to give my friend either a book or some jewelry for her birthday.
11. Yes, either my sister or my brother will meet me at the airport.
12. Yes, they can either go swimming or play tennis.
14. No, neither her husband nor her children speak English.
15. No, they have neither a refrigerator nor a stove for their new apartment.
16. No, the result was neither good nor bad.

Exercise 14, p. 359.
1. b   4. b
2. a   5. b
3. a

Exercise 15, p. 360.
3. Both Tanya and Beth enjoy horseback riding.
4. Neither Arthur nor Ricardo is in class today.
5. Both Arthur and Ricardo **are** absent.
6. We can either fix dinner for them here or take them to a restaurant.
7. Both the leopard and the tiger face extinction.
8. Neither the library nor the bookstore **has** the book I need.
9. We could either fly or take the train.
10. The hospital will neither confirm nor deny the story.
11. Both coal and oil **are** irreplaceable natural resource**s**.
12. Neither her roommates nor her brother **knows** where she is.

Exercise 16, p. 360.
(2) harmless . . . beneficial . . . tangle
(3) attack . . . eating . . . destroy
(4) trainable

Exercise 17, p. 361.
Correct sentences: 1, 3, 4

Exercise 18, p. 361.
2. The boys walked (,) and the girls ran.
3. The teacher lectured. **T**he students took notes.
4. The teacher lectured (,) and the students took notes.
5. Elena came to the meeting, but Pedro stayed home.
6. Elena came to the meeting. **H**er brother stayed home.

Exercise 19, p. 361.
1. Both Jamal and I had many errands to do yesterday. Jamal had to go to the post office and the bookstore. I had to go to the post office, the travel agency, and the bank.
2. Roberto slapped his hand on his desk in frustration. **H**e had failed another examination and had ruined his chances for a passing grade in the course.
3. When Alex got home, he took off his coat and tie, threw his briefcase on the kitchen table, and opened the refrigerator looking for something to eat. Ann found him sitting at the kitchen table when she got home.
4. When Tara went downtown yesterday, she bought birthday presents for her children, shopped for clothes, and saw a movie at the theater. It was a busy day, but she felt fine because it ended on a relaxing note.
5. It was a wonderful picnic. The children waded in the stream, collected rocks and insects, and flew kites. **T**he teenagers played an enthusiastic game of baseball. **T**he adults busied themselves preparing the food, supervising the children, and playing some volleyball.

Exercise 20, p. 362.
1. Janice entered the room and looked around. **S**he knew no one.
2. A thermometer is used to measure temperature. **A** barometer measures air pressure.
3. Derek made many promises, but he had no intention of keeping them.
4. The earthquake was devastating. **T**all buildings crumbled and fell to the ground.

5. Birds have certain characteristics in common. **T**hey have feathers, wings, and a beak with no teeth. Birds lay hard-shelled eggs, and their offspring are dependent on parental care for an extended period after birth.
6. The ancient Egyptians had good dentists. **A**rcheologists have found mummies that had gold fillings in their teeth.

Exercise 21, p. 363.
A butterfly is a marvel. **I**t begins as an ugly caterpillar and turns into a work of art. **T**he sight of a butterfly floating from flower to flower on a warm, sunny day brightens anyone's heart. **A** butterfly is a charming and gentle creature. **C**aterpillars eat plants and cause damage to some crops, but adult butterflies feed principally on nectar from flowers and do not cause any harm. **W**hen cold weather comes, some butterflies travel great distances to reach tropical climates. **T**hey can be found on every continent except Antarctica. **B**ecause they are so colorful and beautiful, butterflies are admired throughout the world.

Exercise 22, p. 363.
Note: Parallel structures that are found within a larger parallel structure are underlined twice.
1. justice, peace, and brotherhood
2. where he stands in moments of comfort and convenience, but where he stands at times of challenge and controversy
3. not the words of our enemies, but the silence of our friends
4. political and moral question . . . oppression and violence . . . oppression and violence . . . revenge, aggression, and retaliation

Chapter 17: Adverb Clauses

Exercise 1, p. 365.
When the adverb clause comes before the main clause, there is a comma. If it comes after the main clause, there is no comma.

Exercise 2, p. 366.
Correct sentences: 4, 5, 6, 7, 10

Exercise 3, p. 366.
2. We went inside when it began to rain.
3. It began to rain. We went inside.
4. When it began to rain, we went inside.
5. When the mail comes, my assistant opens it.
6. My assistant opens the mail when it comes.
7. The mail comes around ten o'clock every morning. My assistant opens it.

Exercise 4, p. 366.
1. As soon as the rain began, the children wanted to go outdoors. They love to play outside in the warm summer rain. I used to do the same thing when I was a child.
2. I had a cup of tea before I left for work this morning, but I didn't have anything to eat. I rarely eat breakfast.
3. When Jack and his wife go on vacation, ...
4. After Ellen gets home from work, she likes to read the newspaper. She follows the same routine every day after work. As soon as she gets home, she changes her clothes, gets a snack and a drink, and sits down in her favorite chair to read the newspaper in peace and quiet. She usually has . . . .
5. When you speak to someone who is hard of hearing, you do not have to shout. It is important to face the person directly and speak clearly. My elderly father is hard of hearing, ...

6. Jane wears contact lenses because she is near-sighted. **W**ithout them, she can't see from one end of a basketball court to the other. **W**hen one of her contacts popped out during a recent game, both teams stopped playing and searched the floor for the lens.

Exercise 5, p. 367.
2. Before I go to bed, I always brush my teeth.
3. Ever since I was a child, I've been interested in butterflies.
4. I'm going to meet some friends after I leave class today.
5. When people speak English too fast, Oscar can't catch the meaning.
6. The next time the teacher speaks too fast, Oscar is going to ask her to slow down.

Exercise 6, p. 369.
Sample answers:

2. did	9. will have been
3. do	10. gets
4. have been	11. go
5. give	12. you graduate
6. had brought	from college
7. was	13. go
8. was driving	14. ate

Exercise 7, p. 369.
Sample answers:
2. I left the room after I turned off the lights.
3. Before I left the room, I turned off the lights.
4. Whenever Suki feels nervous, she bites her nails.
5. The frying pan caught on fire while I was making dinner.
6. Just as we were sitting down to eat, someone knocked on the door.
7. The audience burst into applause as soon as the singer finished her song.
8. We have to wait here until Nancy comes.
9. As soon as Julia comes, we can leave for the theater.
10. Just as soon as my roommate walked into the room, I knew something was wrong.
11. Just before I stood up to give my speech, I got butterflies in my stomach.
12. The first time I saw the great pyramids of Egypt in the moonlight, I was speechless.
13. Since Lori started working at this company six months ago, she has gotten three promotions.
14. Once the weather gets warmer, we can start spending more time outside.
15. By the time Shakespeare died in 1616, he had written more than 37 plays.
16. The next time Sam goes to get his driver's license, he'll remember to take his glasses.

Exercise 8, p. 370.

2. d	7. b	11. b
3. c	8. c	12. a
4. d	9. b	13. d
5. d	10. b	14. b
6. a		

Exercise 9, p. 371.
Sample answers:
1. Just after Judy returned to her car, she called the police.
2. Just as the police arrived, Judy began crying in frustration.
3. When Judy returned to her car, she discovered that her car had been broken into.
4. While Judy was buying jeans, a thief broke into her car.

5. By the time Judy returned to her car, the thief was gone.
6. As soon as Judy got back to her car, she called the police.

Exercise 11, p. 372.
1. he thought the person was asking him about leaving.
2. she gave a long answer.
3. he won't snap his fingers.
4. they have learned that cultural misunderstandings are a normal part of learning another language.
5. they just smile.

Exercise 12, p. 372.
Adverb clauses: 1, 3

Exercise 13, p. 373.
3. Cold air hovers near the earth because it is heavier than hot air.
4. Since you paid for the theater tickets, please let me pay for our dinner.
5. Do you want to go for a walk now that the rain has stopped?
6. Because our TV set was broken, we listened to the news on the radio.
7. Many young people move to the cities in search of employment since there are few jobs available in the rural areas.
8. Now that the civil war has ended, a new government is being formed.
9. Since ninety-two thousand people already have reservations with an airline company for a trip to the moon, I doubt that I'll get the chance to go on one of the first tourist flights.

Exercise 15, p. 375.
Sentence 2

Exercise 16, p. 374.
2. a
3. a
4. b

Exercise 17, p. 375.
3. Even though
4. Because
5. even though
6. because
7. even though
8. even though
9. because
10. Even though . . . because

Exercise 18, p. 375.
1. Yes. Even though I wasn't tired, I went to bed anyway.
2. No. Even though the phone rang many times, I didn't wake up.
3. Yes. Even though the food was terrible, I ate it anyway.
4. Yes. Even though I didn't study, I passed the test anyway.
5. No. Even though the weather is terrible today, I didn't stay home.
6. No. Even though I fell down the stairs, I didn't get hurt.
7. No. Even though I told the truth, no one believed me.
8. Yes. Even though I turned on the air conditioner, it's still hot in here.
9. No. Even though I mailed the letter a week ago, it hasn't arrived yet.

10. No. Even though I have a lot of money, I can't afford to buy an airplane.
11. Yes. Even though my grandmother is ninety years old, she is still young at heart.
12. Yes. Even though I didn't understand the joke, I laughed anyway.

Exercise 19, p. 376.
Sentences: 1, 3

Exercise 20, p. 376.
2. d
3. c
4. c
5. a
6. b

Exercise 22, p. 377.
Correct sentence: 2

Exercise 23, p. 377.
1. If the teacher isn't in class tomorrow, ...
2. If I stay up until two in the morning tonight, ...
3. If the sun is shining when I get up in the morning, ...
4. If predictions about global warming are correct, ...
5. *(Answers will vary.)*

Exercise 24, p. 378.
Correct sentences: 1, 2, 3, 4

Exercise 25, p. 378.
2. a. so
   b. are
3. a. so
   b. do
4. a. so
   b. are
5. a. so
   b. did
6. a. not
   b. can't

Exercise 26, p. 379.
True sentences: 1, 4, 5, 6

Exercise 27, p. 380.
2. b
3. a
4. a
5. b
6. b

Exercise 28, p. 380.
2. a. they are funny
   b. they aren't funny
3. a. you are finished
   b. you aren't finished
4. a. it snows
   b. it snows
5. a. he gets a scholarship
   b. he doesn't get a scholarship
6. a. the weather is cold
   b. the weather is hot
7. a. you approve
   b. you don't approve

Exercise 29, p. 381.
Sentence 1

Exercise 30, p. 381.
2. In case you (should) need to see me, I'll be in my office tomorrow morning around ten.

3. In case you (should) need any more information, you can call me.
4. In case you (should) have any more questions, ask Dr. Smith.
5. In case Russ calls (should call), please tell him that I'm at the library.
6. In case you aren't satisfied with your purchase, you can return it to the store.

Exercise 32, p. 382.
1. isn't
2. is
3. rainy
4. sunny

Exercise 33, p. 382.
2. You can't travel abroad unless you have a passport.
3. You can't get a driver's license unless you are at least sixteen years old.
4. Unless I get some new batteries for my camera, I won't be able to take pictures when Laura and Rob get here.
5. You'll get hungry during class unless you eat breakfast.

Exercise 35, p. 383.
1. No.
2. No.
3. No.
4. Yes.

Exercise 36, p. 383.
True sentences: 1, 3

Exercise 37, p. 384.
Part I.
2. you have an invitation.
3. you have a student visa.
4. chews gum
5. will go to the movie
6. the temperature reaches 32°F / 0°C.
(Notice subject-verb inversion for sentences 7.–10. See Chart 17-11 fn., p. 383.)
7. will you pass the exam.
8. can you get into the soccer stadium.
9. can he watch TV in the evening.
10. will I have enough money to go to school.

Part II. (Answers will vary.)

Exercise 38, p. 385.
2. I can pay my bills only if I get a job.
   I can't pay my bills unless I get a job.
3. Your clothes will get clean only if you use soap.
   Your clothes won't get clean unless you use soap.
4. I can take (some) pictures only if the flash works.
   I can't take any pictures unless the flash works.
5. I wake up only if the alarm clock rings.
   I don't wake up unless the alarm clock rings.
6. Eggs will hatch only if they are kept at the proper temperature.
   Eggs won't hatch unless they are kept at the proper temperature.
7. Borrow money from friends only if you absolutely have to.
   Don't borrow money from friends unless you absolutely have to.
8. Anita talks in class only if the teacher asks her specific questions.
   Anita doesn't talk in class unless the teacher asks her specific questions.

Exercise 39, p. 385.
1. Whether or not it rains, the party will be held outside/inside.
2. Even if it rains, the party will be held outside.
   Even if it doesn't rain, the party will be held inside.
3. In case it rains, the party will be held inside.
4. Unless it rains, the party will be held outside.
5. Only if it rains will be party be held inside.
   Only if it doesn't rain will the party be held outside.

Chapter 18: Reduction of Adverb Clauses to Modifying Adverbial Phrases

Exercise 1, p. 387.
Correct sentences: 1, 2, 4, 6

Exercise 2, p. 388.
Correct sentences: 4, 5, 7

Exercise 3, p. 388.
3. Before I came to class, I had a cup of coffee. / Before coming to class, I had a cup of coffee.
4. Before the student came to class, the teacher had already given a quiz. / (no change)
5. Since I came here, I have learned a lot of English. / Since coming here, I have learned a lot of English.
6. Since Alberto opened his new business, he has been working 16 hours a day. / Since opening his new business, Alberto has been working 16 hours a day.
7. Omar left the house and went to his office after he (had) finished breakfast. / Omar left the house and went to his office after finishing/having finished breakfast.
8. Before the waiter came to our table, I had already made up my mind to order shrimp. / (no change)
9. You should always read a contract before you sign your name. / You should always read a contract before signing your name.
10. While Jack was trying to sleep last night, a mosquito kept buzzing in his ear. / (no change)
11. While Susan was climbing the mountain, she lost her footing and fell onto a ledge several feet below. / While climbing the mountain, Susan lost her footing and fell onto a ledge several feet below.
12. After I heard Marika describe how cold it gets in Minnesota in the winter, I decided not to go there for my vacation in January. / After hearing Marika describe how cold it gets in Minnesota in the winter, I decided not to go there for my vacation in January.

Exercise 5, p. 389.
1. Alan
2. the bear

Exercise 6, p. 390.
Modifying adverbial phrases:
2. Being a widow with three children *(because)*
3. Sitting on the airplane and watching the clouds pass beneath me *(while)*
4. Having guessed at the answers for most of the test *(because)*
5. Realizing that I had made a dreadful mistake when I introduced him as George Johnson *(because)*
6. Tapping his fingers loudly on the airline counter *(while, because)*

Exercise 7, p. 390.

7. Having broken her arm in a fall *(because)*
8. Lying on her bed in peace and quiet *(while, because)*

Exercise 7, p. 390.

2. Believing no one loved him, the little boy ran away from home.
3. Having forgotten to bring a pencil to the examination, I had to borrow one.
4. Being a vegetarian, Chelsea does not eat meat.

Exercise 8, p. 391.

2. a, c
3. a, b
4. a, b, c
5. a, c
6. b, c
7. b, c
8. b
9. a, b

Exercise 9, p. 391.

3. Keeping one hand on the steering wheel, Anna paid the bridge toll with her free hand.
4. *(no change)*
5. Hearing that Nadia was in the hospital, I called her family to find out what was wrong.
6. *(no change)*
7. Living a long distance from my work, I have to commute daily by train.
8. *(no change)*
9. Being a married man, I have many responsibilities.
10. *(no change)*
11. Recognizing his face but having forgotten his name, I just smiled and said, "Hi."
12. (Being) Convinced that she could never learn to play the piano, Ann stopped taking lessons.

Exercise 10, p. 392.

2. Having done very well in her studies, Nancy expects to be hired by a top company after graduation.
3. (Having been) Born two months prematurely, Monique needed special care for the first few days of her life.
4. Having done everything he could for the patient, the doctor left to attend other people.
5. Having never eaten / Never having eaten Thai food before, Marta didn't know what to expect when she went to the Thai restaurant for dinner.
6. Having no one to turn to for help, Sayid was forced to work out the problem by himself.
7. (Being) Extremely hard and nearly indestructible, diamonds are used extensively in industry to cut other hard minerals.
8. (Being) Able to crawl into very small places, mice can hide in almost any part of a house.

Exercise 11, p. 392.

3. *(correct)*
4. Because I was too young to understand death, my mother . . . .
5. *(correct)*
6. While I was working in my office late last night, someone . . . .
7. After we (had) hurried to get ready for the picnic, it . . . .
8. While I was walking across the street at a busy intersection, a truck . . . .

Exercise 12, p. 393.

All three sentences have the same meaning.

Exercise 13, p. 393.

2. Upon crossing the marathon finish line, Tina fell in exhaustion.
3. Upon looking in my wallet, I saw I didn't have enough money to pay my restaurant bill.
4. Sam found that he had made a math error upon re-reading the data.
5. Upon finishing the examination, bring your paper to the front of the room.
6. . . . Upon hearing my name, I raised my hand to identify myself.
7. . . . Upon hearing this, Cook grabbed his telescope and searched the horizon.

Exercise 14, p. 394.

5. Before leaving on my trip, I checked to see what shots I would need.
6. *(no change)*
7. Not having understood the directions, I got lost.
8. My father reluctantly agreed to let me attend the game after having talked/talking it over with my mother.
9. (Upon) Discovering I had lost my key to the apartment, I called the building superintendent.
10. *(no change)*
11. After having to wait for more than half an hour, we were finally seated at the restaurant.

Exercise 16, p. 395.

1. a
2. b
3. b
4. a

Exercise 17, p. 395.

Part I.

The First Telephone

Alexander Graham Bell, a teacher of the deaf in Boston, invented the first telephone. One day in 1875, while running a test on his latest attempt to create a machine that could carry voices, he accidentally spilled acid on his coat. Naturally, he called for his assistant, Thomas A. Watson, who was in another room. Bell said, "Mr. Watson, come here. I want you." Upon hearing words coming from the machine, Watson immediately realized that their experiments had at last been successful. He rushed excitedly into the other room to tell Bell that he had heard his words over the machine.

After successfully testing the new machine again and again, Bell confidently announced his invention to the world. For the most part, scientists appreciated his accomplishment, but the general public did not understand the revolutionary nature of Bell's invention. Believing the telephone was a toy with little practical application, most people paid little attention to Bell's announcement.

Part II.

1. T
2. T
3. F
4. F

Exercise 18, p. 396.

1. T
2. T
3. F
4. T

Exercise 1, p. 397.
All four sentences have the same meaning.

Exercise 2, p. 397.
1. *Cause*: Jon is a heavy smoker.
   Effect: Jon has breathing problems.
   Because Jon is a heavy smoker, he has breathing problems.
2. *Effect*: Martina feels homesick.
   Cause: Martina moved to a new town.
   Martina feels homesick because she moved to a new town.
3. *Effect:* Mr. Jordan's house has no heat.
   Cause: Mr. Jordan lost his job.
   Mr. Jordan's house has no heat because he lost his job.
4. *Cause:* Victor has gained weight.
   Effect: Victor is going to eat less.
   Because Victor has gained weight, he is going to eat less.

Exercise 3, p. 398.
1. because of
2. because
3. because
4. because of
5. Because of
6. Because
7. because of

Exercise 4, p. 398.
2. his wife's illness
3. the noise in the next apartment
4. our parents' generosity
5. circumstances beyond our control

Exercise 5, p. 398.
Sentences: 1, 4, 6

Exercise 6, p. 399.
1. A storm was approaching. **T**herefore, the children stayed home.
2. A storm was approaching. **C**onsequently, the children stayed home.
3. A storm was approaching, so the children stayed home.

Exercise 7, p. 399.
1. Because it was cold, she wore a coat.
2. *(no change)*
3. Because of the cold weather, she wore a coat.
4. *(no change)*
5. The weather was cold. **T**herefore, she wore a coat.
6. The weather was cold. **S**he wore a coat, therefore.
7. The weather was cold, so she wore a coat.

Exercise 8, p. 400.
1. Pat always enjoyed studying sciences in high school. **T**herefore, she decided to major in biology in college.
2. Due to recent improvements in the economy, fewer people are unemployed.
3. Last night's storm damaged the power lines. **C**onsequently, the town was without electricity.
4. Due to the snowstorm, only five students came to class. **T**he teacher, therefore, canceled the class.

Exercise 9, p. 400.
Correct sentences: 3, 4

Exercise 10, p. 401.
1. The weather was bad. **T**herefore, we postponed our trip. OR We, therefore, postponed our trip. OR We postponed our trip, therefore.
2. Since the weather was bad, we postponed our trip. OR We postponed our trip since the weather was bad.
3. The weather was bad, so we postponed our trip.
4. Because of the bad weather, we postponed our trip. OR We postponed our trip because of the bad weather.
5. The weather was bad. **C**onsequently, we postponed our trip. OR We, consequently, postponed our trip. OR We postponed our trip, consequently.
6. Due to the fact that the weather was bad, we postponed our trip. OR We postponed our trip due to the fact that the weather was bad.

Exercise 11, p. 401.
2. Pat doesn't want to return to the Yukon to live because the winters are too severe. OR Because the winters are too severe, Pat doesn't want to return to the Yukon to live.
3. It is important to wear a hat on cold days since we lose sixty percent of our body heat through our head. OR Since we lose sixty percent of our body heat through our head, it is important to wear a hat on cold days.
4. Bill's car wouldn't start. Therefore, he couldn't pick us up after the concert. OR He, therefore, couldn't pick us up after the concert. OR He couldn't pick us up after the concert, therefore.
5. When I was in my teens and twenties, it was easy for me to get into an argument with my father because both of us can be stubborn and opinionated.
6. Due to the fact that a camel can go completely without water for eight to ten days, it is an ideal animal for desert areas. OR A camel is an ideal animal for desert areas due to the fact that it can go completely without water for eight to ten days.
7. Robert got some new business software that didn't work, so he emailed the software company for technical support.
8. A tomato is classified as a fruit, but most people consider it a vegetable since it is often eaten in salads along with lettuce, onions, cucumbers, and other vegetables. OR Since it is often eaten in salads along with lettuce, onions, cucumbers, and other vegetables, a tomato is considered a vegetable.
9. Due to consumer demand for ivory, many African elephants are being slaughtered ruthlessly. Consequently, many people who care about saving these animals from extinction refuse to buy any item made from ivory. OR Many people who care about saving these animals from extinction, consequently, refuse to buy any item made from ivory. OR Many people who care about saving these animals from extinction refuse to buy any item made from ivory, consequently.
10. Because most 15th-century Europeans believed the world was flat and that a ship could conceivably sail off the end of the earth, many sailors of the time refused to venture forth with explorers into unknown waters. OR Many sailors of the 15th century refused to venture forth with explorers into unknown waters because most Europeans of the time believed the world was flat and that a ship could conceivably sail off the end of the earth.

Exercise 13, p. 402.
4. so
5. so
6. so
7. so
8. such
9. so

Exercise 15, p. 403.

2. The radio was so loud that I couldn't hear what Michael was saying.
3. Olga did such poor work that she was fired from her job.
4. The food was so hot that it burned my tongue.
5. There are so many leaves on a single tree that it is impossible to count them.
6. The tornado struck with such great force that it lifted cars off the ground.
7. So few students showed up for class that the teacher postponed the test.
8. Charles used so much paper when he was writing his report that the wastepaper basket overflowed.

Exercise 16, p. 403.
Correct completions: 1, 4

Exercise 17, p. 404.

5. Please be quiet so (that) I can hear what Sharon is saying.
6. I asked the children to be quiet so (that) I could hear what Sharon was saying.
7. I'm going to cash a check so (that) I will have / have enough money to go to the store.
8. I cashed a check yesterday so (that) I would have enough money to go to the store.
9. Tonight Ann and Larry are going to hire a babysitter for their six-year-old child so (that) they can go out with some friends.
10. Last week, Ann and Larry hired a babysitter so (that) they could go to a dinner party at the home of Larry's boss.
11. Be sure to put the meat in the oven at 5:00 so (that) it will be/is ready to eat by 6:30.
12. Yesterday, I put the meat in the oven at 5:00 so (that) it would be ready to eat by 6:30.
13. I'm going to leave the party early so (that) I can get a good night's sleep tonight.
14. When it started to rain, Harry opened his umbrella so (that) he wouldn't get wet.
15. The little boy pretended to be sick so (that) he could stay home from school.

Exercise 18, p. 405.

3. I need a visa so **that** I can travel overseas.
4. I needed a visa, so I went to the embassy to apply for one.
5. Marta is trying to improve her English so **that** she can become a tour guide.
6. Olga wants to improve her English, so she has hired a tutor.
7. Tarek borrowed money from his parents so **that** he could start his own business.
8. I turned off the TV so **that** I could concentrate on my paperwork.

Exercise 19, p. 405.

1. no	4. no	6. yes
2. yes	5. no	7. yes
3. yes		

Exercise 20, p. 406.

1. outside	5. outside
2. inside	6. outside
3. outside	7. outside
4. outside	8. inside

Exercise 21, p. 406.

1. am	5. am
2. am not	6. am not
3. am	7. am
4. am	

Exercise 22, p. 407.

4. but	10. However
5. Nevertheless	11. yet
6. Even though	12. Although
7. even though	13. yet
8. but	14. Although
9. Nevertheless	15. However

Exercise 23, p. 407.

2. Anna's father gave her some good advice, but she didn't follow it.
3. Even though Anna's father gave her some good advice, she didn't follow it.
4. Anna's father gave her some good advice. **S**he did not follow it, however.
5. Thomas was thirsty. I offered him some water. **H**e refused it.
6. *(no change)*
7. Thomas was thirsy. **N**evertheless, he refused the glass of water I brought him.
8. Thomas was thirsty, yet he refused to drink the water that I offered him.

Exercise 24, p. 408.

1. Even though his grades were low, he was admitted to the university. OR He was admitted to the university even though his grades were low.
2. His grades were low, but he was admitted to the university anyway.
3. His grades were low, yet he was still admitted to the university.
4. His grades were low. Nonetheless, he was admitted to the university.
5. Despite his low grades, he was admitted to the university.
6. He wasn't admitted to the university because of his low grades. OR Because of his low grades, he wasn't admitted to the university.

Exercise 25, p. 408.
Sentences: 1, 3, 4, 5

Exercise 26, p. 409.
Possible answers:

1. Florida has a warm climate; however, Alaska has a cold climate. OR Florida has a warm climate. Alaska, on the other hand, has a cold climate.
2. Fred is a good student; however, his brother is lazy. OR Fred is a good student. His brother, on the other hand, is lazy.
3. Elderly people in my country usually live with their children; however, the elderly in the United States often live by themselves. OR The elderly in the United States, on the other hand, often live by themselves.

Exercise 30, p. 410.

1. can	3. can't
2. can't	4. can't

Exercise 31, p. 410.

2. You should / had better / have to / must leave now. Otherwise, you'll be late for class.
3. You should / had better / have to / must have a ticket. Otherwise, you can't get into the theater.
4. You should / had better / have to / must have a passport. Otherwise, you can't enter that country.
5. Tom should / had better / has to / must get a job soon. Otherwise, his family won't have enough money for food.
6. You should / had better / have to / must speak both Japanese and Chinese fluently. Otherwise, you will not be considered for that job.
7. Mary should / had better / has to / must get a scholarship. Otherwise, she cannot go to school.
8. I should / had better / have to / must wash my clothes tonight. Otherwise, I won't have any clean clothes to wear tomorrow.

Exercise 32, p. 411.

Possible completions:
2. I failed the exam because I did not study.
3. Although I studied, I did not pass the exam.
4. I did not study. Therefore, I failed the exam.
5. I did not study. However, I passed the exam.
6. I studied. Nevertheless, I failed the exam.
7. Even though I did not study, I (still) passed the exam.
8. I did not study, so I did not pass the exam.
9. Since I did not study, I did not pass the exam.
10. If I study for the exam, I will pass it.
11. Unless I study for the exam, I will fail it.
12. I must study. Otherwise, I will fail the exam.
13. Even if I study, I won't pass.
14. I did not study. Consequently, I failed the exam.
15. I did not study. Nonetheless, I passed the exam.
16. I will probably fail the exam whether I study or not.
17. Only if I study will I pass the exam.
18. I studied hard, yet I still failed the exam.
19. You'd better study, or else you will fail the exam.

Exercise 33, p. 412.

1. a
2. a
3. b
4. b
5. a
6. b
7. a

Exercise 36, p. 414.

1. T
2. T
3. F
4. F
5. T
6. F

Exercise 37, p. 414.

1. We went shopping after **we** ate / **eating** dinner, **but** the stores were closed. We had to go back home even **though** we hadn't found what we were looking for.
2. I want to explain that I know a lot of **grammar, but my problem is that** I **don't have** enough **vocabulary**.
3. When I got lost in the bus station, a kind man helped me. **He** explained how to read the huge bus schedule on the wall, **t**ook me to the window to buy a ticket, and showed me **where my bus was.** I will always appreciate his kindness.
4. I had never **understood** the **importance** of **knowing the** English language / of **knowing English until** I worked at a large, international company.
5. **When** I was young, my father found an American woman to teach **my brothers and me** English, but when we

moved to **another** town, my father wasn't able to find **another** teacher for **another** five years.
6. I was surprised to see the room that I was given at the dormitory **because** there **wasn't** any **furniture and it was** dirty.
7. When I **met** Mr. Lee for the first time, we played video games at the student center. **Even** though we **couldn't** communicate very well, we had a good time.
8. Because the United States is a large **and big** country, **it** has a diverse population.
9. My grammar class **started** at 10:35. When the teacher **came** to class, she returned the last quiz to my classmates and **me.** After **that, we had** another quiz.
10. If a wife **has to work**, her husband should share the **housework** with her. If both of them help, the **housework** can be **finished** much faster.
11. The first time I went skiing, I was afraid to go down the hill, **but** then I **thought** to myself, "Why not? Give it a try. You'll make it!" After **standing** around for ten minutes without moving, I **finally** decided **to** go down that hill.

Chapter 20: Conditional Sentences and Wishes

Exercise 1, p. 416.

Result clauses:
2. I will buy a new laptop computer next month
3. I would buy a new laptop today or tomorrow
4. I would have bought a new laptop last month

Exercise 2, p. 416.

2. have . . . will send
3. had . . . would send
4. had . . . would send
5. had had . . . would have sent

Exercise 3, p. 417.

a. = habitual activities or situations.
b. = a particular activity or situation in the future OR a predictable fact or general truth

Exercise 5, p. 418.

1. will let
2. (both correct)
3. (both correct)
4. (both correct)
5. (both correct)
6. will recharge

Exercise 6, p. 418.

1. If I'm talking
2. If we get
3. If it's
4. If he's planning
5. If it's not working
6. If she works
7. If I should get

Exercise 7, p. 418.

1. a. isn't
   b. doesn't teach
2. a. isn't
   b. can't

Exercise 8, p. 419.

3. have
4. had
5. will go
6. would go
7. is
8. were

Exercise 10, p. 419.
1. would not be . . . were
2. will float / floats
3. were . . . would not exist
4. doesn't arrive
5. were . . . wouldn't want
6. would human beings live
7. disappears / will disappear
8. had . . . would have to . . . wouldn't be

Exercise 11, p. 420.
1. If there weren't gravity on the earth, ...
2. If people had wings, ...
3. If cars could fly, ...
4. If children got everything they wanted, ...
5. If guns didn't exist, ...
6. If there were enough food on the earth for everyone, ...

Exercise 12, p. 420.
*Sentences with a past **meaning**:* 2, 4

Exercise 13, p. 421.
2. he became a soccer player.
3. I answered my cell phone while I was driving.
4. Professor Stevens didn't give a fair test.

Exercise 14, p. 421.
Conditional clauses:
3. U If the weather had been warm, *(past)*
4. U If I had more money, *(present/future)*
5. U If I had had more money, *(past)*
6. T If I take time off from work, *(present/future)*
7. U If I hadn't had to work, *(past)*
8. U If I didn't have to work, *(present/future)*

Exercise 15, p. 422.
1. will do
2. would do
3. would have done

Exercise 16, p. 422.
1. have
2. had
3. had had
4. will go
5. would go
6. would have gone
7. is
8. were . . . would visit
9. had been . . . would have visited
10. had read . . . wouldn't have washed

Exercise 17, p. 423.
2. a. no
   b. yes
   c. no
3. a. yes
   b. no
   c. yes
4. a. no
   b. yes

Exercise 19, p. 424.
1. T
2. T

Exercise 20, p. 424.
1. If I had known . . . I would have acted
2. If we hadn't believed . . . we wouldn't have felt
3. If you hadn't told . . . I wouldn't have believed
4. If it had been . . . I wouldn't have been
5. If he hadn't lied, I would have had

Exercise 21, p. 425.
1. were . . . would tell
2. had had . . . would have taken
3. have . . . will give
4. had . . . wouldn't have to
5. had been . . . wouldn't have bitten
6. would we use . . . didn't have had
7. doesn't rain . . . will die . . . die . . . will go
8. had realized . . . wouldn't have made
9. B: would/could have come . . . washed . . . had told
   A: would have come . . . had called

Exercise 22, p. 426.
1. a. no
   b. no
2. a. yes
   b. no
3. a. no
   b. yes
   c. no
4. a. no
   b. yes

Exercise 23, p. 426.
4. did
5. weren't
6. had
7. were
8. had
9. didn't
10. weren't
11. hadn't

Exercise 25, p. 427.
1. b
2. a

Exercise 26, p. 427.
2. if you were wearing a coat, you would be cold.
3. if he hadn't been driving so fast, he wouldn't have gotten a ticket.
4. if I weren't enjoying myself, I would leave.
5. if you hadn't been sleeping, I would have told you the news (as soon as I heard it).

Exercise 27, p. 428.
3. weren't drying
4. hadn't been drying
5. were having
6. hadn't been talking

Exercise 28, p. 428.
1. earlier . . . now
2. now . . . earlier

Exercise 29, p. 429.
2. But if you hadn't left the door open, the room wouldn't be full of flies.
3. But if you had gone to bed at a reasonable hour last night, you wouldn't be tired this morning.
4. But if I had finished my report yesterday, I could begin a new project today.
5. But if I were you, I would have told him the truth.
6. But if I knew something about plumbing, I would/could have fixed the leak in the sink myself.
7. But if she had followed the doctor's orders, Anita wouldn't have gotten sick.

Exercise 30, p. 429.
1. If I were the teacher, I would give fewer tests.
2. If I had known about your problem, I would have helped you.
3. If anyone should come, please tell them I'm asleep.

Exercise 31, p. 429.

2. Were I you, ...
3. Had they realized the danger, ...
4. Were I your teacher, ...
5. Should you change your mind, ...
6. . . . had she been better prepared.
7. Were I you, ...
8. . . . Should you need to reach me, ...
9. . . . Had they not dared to be different, ...
10. Should there be a global nuclear war, ...

Exercise 32, p. 430.

1. b   3. c   5. b
2. d   4. a   6. c

Exercise 33, p. 430.

True sentences: 1, 3

Exercise 34, p. 431.

3. I would have answered the phone if I had heard it ring.
4. I couldn't have finished the work if you hadn't helped.
5. I like to travel. I would have gone to Nepal last summer if I had had enough money.
6. If I hadn't stepped on the brakes, I would have hit the child on the bicycle.
7. The neighbors probably would have called to complain about the noise if Olga hadn't turned down the volume on the CD player.
8. Tarek would have finished his education if he hadn't had to quit school and find a job in order to support his family.

Exercise 35, p. 431.

1. a, b   4. a
2. a   5. b
3. b

Exercise 36, p. 431.

1. would/could spend
2. would/could have sent
3. is completed
4. weren't snowing
5. would have gone
6. would be
7. hadn't been sleeping

8. would forget . . . were not
9. A: were not/weren't
   B: would be sleeping
10. were . . . wouldn't be
11. would have been
12. would not ride
13. will tell

Exercise 40, p. 434.

2. were shining   8. would lend
3. had gone   9. were coming
4. knew   10. weren't going to give
5. were wearing   11. could meet
6. had   12. had come
7. could   13. were lying

Exercise 42, p. 435.

6. had   11. were
7. could   12. had
8. did   13. did
9. had   14. were
10. would

Exercise 43, p. 435.

1. now
2. soon

Exercise 44, p. 436.

1. (a) Anna wishes Yoko would come to the concert.
   (b) Anna wishes Yoko would change her mind.

2. (a) Helen wishes Judy would pick up after herself, wash her dirty dishes, pick up her clothes, and make her bed.
   (b) Judy probably wishes Helen didn't nag her to pick up after herself.

Exercise 45, p. 436.

1. she hadn't gone
2. A: we didn't have to
   B: it were
3. you had come . . . you had come . . . we would have had
4. you would tell
5. A: I had worn
   B: I had known

NOTES

NOTES

NOTES

NOTES

NOTES

The PowerPoint presentations are saved as .PPS files, which means that they open in Slide Show view and cannot be edited. The instructions in this section explain the basic steps of opening and using the PowerPoint presentations.

2.1. Start a Presentation

2.1.1. Windows
- Insert the PowerPoint® presentations CD-ROM into the CD-ROM drive. On most computers, a Contents page will open automatically.
- If the Contents page does not open automatically, open **My Computer**, double-click on the CD-ROM drive, and then double-click on the **"Start.html"** file.
- On the Contents page, click the link for **"PowerPoint presentations."**
- Click the link for the presentation you wish to view.

2.1.2. Macintosh
- Insert the PowerPoint® presentations CD-ROM into the CD-ROM drive.
- Double-click on the CD-ROM drive icon, the symbol that looks like a CD.
- Double-click on the **"Start.html"** file.
- On the Contents page, click the link for **"PowerPoint presentations."**
- Click the link for the presentation you wish to view.

2.2. Advance Through Slides
To advance from one slide to the next or from one animation to the next, click the left mouse button, the **Down Arrow** button (↓) or the **Right Arrow** button (→) on the keyboard.

2.3. Go Back Through Slides
To go back to previous slides, or to go back through the animations on a slide, click the **Up Arrow** button (↑) or the **Left Arrow** button (←) on the keyboard.

2.4. Exit a Presentation
Press the **"Esc"** (escape) button on the keyboard.

Technical Support

For Technical Support, email
EPSupport@pearsoned.com

System Requirements

For Windows:
- Windows® 2000 or XP
- 500 MHz Processor
- 256 MB RAM
- Microsoft PowerPoint® (or higher) software

For Mac:
- Mac OS 10.2 or higher
- 500 MHz Processor
- 512 MB RAM
- Microsoft PowerPoint® (or higher) software

For Both:
- 12X CD-ROM drive
- Projector (to display PowerPoint® presentations in class)

License Agreement